EASY-GAITED HORSES

Easy-Gaited Horses

Gentle, humane methods for training and riding
gaited pleasure horses

Lee Ziegler

Foreword by Rhonda Hart Poe
Illustrations by JoAnna Rissanen

Storey Publishing

The mission of Storey Publishing is to serve our customers by publishing practical information that encourages personal independence in harmony with the environment.

Edited by Deborah Burns and Sue Ducharme
Art direction by Kent Lew and Cynthia McFarland
Cover design by Vicky Vaughn
Cover photographs by: © Shawn Hamilton, front cover large, © Bob Langrish, front cover top four (left to right: Missouri Foxtrotter, Rocky Mountain Horse, Tennessee Walker, Rocky Mountain Horse); © Judy Ryder Duffy, back cover.
Cover models: Kathryn Utke on Casey's Last Chance, owned by Kit Darrow.
Illustrations by JoAnna Rissanen
Interior photographs by: © CORBIS 11; © Judy Ryder Duffy 92, 132, 172; © Bill Erickson 206; © Shawn Hamilton ii, 114, 122, 154; © Elisabeth Haug 216; © Bob Langrish 6, 42, 64, 188; © Darlene Wohlart 28.
Text design by Kent Lew
Text production by Eugenie S. Delaney
Indexed by Eileen Clawson

The information in this book is true and complete to the best of our knowledge. All recommendations are made without guarantee on the part of the author or Storey Publishing. The author and publisher disclaim any liability in connection with the use of this information. For additional information, please contact Storey Publishing, 210 MASS MoCA Way, North Adams, MA 01247.

Printed in the United States by Versa Press
10 9 8 7 6 5 4 3
LIBRARY OF CONGRESS CATALOGING-IN-PUBLICATION DATA
Ziegler, Lee, 1949–
    Easy-gaited horses / Lee Ziegler.
        p. cm.
    Includes bibliographical references and index.
    ISBN-13: 978-1-58017-562-3 (pbk. : alk. paper)
    ISBN-13: 978-1-58017-563-0 (hardcover : alk. paper)
    1. Horses—Paces, gaits, etc. I. Title.
SF289.Z54 2005
636.1'089276—dc22
                                                                            2004025043

For the horses, all of them.

ACKNOWLEDGMENTS

This book would not have been possible without the many years of research done in musty libraries, obscure museums, stables (both clean and not so clean), and smoke-filled rooms around the world by my father, Lt. Col. J. W. Bradbury. I thank him for that and for passing on half the genetic makeup that made horses a necessity in my life. It would also not have been possible without the encouragement and kindness of my mother, Roberta, who gave me the rest of the genetic predisposition for horsemanship. And, of course, this book and I both owe more than I can say to my husband, Charles Ziegler, who has supported me quietly from the sidelines for the past 35 years while learning to love most of the objects of my addiction.

Besides my family, I am fortunate to have many friends who helped, taught, and encouraged me to learn more about these wonderful gaited horses. Rob McCartney has been a constant and sane resource for things to do with hooves and Walking Horses for almost 30 years. Carol and Hank Kuiper have provided a doorway into the world of the Paso Fino for more than 25 years. Dave Sena has generously shared his joy in Peruvian Paso horses with me for almost 15 years. And Glenn Clary, who was steeped in the traditions of both the vaquero and the dressage master, shared his methods, his thoughts on riding, and his wonderful understanding of horses of all gaited breeds with me for more than 20 years, until his death. I miss him.

This book exists almost entirely because Rhonda Hart Poe of *The Gaited Horse* magazine convinced me that it was possible and held my hand through it, and Deb Burns at Storey Publishing hung in there for me. I thank them both. I also thank Kit Darrow and Will Chester for helping with organization and clarity and Liz Graves for reviewing, encouraging, and cheering me on. Finally, I am grateful to the many horses, dear friends all, who patiently taught me what little I know during the past 50 years. To them, especially to Metronome, Cinnabar, and "Isabella Louisa," I am eternally grateful. It has been a great ride!

Contents

Foreword

Even among established horsemen, gaited horses represent something of an enigma. So much about them seems so different from "regular" horses. I can't think of another aspect of the horse world with more myths, misunderstandings, and odd (often harmful) traditions than the gaited horse industry. Contradictions run rampant. Bad training techniques, poor riding habits, and quirky, ill-fitting tack are all too common. We have more old wives' tales than a downtown beauty parlor.

Nevertheless, gaited horses represent one of the fastest-growing equine groups in the world. The reason is simple: The horses are wonderful. It's just we folks that are a little confused. What we need is an authoritative, sane, superbly educated, and experienced voice of reason to clear the confusion. Luckily for us, that's exactly what Lee Ziegler offers.

Nobody knows gaited horses better than Lee. With the seamless skill of Isaac Asimov explaining warped dimensions of science, she distills mysterious concepts to their simple truths. Her insight, depth of understanding, and natural talent as a teacher dissolve confusion with logic, clear explanations, and step-by-step, sensible information.

We are fortunate to have Lee Ziegler as a resource. In her youth she received the finest classical equine education from military cavalry officers. She has spent decades delving into the finer points of gait and equine biomechanics at the scientific level. She has observed and critiqued thousands of horses, first as a student, then as a trainer, and ultimately as a horse show judge and clinician. In her years of teaching she has never stopped learning. Her inquisitive nature wouldn't let her settle for less than clear, specific answers.

Because she has done all this, we don't have to. All we have to do to benefit from this amazing wealth of hard-won knowledge is turn the page.

RHONDA HART POE

Co-founder and Editor of *The Gaited Horse* magazine

Introduction

Easy-gaited horses have always been a part of human equestrian culture. Prehistoric drawings on cave walls frequently depict horses moving in gaits other than the walk, trot, and gallop of the non-gaited horse, and stone carvings from many parts of the world show horses that are clearly ambling or pacing.

The earliest text on training horses, which was discovered near present-day Ankara, Turkey, was written around 1360 BCE. Produced as a cavalry manual for the Hittite King Sepululiumas, it was probably dictated to a scribe by the king's horse master, Kikkulis, a member of the Mittanni people who came from an area now part of western Iran. This text, written in Hittite and in Mittanni, refers to training horses in a gait other than a walk or trot, generally translated as an amble. Most ancient peoples, including the Assyrians, the

Chinese, the Greeks, and the Egyptians, depicted ambling horses in their art. The Romans distinguished gaited horses as ambulators, while calling trotting horses tortores or torturers. During the Middle Ages, when European roads were virtually impassable, easy-gaited horses were the prized possessions of the wealthy and were frequently mentioned in their last wills and testaments at ten times the worth of non-gaited horses.

As the Americas were colonized, easy-gaited horses found a new role providing comfortable transportation through the wilderness of the developing colonies. Although they gradually disappeared from Europe during the 1600s, replaced by trotting carriage horses, carthorses, and racehorses, easy-gaited horses were still appreciated in remote areas of Asia and Africa, as well as in rural areas of the Americas. Wherever and whenever humans relied on riding horses rather than driving horses for transportation, the easy-gaited horse was present and valued.

What Is an Easy-Gaited Pleasure Horse?

Times have changed. Today, few people in the world rely on horses for transportation; we ride for sport or recreation, not for necessity. As a result, the term "gaited horse" has in some cases, especially in the United States, become synonymous with the flash and exaggeration of the show ring. Those high-stepping show horses seem to have little in common with the hardy breeds who carried our ancestors through the wilderness of the New World. They may be gaited, but they certainly aren't pleasure horses.

Those of us who prefer the peace and quiet of a shady bridle path or scenic trail to the glamour of show-ring competition want a different type of horse. We want horses that are calm, obedient, relaxed, alert, sure-footed, consistent in gait, and easily maneuvered with little effort from the rider. Fortunately, there are plenty of gaited horses that are not constrained by the demands of the show ring and, when trained correctly, they make ideal pleasure horses because they provide a smooth ride in addition to these other qualities. An easy-gaited pleasure horse may do any of a number of easy gaits, as long as the gait is comfortable and not tiring to him over the course of a long day on the trail. He may belong to any of the known gaited breeds, belong to a breed not known for gait, or simply be a grade horse with an extra gait that allows him to be comfortable on the trail. His smoothness of gait and ease of handling are what make him a pleasure to ride.

The Misplaced Traditional Focus on Legs and Hooves

Because easy-gaited horses often have the ability to perform a number of gaits and some of those gaits are less comfortable to ride than others, trainers have looked for ways to encourage their preferred gaits for many centuries. Several centuries before Christ, the Parthians manipulated hoof flight to change gait by digging a series of trenches a certain distance apart, then riding over them until the horse changed the timing of his footfalls to avoid tripping. Early English texts on training amblers advocated hanging weights on the legs or using shackles and hobbles to force a trotting horse into a more desirable lateral gait.

These days, trainers are more likely to rely on hoof angle changes, special shoes, weights, and chains on the pasterns, but the spirit of the method remains the same: They change the gait by manipulating the feet and legs.

It is easy to understand why people would focus on the pick-up and set-down of the hooves and legs as the most important aspect of a gait; after all, those are the most obviously active parts of a horse in motion. Manipulating the angles of the hooves and the placement of the legs through mechanical means will certainly alter the flight and timing of a horse's hooves and can be a quick and easy, if not lasting, solution to many gait problems. For riders familiar with the precepts of good horsemanship, however, these methods carry with them more than a hint of the spirit of the Spanish Inquisition and certainly do not reflect modern horse training techniques. Because most of today's breeders advertise their easy-gaited horses as naturally gaited, it seems peculiar to rely on such artificial means to train them.

Adjusting gait by using weighted shoes or trimming hooves at angles unnatural to the horse may not be particularly harmful to horses that are ridden for short periods of time in well-groomed arenas. Most veterinarians and honest farriers, however, maintain that to stay sound for long-term riding, any horse, gaited or not, should be trimmed at his anatomically correct angle and shod for protection, traction, or therapeutic purposes with ordinary unweighted, generally caulkless, shoes. Typical shoeing methods for gait adjustment do not fit these criteria and are not an option for the long-term soundness of the easy-gaited pleasure horse. If he is to work well in gait, he must do so without relying on a creative farrier, or he will be at risk of navicular disease, tendonitis, arthroses (arthritis) of the joints, and other conditions that threaten soundness.

Our easy-gaited horses deserve more from us than mechanical attempts to fool Mother Nature through manipulation of their hooves. Other methods of obtaining easy gaits exist. In fact, it is possible to shift easily from one gait to another on a well-trained multi-gaited horse that is barefoot, trimmed to his natural angles, and ridden without a bit. This talented horse changes gait, not due to changes in the angles of his hooves or artificial interference with the timing of his legs, but as a result of complex actions in his entire body that move his legs in his gaits.

The Role of the Horse's Body in Movement

Watch carefully as a horse takes one step forward with a front leg from a square, balanced stop. He first readjusts his weight slightly to the rear, tightening his back and abdominal muscles and increasing the flexion of his hind leg joints. He shifts his head and neck up and away from the advancing front leg and only then takes a step. He uses his whole body to move one front leg. Imagine how complex his body movements are as he moves multiple legs in various patterns to produce the easy gaits.

If you look closely or use slow-motion video, you can observe some of the changes in a horse's back muscles, abdominal muscles, neck carriage, and use of his haunches as he moves in the different gaits. Neck, back, and abdominal muscles contract and stretch, affecting hip muscles, shoulder muscles, leg muscles,

A method of forcing a horse into a lateral gait, circa 1624.

tendons, and ligaments, which all work in groups, at different times, in different sequences. Depending on how he moves his bones and joints, a horse either gallops or walks, trots or paces, fox trots or racks, does a running walk or a stepping pace. Only when the rest of a horse's body works in a certain way do his hooves finally set down in the order of a particular gait.

If you think about a moving horse as a whole, instead of concentrating on his legs, you can see how his entire body position determines how he will move in a gait. This is the key to understanding easy-gaited horses and training them without gimmicks. To feel the changes in a horse's body and experience the way he produces the various gaits, first try riding bareback or in a very light English saddle on a horse that does only one of the easy gaits. Notice how his back feels as it remains in a certain position under your seat during his single gait. If you can, try this experiment with as many horses as possible, while riding bareback or in a light saddle. Feel how each one uses his back and body while he works in a particular gait. The muscle use, body position, and overall feel will be similar in each horse as he does that gait. Next, try riding a multi-gaited horse as he shifts from one gait to another. You can easily feel the changes in the muscles of his back as he changes gaits. If you ride a number of multi-gaited horses, you will experience the same body changes between gaits with each horse, assuming they do the same easy gaits.

Changing Gait by Manipulating the Feet

THE MOST COMMON METHODS for developing easy gaits through mechanical means are based on the idea that changing the flight pattern of hooves will alter the timing of the movement of the horse's legs, and by either speeding up or slowing down that timing, a gait can be manufactured. If the angle of a hoof is made steeper, either by cutting the toe short, letting the heel grow long, nailing on a shoe with a thick turnback or caulk, or raising the heel with a wedge, that hoof will pick up from the ground faster, and will increase speed in its flight pattern. If the angle of a hoof is made lower, either by letting the toe grow long, trimming off heel, or fitting with a shoe that has a thicker toe than heel, that hoof will leave the ground more slowly due to the longer toe, and may reduce speed in its flight pattern.

In addition to this manipulation of timing through hoof angle, the use of weighted shoes or "action devices" that cause the horse to take a higher step will also change the timing of the flight pattern. Generally, when fitted with a weighted shoe, a horse will lift the weighted leg higher than he would with no extra weight. This action changes the timing of the gait by slowing the flight pattern of the weighted leg, which takes longer to lift and set down due to the higher lift in the step.

Higher action can also be encouraged through the use of wooden rattles or chains on the pasterns. These cause the horse to lift his legs higher in response either to the noise of the "bracelets" or to the irritation of the soft tissues of his lower leg from repeated impact on them as he moves. It is also possible to create higher action and a slower step with the use of developers, shackles very similar to those used in the 1600s but made with modern materials such as surgical tubing or bungie cords.

Use of weighted shoes and action devices to develop gait is not an exact science. Often the preferred method for curing a pace is to lower the heels on the front hooves and fit them with weighted shoes or rattles/chains, while raising the heels on the hind hooves and shoeing them with keg or lighter weight shoes. The conventional method for curing a trotty horse is to weight the hind shoes or put rattles/chains on the hind fetlocks, while raising the heels of the front hooves and shoeing them with lighter shoes. But, if these methods don't work for a particular horse, the usual advice is to try the opposite approach, weighting the hind hooves to cure a pace, or weighting the front ones to cure a trot.

Sometimes after a horse has been manipulated into a gait through these methods, he will continue to do the gait, even after he is returned to his natural angles in keg shoes or barefoot. In time, however, he usually reverts to his "default" gait, and the specialized shoeing is again required to get him back in gear.

Training the Whole Horse

To enjoy an easy-gaited horse, you don't need to call in a farrier with a trunk full of weighted shoes or dig up your back pasture into a series of trenches. All you need to do is learn to help him carry his body in the position that works best for his specific gait. Instead of focusing on his legs, you need to focus on his body.

There are three simple rules for developing an easy-gaited pleasure horse.

1. Start with a horse of appropriate conformation and breeding for the desired gait.
2. Reach his mind so that he wants to work for and with you.
3. Develop his muscles through consistent, effective exercise.

When these three factors come together, it is possible to train a horse's whole body for his gaits. At first, this type of training may seem more complicated than training with mechanical gimmicks, but it is more effective in the long run. Whole-body training stays with the horse for a lifetime once he learns the correct body position for his easy gait. The training won't wear off just because he has his hooves trimmed.

Training the whole body allows the horse to be calm, supple, responsive, consistent in his gait, and a pleasure to ride no matter which gait he is doing. The method can be applied to young horses or used in the retraining of those that may have been forced into their gait through mechanical manipulation. Following this approach, it is possible to keep the horse shod or barefoot at his natural angles, preserving the soundness of his legs under the stress of long trail rides. Unlike reliance on shoeing and other gimmicks, this whole-body technique works to develop a desirable easy gait with every horse, every time.

Although some of the techniques can be applied to show horses, this method is not aimed at show riders or aspiring trainers of flashy gaited show horses. It will, however, help an ordinary pleasure rider develop the gaits and responsiveness of the ordinary easy-gaited pleasure horse. Much of it requires only standard horsemanship, the type that has been used for hundreds of years by good riders and trainers in any discipline. Some of it is specific to developing the desired gaits of various breeds or strains of horses. Follow this method and you will be able to ride down the trail on a light rein in a consistent, smooth, relaxing gait. Why would you expect, or accept, less from your easy-gaited pleasure horse?

Note: Throughout this book the horse is referred to as "he" for simplicity. Obviously, everything mentioned will apply equally to a "she!"

CHAPTER ONE

What Are the Easy Gaits?

(Everything You Ever Wanted to Know about Gaits, and More!)

The natural and perfect gaits are those that come from nature,
without having been improved upon by art.
— François Robichon de la Guérinière (1687–1751)

It is easy to fall in love with gaited horses. In addition to their pleasant dispositions and attractive looks, they seduce you with the promise of long rides spent gliding effortlessly along the trail without the hard work of posting or sitting the jarring motion of the trot. Because their gaits are so comfortable to ride, these horses lull you into believing that riding them will be simple. After all, if you don't have to post and you don't have to worry about staying on during a rough trot, riding doesn't appear to take much physical effort. You can just relax and enjoy your wonderful easy-gaited horse.

You may expect that your horse's gait will be automatic because his breed is "supposed to" do that gait. With years of breeding for a specific gait behind your horse, it is reasonable to assume that your Tennessee Walking Horse will do a running walk, your Missouri Fox

Trotter will do a fox trot, your Paso Fino will do a *corto or largo,* your Peruvian Paso will do either a *sobreandando* or a *paso llano,* your Rocky Mountain horse will do a saddle rack, your Icelandic will do a *tolt,* and if your horse is of some other breed, he will do the gait specialty of that breed.

Sometimes, however, a peculiar thing happens as you spend more time riding your new gaited horse. The lovely gait that originally came with him may change or evaporate entirely, often about the time he needs a hoof trim or a new set of shoes. He may start to "wiggle differently" in some other smooth gait. Worse yet, he may start to bounce you in something that is not a trot, but just as uncomfortable. "What happened?" you wonder. How could this horse, the love of your life, change into a rough-riding nightmare?

It happens because easy-gaited horses don't read their registration papers, let alone the glowing accounts that fill the breed literature. No matter what the breed, no matter how pure the bloodlines, no matter how thorough the training may have been, the reality is that almost *all* easy-gaited horses can, on occasion, offer gaits you may have never heard of, some of which are not particularly easy to ride. To enjoy consistently the gliding gait that convinced you to "go gaited," you need to be more than a passive load of freight on your horse's back. You need to figure out what gaits he can do and actively help him perform the one you prefer.

Although every easy-gaited horse has many natural or inborn gaits to choose from, most naturally prefer to do only one intermediate gait. However, your horse may not automatically select the gait you are expecting. Riding one of these horses is like changing from a simple pedal bicycle to a 20-speed version. Trotting horses are pedal bikes, basically doing their gaits according to speed, with no options. Easy-gaited horses are more complex, multi-geared models. If you fail to select a gait from the many they offer, or somehow shift gears without realizing you have done so, you may find yourself riding an unexpected gait.

Before you can select a specific gait "gear" with your easy-gaited horse, you need to figure out what gears he has! Learn to recognize the gaits your horse may slip into so you can identify the difference between what he is doing and the gait you want. This is not terribly difficult, but it takes a little concentration and some practice. To learn the differences between gaits, watch as many horses as possible moving in gait from the ground (preferably on slow-motion video) and feel the gaits of a number of well-gaited horses from the saddle. If you learn to recognize each specific gait by sight and feel, you will develop a good foundation for riding and training in the easy gaits of any breed.

Eadweard Muybridge and the Gait Definition Revolution

IN 1872 EADWEARD MUYBRIDGE (who changed his name from the more prosaic Edward James Muggeridge because he believed that Eadweard was a more correct Anglo-Saxon form of the name) started experimenting with sequential photographs of horses in motion to settle a controversy about the support phases of the trot. He devised a method, using strings and a series of cameras, to take individual pictures of each phase of a horse's stride in gait. This photographic proof of the support and timing of gaits caused a sensation, and soon people on both sides of the Atlantic were conducting studies of gaits using sequential still photographs. Etienne Marey and his fellow Frenchmen Armand Goubaux and Gustave Barrier, among others, devised several systems for differentiating among gaits based on footfall timing and duration. Their relatively simple early graphic representations of locomotion were used for many years to illustrate the various gaits, but, as photography advanced with the invention of extreme slow motion film and video, these graph systems have been refined and replaced by other more complex ways of describing gaits. There are now seemingly hundreds of bar graphs, hoof set-down pattern charts, and timing grids available to define the gaits of horses. No mysteries remain about what a horse does in a particular gait; all we have to do now is look at a video of him in action and apply the specific descriptions developed through the science of gait analysis to determine what he is doing.

Defining the Gaits

The easy gaits are those gaits that are comfortable to ride and faster than an ordinary walk but slower than a canter or gallop. Sometimes called the intermediate gaits, they include the flat-footed walk, the running walk, the fox trot, the broken or stepping pace, the saddle rack, and the true rack. The pace is also sometimes used as a riding gait, but it is not as comfortable as the true easy gaits.

If you try to figure out what a horse is doing as you watch him zip by at top speed, you will probably get only a vague idea of his gait. You might make an educated guess about what his legs are doing, but what you perceive may be as far from reality as those traditional paintings of a horse galloping with two front legs stretched straight in front and two hind legs stretched out behind. Photography has long since proven that horses don't gallop that way, and photography can be a great help in figuring out exactly what a horse is doing in a gait. Using photography, we can view and quantify enough information about gaits to overwhelm anyone who just wants to understand easy gaits for ordinary riding purposes.

For practical gait identification, complex scientific gait graphs are sometimes confusing and difficult to apply. A series of pictures showing how a horse looks in each phase of a gait is easier to understand than a grid showing his hoof supports. To truly understand a gait, however, you need a little help from the scientific definitions of gait to go along with pictures of the horse in the gait. Applying some of these clearly defined elements of gait to your horse's easy gaits will fill in details that are missing from sequential still pictures and give you a clear picture of what your horse is doing with all those different "wiggles" he uses when you ride him.

Useful criteria for categorizing gaits are:

- Footfall sequence
- Footfall timing
- Hoof pick-up timing
- Hoof support sequence
- Hoof-to-hoof weight transfer between the two front hooves or the two hind hooves, also called the **transverse** pairs of hooves. (That is, the transverse pairs are the hooves straight across the horse's body from each other, either the front hooves or the hind hooves.)

In addition, for comparison purposes, some definitions have been adopted as standard by most gait analysis systems.

1. All **gait sequences** start with the set-down of a hind hoof, usually the right, and form a **half stride** with the set-down of the opposite hind hoof or a **full stride** with the set-down of the original hind hoof again.

How weight is transferred from one front hoof to the other.

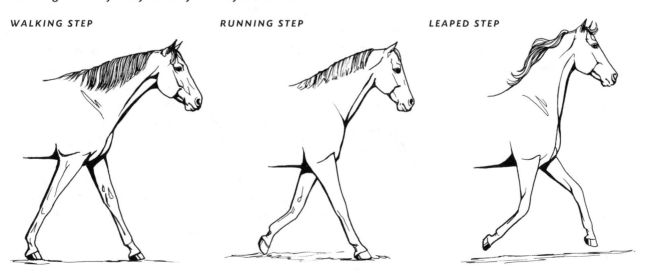

WALKING STEP   RUNNING STEP   LEAPED STEP

2. A **step** is defined as the distance between the set-down of one front hoof and the other or one hind hoof and the other. Steps may be:

- **Walking or marching steps,** in which each hoof of the transverse pair is flat on the ground for a split second as weight is transferred
- **Running steps,** in which one hoof of the transverse pair is in the process of lifting as the other sets down
- **Leaped steps,** in which both hooves are off the ground for a split second

3. The **track** of a gait is the impression left by hooves in the dirt as the horse moves forward. This includes overstride, understride, and capping. Sometimes the track is used as part of the definition process for a gait, along with the less permanent aspects of timing and sequence.

- **Overstride** is defined by the distance a hind hoof sets down in front of the front hoof on the same side, measured from the toe of the hind-hoof track to the toe of the front-hoof track.
- **Understride** is defined as the distance a hind hoof sets down behind the front hoof on the same side, measured from the heel of the front-hoof track to the toe of the hind-hoof track.
- **Capping** is defined as the setting down of the hind hoof in the track of the front hoof on the same side.

These basic terms and definitions are used in most descriptions of the easy gaits and are useful parts of any horseman's vocabulary. It is impossible to describe the different gaits without them.

Hoofprints reflecting hoof placement in the track of a gait.

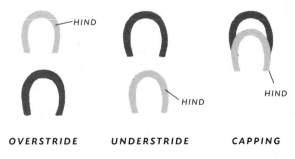

OVERSTRIDE   UNDERSTRIDE   CAPPING

How Many Gaits Are There?

Photography has allowed scientists to determine that horses are theoretically capable of more than 100 different support or timing sequences in addition to the more complex canter and gallop. Horses have actually been observed using more than 50 of these gait variations! Fortunately for those of us who are trying to understand the easy gaits, horses most often use eight or nine clearly defined, symmetrical gaits (gaits in which the movements of legs on one side of the horse mirror those on the other) when they are not cantering or galloping. These gaits, in which the action of the legs on the right of the horse mirrors that of the left, have different names in various languages but are essentially the same no matter what breed of horse is doing them. In English, as well as in the most common foreign terms used in the United States, they are:

1. The walk
2. The flat-footed walk or flat walk (slow paso llano)
3. The running walk (paso llano)
4. The pace (skeith, flug skeith, huachano)
5. The broken or stepping pace, also called the amble (skeith-tolt, sobreandando)
6. The saddle rack, sometimes called the single-foot (slow tolt, fino, corto, largo)
7. The true rack (true tolt, fast largo)
8. The trot
9. The fox trot (brokk tolt, trocha, pasitrote)

Because horses are living creatures with imperfections, within each of these gaits there will be some variations from the ideal gait. For example, a trot is usually defined as a diagonal gait in which the right hind and left front hoof hit the ground at the same time, followed by a moment of suspension when all four legs are off the ground, followed by the simultaneous set-down of the left hind and right front hooves. With some horses, however, the hind hoof of the diagonal pair will hit the ground a split second before the front, and in others the front hoof of the pair will hit first. Because it is almost impossible to see these timing differences without slow-motion video, the variations are accepted as trots, although they may not be as desirable as the ideal type. In the easy gaits, horses

How to Determine Gait Timing Using Stop-Frame Video

IF YOU ARE CURIOUS about the timing or the support of a horse's gait, the best way to find out what he is doing is to view a good, clear video filmed from the side while he does his gait. To videotape gait, use a tripod if possible and tape in an area with firm footing and a contrasting background so you can easily see the hooves as they hit and lift off the ground. You may also want to color code each of your horse's legs with contrasting leg wraps or strips of tape.

Play the video on a VCR with slow-motion and stop-frame features. Watch the horse's hooves and stop the frame just as the right hind hoof sets down flat on the ground. Count that set-down as "one" in your gait sequence. Advance the frames one at a time, counting each frame, until the right front hoof sets down. Stop the video on that frame. (A typical count for a walk might be seven, for a running walk or fox trot it might be six, and for a rack, five, depending on the speed of the horse in the gait.) Remember the number of frames between set-down of the right hind and set-down of the right front, then start the single frame advance again, counting between the set-down of the right front and the set-down of the left hind. The count starts at "one" from the set-down of the right front hoof. Count frames until the left hind sets down, and stop the video. Compare the frame counts between the set-down of the right hind and right front, and the right front and left hind.

When a gait is even in set-down, the number of frames between the set-down of the right hind and right front will be the same as the number of frames between the set-down of the right front and left hind. For a horse in the rack, running walk, or walk, there should be the same number of frames between the set-down of the right hind and right front as between the right front and left hind. When a gait is diagonal in set-down, the number of frames between the set-down of the diagonal hooves will be fewer than between the set-down of the lateral hooves. In a fox trot, there might be six frames between the set-down of the right hind and right front but only four between the set-down of the right front and left hind, depending on the speed of the gait. When a gait is lateral in set-down, there will be fewer frames between the set-down of the right hind and right front than between the set-down of the right front and left hind hooves and more frames between the set-down of the diagonal ones. In a stepping pace there might be four frames between the set-down of the right hind and right front but six frames between the set-down of the right front and left hind, depending on the speed of the gait.

Once you have determined the set-down timing, determine the pick-up timing of the hooves. Start counting frames as the right hind hoof leaves the ground and stop when the right front hoof leaves the ground. In a typical rack that has a five-frame timing between the set-down of each hoof, the pick-up timing of these lateral hooves will be at four frames. In a typical running walk, the lateral hooves will leave the ground with the same timing as the set-down, about six frames between pick-up and between set-down, depending on speed.

Seven Steps for Identifying a Gait without Slow-Motion Video

1. Look at the legs on the right side of the horse. Look only at these two legs, one front, one hind.

▸ Do these legs appear to move forward at exactly the same time? If so, the gait is a *pace*.

▸ Do they appear to move forward close to but not exactly at the same time? If so, the gait is a *stepping pace/amble*.

▸ Do they appear to move forward singly, not paired together? If so, the gait may be a *walk, flat walk, running walk, saddle rack,* or *rack*.

▸ Do they appear to move toward one another, forming a V as the horse moves? If so, the gait is either a *trot* or a *fox trot*.

2. Look at one hind leg and the opposite front leg. Look at only two diagonal legs.

▸ Do they appear to move forward exactly together? If so, the gait is a *trot*.

▸ Do they appear to move forward not quite exactly together? If so, the gait is a *fox trot*.

▸ Do they appear to move forward at distinctly separate times? If so, and the legs on the same side also appear to move forward at distinctly separate times, the gait is either a *walk, flat walk, running walk, saddle rack,* or *rack*.

3. Look at the hooves of the legs on the side of the horse closest to you.

▸ Do they appear to leave the ground very close in time to one another? Can you see the bottom of both of them at the same time? If so, and the legs on the same side move forward together as well, the horse is *pacing* or *step pacing/ambling*.

▸ If so, and the legs on one side do *not* appear to move forward together, the horse is doing a *saddle rack* or *rack*.

4. Look at the bottom of the hooves on the legs diagonal from one another. (Right hind, left front.)

▸ Do they appear to set down at exactly the same moment? If so, the gait is a *trot*.

▸ Do they appear to set down with the front hitting just before the diagonal hind? If so, the gait is a *fox trot*.

▸ Do they appear to set down separately at evenly timed intervals? If so, the gait is a *walk, flat walk, running walk, saddle rack,* or *rack*.

5. Look at the head and neck of the horse.

▸ Do they bob up and down? If so, the gait is a *walk, flat walk, running walk,* or *fox trot*.

▸ Do they stay still as the horse moves? The gait is either a *saddle rack, rack,* or *true trot*.

▸ Do they swing from side to side? If so, the gait is either a *stepping pace/amble* or a *pace*.

6. Look at the croup and tail.

▸ Does the tail swing from side to side? If so, the gait may be a *hard trot, stepping pace/amble,* or *pace*.

▸ Does the tail bob up and down? If so, the gait may be a *fox trot, saddle rack,* or *rack*.

▸ Does the tail stay relatively still and the croup level? If so, the gait is either a *flat walk* or a *running walk*.

7. Add up the clues:

▸ If the legs on one side move forward together at exactly the same time, the hooves on one side lift and set down at the same time, and the head, neck, and tail move from side to side, the gait is a *pace*.

▸ If the legs on one side move forward at about the same time, the hooves on one side set down with the hind just before the front, and the head, neck, and tail move from side to side, the gait is a *stepping pace/amble*.

▸ If the diagonal legs move forward at exactly the same time, the head and neck remain relatively still, and the tail swings just a little from side to side, the gait is a *trot*.

▸ If the diagonal legs move forward at about the same time, the front hoof lands just before the diagonal hind, the croup and tail bob up and down, and the head and neck also nod up and down, the gait is a *fox trot*.

▸ If the legs move forward separately (not paired laterally or diagonally), the croup remains level, the head and neck move up and down, and each hoof lifts and sets down at a distinct, even interval, the gait is a *walk, flat walk,* or *running walk*. (Speed is the main difference between these gaits.)

▸ If the legs move forward separately (not paired laterally or diagonally), the croup and tail bob up and down, the head and neck remain relatively still, and the hooves on one side appear to leave the ground slightly closer in time than the diagonal ones, the gait is a *saddle rack* or *rack*, again depending on speed.

will also vary slightly in timing and support from the ideal version of the gait, but as long as these variations are not obvious to the naked eye, they are accepted as falling within the definition of that particular gait.

How the Gaits Look and Feel

The easy gaits fall into three main groups, according to the timing of their footfalls and hoof pick-up.

The Square Gaits

These gaits are "square" because hooves leave the ground and set down at even intervals. In all of these gaits, there is no obvious diagonal or lateral pairing in the timing of the set-down or pick-up of the hooves. Each leg works alone, independent of the other three. The gaits differ from one another in their speed and in the way weight is shifted between the transverse pairs of legs. Horses also do them with slightly different "body language."

The Walk

All horses do an ordinary walk, sometimes called a "dog walk" in gaited breeds. In the walk, each hoof lifts and contacts the ground at equal, separate intervals. The speed is relatively slow, at most four miles

per hour. The sound, or rhythm, is an even 1-2-3-4 beat. In the walk, there are two periods during which three hooves are solidly on the ground, and two periods during which only two hooves are in contact with the ground. The walk is a two-foot, three-foot support gait that can be seen as the "mother gait" of all the easy gaits, which are all variations of the timing and support of this basic four-beat gait.

HOW IT LOOKS: In an ordinary walk, there is a gentle, rhythmic up-and-down motion of the head and neck, in time with the forward motion of the front legs. The head rises as each forefoot is about to set down and reaches its lowest position as each front hoof is halfway through its step. The back may seem to undulate as the horse moves, but his croup stays relatively level, without up-and-down motion.

No two legs appear to move together; each lifts and sets down independently. The horse nods his head and neck up and down in time with his leg movements, moving slowly.

HOW IT FEELS: The walk rocks you gently from front to back in the saddle. You can clearly feel each hoof hit the ground at even intervals as the back gently rises and falls in a rolling motion under your seat.

The Flat-Footed or Flat Walk/Slow Paso Llano

Although some non-gaited horses can be taught to do this gait, it is mostly seen in the easy-gaited breeds. It

THE SUPPORT SEQUENCE OF THE ORDINARY WALK

is identical to the ordinary walk in footfall sequence, footfall timing, support sequence, and weight transfer. The flat walk, however, is faster than the ordinary walk, ranging from four to six miles per hour. The speed comes from longer steps and increased overstride. The sound is an even 1-2-3-4 beat.

HOW IT LOOKS: Horses nod their heads up and down a little more obviously in the flat walk than they do in the ordinary walk. The back does not seem to undulate as much, and the motion of the horse's body is tighter, less "sloppy," in this type of walk. The horse's croup remains level, but the hind legs push a little more strongly than they do in the ordinary walk. Each hoof leaves the ground and sets down independently; no two legs appear to move together. The horse appears energetic but relaxed in this fast walk. A good description of this gait is that it is the walk a horse uses when he has worked hard during the day and is heading home. He speeds up his walk, but doesn't take rapid steps.

HOW IT FEELS: The flat walk is often more comfortable to ride than the ordinary walk, especially if the horse is long legged. In this gait any rolling motion of the back that was noticeable in an ordinary walk disappears, but you do feel some front-to-back movement in the saddle. You feel each hoof hit the ground separately, with a strong push from each hind leg. You feel an energetic connection through the horse's body as he moves in a flat walk, unlike the more relaxed and lazy feel of the ordinary walk.

The Running Walk

In this gait, the hooves leave the ground and set down at even intervals, as they do in the walk and flat walk. The speed ranges from seven to ten miles per hour, with a few individuals able to perform the gait correctly at higher speeds. The sound is an even 1-2-3-4 beat. You can easily recite the little phrase "let's go along" to the beats of the gait when riding on a firm surface. The footfall sequence and timing are the same in this gait as they are in the ordinary and flat walk. The basic support sequence is also the same, although when it is done at faster speeds there is a change in the weight transfer from a walking step to a running step. That means that one hoof sets down as the other lifts, with only part of the lifting hoof still in contact with

The Paso Llano
Stylistic Differences from the Running Walk

FOR PERUVIAN HORSES, the running walk or flat walk is called the paso llano. Although they are essentially the same gait, there are some differences between the running walk and the paso llano. The most obvious difference is that there is little or no head nod in the paso llano. Instead, the horse performing a paso llano travels with upward and outward rotation of the front legs from the shoulders, called termino. The horse may also show less overstride, called advance, than a horse in a running walk, although he ordinarily will not cap his tracks and should never understride. Other aspects of the gait remain the same. No two legs move paired in time; hooves leave the ground and set down in even, equal intervals; and the transfer of weight becomes a running step only at higher speeds.

Termino, the outward rotation of the front leg from the shoulder, is not the same as the paddling that occurs in horses with crooked front legs.

the ground as the transfer is made. The overstride is also longer in the running walk than it is in the flat walk or ordinary walk. Some of the increase in speed between the ordinary walk and the running walk is the result of this increased length of step.

HOW IT LOOKS: Horses doing a running walk continue to nod their heads and necks, although they may not move quite as far up and down as they do in the slower walks. The back is steady, with no obvious undulations, and the croup stays level, with no up and down bounce to the tail. The hind step is long and sweeping, while the front may be a little higher than in the ordinary walk for some horses. The hooves leave the ground and set down at even, equal intervals, with no pairing in time of any two legs. The horse appears energetic but relaxed, with long sweeping steps from his hind legs pushing him strongly forward.

THE RUNNING WALK

The running walk and paso llano: Similar gaits with stylistic differences.

THE PASO LLANO

HOW IT FEELS: You will feel a gentle front-to-back rock in the saddle, with a rolling motion in the shoulders. There is no noticeable up-and-down motion in the hindquarters, but there is a strong feeling of forward thrust and power from each hind leg. The sensation is a little like riding on a riverboat with a paddle wheel turning just out of phase on each side.

The Lateral Gaits

Lateral gaits are those in which the pick-up or set-down of the hooves on one side of the horse is closer in time than the pick-up or set-down of the diagonal hooves. All of the easy gaits are lateral in *sequence;* that is, the set-down of the right hind hoof is followed by the set-down of the right front. They are not, however, all lateral in *timing* of set-down and pick-up. For a gait to fall into the lateral gait category, there must be some lateral element in its timing. This category contains the most common of the easy gaits, those seen in the most breeds worldwide.

The Pace

The pace is not usually considered an easy gait because it can be very uncomfortable to ride. Icelandic horses are ridden at this gait, however, and the pace appears in most of the other gaited breeds from time to time. It is a totally lateral gait, in which the hooves on one side of the horse lift from the ground at the same time, advance forward at the same time, and hit the ground at the same time. It is a two-beat gait in which there is a moment of suspension when all four hooves are off the ground between the set-down of each set of lateral legs. The pace can be done at a variety of speeds, but is usually done at a fast, racing speed. The sound is a 1-2 beat, with the beats coming from the set-down of the lateral hooves. Occasionally, the track may be capped, with the hind hoof setting down in the track of the front, but usually there is considerable overstride in the gait.

HOW IT LOOKS: A horse moving in a pace will have no up-and-down motion to his head and neck, but they may swing from side to side, away from each advancing foreleg. He may also swing or wag his hindquarters from side to side. His entire body will rise and fall with the motion of his legs, lifting for the moment of suspension when all four hooves are clear of the ground, then falling with the set-down of each lateral set of hooves. The horse's barrel will swing from side to side as his whole body balances first on one lateral set of legs, then on the other.

HOW IT FEELS: A horse in a true pace usually throws you abruptly from side to side in the saddle. The motion can be as bouncy as a hard trot, and for this reason the pace is not favored as a riding gait by most people. It is possible to post to a hard pace, rising and sitting with alternating lateral sets of legs, but those who ride it at racing speeds sit down to the gait. At a very fast speed, it can be relatively smooth to ride, but it is not as comfortable as a true easy gait for distance riding.

The Amble or Broken/Stepping Pace

The amble is probably the most common of the easy gaits. It is a broken lateral gait in which the hooves on one side of the horse lift from the ground close in time and set down close in time, but not at exactly the same moment, as they do in the true pace. The hind hoof sets down noticeably before the front on the same

THE PACE

side. The speed of this gait ranges from less than three miles per hour to more than fifteen miles per hour. The sound is a broken 1-2, 3-4 beat, with the beats closest together coming from the set-down of the lateral hooves. Notice that this gait has the same sound and beat as the fox trot. You can recite the same "ka-chunk, ka-chunk" sound for this gait as well as for the fox trot.

The amble is a three-foot, two-foot support gait, like the walk. At very slow speeds, however, there may be a moment when all four hooves are in solid contact with the ground.

HOW IT LOOKS: In an amble, your horse will sway his head and neck from side to side and may sway his body from side to side as well, but not as strongly as he does in a true pace. He may also have some up-and-down motion in his head and neck. There will be no up-and-down bob of his croup or tail.

HOW IT FEELS: The amble is a comfortable gait that rocks you gently from side to side in the saddle. There is no jolting or jarring, but the side-to-side motion can make some people seasick. You can sometimes feel the horse's back tighten first on one side, then on the other as he moves in this gait.

The Saddle Rack/Singlefoot/Corto/Slow Tolt

This gait is the second most common of the easy gaits among breeds of horses. As a result, it has many names in many languages, and only a few of them are mentioned here. The gait is sometimes classified as a square gait, because, like the walk and running walk, it has even footfall set-down timing and a 1-2-3-4 beat. It also, however, has lateral hoof pick-up timing and a lateral footfall sequence; for these reasons it can be classified with the lateral gaits. This lateral pick-up and even set-down timing is possible because the horse takes slightly higher (and therefore more time-consuming) steps with his front legs in the saddle rack than he does in the truly square gaits. The speed of this gait ranges from the very slow fino fino gait of the Paso Fino (which is done almost in place) to about eight miles per hour.

The saddle rack is usually a three-foot, two-foot support gait, with the same sequence as a walk, but at moderate speed the support changes to a three-foot, two-foot, one-foot support, because there is a moment in the stride when both front (but never both hind) hooves are clear of the ground. Weight is transferred between the front hooves with a walking step at slowest speeds in this gait. With increased speed this becomes a running step and with even more speed it becomes a leaping step. Weight is transferred between the hind hooves with a walking step at slow speeds and a running step at both moderate and fast speed. There is usually some overstride in the saddle rack at

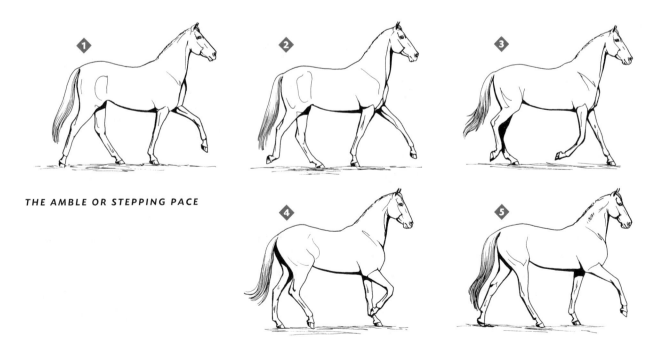

THE AMBLE OR STEPPING PACE

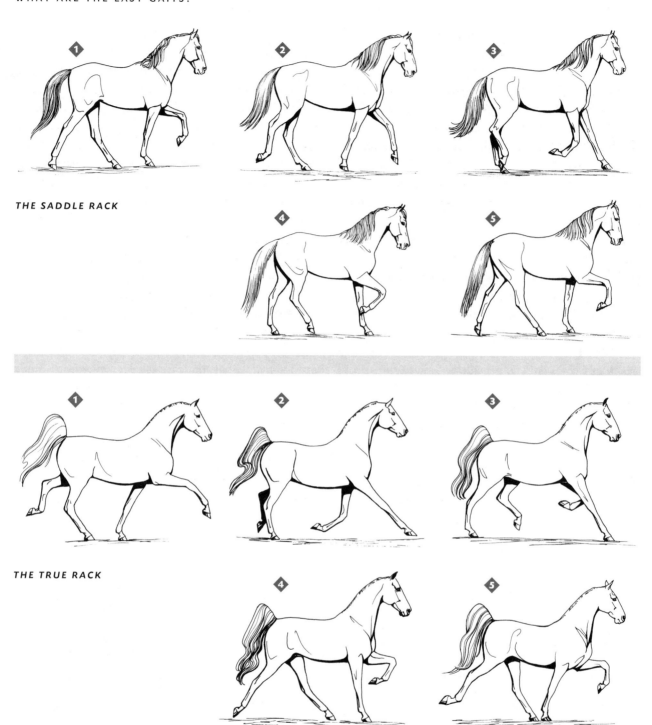

THE SADDLE RACK

THE TRUE RACK

higher speeds, but at the very slowest speeds the gait track may show capping or even understride.

HOW IT LOOKS: A horse saddle-racks with a high, steady head and neck without noticeable up-and-down nod or side-to-side sway. His croup rises and falls with the active use of his hocks, which flex sharply at each step. His tail also bobs up and down with the motion of his croup. The horse also has some animation or higher action in his front legs than he normally exhibits in a walk. The hooves on one side of the horse appear to leave the ground close in time to one another, allowing you to see the bottoms of both hooves at the same time as they lift. No two legs will appear to move forward together, however, and the diagonal and the lateral legs move independently, as they do in a walk.

HOW IT FEELS: The saddle rack is a very comfortable gait to ride. The movement is a slight side-to-side sway and produces a strong sensation of each leg moving rapidly and independently. The rider sits in the smooth center while the shoulders and hindquarters move energetically up and down. The horse may feel as if he is climbing a ladder in front and "shaking his tail" in back.

The Rack/Fast Tolt/Largo

This gait is a much faster version of the saddle rack. Some individual horses have been clocked at more than 25 miles per hour in the true rack. The gait is identical to the saddle rack in sequence, timing, body language, and feel. The sound of the gait is also an even 1-2-3-4 beat. The rack, however, is slightly different in support and weight transfer than the slower saddle rack.

In the true rack, there is never a three-foot, two-foot support for the horse. Instead, one hoof, then two hooves support him alternately. The weight transfers between both sets of transverse pairs of hooves are leaped. That is, there is never a moment when both front hooves are in contact with the ground, and there is also never a moment when both hind hooves are in contact with the ground. There is some overstride in the rack, although usually not as much as in the running walk.

In all other ways, the rack and saddle rack are identical. They look and feel the same, although the true rack is faster than the saddle rack.

The Diagonal Gaits

The diagonal gaits are those in which the pick-up and set-down of the diagonal hooves (right front, left hind) are closer in time than the pick-up or set-down of the lateral hooves. A gait with a lateral footfall sequence is still considered diagonal if it has diagonal timing in the pick-up and set-down of the hooves. There are two diagonally timed gaits.

The Trot

The most familiar of all the intermediate gaits is the trot. It is the only intermediate gait of non-gaited horses and may be used in addition to one of the easy gaits by some gaited horses. In a trot, the diagonal hooves leave the ground at the same time, move forward at the same time, and set down at the same time. The gait has two clear beats, one as each set of diagonal hooves set down. It also has a moment of suspension when all four hooves are off the ground, similar to that of the hard pace. This gives it the same 1-2 beat as the pace and usually the same degree of comfort or

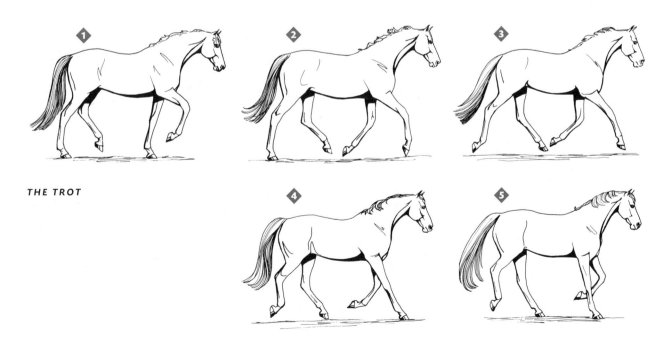

THE TROT

discomfort for the rider. The speed of the trot can vary between the very slow jog trot at less than four miles per hour to the very fast racing trot of the Standard-bred, at well over fifteen miles per hour.

HOW IT LOOKS: In the trot, a horse maintains a steady head and neck carriage with no visible head-nod. His entire body will rise and fall with the motion of his legs, lifting for the moment of suspension when all four hooves are clear of the ground, then falling with the set-down of each diagonal set of hooves. The horse's back and tail may swing from side to side as his whole body balances first on one diagonal set of legs, then on the other.

HOW IT FEELS: The trot will bounce you up and down in the saddle, unless you have learned to adapt to the motion of the gait by either sitting or posting it. If you have learned to sit it, you will often feel a swinging motion in the horse's back as he jumps from one diagonal set of hooves to the other.

The Fox Trot/Trocha/Pasitrote

The fox trot is the *only* diagonally timed easy gait. It is a broken diagonal gait in which the hooves set down at separate intervals, not at the same time as they do in the trot. The diagonal hooves leave the ground close in time and set down close in time, with the front hoof hitting the ground noticeably before the diagonal hind. At slow speeds in this gait (sometimes called a fox walk), the weight transfer between front hooves is a walking step, with each hoof flat on the ground. With some increase in speed, the transfer becomes a running step, with one hoof lifting as the other sets down. At some show-ring speeds, the transfer becomes a leaped step, with both front hooves clear of the ground for a split second. In the hind hooves, the weight transfer is most frequently a running step, one hoof lifting as the other sets down, but it may be a walked step at slow speeds. The comfortable, pleasure fox trot is always a gait with a two-foot, three-foot support sequence.

The speed of this gait ranges from about six miles per hour to, at most, 10 miles per hour before it loses form. The sound of this gait is an uneven, 1-2, 3-4 beat, with the beats closest in time coming from the diagonal hooves. You can easily recite the sound "ka-chunck, ka-chunck" to the beats of this gait if you ride on a firm surface.

HOW IT LOOKS: When a horse fox trots, he nods his head and neck up and down at least a little. The nod may appear to be more of a V-shape than a simple vertical motion. The horse's croup and tail bounce up and down. The hind legs appear to "break" or bend sharply at the hocks, taking a less sweeping step than they do in the running walk. The diagonal pairs of hooves lift off from the ground relatively close in time, although not at the exact same moment as they do in

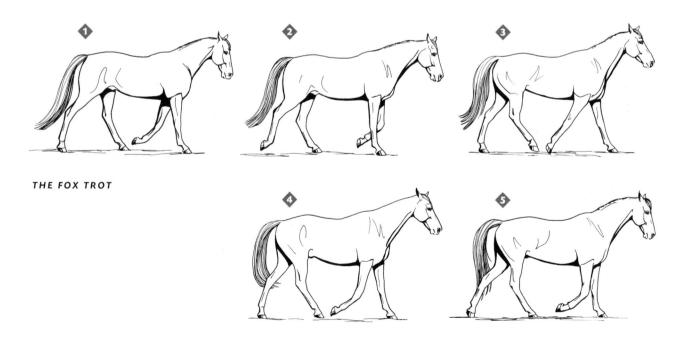

THE FOX TROT

WHAT ARE THE EASY GAITS?

the trot. The diagonal legs move forward together but not at the same moment, and the front hoof lands noticeably before the diagonal hind.

HOW IT FEELS: In the saddle, the fox trot pushes you from front to back with a slight stutter-step or bounce in the hindquarters. There is never a side-to-side motion, but there is a feeling that the shoulders are reaching and pulling and the hindquarters are actively moving up and down without jarring the rider's body.

Elements of Style and Quality in the Easy Gaits

Over time, people associated with each breed of gaited horse have developed ideas about the quality of performance in the easy gaits. Most of these characteristics, while prized in the show ring, do not matter much to pleasure or trail riders. In fact, some of these qualities may actually be somewhat detrimental to a sound performance on the trail. Because these characteristics are often easily visible, they can sometimes be confused with the elements that truly define the easy gaits. If you know how to recognize the gait itself under these "decorations" you can think of them as additions to the gait, some useful for distance riding, some just pleasing to look at.

Overstride, Understride, and Capping

The elements of track seem to get a lot of attention in the show ring. Horses in a running walk are expected to show a lot of overstride. Horses in a fino fino are expected to show understride. Horses in a fox trot, while once expected to cap their tracks, are now more desirable in the show ring if they show overstride. Long overstride can mean that a horse takes long, effortless steps, and therefore covers ground well. It can also mean that the horse's gait is to the lateral side of square or that his hind legs are longer than his front legs. An extremely long overstride may be a detriment on the trail in rough ground, because it can cause the horse to stumble. Understride, on the other hand, often indicates that the horse is not using his hindquarters very effectively to thrust himself for-

ward. He may be stiff in the hind legs and, therefore, take very short steps that require more energy to cover the same amount of ground as a long-striding horse. A horse that caps his tracks may be more sure-footed in rough terrain than one that overstrides, or he may have a choppy gait that does not cover ground well. When choosing an easy-gaited horse, consider these elements of track and the type of riding you plan to do. Choose a horse that fits your needs. What works for you may not necessarily be the type that is considered the best by show-ring standards.

Head Nod, Ear Flop, and Tooth Click

These small aspects of the way a horse's body moves in gait also receive a lot of attention in the show ring. Horses in a running walk and fox trot are expected to nod their heads and necks actively. Horses that fox trot are expected to flop their ears in time with their nodding heads. Horses in other easy gaits are not expected to exhibit these traits.

Although perhaps useful for shooing away flies, a lot of head nod and ear flop is not particularly important for trail or pleasure riding *except* when it occurs as a result of the relaxation and rhythm of a horse that is moving correctly in gait. Some horses naturally nod in their gaits and some don't move their necks so obviously. Some horses relax and allow their ears to flop in time with the way their heads nod, some don't. And some horses that nod also relax their jaws to the point that their teeth click as they nod. Others do not. Although in some horses a deep, relaxed nodding motion, flopping ears, and clicking teeth *are* results of relaxed, elastic use of the body in a particular gait, the comfort of the gait is not particularly affected by how obviously the horse does these things.

Be aware that it is possible to manufacture head nod and ear flop in horses that do not use their bodies with the elasticity and relaxation to produce those motions naturally. Horses may nod strongly in a rack or even a hard trot, if they have been made to do so through training gimmicks. Their ears may flop because they have been anesthetized or are full of oil or pebbles. Look at the legs, not the head and neck alone, to determine what gait a horse is doing and how well he does it.

Which Gait and Gaited Breed Should You Choose?

REMEMBER THAT ALL GAITED BREEDS include individual horses that may prefer a gait other than the one officially identified with that breed. Before you buy an easy gaited horse, ride him and decide whether you like the way he travels, even if he is not doing the signature gait of his breed. What do you want in a pleasure horse?

Do you enjoy excitement and speed on the trail? If so, a horse that specializes in one of the racking family of gaits may be for you.

Do you prefer a horse that approaches life with a more laid-back attitude, covering ground comfortably, but not a speed demon when you go out for a ride? If that type of horse is your ideal pleasure mount, consider a horse with an inclination to do a running walk or fox trot.

Do you plan on working cattle or riding in extremely rough country? Your best choice for those activities may be a horse that fox trots.

Do you plan to do competitive trail or endurance riding? Your best choice may be a horse that does several easy gaits as well as the trot.

Consider also your physical size relative to that of the horse. The Paso breeds, although they do produce some taller and larger-boned individuals, tend to be smaller and finer-boned than some of the other gaited breeds. If you are a tall or heavy person, those horses may not be the best choice for you. Icelandic horses, although most are well under 14.2 hands in height, tend to have heavier bone and better weight-bearing ability than their size might indicate. However, if you have very long legs, and are well over 6 feet tall, you may feel that an Icelandic is not tall enough to carry you well. Most of the other gaited breeds include individuals of all sizes, from almost pony height to well over 16 hands. You should be able to find one that fits you fairly easily.

Finally, consider the temperament of the horse you plan to spend all those hours with on the trail. All gaited breeds contain individuals of all temperaments, but strong inclinations to certain personality traits have been encouraged in some breeds. If you prefer a rather stoic horse, one that is a no-nonsense worker, you may find more of that personality type among Icelandic horses or some of the Rocky or Kentucky Mountain horse breeds. If you like a horse with an unflappable disposition, you may find more of that type in the Tennessee Walking Horse or Fox Trotting Horse breeds. For fiery spirit, tempered by kindness and willingness to please, the Paso Fino or Peruvian Paso horses are a good place to start. They are specifically bred for *brio,* a quality of controlled enthusiasm coupled with tractability that may be too hot for some people, but is exactly the quality others prize. There are certainly some hot-blooded Tennessee Walkers and Fox Trotters, as well as laid-back, lazy Paso Finos, but they are not as common as the others. It makes sense to consider horses from a breed that is known for a certain temperament that you prefer, rather than try to find that disposition in a breed that is not known for it.

Choose the gait and the horse that will work best for you physically. Many people with arthritis or other physical problems start to ride gaited horses because they are less stressful to ride than trotting horses. All easy gaits do not feel the same, however, and you are the only one who can decide which one is best for you. Although the easy gaits are all more comfortable to ride than the trot, some feel better than others to people with different physical needs. If at all possible, before you decide on a gaited horse, ride several horses that perform different gaits to see which is best for you. Some people with back problems find the motion of a running walk less comfortable than that of a rack, while others with arthritic hip joints may find the running walk more comfortable than the racking gaits. Others with neck problems may find the fox trot more comfortable than the running walk. Explore the different gaits available, and you will soon agree that once you "go gaited" you won't want to go back to a horse that only trots.

Front Leg Action

In some gaited breeds, the desired style is high, animated front leg action. For show-ring success, this action should be even in both legs, with the knees rising to the same height, and no indication of uneven steps. While high action is flashy to watch in a groomed arena, it may not be particularly valuable on the trail or for pleasure riding. High action can waste energy and tire a horse more quickly than lower, less animated use of the front legs. On long trail rides, a horse with extremely high action may wear down while others with lower action are still going strong.

In other breeds, a long, low, reaching step in the front is rewarded. Again, this may be exciting to watch, but a horse that takes a low step in front may trip more easily than one with less reach and more lift to the step. Evaluate leg action in light of the type of riding you plan to do with your horse, and decide how valuable front leg action is for that activity. Remember that gaits are not defined by action in the front legs and can be very comfortable with moderate leg motion.

You Be the Judge

Beneath the elements of style and quality, an easy gait is still defined by footfall sequence, footfall pick-up and set-down timing, support sequence, and weight transfer. Look for those basics to decide whether the horse is doing a specific gait, and decide for yourself whether the quality of his gait fits in with the type of riding you plan to do. In the end, your judgment matters most when it comes to enjoying your easy-gaited horse.

Support Patterns of the Symmetrical Gaits

1–4 ARE SQUARE GAITS, 5–8 ARE LATERAL GAITS, 9 & 10 ARE DIAGONAL GAITS

1. THE ORDINARY WALK

2. THE FLAT WALK

3. THE RUNNING WALK

4. THE PASO LLANO

5. THE TRUE PACE

6. THE AMBLE

7. THE SADDLE RACK

8. THE TRUE RACK

9. THE TROT

10. THE FOX TROT

FOOTFALLS & SUPPORTS OF THE SYMMETRICAL GAITS

	GAIT	FOOTFALL SEQUENCE	FOOTFALL TIMING
EVEN OR SQUARE GAITS	Ordinary and flat walk	Right hind, right front, left hind, left front	Even pick-up, even set-down, 1-2-3-4 beat
	Running walk/paso llano	Right hind, right front, left hind, left front	Even pick-up, even set-down, 1-2-3-4 beat
LATERAL GAITS	Pace	Right hind, right front hit at same time, moment of suspension, then left hind, left front	Lateral even two-beat timed gait, 1-2 beat
	Stepping/broken pace/ amble	Right hind, right front, left hind, left front	Uneven lateral pick-up and set-down, 1-2—3-4 beat, lateral hooves paired
	Saddle rack (fino, corto, largo)	Right hind, right front, left hind, left front	Lateral pick-up, even set-down, 1-2-3-4 beat
	True rack	Right hind, right front, left hind, left front	Lateral pick-up, even set-down, 1-2-3-4 beat
DIAGONAL GAITS	Trot	Right hind, left front hit at same time, moment of suspension, then left hind, right front	Diagonal even pick-up and set-down, 1-2 beat
	Fox trot	Right hind, right front, left hind, left front	Diagonal uneven pick-up and set-down, 1-2—3-4 beat, closest beats from diagonals

SUPPORT SEQUENCE	WEIGHT TRANSFER TO TRANSVERSE HOOVES	TRACK	SPEED
Three foot, two foot	Walking step, front and hind	Overstride more than in ordinary walk	4–6 miles per hour
Three foot, two foot	Running step in front, walking in hind	Overstride more than in flat walk	7–10 miles per hour, some horses faster
Two foot, no foot, two foot	Weight transfers in air, transverse pairs never on ground at the same time	Can be short or long overstride	Fast speed, more than 10 miles per hour, much faster when used for racing
Three foot, two foot	Walking step at slow speeds, running step at fast speeds	Varies from short to long overstride, depending on speed and horse	4–10 miles per hour
At slow speed, two foot, three foot; at moderate speed, three foot, two foot, one foot, two foot, three foot	Running step, front and hind	Some overstride, less than running walk	3–12 miles per hour
One foot, two foot	Leaping step, weight transfers in midair, front and hind	Some overstride, less than running walk	Up to 25 miles per hour
Two foot, no foot, two foot	Weight transfers in mid-air, transverse pairs never on ground at same time	May cap or overstride, depending on horse	About 6 miles per hour, faster when used for racing
Three foot, two foot	Walking step front and hind at slow speed, running step in front at fast speed	May cap or overstride, depending on speed and horse	6–10 miles per hour, faster speeds rougher to ride, slower called "fox walk"

CHAPTER TWO

The Why and How of Easy Gaits

Body Position, Conformation, and Gait

How can the foal amble, when the horse and mare only trot?
—WILLIAM CAMDEN (1551–1623)

Now that you know which gaits your horse may surprise you with, the next thing you'll probably wonder about is why he does them. The simple answer is usually, "It's genetic." Since just about everything in life is genetic in origin, that isn't much help. Even if there is a "gait gene" or gene complex, it does more than crank out gaits from a mysterious black box. Genes regulate physical properties of the body. Just as the genes that determine color regulate the chemical composition of pigment in hair shafts, any genes that determine gait will regulate the parts of the body that cause horses to move.

Although great strides have been made in mapping the genetic makeup of horses, there is still a lot of work to do, and no one can reasonably state which specific genes are associated with motion. As yet, there have been no solid, scientific studies on the inheritance of the easy gaits in general, let alone specific easy gaits. Any speculation on the way genetic inheritance affects gaits is just that, speculation. But it is possible to observe some physical traits that might be connected with the ability of horses to perform the easy gaits.

Gait Genes?

What exactly do those "gait genes" contribute? Most non-gaited foals will show some lateral gait for the first few months of life, but lose those gaits as they mature. Do their inborn gait genes change as they age, or do their muscles lose flexibility as their body proportions change? Some gaited horses only hard trot at liberty, never offering to do it under saddle. Do their gait genes switch on when they feel weight on their backs, or are other factors involved? Rather than trigger a specific gait, genetic material in all horses most likely contributes to gait by weaving a complex tapestry of factors that are related to motion. We don't know much about the specific genes involved, but we can observe the physical causes of movement.

You may have taken your horse out for a nice ride on a scenic trail, started out happily in his easy gait on firm level ground, then noticed that he changed into another gait as you climbed a small hill. Perhaps he changed gait again as you came back down the hill, and then changed yet *again* when you rode across some deep sand. While you sat there perplexed in the saddle, you accidentally discovered the role balance, weight distribution, and general body position play in the easy gaits. If you took a typical non-gaited horse on the same ride, he would probably only trot with you, no matter how much his balance changed as he covered the same terrain. What makes your gaited horse so susceptible to shifts in balance, and why does he respond to these shifts by changing gait?

The Source of the Easy Gaits

Three elements work together to produce movement in all horses, including the complicated coordination of the easy gaits. These elements are the neurological system, the muscular and ligament systems, and

An easy-gaited horse may fox trot on flat ground (A), hard trot uphill (B), and do a stepping pace on a slight downhill slant (C). His gait shifts with his balance and the position of his spine.

the skeletal system. The process is simple: The brain/nerves fire the muscles/tendons/ligaments, and they in turn move the bones of the skeleton. Your gaited horse changes gait according to changes in terrain because the use of his vertebral system, which is strongly related to his balance, changes with that terrain. When his body position changes with the use of his back and neck muscles and ligament system, it affects the way he moves his legs. That movement determines his gait. The source of his gaits is in his body.

The Brain and Nerves

When we look at a horse in motion, we can't see his neurological system or brain working. We can only guess how they operate to produce gait. It is possible that horses inherit favored "neural pathways" that predispose them to certain gaits. However, we also know from experience that a horse's gait and movement can be both involuntary and voluntary. The fact that a startled horse will take off at a dead run in a split second, long before he can process information through his brain that it is time to get out of Dodge, is evidence that his ability to move can be involuntary, or reflexive. The fact that we can ride a horse and cue him to walk slowly as he picks his way a step at a time through an obstacle course is evidence that his ability to move can be voluntary, or regulated by conscious thought.

Did your horse make a conscious decision to adjust his balance and change gait when he came to that first hill on the trail? Or was he somehow genetically programmed to shift neural pathways and use different gaits as the terrain changed? Probably not. Most likely, his balance shifted to the rear in response to gravity as he started up the hill. His nervous system registered that fact, and it sent signals to the muscles in his back and hindquarters to work a little differently than they did when he was on flat ground. This, in turn, changed the position of his spine and caused him to push more with his hind legs. Voilá, a different gait!

Are you stuck with whatever gait your horse's reflexes tell him he should do when he encounters a hill? No. Because horses can learn and because movement can be a voluntary behavior, with consistent training and conditioning you can eventually teach your horse to use the same gait up the hill that he chose on flat ground, overcoming his reflexive response to gravity. Few horses are "hard-wired" to do a specific gait in all circumstances because gait is a behavior, and it is subject to modification through conditioning. Even a horse that starts life with weak or incomplete "wiring" for a specific gait can learn to do that gait through repetition and through physical conditioning that encourages the development of new neural pathways.

The Muscular/Tendon/Ligament System

In contrast to the invisible action of the nervous system, it is possible to see parts of a horse's muscular/tendon/ligament system at work without dissecting him. Many muscles, which enlarge with work and shrink with disuse, are partly visible under the horse's skin. Work in the easy gaits can cause visible changes in muscle groups of the back and neck, which develop in different ways in gaited horses than in horses that only trot. A horse's ligaments and tendons are deeper below the surface of his skin, but their actions are visibly reflected in his body position and how he moves his legs.

The reason your gaited horse is able to use so many gaits on the varied terrain of the trail while the trotting horse only trots is directly related to your gaited horse's muscle tone and the elasticity of his ligaments and tendons. Although many trotting horses do have looseness in their back ligaments and stretch in their muscles and tendons similar to that of their gaited cousins when they are young foals, they don't retain these qualities as adults. They stay in their trot despite changes in balance because their backs do not change position very much as their balance shifts. Your gaited horse's entire body shifted a fair amount when he went uphill, causing his spine to rise a little, and changed again when he went downhill, causing his spine to sag a little. Those variations of posture were enough to change his gait because his back was affected much more strongly than that of a trotting horse.

Any gait gene discovered in the future is likely to have some connection with the type of muscle fibers, tendon elasticity, and ligament flexibility that a horse inherits. Because muscle composition and tone can be modified through exercise, however, you can help your horse develop the strength to maintain his gait no matter what type of muscle tone he was born with. He can learn to do the same gait on level ground and up and down hills if you help him build his body for that gait through consistent exercise.

The Bones

The most apparent element of the three that combine to move a horse is the skeletal system, the solid structure that underlies the soft tissue of the nerves, ligaments, tendons, and muscles. The proportions of his bones and the angles of his joints determine how a horse moves, how far and how high he can reach with his legs, and which body position will be most natural for him. Your horse may have had difficulty maintaining his balance and gait on that downhill trail because his bone structure made it difficult for him to do so.

Obviously, bone structure is the one part of the movement equation that can't be modified through training. It can be changed only in the breeding shed for the next generation. You can sometimes partially overcome his bone structure through conditioning your horse's muscles, tendons, and ligaments, or "rewiring" his habitual neural pathways, but his skeletal proportions dictate how he will carry his body and how he will move. Because the position of his back is

so important to the way a horse moves, the proportions of your horse's spine and hindquarters are vital to the ability to do his gait. The genes that determine the proportions of a horse's spine and hindquarters will most likely be a major part of any gait gene complex, if one is ever identified.

Simple Mechanics of the Horse's Body

The structure of the horse's body has been compared to a suspension bridge, a cantilever, a combination of the two, and a string and bow with a beam hung off both ends. Whether you see the Golden Gate Bridge, a construction crane/cantilever, or Robin Hood's bow when you look at your horse, underneath his skin he has a somewhat flexible system of vertebrae that is supported by the action of muscles and ligaments. These living "cables" operate above and below the bones of the spine to hold the structure together.

Very simply, when tension is increased in the ligament system, the back rises and is said to *bascule*, or round. When it is decreased, the back sags downward and is said to *invert*, or hollow. When tension is maintained at a moderate, resting level, the back is carried in a *neutral* position.

There are two locations where it is possible to tighten or loosen the system and adjust the position of the back. These "ratcheting points" are located at the withers and the lumbosacral junction of the spine, where the relatively flexible lumbar vertebrae meet the

Different views of the mechanics of the horse's back.

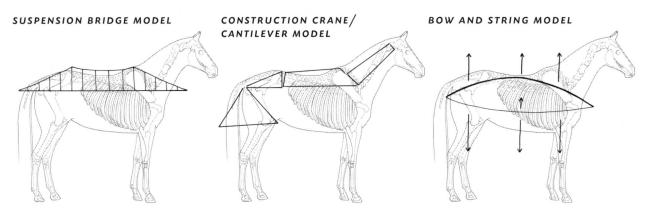

SUSPENSION BRIDGE MODEL

CONSTRUCTION CRANE/ CANTILEVER MODEL

BOW AND STRING MODEL

fixed sacral vertebrae, or sacrum, located just below the sacroiliac in the hindquarters.

In a real horse, the position of the head and neck combine with the position of the hindquarters to determine how much tension there will be in the living cable system that supports the spine. If a horse lowers his head and neck, the tension in the cable system is increased as the neck ligaments stretch over the

The basic bone structure of the horse.

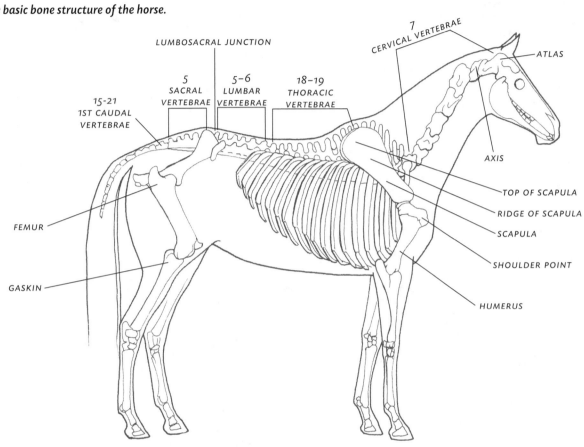

The living cable system of the horse.

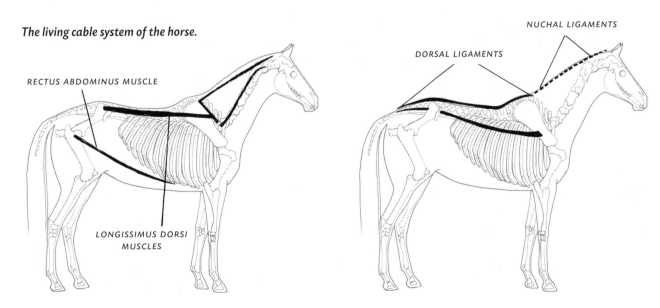

The three general back and body positions.

Round: *A tightened dorsal ligament system with strong abdominal muscles and flexed hind legs combining to lower the hindquarters from the lumbosacral junction.*

Neutral: *A working dorsal ligament system, functioning without being stretched through lowering the hindquarters and with no downward flexion at the lumbosacral junction.*

Hollow: *A relatively slack dorsal ligament system combined with slack abdominal muscles and no sustained downward flexion at the lumbosacral junction.*

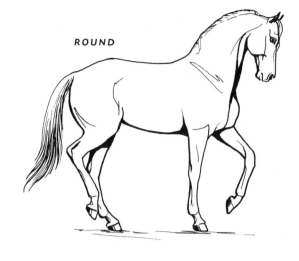

ROUND

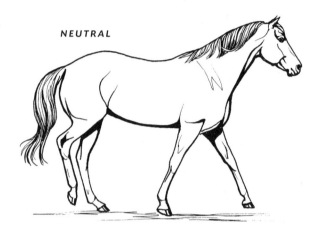

NEUTRAL

HOLLOW

withers. This results in a slightly raised back. If a horse lowers his hindquarters by tightening his abdominal muscles and flexing his pelvis downward from the lumbosacral junction, the entire cable system tightens. His withers, neck, and head rise as a result of stronger tension in the back ligaments. If a horse raises just his head and neck, without raising the base of his neck and without lowering his hindquarters, his back inverts slightly because the neck ligaments loosen over the withers. If a horse carries his neck at a medium height without flexing his pelvis downward, his back stays in a neutral position. At liberty, your horse probably uses whatever muscle and ligament tension is easiest at the time, sometimes raising his back, very rarely inverting it, and mostly staying in the neutral position.

The Three General Body Positions and the Easy Gaits

Depending on how much tension or slack there is in his living cable system, your horse will carry himself in a round, neutral, or hollow body position.

These body positions are the major points of a continuum that runs from "most round" to "most hollow" and includes many possible positions between the two extremes, as well as a large gray area in the center made up of variations of neutral.

The Neutral/Working Position

Most horses, gaited or non-gaited, spend most of their time in some degree of the neutral position. A horse in this position maintains just enough tension in his ligament cable system to hold his back level, with no obvious sag or rise to his spine. His abdominal muscles work just enough to keep his belly from sagging downward, but not enough to tip his pelvis or flex his lumbosacral junction. There is no strong tension or stretching in his neck ligament system, but he does keep his neck raised a little, not showing a dip in front of the withers or an inverted, ewe neck. In this position his back muscles remain elastic, allowing the legs to move freely with some energy coming from the hindquarters to thrust him forward. For gaited horses, very slight variations in the neutral position determine whether the horse will perform a true running walk or a fox trot. Horses that fox trot tend to have just slightly more rounded or raised backs than those that do a running walk, although both types can work correctly in gait in a basically neutral position.

The Rounded/Collected Position

A horse rounds his back and starts to *collect* his body by tightening his abdominal muscles, causing his pelvis to tip downward from the lumbosacral junction and increasing tension in his ligament system. This, in turn, increases the bend in all the joints of his hind legs as they reach under his body. As a result of this flexion in his spine, the base of his neck lifts and, eventually, his entire neck and head also rise. While ten-

sion increases in his ligament system, his large back muscles become more elastic, working to transfer efficiently the energy developed in his lowered hindquarters through his body.

There are many degrees of collection possible, from the slightly raised back of a horse just beginning to come away from a neutral position to the completely rounded frame of a horse working in a good piaffe.

> ## Indications That a Horse Has Been Working in a Rounded Position
>
> ▸ A well-defined line along the abdomen, at the rectus abdominus muscle, and a tight belly.
> ▸ Full muscles in the haunches.
> ▸ Full, strong muscles on either side of the backbone.
> ▸ Smooth, full muscling along the top of the neck, along the crest, and just in front of the withers.
> ▸ No obvious enlargement of muscles on the underside of the neck or in the shoulders.

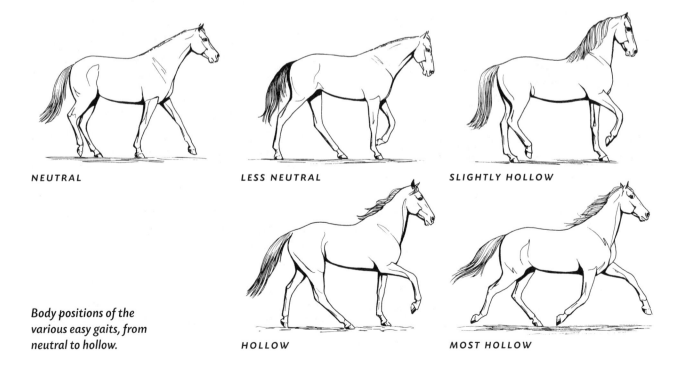

NEUTRAL   LESS NEUTRAL   SLIGHTLY HOLLOW

HOLLOW   MOST HOLLOW

Body positions of the various easy gaits, from neutral to hollow.

Easy-gaited horses do not reach the degree of roundness necessary for collected trot work, let alone that needed for a correct piaffe. Because the easy gaits require a type of elasticity in the back that is reduced when there is much tension in the ligament cable system (the same elasticity that allows non-gaited foals to do easy gaits for a short time in their lives), gaited horses do most of their gaits in a neutral to somewhat hollow position.

Despite the arched necks and high heads you may see in some gaited horses, very few of them work with their bodies in more than a slightly rounded neutral position. To test the degree of true collection possible in any particular easy gait, ride a gaited horse in his gait. Then teach him to round his body correctly, raising the base of his neck, creating a bascule in his back, and working with sustained downward flexion at the lumbosacral junction in a truly collected position. As he becomes more round, he will generally lose his easy gait and start trotting.

The Hollow/Inverted Position

A horse travels in a hollow or inverted position if he has some slack in his ligament system accompanied by tight or clamped large muscles in his back. If he raises his head and neck, loosening his neck ligaments, without lowering his pelvis by flexing downward at the lumbosacral junction, he loosens his living cable system from poll to tail and the "roadway" of his spine will sag down slightly. This slack in the ligament system is usually accompanied by a dip in his neck in front of his withers, an up and down bobbing of his hindquarters on the "hinge" of the lumbosacral junction, and sometimes a sagging belly as his abdominal muscles go slack. Without sustained downward flexion at the lumbosacral junction, a horse can carry a high head and flex at or near the poll, appearing to have a "collected" head-set, but his body will be inverted because of the lack of tension in his cable system.

While horses can and do trot and gallop with their backs in a hollow position, you will most often see this posture in horses doing the lateral gaits. Horses pace or do a stepping pace with inverted backs and tight, large back muscles. They rack or saddle rack with some inversion at the base of the neck and some tight-

ening of their back muscles over the loin. Just where along the spine this inversion is located and how deep it is determines which lateral gaits a horse uses.

If you watch a lot of horses move in their gaits, you will begin to notice that they pace with the most hollow back position, do a stepping pace with a slightly less hollow back, and do the various racking gaits with a slight inversion and a certain essential tension or tightening at the base of the neck and upper shoulder muscles. Horses doing the slower racking gaits, such as the corto or fino, can be confusing to watch because they take very short steps and compress the lengths of their bodies, moving in a position that looks a little like the rounded position of true collection. If you look closely, however, you will see that they don't move with sustained downward flexion at the lumbosacral junction or with visibly raised backs. These horses raise their necks and often flex at the poll, but they

Hunter's or Racker's Bump

IN SOME HORSES that have spent a lot of time working in an inverted position, a hard lump forms at the highest point of the croup, over the lumbosacral junction and the sacroiliac. The lump can be a result of trauma to this area of the back as the horse flexes up and down at the lumbosacral junction. Such motion creates tearing, scarring, and eventual ossification or hardening of the ligaments and muscles that surround the joint, enlarging it and forming a bump. In extreme cases the bump can be caused by dislocation of the sacroiliac as a result of stress to this part of the spine. This condition also occurs in horses that jump with their backs in a hollow position and in broodmares who have had several foals, because the process of labor can cause tearing at this joint.

Ossification at the lumbosacral junction reduces the flexibility of the horse's spine and can lead to stumbling and poor hind leg coordination. You can prevent this problem in your gaited horse by avoiding long periods of work in an inverted or hollow position and by encouraging the horse to raise his back while you ride in a walk, trot, or other gait between periods of work in gaits that are done in a more inverted position.

also travel with tightness at the base of the neck and without any stretch in the ligaments over the withers. Sometimes the tension in the muscles at the base and underside of the neck and over the top of the shoulder blades will cause horses working in these gaits to bow out their necks on the underside, a position never seen in horses traveling in true collection.

This tight body use compresses the movement of a horse's legs into short, high steps by containing his forward momentum and restricting the flexibility of his back. This position is not the same as the rounded position of the neck and back in true collection, but it is certainly not the same as the complete inversion of the entire spine of a horse doing a hard pace or the moderate inversion along the spine of a horse doing a stepping pace. It is not really collection in the classical sense. It is *containment*.

Conformation and the Easy Gaits

Most of the accepted traits of good conformation for trotting horses are desirable in gaited horses as well.

Straight front legs with no angular limb deviations (as in toe in or toe out) from elbow to ground; hind legs built for strength, with the hock joint lying

Indications That a Horse Has Been Working in an Inverted Position

▸ A sagging belly, with no visible muscle tone in the abdominal muscles.
▸ Flat muscles on either side of the backbone, a prominent spine, some downward sway in the back.
▸ Heavy muscling on the underside of the neck.
▸ A hunter's bump or knot at the highest point of the croup over the lumbosacral junction.

directly under the back of the buttock when a plumb line is dropped from it; deep hips about a third the length of the body — all contribute to strong, sound horses, no matter what the gait or the breed. Gaited horses, however, have different proportions because they use their bodies differently than their non-gaited cousins, and horses that prefer each specific easy gait tend to resemble one another in conformation. The nerves and muscles/ligaments can do a lot to move horses in specific easy gaits, but they work best when bone structure also encourages those gaits. Skeletal proportions can make it easy or very difficult for a

The horse on the left is contained. Note the lack of lowering at the lumbosacral junction and bowing out of the underside of the neck.

The horse on the right is truly collected. Notice the sustained lowering of the hindquarters from the lumbosacral junction, the arching of the neck, and the placement of the hind leg under the horse.

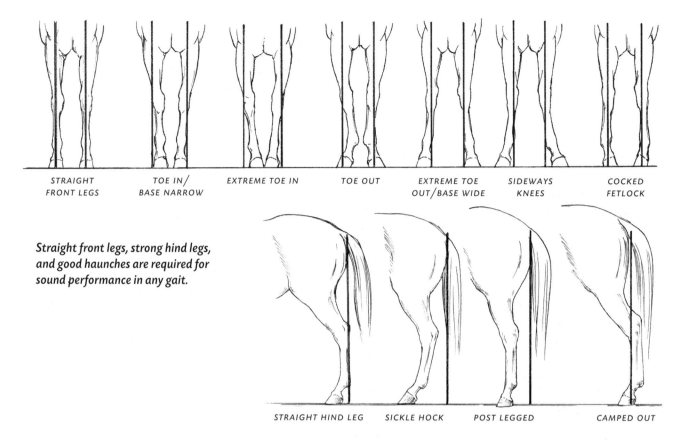

STRAIGHT FRONT LEGS   TOE IN/ BASE NARROW   EXTREME TOE IN   TOE OUT   EXTREME TOE OUT/BASE WIDE   SIDEWAYS KNEES   COCKED FETLOCK

Straight front legs, strong hind legs, and good haunches are required for sound performance in any gait.

STRAIGHT HIND LEG   SICKLE HOCK   POST LEGGED   CAMPED OUT

horse to adjust his living cable system. Bone structure isn't a perfect clue to gait, but it can give a pretty fair picture of which body position will be easiest for your horse and which gaits he is likely to prefer as a result.

Neck and Back Proportions

If you think of the suspension bridge/cantilever model of the horse's body, it is pretty obvious that the longer the span of skeletal "roadway" the horse holds up between supports, the harder it will be to tighten the cables that lift it. In the living horse, the proportions of the back between poll and lumbosacral junction are strongly related to the way he will carry his entire body.

Hindquarter Proportions

In addition to the way he carries his neck and stretches his ligaments over the withers, the second major "ratcheting point" for the horse's living cable system is the position of his hindquarters, including his hind legs. If the proportions of his pelvis and hind legs make it difficult for him to tighten his back ligament

Conformation Traits:
Inverted and Rounded

Conformation traits inclining a horse to an **inverted position** and often to the pace or stepping pace:
  ▸ A long back (the span from withers to the lumbosacral junction). A long span is harder to lift than a short one.
  ▸ A short neck. A thick, short neck may make it difficult for a horse to stretch his neck ligaments.
  ▸ A long loin, measured from the last rib to the lumbosacral junction. The loin has no support from the ribs, and a long loin is difficult to lift and round.

Conformation traits inclining a horse to a **rounded position** and often to the trot:
  ▸ A short back, from withers to lumbosacral junction.
  ▸ A moderately long neck. A longer neck may make it easier for a horse to tighten his neck ligament and, through it, the back ligament system.
  ▸ A short loin. A shorter loin may be easier lift and round.

Hindquarter Traits: *Inverted and Rounded*

Conformation traits inclining a horse to an **inverted position** and often to the pace or stepping pace:

▶ A short, steep pelvis. The shorter the pelvis, the less power there is in the attached muscles to lower it and tighten the back ligaments. The steeper the pelvic angle, the less able the horse is to tip it downward with the abdominal muscles because it is already tipped when the horse is in the resting position.

▶ Placement of the hip socket toward the rear of the pelvis. The closer the hip socket is located toward the tail from the midpoint of the pelvis, the more difficult it will be for the horse to flex his hind leg at that joint and reach strongly under himself.

▶ Short femur/thigh, long gaskin ratio. A shorter thigh in relation to the gaskin (stifle to hock) tends to place a horse's hocks behind him with a camped-out conformation. This makes it harder for him to raise and round his back because he can't easily increase the bend of the joints in his hind legs to lower his croup.

▶ Long hind legs in relation to front legs/rump high horse. If a horse stands with his croup higher than his withers and his stifles are above his elbows, he will have to work harder to lower his hindquarters and tighten his ligament system.

Conformation traits inclining a horse to a **rounded position** and often to the trot:

▶ A long, well-angled pelvis and hip/haunch. A pelvis and hip or haunch approaching one-third the body length of a horse (which is neither goose-rumped nor flat-crouped) provides a large, strong attachment point for the muscles that work to lower the hindquarters. This sort of pelvis can flex downward and tighten the back ligament system efficiently, contributing to a raised back.

▶ Placement of the hip socket toward the center of the pelvis. This placement allows the hip joint to flex more easily and can help lower the hindquarters.

▶ Equal femur/gaskin ratio. If the thigh and the gaskin are about equal in length, the hind leg can flex more strongly at the stifle and hock, lower the hindquarters, and stretch the back ligament system.

▶ Equal height in hind and front legs/rump and withers even. If the elbow and stifle are almost the same distance from the ground, the horse will be more likely to have equal height at the withers and croup. He will not have to work as hard to lower his hindquarters below the level of his withers to tighten the back ligaments, and it will be relatively easy for him to round his back.

system, he will probably move in an inverted position. If they allow him to easily lower his haunches and use his hind legs to reach strongly under him, he will be more likely to travel in a rounded position.

Few gaited horses have all the traits that can lead to a hollow body position, and even fewer have all the traits that incline to a rounded position. If you expect your horse to do a gait that requires a neutral to round position, he will have a better chance if he doesn't have more than a couple of traits that contribute to an inverted posture mixed with some that incline to a more rounded position. If you expect your gaited horse to do a gait that requires a neutral to slightly inverted position, he should not have all the traits that produce a rounded posture and facilitate a hard trot.

This is where breeding and breed registries enter the picture. Because most breeds have been specifi-

cally selecting horses for particular easy gaits for a long time, the conformation proportions in horses of those breeds will result in a higher number of horses that do those specific gaits. Horses that are expected to do a pace or stepping pace will have slightly longer backs and loins, shorter necks, and steeper, shorter hips than those that work in more neutral frames. Horses that are expected to work in the racking gaits often have longer loins and shorter hips than those that work in the more neutral position gaits. Horses that work in neutral positions in the running walk or paso llano tend to have moderate to long necks, long backs, and relatively long hips. Horses that work in neutral to round positions in the fox trot may have shorter backs and loins than those that prefer the running walk or paso llano, but they will also have long necks and relatively long hips. While these proportions are not absolute guarantees of these specific easy gaits, they are good indicators of which gaits a horse is most likely to prefer. It is a good idea to pay some attention to them if you are selecting a horse for a specific gait.

Conformation and Quality or Style of Gait

Along with strongly influencing which gait your horse prefers, conformation also contributes to the way he does the gait. High action, long step, and overstride or understride are all the direct result of the type of conformation a horse is born with. Whether these things are important to you or not, they are considered important in the highly subjective world of the show ring. Of course, the qualities that make a gait exciting to watch in a show may make it pretty useless for trail riding. Because show-ring style has an effect on the breeding pool for pleasure and trail horses, however, it is a good idea to know which conformation features will produce which type of gait.

Traits that Determine Front Leg Motion

The range of motion in a horse's front legs is determined by the length and angles of his shoulder and humerus bones.

The Special Case of Termino

PERUVIAN PASO HORSES, some Paso Fino horses, and some others that perform the racking family of gaits move their front legs in an upward and outward rotation from the shoulder that has nothing to do with bone conformation. Horses with perfectly straight legs will display *termino*, which is quite different from the paddling of horses with crooked front legs. Equal, moderately high termino is often desired for Peruvian Pasos in the show ring, but is not as important in a trail or pleasure horse. If your horse shows equal, natural termino, do not try to alter it through shoeing or trimming. It is the result of the way he uses his body in his gait, not a sign of some structural flaw. If his termino is uneven, however, it can be a sign of a physical problem in his leg or shoulder and may indicate a need for veterinary evaluation.

An ideal shoulder for long reach is set close to 45 degrees, measuring along the ridge in the shoulder blade (spine of the scapula) to the top of the shoulder (a flat, fan-shaped bone). Measured this way, few horses of any breed have shoulders that are actually 45 degrees. The ideal 45-degree shoulder that has been adopted by many breeds is likely only if you measure

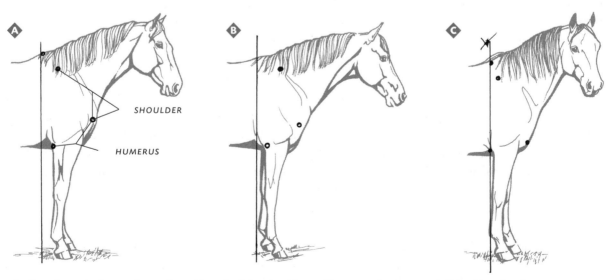

*In the front legs of a horse, the angle and length of the shoulder and humerus determine reach and height of motion. Horse **A** will have moderate reach and height; horse **B** will have high action but not much reach; and horse **C** will have a long, low step.*

Hind leg conformation.

A: *Equal femur and gaskin, open stifle, open hock, horse takes moderate long steps.*

B: *Short femur, long gaskin and cannon, closed stifle, closed hock, horse takes long steps, may be "hocky" in his action.*

C: *Equal femur and gaskin, open stifle, more closed hock, horse takes short but hocky steps.*

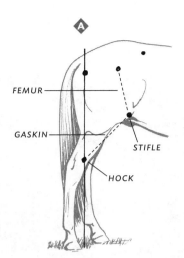

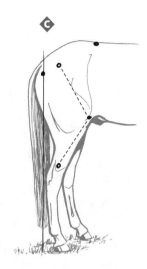

FEMUR

GASKIN

STIFLE

HOCK

the angle of the shoulder to the crest of the withers, not to the top of the shoulder blade. Try measuring your own horse, first to the top of his real shoulder blade, then to the crest of his withers. He may have a 45-degree shoulder using his withers as the top, but a much steeper one if you measure his actual shoulder blade. Most shoulders with adequate reach range between 50 to 53 degrees in slope. In horses that take short, upright steps, the shoulder may be closer to 60 degrees.

Another factor in front leg action is the humerus bone, which runs from the point of the shoulder to the elbow, determining reach and lift in gait. The more upright and shorter the humerus bone, the less reach the horse will have, but the higher his steps will be. The longer and more horizontal the humerus, the longer but less lofty his steps will be. For pleasure riding, when you want moderate reach and height of step, the angles and proportions of the humerus should place the point of the elbow in a direct line under the crest of the withers. Much in front of that, the horse will take short, choppy steps; much behind it, he will be inclined to stumble because he does not have much scope in his front leg motion.

Traits That Determine Hind Leg Motion

The range of motion of the hind legs of a horse is determined by the proportions of the femur/thigh and gaskin and by the angles of the hip, stifle, and hock.

Horses that take short or moderate steps behind often have nearly equal femur-to-gaskin ratios. Horses that take long steps behind and show a lot of overstride in their gait track frequently have much longer gaskins than femurs, often as much as a 1:1.5 ratio, with the gaskin being half again as long as the femur.

The angles of the joints of the hind legs also contribute to the type of steps horses take. Sickle hocks are relatively common in gaited horses, sometimes deliberately bred into them with the expectation of producing long steps in back. Horses with more closed hock angles and truly sickle-hocked horses, however, may not take long steps with their hind legs unless they also have long cannons and very long gaskins. They may be susceptible to hock and stifle injuries that negate any advantage of this type of hind leg conformation for producing longer steps.

Why Structure Matters

A horse can do only what his body allows him to do. If his bone structure inclines him to use his body in a particular easy gait, his muscles and nervous system will have an easier time moving him in that gait. When he doesn't have to work hard to do his gait, you don't have to work very hard to ride or train him in that gait. Make life easy for yourself and your horse by learning to understand what his body can tell you about the gait that suits him best.

CHAPTER THREE

Before You Ride

Attitude, Equipment, and Equitation for Your Easy-Gaited Pleasure Horse

You can't out-stout a horse, but you ought to be able to out-think one.
— DOUG ANDERSON, DVM

You can work through a horse's body to help him do his easy gaits only if he wants to cooperate, his body is comfortable, and you ride him effectively. The attitude you have about working with him and the attitude he has about working with you form the foundation for riding him in his easy gait. Equipment that fits him and helps you give him clear signals for gait work strengthens this foundation and makes it easier to ride him in his gait. And, finally, sitting well in the saddle and using effective aids to cue him for his gait builds on that foundation to help him use his body correctly for whichever easy gait is most natural to him.

Attitude, Yours and His

To gait well, your horse must trust you, respect you, and work willingly for you. A confused, resistant, or fearful horse will have a stiff body and most likely travel with his head high and his back muscles clamped, physical reactions that can make any horse do a hard pace. You want your horse to be relaxed, willing, and responsive, so he can do his easy gait effortlessly and will listen to you when you ask him to use his body in that gait. How do you develop a co-operative, relaxed horse? The secret is in the way you interact with him on the ground and in the saddle.

Basic Approaches to Training

Horses, if left to their own devices, would probably be content to do nothing but eat, sleep, hang around with their buddies, and occasionally show an interest in the opposite sex. Humans are the ones who decide there should be more to a horse's life than those basic activities. What is absolutely amazing, if you think about it, is that these large animals actually allow us to decide what they are going to do and, for the most part, willingly do all sorts of things for us that they would never do without us. Why do they do it?

There are a couple of possible answers to this question and two types of horse training that come from them.

Approach 1

The first answer, and one that has been around since people domesticated horses, is that horses do what we want because we **make** them do it. According to this approach, the horse/human relationship is mostly adversarial, meaning that one must conquer the other. The logic is that by overpowering horses and forcing them to accept our dominance, we break them to our will and make them our servants. This approach often requires the use of snubbing posts, trip ropes, side-lines, running W's, and other mechanical devices that physically restrain and subdue a horse as he is "broke" and strong leverage bits to "keep him under control" once he has been forced under saddle. This way of doing things often produces a horse with a stiff body and either a resistant attitude or a fearful one.

Approach 2

The second answer, and one almost as ancient, is that horses become our partners because, as herd animals, they require a leader. According to this view of the relationship, horses somehow see us as leaders and willingly do what we ask because of an innate desire to "get along" in the herd. The horse/human relationship is seen as a partnership, with the human as the managing partner, not an adversary or conqueror. The main responsibility for people who believe that a horse responds to humans out of redirected herd instinct is to convince the horse that human beings are actually odd-looking but superior members of his herd. Through kind, firm, consistent handling, it is possible to teach the horse in a way that is comprehensible to him, without force.

Most people beyond a certain age or level of experience opt for the second method because it works with less strain on both horse and trainer. The second approach is useful for working through the horse's body to develop the easy gaits because it creates less mental and physical tension in the horse, tension that often goes with an undesirable hard pace. Think of yourself as your horse's leader, not his conqueror, and his gaits will reflect your attitude.

Who's in Charge Here?

Although your horse sees you as a herd member and not an adversary (or worse, a predator), he should not be the dominant member of the partnership! Horses are large, heavy animals that can and do injure or kill humans out of fear or aggression. To be safe with your horse, your job is to become the unquestioned leader in the small herd consisting of you and him, because, after all, riding was your idea, not his. If he doesn't see you as his leader and trust your judgment, he will not see any point in doing all the odd things you may think he should do when you ride. To convince your horse that you are his managing partner, first examine the way horses organize themselves in herds.

If you watch horses in an established group, you will soon notice that one (usually a mare) is definitely in charge. She eats where she wants, drinks first, decides when the group will move to a different place to graze, and basically runs the show. Others stay "out of her space" unless she invites them to come close, wait for her to go through narrow passages ahead of them, and give her the respect she feels she is owed. This horse is the alpha mare, and her position is important in keeping the group in order, preventing fights among underlings, and preserving the well-being of the herd. Horses that are lower than alpha are usually ignored if they try to lead the group. They are fair game for play fights, bossing around, and general lack of respect from others in the group. The alpha is not. If you are going to have much success riding and training any horse, you absolutely must convince him that you are the alpha in the little herd consisting of the two of you.

Most alpha mares establish their position through personality, intelligence, and willingness to back up the threats they make to any potential challenger. These mares simply act like they are in charge, and the others (the betas and zetas) hang back and let them lead. These leaders rarely kick or bite a subordinate horse. A glare and threatening expression are usually enough to keep the underlings in line. In most conditions, an alpha will use physical violence only if challenged for authority. Then, after a short (or long) kicking match, things are resolved and the top alpha wins position and, usually, is not challenged again by the defeated party for a time.

You can establish your alpha position the same way a mare does, through strength of personality, intelligence, and willingness to back up your authority with physical force if necessary. If you deal with your horse in a confident, consistent way, rewarding him with kind words or strokes when he does what you want, asking him to do only what he can reasonably be expected to do, and resorting to force only when absolutely necessary to reprimand him for major disobedience or dangerous behavior, you will have no trouble being the lead partner in the relationship.

Friendly But Firm Persuasion

When is force necessary? This can be a touchy subject. Some people think that hitting a horse in any way at any time is abuse, and others believe that hitting a horse with a whip is the only way to get him to do anything. Both approaches are equally flawed. As with everything else in horsemanship, how you reprimand a horse depends on the personality of the horse involved. Some horses are so timid that a slightly raised tone of voice will reduce them to complete submission and earn you apologetic looks. Others are so tough that a strong whack from a thick crop is about the only thing that gets the idea across that they have done something potentially dangerous that you won't tolerate, such as kicking out or slamming you against a wall. Think of how an alpha mare reacts to the other horses in her herd. For the timid ones, she may flick an ear at what she sees as disobedience; for the more aggressive ones, she will bite or kick to move them out of her way and get her message across. Adjust your reactions to the personality of your horse.

Mild Reprimands

If your horse is basically a timid soul, and he does something less than respectful, such as walk too close to you, invade what you consider your personal space, or step on you, **tell** him that he has gone over the boundaries of good behavior. Say *No!* forcefully as he misbehaves. Raise your arms to make yourself appear larger than life and walk purposefully toward him to back him away from you. If he is in a halter, give a single, sharp, quick tug/release on the lead rope as you correct him. If necessary, back this up with a single hard slap from your open hand on his chest or neck. With this type of horse, "spare the rod" or you could easily make him fearful and permanently damage him mentally.

Stronger Measures

Sometimes a milder form of discipline such as a harsh word or a tug and release on the lead rope fails. If you feel that what your horse is doing is likely to be dangerous to you or reflects a total lack of respect or "testing" of your authority, take charge. As soon as possible after the disobedient act, but preferably during it, use a stern, loud voice to say *No!* Back him away from you and, if he did something really dangerous such as bite hard or kick, whack him hard once on the neck, shoulder, or rump with your open hand or a crop, again moving him away from you. Then stop and give the horse a chance to understand that you won't allow his misbehavior. See whether he tries it again.

He probably won't, at least for a while. Some horses test constantly until they are convinced that you are truly alpha, then they settle down and don't challenge again. If he has a tough personality, a quick single whack on the neck or shoulder from a hand or crop will not permanently injure your horse, either physically or mentally. It will remind him that you are able to back up your commands with force if necessary, the same way an alpha mare would discipline him. Horses are physically very strong and, short of leverage devices, bats, clubs or restraints, there is not much you can do to one that will be as severe as the type of damage an alpha mare can dish out.

There is, however, *never* any reason to beat a horse, even one that is tough mentally. Physical punishment that goes beyond a quick reminder that he should not do whatever he did wrong can make any horse tense, confused, and sometimes aggressive. In addition to being cruel, this type of punishment works against developing a relaxed, willing horse that is able to work in a pleasant easy gait. Horses seem to have a well-developed sense of personal justice. They are willing to respect you as long as you deal with them fairly. If you go beyond that into abuse, they will become sullen and sour and you will have little success in trying to train them. Horses can be spoiled just as easily by too much physical discipline as by too little.

Treats and Rewards

This topic is almost as controversial a subject as punishment. Again, how you reward a horse depends on the personality of the horse. A kind word of praise and a gentle stroke are necessary to all horse/human relationships. Relaxing pressure from legs or reins as a reward is an essential part of riding. Hand-fed treats are another story. Some horses that are fed treats for no reason rather than as a reward for a specific performance can become obnoxious pests, nipping and shoving, demanding to be fed. These are usually horses that have not fully accepted you as alpha, and it is not a good idea to give them anything by hand. Feed them only in their feed boxes if you want to reward them with treats. You can, however, give most horses a piece of apple or an alfalfa cube once in a while, as a

reward for an exceptional ride or work session, without turning them into cookie monsters. As long as a horse respects you on the ground and doesn't pester for his treat, there is no harm and some good in finishing a session with a fed reward. Just stop doing it if the horse starts to get pushy.

Will feeding treats and petting your horse somehow spoil him? As always, know your horse. Only if he is fed treats for no reason or allowed to demand them with no correction for pushy behavior will you be spoiling him by feeding him by hand. Obviously, pushy mares or mouthy geldings or stallions are not good candidates for treats. With most horses, though, once you are clearly alpha, you can feed by hand and you will not lose status. Horses in a herd are frequently the objects of affectionate treatment by the alpha mare, but they know better than to challenge her authority even if she does occasionally nicker to them or groom their backs. You can handle your horse kindly and with affection, and not ruin his spirit or turn him into a disrespectful, spoiled animal, as long as you are clearly the lead partner in the relationship.

Dealing with Alpha Horses

You will not have much trouble becoming alpha to most horses. In the natural scheme of things, more horses are betas or zetas than are true alphas. However, once in a while you will run across a horse that is accustomed to alpha status herself (again, it is very frequently a mare). These horses often do not recognize a human as an authority figure and do not want to give up their dominant role. Sometimes they can be convinced that they are not so dominant by spending time at pasture with an older alpha who can teach the young one some manners. Of course, this only works if the older mare keeps her status in the resulting struggle! If that is not possible or for some reason fails, you can work things out with her on your own, using round pen and ground work techniques to remind her that you really are the managing partner in the relationship. There are a number of sources on round pen work for discipline available and some are listed in the bibliography (see page 241). If you have a definite alpha horse that does not accept you as dominant, by all means learn about and apply these techniques. They work as well for gaited horses as they do for non-gaited ones.

You may also discover that the only way to get along with an alpha horse is to devise a "division of power" in which she is allowed some decision-making authority under your guidance. This arrangement is sometimes seen in the wild with co-alpha mares in small herds. One is the leader, but she shares authority with another strong alpha. With a horse like this, you can insist on alpha status on the ground, but allow her some leeway from the saddle. Let her decide if trails are safe. If a bog looks dicey, listen to her if she is unwilling to cross it. She may have better judgment about footing than you do. If you can work with rather than against the alpha personality of your horse, you may be pleasantly surprised. These horses make great trail and working cattle horses because they can and do think on their own, are usually fearless, and will take care of a rider as long as he doesn't get in their way. Sadly, they also make good rodeo broncs if they can't be convinced to at least share status with a human.

Probably the best way to deal with alpha types is to start at birth convincing them that you are a superior being, while letting them have plenty of time out with a herd of older horses that will not tolerate misbehavior. If they are worked sensibly and consistently from earliest foalhood, these fillies (and sometimes colts) will see you in the same way they see their own alpha mothers, and you will be able to channel their talents in the direction you want. If left on their own in a herd of young submissive horses from weaning until they are two, or if allowed to live only with submissive older horses while being fed treats and never having a human insist they do anything they don't want to do, they can be difficult, stubborn, and downright dangerous.

Building a Cooperative Attitude in Your Horse

Whenever you ride, no matter how casually you do it, you are training your horse. The end result of good riding and good training should be a nicely gaited horse that is calm, obedient, forward moving, supple, straight, and, eventually, light. To develop this type of horse, approach riding and training quietly, patiently, and systematically. Don't ride or try to train when you are angry, unhappy, nervous, or in a bad mood, and don't take your emotional problems out on your horse. He will pick up on your attitude, reflect it in his behavior, and you both will be miserable.

Traits of Good Riding and Training

To be successful in riding and training, you must be **consistent** in the way you deal with your horse. Don't confuse your horse by allowing him one day to shove you with his head because it is "cute" and punishing him for the same behavior the next. Use the same leg cues each time you ask him to move, and use the same rein cues when you ask him to turn or stop. Don't suddenly change your weight or leg cues and expect him to adjust instantly.

Horses learn by progressing from familiar experiences to unfamiliar ones. To teach your horse, work in **small increments**, building on what he already knows. Start with easy things and very gradually add more complicated ones. Don't ask him to do flying lead changes if he hasn't learned how to canter reliably on both leads!

Although this is not as important in pleasure riding a trained horse, while you are working with your horse to do his best easy gait, your riding should be **goal-oriented**. Before each training session, decide what you want to work on, set out a reasonable plan of action that will allow you to reach that goal, then follow it as closely as possible.

You should set goals, but do not expect instant perfection from your horse. Be **flexible** and realistic about what he can learn. If your horse is just not responding to whatever you are doing, it is a good idea to relax and analyze the situation.

Don't be too stubborn to take a different approach and work around the problem. Maybe you both need a change of scenery. Stop work on whatever he is not able to understand and take a relaxed trail ride in whatever gait he feels like doing. No law says that what you decided to do for the day absolutely must be accomplished according to your timetable. Stop and smell the roses!

Horses get dull and "sour" if they are kept at one thing for long periods of time, so avoid drilling a horse in any particular exercise for more than a few minutes at a time. Instead, be **tactful and moderate**. Notice if the horse is acting confused or resentful and instantly go on to something he does well. Always end your sessions on a successful note, even if the whole episode from start to finish has been a mess. Let the horse feel as though he has done at least one thing to please you, even if it is just walking quietly and stopping.

In setting goals and working with your horse, do not give up the first time he misunderstands what you are trying to teach, but be **reasonable**. Don't ask him to do things he is not mentally or physically able to do. If your horse has been crossing small puddles with no problem, it is reasonable to expect him to cross a brook and to insist that he do it, even if you do have to dismount and lead him through the first time. It is not reasonable to expect him to swim a river if he has never seen moving water!

Perhaps the best thing you can do when riding or training is to be **sensible**. Take advantage of your horse's moods. On a cool, windy day, when he is bursting with energy, don't spend your time trying to teach him slow little exercises such as walking with small steps. Work on his extended gaits instead. On hot, humid days, work him in slow circles or a little collected canter, not on great gait extensions.

Plan Ahead

Never do anything that will put your horse in a position to become hurt or scared if you can possibly avoid it. If he appears frightened of something (the world is full of horse-eating monsters for some horses), don't be too proud to get off and show him that he is safe by putting yourself between "it" and him. Use good judgment and avoid dangerous and useless stunts, such as riding him full speed down crumbling cliffs where he could take a bad fall and hurt both of you. Let him know that you will look out for him just as well as a real alpha mare, earn his trust, and he will work willingly for you. Confuse or frighten him and he may not be very reliable.

Pleasure Riding Versus Training

So, when can you relax and just ride as a passenger, instead of training your gaited pleasure horse? If you expect good, consistent gaits from your horse, you won't ever "just ride" him, although once he has become fit and learned his gait you can certainly relax while riding him. Remember, however, that every time you ride your horse or handle him on the ground, whether you mean to or not, you are training him, and if you are observant, you can also learn from him. Eventually, you will probably stop teaching your horse specific skills, but whenever you ride new things will happen to you both. One of the main joys of riding is that the experience is always different. You and your horse may dance the same dance over and over, but the tune is always changing. If you ride with an open and interested mind, you will never be bored, and neither one of you will ever stop learning!

Equipment for Gaited Horses

Although each breed has its own rules for tack in the show ring and many things are marketed specifically for gaited horses, for pleasure riding you need only tack that fits the horse and that works to help him do his gait. There are no magic saddles or headgear that work on every horse of a particular gaited breed, only tack that fits and works for an individual horse, no matter what his breed.

Saddles

Look in any saddle shop or catalog and you will probably be confused by the variety of saddles available. Where once saddles were divided into English or Western designs, now there are many different types that do not fit into any particular category, many of them marketed for easy-gaited horses. No matter what the design, there are only three things that really matter when deciding on a saddle for your gaited horse. To work well for a gaited horse, a saddle must fit his back, place you in the best position to encourage his gait, and be comfortable to ride in. There is no one brand or style of saddle that will work for all gaited horses nor one that will be appropriate for all horses of a particular breed. Look beyond the label and see how a saddle actually works for your horse before you choose it.

Fitting a Saddle

The best, or most expensive, saddle in the world is not going to help your horse do his gait if it does not fit his back. A horse with a sore back caused by poor saddle fit will not be willing or able to do his easy gait easily because his long back muscles will lose elasticity if they are cramped from pain caused by a saddle that digs into them.

In addition to the way the tree fits on the horse's back, the shape and set of the bars of a saddle and its placement on his back will have an effect on how well a horse can do the easy gaits. Carefully consider the shape of the gullet and the front of the bars of a saddle when you choose one for your gaited horse. Many gaited horses have wide and long shoulders. To gait well, they need freedom in those shoulders that can be restricted by the skirt, flap, or bar design of some saddles, even those that otherwise fit the horse. Jumping saddles or all-purpose saddles and some Western saddles can interfere with the shoulders of gaited horses. Saddles with long bars, whether the bars are flexible or fixed, will go over the top of your horse's shoulders, no matter how well they are flared and placed, and will interfere with his shoulder motion. Dressage saddles and cut-back saddles usually leave the shoulders free, as do some plantation or endurance designs and some of the wide-flare Western saddles.

The shape of skirting over the tree and the length of the bars over the loin of the horse also have an effect on saddle fit for gaited horses. Some gaited horses have prominent hips and a short length between the shoulders and the hipbones. Western saddles with square skirts will often rub on those hipbones or sit over the top of them. Round-skirted Western saddles are a better solution for those horses. Some saddles have very long, narrow bars that project over the loins. Whether they flex or are fixed, these saddles may dig into the thick back muscles and cause the horse to tighten them, losing elasticity and creating a body position favoring the pace. These saddles are not a good choice for a gaited pleasure horse.

Even the best fitting saddle can interfere with your

Signs of Poor Saddle Fit

▶ Gullet presses down on withers, tree or weight sits directly on spine.
▶ Bars cover shoulder blades, pinching or pressing on them. No flare to allow the shoulders to move.
▶ Back of bars presses into the loin, back skirts hit the hipbones or lie over them.
▶ Uneven sweat marks or dry spots on the back after work, which can be signs of saddles "bridging" on the back, putting strong pressure in some places and not touching others.
▶ Shearing or rubbing of hair on the back, especially in the loin area.
▶ White hairs on either side of the withers or loin caused by continued excess pressure.
▶ Back palpation causes the horse to flinch or squat downward after a ride. Or, in a horse with a back blocked by pain, no reaction at all from firm downward pressure on either side of the backbone at the loin.
▶ Behavior patterns such as tail swishing, balking, rearing, bucking, or fidgeting when being saddled. Pacing when under saddle can also be caused by back pain.

horse's easy gait if it is not set on his back correctly. For the best placement, set the saddle so that the gullet is over the highest point of the withers and the front edge of the tree is set approximately an inch behind the shoulder blade. This will allow his shoulders to move freely in his gait without pressure from the saddle. You may find that setting a saddle in this position will put the seat of the saddle too far back toward the horse's loin. If this is the case, consider a saddle with a different seat design that will allow you to sit more centered on the horse's back.

There are a number of saddle-fitting systems listed in the bibliography of this book (see page 241) that can help you determine whether a particular saddle fits or can be adjusted to fit your horse. Whether you use a gauge, a gel-filled impression pad, or a computerized pressure monitoring system, if you are concerned about saddle fit, do yourself and your horse a favor and find out how your saddle works on his back.

Seat Design

The design of the seat determines where a saddle places your weight on the horse's back. For gaited horses, as for the non-gaited type, the best place to carry weight is over the strongest part of the back, just behind the withers, where the large ribs provide stability for the backbone. This point is also directly above the horse's resting center of gravity. Sitting here, you can modify the horse's balance and back position with very slight shifts in your pelvic position. A saddle that places you in this balanced position is very important for riding your gaited horse because to overcome any gait problems he may have, you must be able to adjust your weight and his balance as easily as possible. Any saddle that by design forces your weight and center of gravity either in front of this point or behind it will limit your ability to use seat or weight aids for the easy gaits.

The best and most versatile seat design for pleasure riding a gaited horse is flat, with no large hump behind the pommel to throw you back toward the cantle, with stirrups that hang directly under your seat, not toward the front of the saddle or behind the deepest point of the seat.

Both English- and Western-style saddles are available with flat seats. While you can certainly ride in other seat designs, you will have to work harder in them to stay balanced over the strongest part of the horse's back.

There are also other types of saddles available with flat seats that work well for gaited horses. Some of the endurance-type saddles are made this way, as are some Australian saddles and some plantation-design saddles. Any of these that fit your horse and you while allowing you to adjust your seat position and your horse's back position will work well.

THREE DISTINCT TYPES OF ENGLISH SADDLES

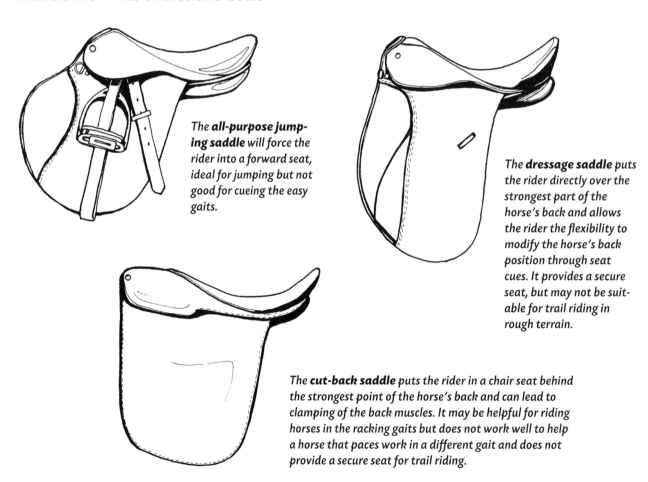

The **all-purpose jumping saddle** will force the rider into a forward seat, ideal for jumping but not good for cueing the easy gaits.

The **dressage saddle** puts the rider directly over the strongest part of the horse's back and allows the rider the flexibility to modify the horse's back position through seat cues. It provides a secure seat, but may not be suitable for trail riding in rough terrain.

The **cut-back saddle** puts the rider in a chair seat behind the strongest point of the horse's back and can lead to clamping of the back muscles. It may be helpful for riding horses in the racking gaits but does not work well to help a horse that paces work in a different gait and does not provide a secure seat for trail riding.

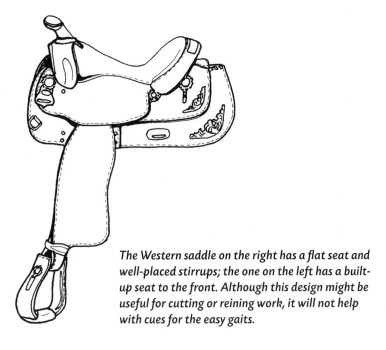

The Western saddle on the right has a flat seat and well-placed stirrups; the one on the left has a built-up seat to the front. Although this design might be useful for cutting or reining work, it will not help with cues for the easy gaits.

There is no one brand or one style of saddle that is perfect for all gaited horses. Find one that fits, that allows you to sit easily in the best position to encourage your horse's gait, and that is comfortable to ride in. You may be surprised to find that the fanciest or most expensive saddle might not be the best for you and your horse.

Bridles and Bitless Headgear

If the number of saddle designs available is confusing, the types of headgear offered for sale can be mind-boggling! The purpose of headgear is to allow easy communication with the horse; it helps you tell him to slow down, stop, turn, or back up. In addition to these basics, headgear also helps you tell him where and how to carry his head and neck, a vital element in adjusting his dorsal ligament system and developing his gait. Effective headgear makes it possible for you to do these things efficiently, without causing pain and resistance from the horse. Although certain breeds have become identified with specific headgear and those bridles or bits may be required for show-ring exhibition, outside of the show world, your gaited pleasure horse can be ridden in any headgear that

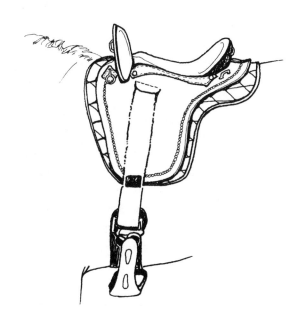

A modern endurance saddle that is similar to the plantation saddles used for gaited horses in the 1800s.

works for him. Keep in mind, however, that some traditional gear may have become traditional because it works well to develop the gaits of a particular breed.

If you plan to ride your gaited horse with a bit, you will need a simple bridle that fits him. You can also use a combination halter/bridle for your gaited horse. It is a good idea to avoid the types that attach to the bit with metal snaps, however, as these can vibrate against the metal of the bit and irritate the horse's mouth. Although many bridles come equipped with cavessons or other types of nosebands, these are not a requirement for riding a gaited horse. If your horse carries his bit quietly, there is no need for a noseband to stabilize the cheekpieces of his bridle, and you can use a typical Western bridle without one. If you do use a noseband or cavesson to finish off the look of the bridle or to keep the cheekpieces still, leave it loose enough so that you can easily slip two fingers sideways between the horse's jaw and the band. Don't use a tight cavesson or noseband to clamp a horse's mouth shut over the bit. A tight cavesson that prevents a horse from opening his mouth will create tension in his jaw that can be reflected in his entire body and in his gaits. Allow your horse room to open his mouth so that he can learn to accept signals from the bit without force.

Whether you use a traditional bridle or bitless headgear, for training purposes you will need at least one set of smooth, buckle-end or tie-end leather reins. Each rein must be at least 4½ feet (approximately 1 meter) long, no thicker than ¾ inch (approximately 1.5 cm), and either split or joined with a buckle. These reins will allow you to feel your horse's mouth clearly and will slip easily through your fingers so that you can instantly release or take contact with the bit. Rope and braided reins are not as easy to adjust and can muffle the feel of your horse's mouth if you use a bit, although with bitless headgear they may allow adequate feel of the nose. Rope reins with slobber straps are also not a good idea because they swing if a horse nods his head, and may irritate him or disrupt the natural rhythm of his nod. They also can reduce the communication between your hands and the horse's mouth when used with a bit. For noseband bridles, snap-end reins are not much of a problem, but avoid them if you ride in a bit. They will bounce and swing and can jar a horse's mouth, confusing him as well as deadening your rein cues. You can overcome the metal-on-metal vibration of these reins for trail riding if you attach a small loop of leather to your bit and snap the reins to that instead of to the bit itself, although they will still swing more than buckle-end reins.

Bitless Headgear

Horsemen have trained and ridden both gaited and non-gaited horses without bits for centuries. The traditions of bitless riding go back to the Numidians, long before the Moorish invasion of Spain brought the jaquima and bosal into Iberian tradition. For early training of gaited horses or for later pleasure riding, headgear without bits can work very well. Some gear seems to work better on some breeds of horses than others. Again, which type of gear is most useful depends on the individual horse.

Nosebands and Jaquimas

Paso Finos seem to work very well in nosebands and leather curb straps or barbadas under the jaw, with rings placed for rein attachment under the jaw as well as higher to either side of the nose.

This versatile equipment can be used with one or two sets of reins to help the horse position his head. Generally, reins placed on the rings under the jaw will cause the horse to raise his head, and those placed on the sides of the noseband will bring the nose in, although with some horses, the reverse is true. This

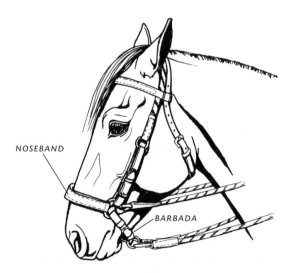

Noseband with leather barbada; typical training headgear for Paso Fino horses. *This bitless gear may also be used for mature trained horses for trail riding. It works to help the horse carry his head in the position necessary to develop the essential tension at the root of the neck that accompanies the corto and largo gaits.*

implement works with steady, light pressure on the reins to keep the horse's head in position for his gait. Another variation on traditional headgear for Paso Fino horses is the Colombian jaquima, which is very similar in design to the noseband/barbada gear but with the addition of a pisador, which is a type of permanently attached longe line, and a strap under the jaw without rings. Colombian jaquimas are often made of stiff rawhide, and because the material is not very supple, they can be more severe on the nose than some of the simpler noseband bridles. Both of these types of headgear often come with a handy additional strap with buckles called a bit hanger, for later attachment of a bit in addition to the noseband. Whether you ever use a bit on a horse trained in one of these bitless bridles is up to you, but the bit hanger makes adding one to the basic bitless gear very easy.

Sidepulls

Although horses can be ridden in sidepulls at any age, they are especially useful for young horses that are just being started under saddle, because they do not bruise a colt's mouth the way a bit might when he is being taught to turn, stop, and back up. Sidepulls are also useful for mature gaited horses that need to learn to relax and reach forward and down to stretch their necks, and for those with tooth problems or mouth injuries that cause them to overreact to a bit. The key to using a sidepull effectively is to avoid taking a steady pull on the reins while riding in it, but to signal the horse with light pulls and slack on the reins while riding mostly with slack reins. Keeping the reins slack will often encourage a horse to relax and lower his head and neck, an important first step in developing some of the easy gaits. A sidepull will not be as effective as a noseband/jaquima for raising a horse's head because the single ring placement on either side of the nose does not encourage lift. It is not a good choice for riding a horse that prefers to trot and needs to lift his head to adjust his ligament system to perform an easy gait. This ring placement is, however, very effective for teaching a stiff horse to bend to each side because it works with a direct rein, pulling to the side, to bend the horse's head and neck.

There are a number of sidepull noseband designs, including single-rope types that can be fairly severe

Colombia jaquima. Note pisador under neck. *This traditional Paso Fino headgear can be more severe on the horse's nose if the rawhide is stiff. It may provide more control than the leather noseband bridle.*

Single-rope sidepull. *This has been padded to prevent chafing on the horse's nose. It is adjusted with a two-finger space between the chin strap and the jaw.*

(because they bite into the horse's nose with pressure from the reins), double-rope types that are less severe, leather-wrapped rope, and wide leather straps that are so mild horses may not respond to them. If you use a single, stiff-rope nose sidepull, it is a good idea to wrap it with fleece to prevent it from rubbing the nose of a sensitive-skinned horse. Some sidepulls have both a chin and a cheek strap to prevent the headstall cheeks from being pulled into the horse's eye when you use a strong direct rein. Others have wider browbands to prevent this problem.

Bozals

Peruvian horses are traditionally started under saddle in bozals, somewhat flexible braided-leather nosebands that are attached snuggly under the jaw with a flat leather strap. The more tightly these nosebands are attached, the more the horse is likely to raise his head and nose. For ordinary pleasure riding, attach this equipment to allow one or two fingers sideways between the bozal and the underside of the jaw. Reins are attached toward the top of the noseband, above the sidepieces of the headstall, making it easy to teach the horse to bend his neck. The key to using this gear is to avoid a steady, strong pull on the reins, which will often make the horse too high-headed, and to keep your hands elastic and quiet. This equipment can encourage a horse to raise his nose and neck, and may help a horse that is inclined to trot or fox trot work in a stepping pace/sobreandando or running walk/paso llano. It may also cause a horse to become too high-headed and more lateral than desirable in his gait. While a too-high position can be adjusted when the horse "graduates" to a bit, for ordinary pleasure riding, because of the single position for rein attachment, the bozal may not be as versatile as some other bitless headgear.

California Bosal Hackamores

Another type of bitless bridle that can work for gaited horses is the traditional California bosal hackamore, or jaquima. This is a stiff, braided rawhide bosal noseband attached to a headstall with a fiador rope throatlatch and used with rope reins formed by a mecate or single long length of cotton rope or braided horsehair wrapped under the jaw.

The bosal is traditionally adjusted loosely, not snugged to the horse's jaw as a Peruvian bozal is. These nosebands are available in different widths,

Peruvian bozal with additional jaquima noseband. Reins attach toward top of nose to lift head.

California bosal with fiador throatlatch. Reins attach under jaw to lower nose.

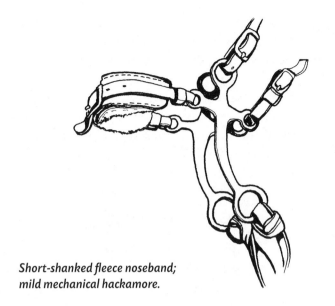

Short-shanked fleece noseband; mild mechanical hackamore.

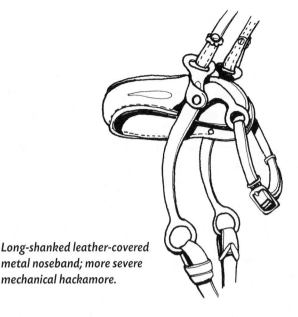

Long-shanked leather-covered metal noseband; more severe mechanical hackamore.

from extremely thick and heavy for initial training to the width of a pencil for an advanced horse. They can be useful for starting a gaited horse, but because they hang loose on the jaw, they are not a good choice in the long run for Walking Horses or Fox Trotters that have a lot of head-nod in their gaits. With each nod of his head, the loose bosal will bang a Walker or Fox Trotter on the nose, in effect punishing him for a natural part of the way he moves. Since you must ride in a bosal with slack reins, there is not much you can do to prevent this banging on the nose. For gaited horses that nod their heads, a sidepull is a better solution than this type of bosal after the horse is started under saddle.

Mechanical Hackamores

Mechanical hackamores put pressure on the nose and the lower jaw of a horse, clamping around his muzzle when the reins are tightened. This clamping action is not effective for teaching horses to bend their necks because it can confuse them and cause them to brace against the turn. It will not work to lower a horse's head, but it can cause a horse that is low-headed to raise his head and neck, if it is used with constant rein pressure. Some styles of mechanical hackamores have a much stronger clamping effect than others. The mildest ones have very short shanks and sheepskin-lined wide leather nosebands, while the most severe have chain noses and very long shanks on swivels. On a trained gaited horse with no gait problems, a mild

one can be useful for pleasure riding, assuming that you ride with slack reins and the horse knows how to neck rein. For working on gait problems or training a young horse, however, if you want to go bitless, a sidepull will work much better than any mechanical hackamore.

Patented "Bitless" Bridles

There are a number of bitless bridle designs now available that have several leverage points using pulley action with various straps that cross parts of the horse's head. They put pressure on the nose, under the jaw, and on the poll, sometimes with much stronger force than is possible in a simple sidepull or even a jaquima. Pressure in multiple locations makes the signals from these bridles more complicated for the horse and will not necessarily help you encourage him to place his head and neck in the best position for his gait. Simple, direct pressure cues from straightforward non-pulley type nosebands are easier for the horse to understand and less likely to have unintended results than pressure from these complicated devices.

Bits

Although bitless headgear works well for starting horses under saddle, and some continue in that type of gear for their entire lives, most easy-gaited horses eventually will be ridden in a bit of some sort. Bits should be used to refine the communication you have with your horse, not to control him by causing him pain. In addition to the basics of turning, bending, slowing down, stopping, and backing up, bits communicate four things: head up, head down, nose in, and nose out. The standard bits that have been used for centuries to give these signals work as well for gaited horses as they do for non-gaited ones. If a standard bit fits your horse's mouth shape and communicates what you want to tell him, you do not need to use a special bit that may be marketed for his breed to help him do his gait. Keep it simple!

Non-Leverage Bits, True Snaffles

These bits, without shanks or pulley action, operate with direct pressure on the tongue, bars, and lips of the horse's mouth. They can easily encourage a horse to lower his head, nose out, and take contact with or "feel" your fingers on the reins. If your horse needs to learn to stretch out his ligament cable system, these bits are a very useful communication tool. If he needs to raise his head to gait better, however, they are probably not so useful.

There are hundreds of snaffles available, but some of them work better than others for gaited horses. If you do use a snaffle, pay attention to how your horse reacts in the bit, and find one he accepts easily. If your horse is annoyed by a bit, he will let you know by gaping his mouth, chewing on the bit, shaking his head, and sometimes putting his tongue over it. Don't try to force him to tolerate a bit that irritates him by using a tight cavesson around his muzzle to keep his mouth shut. Some breeds, especially Fox Trotters, but also some Walking Horses and others, have thick tongues and low palates and are very uncomfortable in standard single-jointed snaffle bits. These horses sometimes accept the shape and feel of French link, double-jointed snaffles, but many prefer the feel of a roller mouth, Billy Allen–type design, or a simple mullen bar to the looser motion of a typical jointed bit. The mullen or Billy Allen–design snaffle bits with limited mobility in the mouth are not as effective in teaching lateral bending as the jointed snaffles, but they are excellent for teaching any horse to reach down and forward and to take contact with your hands.

Although snaffle bits have a reputation for being mild, they are not all created equal. Very thin mouthpieces made of twisted wire can cut through a horse's tongue, whether they are used with leverage or not. Bits that bend around the lower jaw, putting pressure on the sides as well as the tops of the bars, can bruise a horse's mouth and may cause him to overreact to any

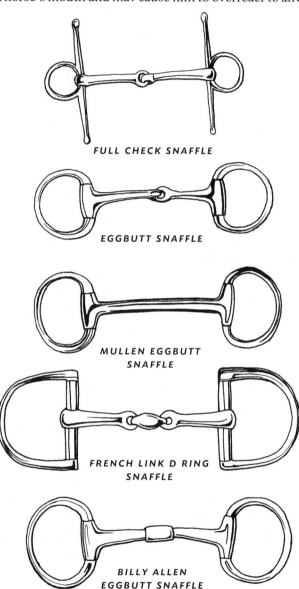

FULL CHECK SNAFFLE

EGGBUTT SNAFFLE

MULLEN EGGBUTT SNAFFLE

FRENCH LINK D RING SNAFFLE

BILLY ALLEN EGGBUTT SNAFFLE

Some useful snaffle bits. From top to bottom: full check snaffle, useful for teaching lateral bending; eggbutt snaffle, a mild, stable, single-joint snaffle; mullen eggbutt snaffle, a very stable bit for horses that are not comfortable with motion in the bit; French link D ring snaffle, comfortable for some horses with low palates; Billy Allen eggbutt snaffle, a stable bit with some give for horses with low palates.

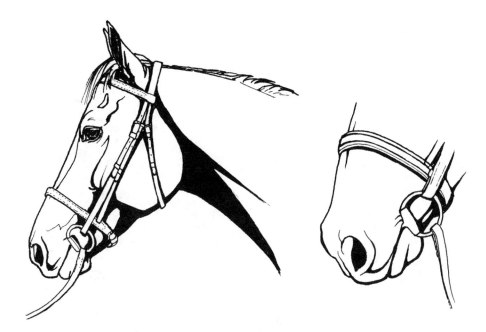

Adjust the snaffle so that there is one fold at each corner of the horse's mouth, and so that there is about ¼ inch (approximately .5 cm) between his lips and the ring or sidepiece of the bit. Adjust the bridle so that you can fit four fingers sideways between the throatlatch and the horse's throat to ensure that he can breathe easily when he flexes at the poll. Fit two fingers between any cavesson and his jaw to allow him free movement of his jaw and mouth. Never force a horse's mouth shut with a tight cavesson.

pressure, putting his forehead behind vertical, or over-tucking behind the bit. Bits that are single jointed and poke into his palate can also cause pain and cause him to stargaze or nose out with a high head. If they are not well made, loose rings can catch the corner of a horse's mouth and pinch his lips, again making him stargaze. A bit that is too small, too wide, or adjusted too high or low for the horse's mouth will also irritate him and can cause him to go with his forehead behind vertical or to star gaze. None of these actions will help your horse work well in his gait, and some of them may make him stiff and inclined to pace as the result of pain.

Leverage Bits/Curbs

These bits, with shanks and a strap or chain under the jaw, put pressure on the tongue, bars, lips, lower jaw, and poll to encourage a horse to raise his head and neck, flex at the poll, and bring his nose in toward vertical. Any bit with a shank and curb strap is a curb, no matter what the mouthpiece design. The degree and location of pressure from a curb bit depends on the length and shape of the shanks, the length of the purchase above the mouthpiece to where it attaches to the bridle, and the height and shape of the port or mouthpiece. Bits with long shanks put more pressure on the jaw than bits with short ones; bits with long purchases put more pressure on the poll than those with shorter

ones. Curb bits with high, narrow ports restrict the tongue and put more pressure on the palate than those with low, wide ports. Curb bits with broken mouthpieces put pressure on the bars, lower jaw, and palate and can be much more severe than those with low port or mullen mouthpieces.

Curb bits may have either fixed or loose shanks. If a horse does not know how to neck rein, a loose shanked bit will work better for direct reining than a fixed shank bit.

Curb bits are used with chain, leather, or combination leather/chain or nylon/chain curb straps. The material in the strap is not particularly important, as long as it lies flat on the horse's jaw and is adjusted so that the strap contacts the horse's jaw when the shank is pulled back between 30 and 35 degrees from vertical. A loose strap will cause the bit to rotate too far in the horse's mouth, making rein cues ineffective. A tight one will dig in with virtually no rein pressure at all and can put too much pressure on the jaw. A rough strap or one with a coarse chain will dig into the jaw and cause more intense pressure and possible pain than a flat, smooth one. Some Western-style leather or combination leather/chain straps may stretch with wear and should be checked often to see that they are adjusted correctly. If you use an English-style curb chain that attaches to the bit with hooks, put the bridle on with it unhooked and adjust it so that it is flat against the

The purchase, shank, and port, and the correct adjustment of the curb strap.

A. *Purchase. Length affects the pressure of the bit on the horse's poll. A long purchase increases pressure on the top of the horse's head.*

B. *Shank. Length affects the leverage of bit on the horse's jaw.*

C. *Port. The port affects pressure on the horse's tongue and soft palate. A high port presses more on the tongue than a low, wide port.*

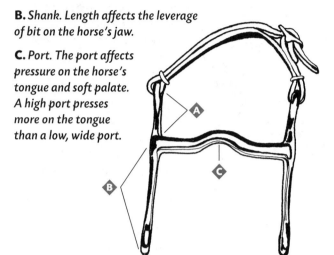

30°–35°

horse's jaw before you fasten it. Unfasten it before you take off the bridle to keep it from digging in to the horse's chin when it is removed.

Despite what you might see in the show ring, easy-gaited horses do not need curb bits to do their gaits. They can gait nicely and be controlled easily without leverage working on their jaws. The action of a mild curb, however, may make it easier to ride a trained horse in the body positions that favor some of the easy gaits and can encourage better response to neck reining and to being ridden with one hand on the reins.

Of the many curbs that are available, the mildest and most acceptable to gaited horses is the simple grazing type. Other mild types that work with many of them are the low port Kimberwicke or Uxeter, which have very short D-shaped shanks with slots for different degrees of very light curb action. For the Paso breeds, the short-shanked, spoon-type traditional curb bits with smooth curb chains may restrict the tongue but have a mild leverage effect under the jaw. A mild curb bit will help a horse raise his head and bring his forehead toward vertical without putting extreme pressure on his jaw or poll. Try to use the mildest curb possible for your horse if he has been trained in that type of bit.

Combination Bits

In addition to snaffle and curb bits, there are also some bits that combine the action of the two. These Pelham bits, fitted with two sets of reins, are useful for teaching horses to make the transition from the snaffle to the curb and for retraining horses that have numb mouths from being ridden in severe curbs but that need to learn to reach down and forward to stretch their ligament systems to develop their easy gaits. The mullen mouth Pelham is a good tool for this type of retraining; the roller Western Pelham works even better for horses that have the bad habit of putting their tongues over the bit. Broken mouth Pelhams, also known as Argentine snaffles, are not as effective because they can have a strong nutcracker effect on the jaw when the curb rein is used, often causing the horse to throw his nose into the air rather than tuck it toward vertical. The Pelham bit allows you to ask a horse either to lower and stretch his neck or to raise it and tuck his nose toward vertical without changing tack. It is a little more complicated to use than a single purpose bit, but it can be very useful for riding and training easy-gaited horses. Pelham bits are readily available in most tack shops and catalogs and are reasonably priced.

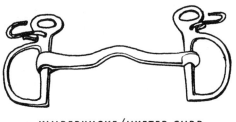

KIMBERWICKE/UXETER CURB
the mildest of curb actions possible.

A SIMPLE GRAZING CURB BIT
with short shanks and a low port, a very mild bit.

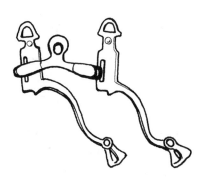

PASO FINO SPOON BIT
has short shanks and mild leverage, but the spoon limits tongue relief and may make it more severe than some other designs.

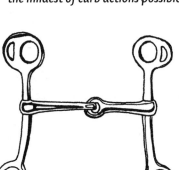

THE "COWBOY SNAFFLE" CURB
may look mild, but it works like a nutcracker in the horse's mouth, putting pressure on the bars, jaw, and roof of the mouth.

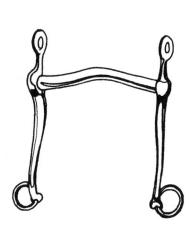

THE MULLEN MOUTH TRADITIONAL WALKING HORSE CURB
allows tongue relief, but can have strong leverage due to long shanks.

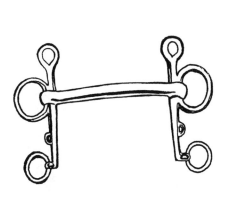

MULLEN PELHAM BIT

ROLLER WESTERN PELHAM BIT

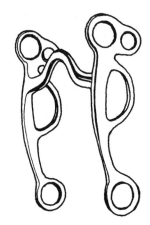

PLAIN WESTERN PELHAM BIT

Other Types of Bits

Bits that operate by rising in the mouth with or without shanks and curb straps and with solid or broken mouthpieces are gag bits. These are sometimes called elevator bits, because they work to raise the horse's head. That is what they are designed to do, and that is the only thing they do better than standard snaffles or curbs. Since most gaited horses need to learn to lower their heads and stretch their ligament systems so that they can do their gaits and do not need encouragement to pace with a high head and hollow back, these bits are not the most useful type to use on them. Gag bits may, however, work for a short time to retrain a horse that presents control problems by habitually overtucking his forehead behind vertical when ridden with other bits.

Use the type of headgear, bitless or bitted, that works best to help you communicate with your horse. Don't worry about following breed style or tradition, especially while you are working to develop his easy gait. When he understands what you want, is obedient to your cues, and is physically conditioned to carry himself in his gait, you may be able to ride him with a string around his neck and he will happily work without any headgear at all!

Other Equipment

In addition to riding tack, you will probably need a longe line about 25 feet long, with a plain, chainless snap on one end and without a doughnut at the other. A longeing cavesson may also come in handy, although you can use a standard nylon web halter with metal fittings. A longe whip with at least a 5-foot (approximately 1.2 meters) stock and lash is an essential tool, as is a dressage whip about 4 feet long (approximately 1.1 meters) with a wrist loop, if you can find one. A round pen with a 60-foot (approximately 15-meter) diameter, made of stout material (not loose panels or wire) is useful, although not strictly necessary for

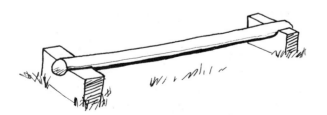

A set of at least four cavalletti can be a valuable tool for training your easy-gaited horse. You can make your own or buy them ready-made.

most gaited work. You will definitely need a flat, relatively large area at least 80 by 120 feet (approximately 20 by 40 meters) enclosed by a rail, not wire, fence. You may need at least six logs or fence poles about 8 feet (approximately 2 meters) long and 6 to 8 inches (approximately 12 to 16 cm) in diameter and four to six concrete blocks to fit them into to make cavalletti, or a set of four true cavalletti.

At least four cones or other markers will also be very useful. If you can locate one, a nice gradually sloping hill with good footing is a very good tool for developing the easy gaits. A safe, solid mounting block is also useful. And finally, do yourself and your family a favor and buy and wear a good, well-fitted, certified equestrian helmet. A bee can sting even the quietest horse, and the ground is not a good place to meet head on.

Equitation

It sounds intimidating, but equitation is really only a word for "how you ride your horse." Basically, equitation is the way you sit on your horse and the way you hold your reins and use your body to tell him what you want him to do. Everyone has some style of equitation, even if it is unrecognized by any rulebook. There are some riding styles that work better than others to help an easy-gaited horse develop his gait.

Seat and Leg Position

There are three basic seat positions for riding pleasure horses.

The *forward*, or hunt, seat, with the legs under the rider's body but the shoulders in front of the hips, is used most often for jumping or cross-country riding, when it is important to help a horse have his balance point forward in his body so he can stretch out and extend himself. It can encourage a gaited horse to hard trot by causing him to shift his balance forward, changing the amount of containment in his body necessary for his gait. You can use this seat on gaited horses that tend to pace to help them stretch their backs and necks and on horses that rack when you are asking for a transition into a hard trot. This seat is

THE CHAIR SEAT

THE STRAIGHT SEAT

THE FORWARD SEAT

easiest to use in a forward seat or jumping-style English saddle.

The *chair* seat, with the legs sometimes braced in front of the rider's body, puts the rider behind the normal balance point of the horse. It is used by many people for any type of riding and can encourage a horse to rack by making him tighten his back muscles and move in a slightly inverted position, with slack in his dorsal ligament. You may sometimes need to use this seat, very sparingly, on gaited horses that tend to hard trot. It is not an appropriate seat for long-term riding because in addition to putting your weight far behind the strongest point of your horse's back, which can tire him, too much work in a chair seat can encourage a pace. You can ride this seat in any type of saddle, although it is easiest in cutback flat English saddles or any saddle designed with a seat slanted toward the cantle.

The *straight* seat, with the legs directly under the rider and the rider's center of gravity directly over the normal resting balance point of the horse, is the most versatile for riding any horse on flat ground and the ideal position for riding easy-gaited horses. In this position your ear, shoulder, hip, and heel are in alignment, balanced straight over the strongest part of the horse's back. To achieve it, sit erect in the saddle, balanced on the triangle formed by your seat bones and the soft flesh between them and your crotch. Stretch your legs down from your hips, letting your thighs hang as straight as possible, with a slight bend in your knees to bring your ankles under your hips. Keep your feet flat, your toes barely pointed up into the stirrups,

VARIATIONS OF THE STRAIGHT SEAT

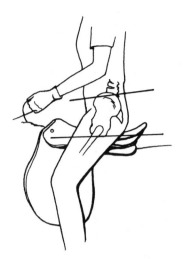

The base position.

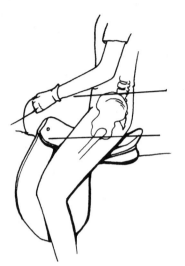

Pelvis tilted toward the rear, a heavy seat useful for riding the rack and discouraging the trot.

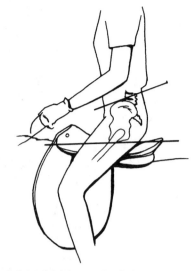

Pelvis tilted forward, a lighter, "allowing" seat useful for discouraging the pace.

heels only slightly lower than your toes, without tension in your ankles.

This position is not easy to learn if you have spent most of your life riding in either a forward or chair seat, but it is so useful for riding all gaited breeds that it is worth the effort. One of the better ways to learn it is to ride with your feet out of the stirrups on a quiet, gentle horse, relaxing and stretching your legs down as far as possible, imagining yourself as a giant tuning fork positioned over your horse's body. Know where your feet are in relation to your hips and try to sit so that if the horse should vanish, you would still be able to stand upright. (Hint: That disappearing horse, with a chair seat, will leave you on the ground sitting on your rump, and with a forward seat, will leave you with your nose in the dirt.) Once you have learned to relax into this position, you may find that you can maintain it with less strain to your back, knees, and ankles than you feel as a result of sitting in other positions. This seat is easiest to use in a Western saddle with a flat seat, an old-style plantation saddle, or a dressage saddle.

Variations of the Straight Seat

The balanced, straight position works well as a base because in it you can adjust your weight forward or backward by slightly tilting your pelvis while keeping your body in balance with the horse. These small weight changes work to influence the horse's back position and his gaits by helping him adjust his ligament system. If a horse is inclined to trot or do a fox trot, you can discourage the gait from your base seat position by tilting your pelvis so that your tailbone is closer to the saddle than your crotch, while still maintaining a straight and balanced upper body. This "heavy" seat pushes the horse's back into a slightly hollow position by adjusting your weight closer to his loin. Be careful not to slouch back in the saddle or slump into a chair seat when you sit heavy in the saddle. Just a little rotation of your pelvis will be enough to encourage your horse to use his back in a different way, without putting you out of balance behind the strongest point of his back. If your horse is inclined to pace, you can discourage the gait by tilting your pelvis so that your pubic bone is closer to the saddle than your tailbone, putting a slight sway in your back, but still keeping a balanced upper body. This "allowing" seat helps the horse's back to rise by lightening your weight in the saddle. Be careful not to put too much of a sway in your lower back, or to ride with your pubic bone pressed into the saddle in what is sometimes called a "crotch" seat. Just a slight forward tilt of your pelvis from the base position is enough to allow your horse to raise his back more easily. It is a good idea to

Riding with Two Hands Versus One

UNTIL THEY ARE VERY WELL SET in their gaits, most gaited horses will need the support of two hands on the reins. If you normally ride Western style with one hand, this can be a challenge, but it is the best way to help your horse learn to use just the right tension in his ligament system for his easy gait. Hold the reins singly in each hand, not crossed, so that you can separate your hands when you need to and can use one rein without the other for turns or other bending exercises. Once your horse is set in his gait, you can go back to riding with the reins held in one hand.

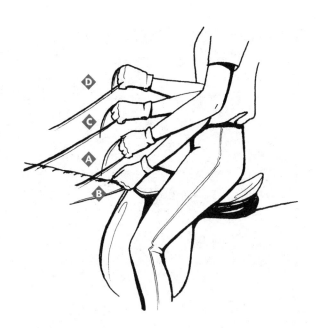

*Adjust your hand and arm positions according to where you want your horse to carry his head and neck. **A.** Base position. **B.** Low position, to lower his head and neck. **C.** Raised position, to raise his head and neck and change tension in his neck ligaments. **D.** Highest position, for the most head elevation.*

practice tilting your pelvis into the heavy and allowing positions while your horse is standing still or moving at a slow walk, to develop a feel for the different ways you can use your weight before you try to adapt your seat to a faster gait.

Whenever you use one of these variations, try to return to the base straight position as soon as possible so that you are riding in balance with your horse.

Hand and Arm Position

Where you hold your hands and arms can have as much effect on the way your horse uses his back and body as how you sit on him. Although it is a good idea to carry your hands so that you can draw a straight line from your elbow, through your wrists to your horse's mouth, sometimes you will need to vary from that position to ask the horse to change his head and neck position so he can do his easy gait.

Start at the base position, upper arms relaxed, elbows close to your body but not clamped to your sides, one rein held in each hand about 6 inches apart and below your waist level. From that position, you may need to lower your hands by opening and relaxing your elbows or raise your hands slightly above waist level by tightening the bend in your elbows.

Try to keep your hands relaxed on the reins, using your fingers instead of a closed fist to hold them with elastic, soft fingers. As you ride, think of warm honey

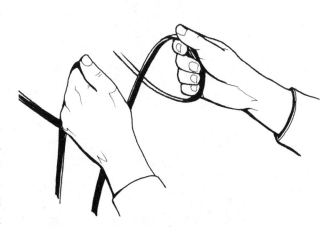

Whether you use English reins or open, split-end reins, hold them one to each hand, without crossing them. This will allow you to use each rein independently of the other.

dripping from the ends of your fingers, all tension released but enough strength left to hold the reins.

These basic seat and hand positions are the starting points for riding your easy-gaited pleasure horse. As you begin to work with him in his gait you will add weight and leg cues as well as more complicated rein and bit cues, called aids, to refine the way he moves.

CHAPTER FOUR

Ground Work

The Basics for Developing Your Easy-Gaited Horse's Cooperation and Flexibility

*Any system of training that neglects the conditioning or which destroys
the tranquility of horses is defective.*
— THE CAVALRY SCHOOL, FT. RILEY, KANSAS, 1942

All systems for training horses involve ground work. Some techniques may be as crude and brutal as halter breaking by snubbing the horse to a post and sacking him out by bombarding him with blankets, slickers, and sacks full of tin cans as he struggles, tied short. Others are as complicated and sophisticated as work in hand with a double bridle at the shoulder-in, piaffe, and movements of the haute école. Between these two extremes, there are practical ground exercises you can do to help your gaited horse develop the coordination, flexibility, and physical condition that will improve his easy gait. You may certainly explore more ground exercises if you want, but at the very minimum you should help your horse realize where his legs are, gain muscle tone and elasticity that will improve his ability to use his body, and enhance his trust in you as his managing partner. Whether he has been ridden for a number of years or is just starting out, any gaited pleasure horse benefits from practicing at least some ground work for improving physical development and mental confidence.

Making the Connection Between Brain and Legs

Some gaited horses seem to have no idea that their legs are attached to their bodies. They stumble and trip when they move and can't even stand still with very good balance. In addition, many of them have never learned how to back up easily on the ground or how to be led freely next to a handler. To help your horse begin to pay attention to where he places his hooves, take time to teach him to stand squarely balanced, to back up easily with little or no pressure from a halter, and to lead on a slack line while walking beside you. These small exercises will also teach him basic ground manners and help develop his respect for your "personal space."

Standing Balanced

Using a web halter and cotton lead rope, lead your horse forward a few steps, stop him by using the verbal command *whoa* and a light tug and slack on the lead rope, if necessary, then check the position of his legs. They will probably point in several directions, one hind trailing and no two legs aligned. To teach your horse to be more aware of his legs so that he can stop and stand balanced evenly on all four hooves, first you will need to teach him to respond when you ask him to move a particular leg or hoof and, in the process, realize that his hooves are attached to his body. Because he naturally carries more of his weight on his front legs, it is usually easier to start teaching a horse to make the connection with his hind legs first and then move on to the front when the hind are set. Start by asking him to move his left hind hoof.

- Standing in front and slightly to the *right* side of the horse, hold the lead rope under his chin.
- Tip his head to the *right* so that he is looking toward you, not straight ahead.

- Tug and slack the lead rope directly under his chin and toward his chest, angling the force of the pull toward the *left* hind part of his body. (It helps to picture an arrow traveling through his body diagonally from his nose through his chest toward the hind hoof that you are asking him to move.)
- Ask him to move the left hoof back, so that it is even with the right. He may move it too far back, in which case, reverse your signals, pulling his nose forward and to the right. He should move the hoof back to its original position.

If you want to move the right hind hoof, reverse all the signals.

With some jockeying around, you will eventually be able to influence his hind hooves so that they are even with one another. Praise him, pet him, let him stand still a short time, then lead him forward a few steps. Practice until you can move either hind hoof forward or back a step or a half step to line them up. Repeat only a few times, keeping your lesson short to keep your horse from becoming sour from too much repetition.

Practice a few times, moving the hind hooves where you want them, then proceed to moving the front legs. To move a right front hoof forward, first set the hind legs, and then stand at the horse's right shoulder. You have several options for moving the front hoof.

- Touch the back of his fetlock with your toe and nudge it forward. Or:
- Use a whip to touch (*not* hit) his leg and annoy him into noticing it and moving it forward. Or:
- Push against his shoulder, tipping him off balance so that he must move it forward. Or:
- Manually pick up and move the foot (not recommended unless he absolutely will not move it any other way). Finally:
- Lift up and forward on the lead rope to cue him to move a front leg. This will change his balance and is the approach you should aim for once he has figured out that you want him to move his legs.

It is probably easiest at first simply to tap the back of his fetlock with your toe until your horse lifts the hoof, then nudge it forward into position. Practice moving both front hooves until you can easily move them forward with your toe. Then use the lead rope, lifting it up and away from each hoof as you ask him to move. By directing his head and neck away from the hoof you want him to lift, you lighten the weight on that leg and make it easier for him to move. If your horse moves a front leg too far forward, direct his nose back and toward the hoof to shift only that leg until it is even with the other.

You can use a verbal cue, such as *stand up*, while you are moving the legs forward, and soon the horse will respond to that when you ask him to stand in a balanced position. Practice over several lessons and several weeks until the horse will stand balanced on all his legs and stay in that position when you ask him for it. Eventually he will develop the habit of standing squarely whenever you stop him on the lead line.

Backing Up

To be safe, pleasant to ride, and maneuverable, trail and pleasure horses need to know how to back up. Your easy-gaited horse may not back up at all or may have learned to back up only in response to strong, steady pressure on his nose from his halter. A better way to work on his reverse gear is to use light, pull/slack vibrations on his halter to ask him to back and to reinforce them with your body position while using a dressage whip as a spacing or signaling tool.

• Stand facing your horse, just slightly to the side, not directly in front of him. Hold the lead rope in your right hand, about 10 inches from the halter, and hold the dressage whip and the rest of the lead rope folded in your left hand.
• Saying the word *back*, alternately pull and slack the lead rope, holding your hand under the horse's chin, directing the pull toward the center of his chest. The horse might instantly back up, or he may just bend his nose to his chest and stand still.
• If he does not move, tap him lightly on the chest with the butt end of the dressage whip,

pull once again, firmly, on the lead rope, followed by in instant slack of pressure, and take a step toward him, again repeating the word *back*. You may instead use the tips of your fingers to pinch lightly on the chest to encourage him to back, "nipping" him as a boss mare might to move him out of her space.
• Keep walking toward your horse, pinching or tapping with the butt of the whip as necessary, vibrating the lead rope under his jaw with light tug/releases, until he takes two steps back. He should eventually back up from the vibration signals of the halter on his nose, not just from the sight of you walking toward him or the physical cue of the pinches or touches on his chest. This will prepare him for later backing under saddle.
• Stop, praise, and reward your horse for backing and go on to something else.

If you practice backing your horse a few steps every day, he will soon back away from you when you stand in front of him, say *back*, and move toward him. He will not care whether you are facing him or not, as long as you move toward him and give a light tug/release on the lead rope under his jaw, toward his chest, as you ask him to back. In a few lessons, he will learn to respond to your body language alone as you move toward him, without the pressure/release on the lead rope. You can then combine backing and walking forward into a pattern. Walk forward a few steps, stop (using the word *whoa*), and then back a few steps (using the word *back*), all on a slack lead. This exercise is good for developing the horse's balance and obedience to your signals.

Leading Next to You

Although all horses should lead on a slack line, gaited horses especially need slack in the lead rope to allow their natural head motion. In addition to going on a slack line, your horse should also learn to lead next to you for safety on the trail. If your horse only understands being led by constant pressure on the line as he trails along behind you, teach him to walk beside you instead. For this exercise, you will need to carry a dressage whip and work inside a corral with a good fence or along an arena rail. Show the horse the whip, let him sniff it, and rub it all over his body so that he is not afraid of it. If he is afraid of the whip as the result of previous training, point with your hand and arm in place of it to keep him calm as he learns.

- Lead him around your enclosure on your right side as you normally do, next to the fence.
- Carrying the whip in your right hand, hold the lead rope in your left hand out in front of your horse as you walk along, parallel to the fence.
- Drop back next to the horse's shoulder, still holding the line in front of you, keeping it slack. He may be confused and stop.
- Use the butt end of the dressage whip to touch (*not* hit) him on the side, toward the flank, and walk forward with him. Make sure the lead line is slack and you do not pull on it in any way.
- He will move forward, but may stop again in a few steps and try to turn to face you.
- Move with him, angling your body toward him to block him from turning toward you. You will be walking sideways, facing the horse's neck and shoulder at this point, urging him to move along parallel to the fence on his far side.

Your progress will be jerky at first. If he starts to move ahead of you, remind him with a light pull/slack on the lead rope to keep his shoulder even with yours. If he tries to pull ahead and then turns sideways toward you, use your dressage whip as a visual cue in front of his nose to block him and slow him down. Do *not* hit him with the whip on his nose. Simply hold the butt end of it in front of him as a barrier. Practice until he moves easily along with you beside him, his shoulder even with your chest as you walk sideways, on a slack line, with only an occasional reminder from the whip that he is expected to keep moving but not allowed to go ahead of you. You can now start to face forward as you lead him, keeping your shoulder even with his, and continuing to keep the line slack. While leading the horse this way, you are pushing him forward with the touches from the whip and the position of your body, rather than leading or pulling him forward with the lead line.

For several lessons, practice leading with your left hand and holding the whip in your right. When your horse seems to understand what you want and walks shoulder to shoulder with you on a loose line, switch hands so that you are now holding the lead rope in your right hand and the whip in your left. If he stops, reach behind your back and touch him with the whip to remind him to move forward. If he tries to go too far ahead, give a light tug and release on the lead rope to remind him to keep his shoulder even with yours and reinforce this by holding the whip in front of his nose to slow him down. Discontinue carrying the whip when he moves easily forward beside you with no reminders.

Be sure to practice leading from both sides, reversing the way you hold the whip and lead rope. Working both sides will help your horse become flexible in both directions and will improve his mental responsiveness.

Obstacle Work to Build Coordination and Manners

As soon as your horse has learned to move each hoof on cue, to stay out of your personal space while being led next to you on a slack line, and to back easily, you can begin to work on pole obstacles with him. These will improve his coordination as well as develop his confidence and trust in you.

Walk-Over Poles

To help your horse find his hooves, start by teaching him to walk over poles set at various heights and patterns on the ground. These exercises will improve his surefootedness and familiarize him with poles that may be needed for later work to improve his easy gait.

For a simple pole pattern, lay out two 8-foot-long poles spaced 5 feet apart and parallel to one another.

- Stand beside your horse, facing the line of poles, and, with light downward tug/releases on his lead rope, ask him to lower his head to look at the poles. Tap the first pole with your foot, so he notices it.
- Walk beside the horse, on a slack lead, over

Patterns of walk-over poles, simple through more advanced.

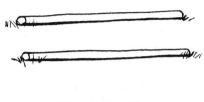

STRAIGHT LINE

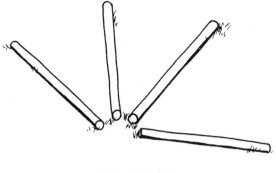

STAR PATTERN

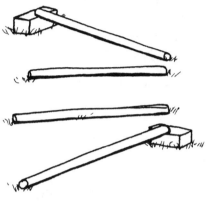

DIFFERENT HEIGHTS

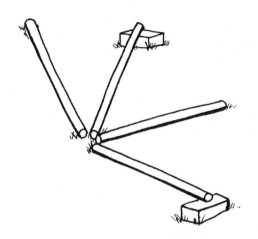

DIFFERENT HEIGHT STAR PATTERN

the poles. Let him watch you pick up your feet to step over the poles.

• Walk him slowly over the poles until he steps over them without tripping or hitting them.

• Lead him back and forth over the line of poles, from both sides and in both directions. Repeat three or four times in each direction, then go on to something else to keep the horse willing and relaxed about walking over the poles.

• Increase the number of poles in the line over several sessions, as the horse learns to walk over them without tripping, ending with five or six in a row.

• Decrease the spacing between some of the poles as your horse becomes able to walk over more poles in a row without tripping, teaching him to vary the length of his steps.

• Praise and reward the horse every time he walks through the poles without stepping on them.

The best way to approach pole work is to start with the easiest possible pattern and then gradually build difficulty as the horse develops confidence and learns to focus on where he puts his hooves. You can eventually reduce the distance between some of the poles to 1 foot or less, if you take the horse slowly over them and stop between each step if necessary. Don't let your horse rush or panic in the poles. Keep the obstacle easy and let him get accustomed to it gradually. It takes time for a horse to learn the coordination to step over poles placed close together, and if he is forced to negotiate a long row of poles with very close spacing, he may become claustrophobic or sour on the exercise. Add poles only when your horse is comfortable walking over two or three in a row. Be sure to increase the number of poles gradually. It may take several months of practice sessions before your horse can negotiate the 1-foot distance with more than two or three poles in a row. Don't keep working at this exercise if your horse has a lot of trouble with it! Walking over a few moderately spaced poles will help his coordination, but trying to pick his way through a number of very close poles may sour him on the whole idea.

Horses with long legs naturally take very long steps and will find it difficult to walk over poles set close together. If your horse seems to have trouble walking over the poles because his steps are too long, help him shorten his steps. To do that, tug/release on the lead rope as he lifts a foot over a pole, causing him to hesitate in the step. Just as he learned to take a short half step back or forward when you were teaching him to stand square and balanced, he can learn to take a shorter step over poles to keep from hitting them.

When your horse walks easily over four or five poles laid flat on the ground, go back to about a 3-foot spacing and raise every other one a few inches by propping one end in the upper hole of a cement block set on end. Be sure to place the block on a firm surface so it doesn't tip over easily. This will only raise the pole a little bit at the center, but it will give the horse a more challenging obstacle to step over. Again, help him focus on the pole by lowering his head and walking over the pole next to him. Practice walking with your horse over these raised poles, a few repetitions at a time, until he can walk over them without hitting either the raised or ground-level poles. Then adjust the spacing between the poles to about 2 feet. When your horse masters the poles in a straight line, set them in a star pattern, with wide spacing at one end and poles touching at the other. Walk over those with him, until he can confidently pick his way through the pattern at the center of each pole. With time and practice, even a very clumsy, long-striding, long-legged horse can learn to pick his way through a set of five poles of different heights and spacing without hitting them.

More Walk-Overs

Walk-over poles build coordination and focus, but other types of walk-over obstacles help build good manners and confidence. Pleasure horses that are ridden on the trail should learn to walk over bridges and through water without hesitation. While you may not have a real bridge or stream handy, you can use some other obstacles in place of them, to help your horse understand that he must go where you ask. Practice over these obstacles will not improve your horse's easy gait, but it will make him more pleasant to ride on the trail.

The bridge obstacle. You can make a small trail obstacle bridge from a couple of wooden pallets with heavy planks or ¾-inch plywood screwed onto them. To increase the obstacle value, you can paint the bridge in stripes, throwing sand on the wet paint for traction. This type of bridge works well as an obstacle, because the horse must step up to get on it, and it makes a nice echo noise under his hooves. If you don't have this type of pallet bridge, you can start with a large sheet of heavy plywood placed on the ground and work up to a more advanced obstacle later.

- Lead your horse up to the bridge, ask him to lower his head, and let him look at it and sniff it.
- Walk over it a couple of times yourself as he watches.
- Standing next to him, ask him to step forward onto it, pulling and slacking on the lead rope.
- Reward and praise him as he steps onto the bridge.
- Lead him across the bridge, stopping in the center before continuing off the far side.

Of course, in the real world, your horse may be reluctant to step on the bridge. You can help him overcome his fear by sprinkling a little grain in the middle of the bridge to entice him to walk on it. You can also lift and place his front hooves on the bridge by hand, showing him that it is not dangerous. Some horses may put their front hooves on the bridge, but refuse to step up with the hind ones. To overcome that problem, set the bridge obstacle with one side against a sturdy rail or pipe panel, and lead the horse over it from the side, just as you did when teaching him to walk next to you, using your dressage whip to remind him to move forward. Do not force your horse over the bridge. Take your time and be happy if he puts one or two hooves on it the first lesson. Build on those tentative steps until your horse easily and confidently walks beside you over the bridge.

The tarp obstacle. There is no similarity at all between a blue plastic tarp spread on the ground and a water crossing. However, if you do not have a handy creek or large puddle, teaching your horse to walk across a tarp will help prepare him for the idea of putting his feet in places he would not ordinarily want to go and may make it easier for him to cross water when you do run across it on the trail.

Start with a woven plastic tarp or a solid canvas one, if you can find one. Fold it over until it is about a foot across and lay it out on the ground with a cement block or rock on each end to keep it from blowing around.

  • Lead your horse up to the tarp, and let him look at it, asking him to lower his head by tugging downward on the lead line.
  • Put some grain on top of the tarp so that he will be encouraged to put his head down and sniff the tarp while eating it.
  • Walk across the tarp yourself, letting him see that it has not harmed you.
  • Ask him to follow you across the tarp, using tugs and slacks on the lead rope. It may take a while, but he will walk over it to you, probably not putting one foot on the tarp.
  • Praise him and pet him, then go on to something else.

Later in the lesson or the next time you work with him, unfold the tarp until it is about 2 feet wide, and repeat the process, again using grain on the tarp.

If he is a bold fellow, he will walk right over it. If he is timid, it may take some persuasion and practice to convince him to follow you. Work on the obstacle gradually, unfolding the tarp a little at a time and using plenty of grain for bribes. Walk over it yourself in a confident way. If you are persistent, but don't overdo work on the tarp obstacle, your horse will eventually stand in the middle of the unfolded tarp and quietly eat grain from it.

Crossing water. Once your horse has mastered walking over the tarp, take the next step and find either a large puddle he can't skip around or a shallow stream with a firm bottom. Carry some treats in your pocket, and wear rubber boots to keep your own feet dry. Approach the water and let the horse see you splash your feet in it. Standing in the water, to the side, not directly in front of him, ask him with a pull/slack on the lead rope to put a foot in the water. He may back away from it at first, but be persistent, holding a treat just in front of his nose to entice him. He will probably put one foot in the water and paw it. Let him play in it a while, then ask again for him to walk into it. Reward him with the treat when he does. If he is reluctant to follow when you lead him into the water this way, try walking at his shoulder carrying your dressage whip, driving him forward into the water with your body language and touches from the whip, as you did when you taught him to lead beside you. Ask for only a step or two the first lesson and then walk him farther into the water as he accepts having wet feet.

Ground Exercises for Flexibility

Many gaited horses are extremely stiff from side to side, with their lateral motion restricted by tense or unconditioned muscles. To work well in their easy gaits, as well as to be maneuverable on the trail, such horses need help to overcome this stiffness. Some basic ground exercises can help develop flexibility and reduce the muscle tension that may cause gaited horses to do an unwanted pace.

Neck Lowering and Stretching

A horse's neck is the longest flexible span of vertebrae in his spine. While elastic neck muscles that allow him to turn easily and to stretch his neck ligaments help him do his easy gait, a stiff neck prevents good body use for his gait and may cause him to do a hard pace instead. The first and most important exercise for overcoming a stiff neck is lowering and stretching the head and neck on cue. This exercise is the basis for later ridden work on gait problems and has the added benefit of releasing tension at the poll and relaxing the horse mentally.

Start this neck-stretching exercise with your horse wearing a wide web halter. A thinner rope halter may be useful for other exercises, but to teach a horse to relax tension in his neck and stretch downward, milder pressure behind the poll from a wider halter is more effective.

*Standing with his head and neck lowered, the horse relaxes tension at the poll and stretches his neck ligaments. Cue the horse first by massaging behind the poll **(A, B)**, using light tugs downward from the halter **(C)** if necessary.*

• Stand beside your horse at his head, one hand on the top of his neck about 6 inches behind the poll, the other holding the lead rope with some slack in it under his jaw.

• Gently knead the muscles at the top of his poll, behind his ears, while pushing slightly downward.

• At the same time, give a light downward tug and release on the lead rope.

• As the tension in the muscles behind the poll begins to release, the horse will start to lower his head a little. He may only lower it a tiny bit and then instantly return it to a higher position. Continue kneading gently and use very light downward tugs with the lead rope until he relaxes and lowers his head a few inches without throwing it back up. He may begin to lick his lips or chew quietly as the tension in his neck is released.

• Reward the horse for lowering his head by petting and praising him and feeding him a treat when he has lowered it.

• Practice this exercise until your horse automatically lowers his head to the ground when you place your hand on the top of his neck behind the poll.

Your horse's neck may be so stiff that he will not respond to simple kneading by lowering his head. For a horse like this, it is a good idea to start the exercise by luring his head down with a treat. Hold the treat under his nose, and lower your hand until the horse follows the smell of the treat down toward the ground, while kneading behind his poll with the other hand. Repeat this a couple of times before you let him eat the treat. Discontinue using the treat as a lure when he responds to the kneading by lowering his head.

Sometimes a horse is so stiff and resistant that he can't follow a treat to the ground. If your horse has this much tension in his neck, try lowering his head by standing in front of him, grasping each side of the halter at the fittings, and pulling down and to the side with one hand, then the other. This side-to-side motion with his head will often loosen tight muscles and allow him to reach down more easily. Be careful, because to do this you will be standing directly in front of the horse, where he can easily step forward on you or even strike you. If you have any question about the safety of standing in front of him, try to approximate this exercise while standing slightly to the side of him, reaching under his jaw to the far side of his halter.

Occasionally a horse will be able to lower his head and neck, but will keep his forehead vertical, not stretching his nose forward. This type of head lowering does nothing to release tension at the poll. To help a horse like this stretch effectively, first ask him to raise his nose above vertical, pushing up on his lower jaw, releasing the tension in his poll. Then, again standing in front of him, ask him to lower his head with your hands on either side of the halter, pulling his nose forward and down. As always, be careful, because you could be standing in a vulnerable position in front of the horse. Stand to the side if you have any question about your horse's reaction to this exercise from the front.

Practice this head and neck stretching exercise several times every time you groom or handle your horse. In addition, if he is a very stiff-necked horse, try feeding him at ground level from a tub and allowing him to graze in a pasture if possible. Over time, even the most stiff and resistant horse can learn to lower and stretch his head and neck on cue.

Bending the Neck at the Poll

The opposite but complimentary exercise to the neck-stretching exercise is flexing the neck at the poll. This exercise, sometimes called direct flexion, stretches the neck ligaments over the poll and encourages the horse to relax his jaw at the same time. It is one of the ground exercises first taught by the nineteenth-century French riding master François Baucher. His philosophy of "position before movement" remains controversial, but his idea of helping the horse develop flexibility in the neck and relax his jaw from the ground before being ridden can be very useful. His method works well to prepare a horse for later ridden work if you are careful not to try to "set" the horse's head in position by strong force.

- With your horse in a snaffle bridle, sidepull, or jaquima, stand at his head, facing him. You may also stand beside his head if he is likely to strike or step on you.
- Hold one rein in each hand, near his mouth.
- Very gently alternate pressure with the reins, drawing the horse's nose toward his chest. If he is in a snaffle bit, he may stiffen his jaw in resistance to this pressure at first. But if you continue to vibrate one rein, then the other, his jaw will begin to relax and he will "give" you his head and start to chew or mouth the bit.

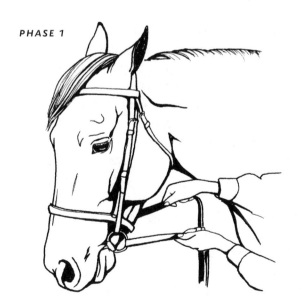

PHASE 1

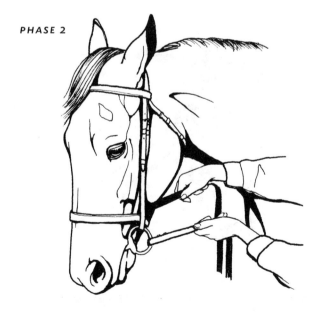

PHASE 2

Direct flexion at the poll. Ask the horse gently to relax his jaw and flex at the poll to prepare him for later ridden work. In phase 1, the horse begins to relax his jaw and chew the bit. In phase 2, the horse flexes at the poll with his mouth quiet and jaw relaxed.

Ask the horse to flex his neck just behind the poll, at the center point of his neck, and just in front of the withers. Gradual bending at these points will loosen the neck better than forcing him to put his nose on his girth while he ducks his head down.

• Relax all tension on the reins when the horse gives his head and brings his forehead toward the vertical. Ask him to maintain the flexed position for a second, then allow his head to return to a more nose-out position, releasing any tension on the reins.

• Practice over the course of several sessions until the horse drops his forehead toward vertical, flexing at the poll, with just a light vibration from each hand on the reins. Do not force the horse's head into position with steady pressure or allow him to bend in the middle of the neck to duck behind the vibrations on the reins. Keep your hands high enough to encourage him to flex only at the poll.

Flexing the Neck to the Side

This is a gentler version of the neck flexing that is used by horse chiropractors. Parts of this exercise are also in Baucher's method for developing light horses, although he was more concerned with the flexion in the poll area than the bend of the entire neck.

To increase lateral (sideways) flexibility in your horse's neck, practice a series of gradual, gentle bending exercises from the ground.

• With the horse facing forward in a halter or sidepull, stand at his head, facing his neck.

• Place one hand on his neck, the heel of your hand on his jawbone, the rest laid against his neck about 4 to 5 inches behind the poll. This establishes the flexion point.

• With the other hand, tip the horse's head toward you by gently drawing his nose toward you from the far side, or pulling steadily on the near ring of the halter or sidepull. Pull his head only slightly at first, tipping his nose a few inches toward you.

• Hold his head bent toward you for a count of five, then release. Repeat on the other side. Practice several times, then go on to other ground work.

• Repeat over several sessions, until the horse can turn his head easily from the poll at a 90-degree angle.

Be careful not to strain the horse's neck by turning it too far at first or to let him cheat by trying to bend farther down his neck. This exercise works well to loosen up tension in the poll area, but only if you actually bend the horse in the poll area.

Once the horse has developed some flexibility at the poll, begin to ask him to flex farther down his neck. Follow the same steps you used above for lateral flexion at the poll to ask for lateral flexibility in the neck. Use your hand as a flexion point, first about a foot behind the poll, then as the horse bends easily there, farther down his neck, gradually working your way to a point close to the withers. Ask for only a tiny bend at first, then, as the horse becomes more flexible, ask him to flex his neck in increasing increments. Do not ask him to bend so far that his head is angled so that he is looking straight behind him. Although that position appears to demonstrate that he has a lot of neck flexibility, most horses can do it only by twisting and ducking under with their necks, not by bending at each vertebra along the neck.

If your horse has a very stiff neck and does not seem able to respond to this gradual bending, consider arranging for an equine therapeutic massage or chiropractic adjustment. These treatments can help unblock cramped necks and, if performed by a qualified person, can be very beneficial for any easy-gaited horse.

Turns on the Forehand, Turns on the Haunches, and Side Step

These exercises teach a horse to move his body away from soft pressure on his side, preparing him for later flexibility exercises under saddle. They contribute to maneuverability on the trail, help the horse improve his leg coordination, and work to loosen stiff muscles in the trunk area of his body. There are a number of ways to teach these exercises using visual cues or pressure on the side, but cueing with the flat of your hand exactly where you will use your leg in the saddle is less mentally threatening and is the easiest method for the horse to carry with him to later ridden work.

In the turn on the forehand described below, the hindquarters move to the left, away from pressure.

- Walk the horse forward a few steps, stop, and ask him to stand square and balanced over all four legs.
- Standing at his right shoulder, tip his nose just a bit toward you with a light pressure on the lead rope.
- Press your palm straight into his side, just behind where your lower leg would hang if he were under saddle. (You can use a verbal command such as *turn* to accompany your hand pressure.)

WHERE TO PRESS WITH YOUR HANDS

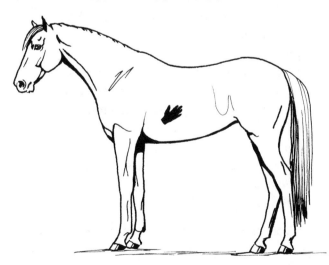

1. *Turn on forehand, hand just behind girth area.*

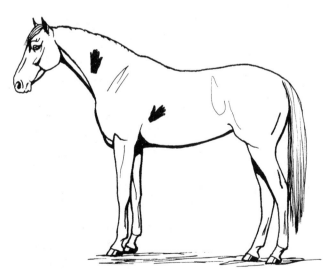

2. *Turn on haunches, one hand at girth area, one hand on the horse's neck.*

• Release all pressure from your hand and from the lead rope when he takes one step to the side.
• Praise him, walk forward, and repeat on the opposite side, asking for only *one* step away with his hindquarters.

Practice a couple of repetitions of this exercise in each direction, then go on to the next exercise. Over time, increase the number of steps to the side with the hind legs until the horse is able to turn first a quarter, then a half, then all the way around his front legs, eventually moving his front legs up and down as he swings his hind legs away from your hand pressure. Always finish the exercise with several steps forward, to help him regain his balance and straighten his front legs.

At the same time you work on the turn of the forehand, teach the horse to begin to turn on his haunches. This is a slightly more complicated movement. Because a horse standing still naturally carries a bit more weight on his front legs than on his hind, he will need to shift his balance slightly to the rear to move his front legs. At first this exercise will be fairly awkward for your horse, but with practice he will be able to easily yield his front quarters to both leg and rein pressure.

In the turn on the haunches described below, the horse's front quarters move away from pressure.

• Lead your horse forward, stop, and ask him to stand square.
• Stand at the side of the horse, even with his shoulder.
• Place your open hand on his girth area, just slightly in front of where your leg would hang if you were in the saddle.
• With the other hand, hold the lead rope against his neck, about halfway between his head and shoulders, keeping the side of your hand against his neck.
• Push straight into his girth area with your open hand, at the same time pressing against his neck with the lead rope and the side of your hand. Avoid pulling back on the lead rope and tipping his nose toward you. He should face straight to the front as he steps over with his front legs.

• The horse should take one step to the side with his front feet, not moving his hind feet, crossing the near front leg over the off front leg.
• Release all pressure on the lead rope and your hand as soon as he steps to the side.
• Praise him, lead him forward, and then repeat the exercise in the other direction.

Practice the exercise a couple of times in each direction, moving only one step at a time, then go on to something else. Gradually increase the number of steps until your horse is able to do a complete turn around his hindquarters, pivoting on the outside hind hoof. Do *not* do this exercise for more than one step in either direction if your horse is shod with caulks for traction because they will "stick" his hooves to the ground, create torque in his hind legs, and damage his joints.

After your horse has learned to give to pressure and move his hindquarters and his forequarters over, you can combine the cues for the two exercises and ask him to move his entire body over one step. This side-step is useful for opening gates and prepares your horse for the more complicated leg yield, which is very useful for trail riding. While the leg-yielding exercise is not necessary for gait development, it can make a horse of any type more maneuverable and pleasant to ride.

• Stand at your horse's side, about even with the girth area.
• Push straight into his side with the flat of your hand, about where your calf would hang if you were in the saddle.
• At the same time, push strongly against the center of your horse's neck with the side of your other hand, holding the lead rope.
• Repeat the word *over* as you push against the horse.
• Your horse should take one step to the side, using both front and hind legs.
• Praise him, then repeat from the other side.

If your horse does not respond by taking a step to the side, try an alternate method and ask for first one step with the hind legs, then one with the front, using the cues for the turn on the haunches alternated with the cues for the turn on the forehand. Repeat several times, gradually shortening the time between cues, until you are giving the side-step cue. Practice until your horse will move over one step from the side-step cue alone. Once he understands moving over one step, you can increase the number of steps to the side.

Your horse may not bend his body a great deal while practicing these exercises from the ground. Through them, however, he is learning to respond to pressure that is released as a reward for his action, preparing him for the more complicated exercises that will help his gait under saddle.

Horse "Sit-Ups" for Back Health

While you are handling your horse's body, add one more little exercise to the program; teach him to raise his back, lifting and expanding his vertebrae and tightening his abdominal muscles in response to pressure under his belly. When he does this lift he will tighten his tummy muscles and raise his back, flexing downward just a little from the lumbosacral junction as he also tips the back of his pelvis down.

- Stand at your horse's side, about halfway down his body, holding the lead rope with one hand.
- Reach under his belly with the other hand, placing the tips of your fingers on his midline, between the lower part of his rib cage and his navel.
- Press firmly into his midline, pushing up and wiggling your fingertips to cause your horse to tighten his abdominal muscles. Watch his back to see whether it rises. If it does not, try again in a slightly different location and press a little more strongly into his midline with your fingertips.

Be careful to stand clear of your horse's hind legs as you do this; some horses may resent the pressure on their bellies and cow kick. Don't do it with long acrylic fingernails! If you have claws on your fingers, use your knuckles instead to ask your horse to lift his back. Be persistent and experiment with the amount of pressure you use as well as the location of your fingers along his midline. Your horse should soon react to light finger pressure under his belly by lifting his back.

Practice this exercise before and after you ride and whenever you groom your horse. If you cue him for back lifts often, you can help your horse maintain healthy separation between his back vertebrae. You can also help him avoid swayback in his old age by practicing these horsey "sit-ups."

The Round Pen and the Longe Line

Working a horse in a round pen is a very popular method for developing respect and agility, and giving

The back lift stretches and raises the horse's back by causing him to tighten his abdominal muscles. Reach under your horse's belly and stimulate his abdominal muscles to lift his back with your fingertips. Practice this exercise before and after you ride to keep his back strong, especially if your horse does one of the gaits in the racking family.

the horse some basic training before he starts work under saddle. The communication possible between trainer and horse in liberty round-pen work is of a fairly large scale, including such commands as *stop, go, turn around, speed up, slow down, get away,* and *come here.* This works well for teaching basic manners as well as changes between gaits, roll backs, sliding stops, and other reining maneuvers. While liberty round-pen work is very useful for those things, it is not the best tool for teaching a horse to rate or adjust his speed in gait, to carry his head in a position that is effective for a particular gait (while discouraging an undesirable one), or to differentiate between gaits that are approximately the same speed (for example, encouraging a flat walk while discouraging a slow fox trot).

Training with a longe line is not quite as useful for teaching agility as round-pen work, but it can be just as effective for teaching manners and is better than round-pen work for teaching the fine body movements necessary to perfect an easy gait. If you are accustomed to working horses in a round pen, continue to use that tool if you wish. For gaited horses, however, work on the longe adds an extra dimension to basic ground work by allowing the finesse needed for work in gait.

What Can You Teach on the Longe?

Unfortunately, the longe (from old French, meaning long) line is often misunderstood and misused in horse training. For some reason, perhaps because the English pronounce the word "lunge," many people think that the only way to use this piece of equipment is to force a horse into trotting or galloping around a circle at top speed, head cocked to the outside, neck and shoulders stiff, while he wears off excess energy. Since running stiffly around a tight circle can be very harmful to the mind, legs, and body of any horse, it is no wonder that some people shudder at the idea of longe-line work. Used correctly, the longe is much more than a human-powered, high-speed hot walker.

Longe-line work can be as effective as round-pen work for teaching a horse obedience to verbal and visual cues at a distance from his trainer. In addition, it can improve a horse's balance and flexibility by allowing you to enforce instantly transitions in speed, not only between the gaits, but also within specific gaits. On the longe, you can help your horse perform a slow, medium, and fast ordinary walk or a slow, medium, or fast flat walk with tiny increments of change in speed. You can ask your horse to change

Attach the longe line to the far ring of a web halter, running it under the jaw through the near ring and to your hand. This method of attachment may encourage a horse to raise his head.

To encourage a lower head, run the line over the nose. Don't attach the longe to the side ring nearest you or to a loose ring under the horse's jaw because that will make it more difficult to position his head.

Attach the line to the far side of the snaffle bridle, running under the jaw and through the near ring to your hand. Do not attach the line over the top of the horse's head because this will convert the snaffle bit into a gag action and may work to raise the horse's head when you use any pressure on the line. Attach the line to the top ring of a longeing cavesson to prevent the noseband from turning on the horse's head.

from one gait to another by speeding up or slowing down or ask for different gaits that are about the same speed by using the line to tell your horse where to carry his head and neck. On the longe, you can ask a horse to do a fox trot, running walk, or hard trot (gaits that are done at about the same speed) by adjusting his head and neck and his balance through signals on the line. Most important for gaited horses, longe-line work can also help them learn better coordination and overcome gait problems by practicing specific exercises and body positions in the ordinary walk.

Longeing Equipment

You will need a longe line, a longeing whip, longeing headgear, and a round pen or other relatively small enclosed area with firm but not hard footing to work in. You can longe a horse in an ordinary halter, a jaquima, a California bosal hackamore, a snaffle bit bridle, or a longeing cavesson.

You will not necessarily need splint boots for your horse, although many people prefer to longe a horse in them. Remember, he will not be dashing around putting stress on his legs and joints the way some horses do when worked on a longe. Because you will not be setting your horse's head artificially on the longe, you will not need side reins, a surcingle, a crupper, or any other strapwork paraphernalia. A light fishing pole may come in handy, though.

Starting Work on the Longe

Lead your horse into a small corral or round pen. Coil the longe line, then hold it in your left hand, fingers *over* the coils so that it can't tighten on your hand if the horse suddenly pulls on it. Lead him a few steps with the longe line, then ask him to stop and stand still. Show him the longe whip, let him sniff it, and rub it all over his body, up and down his legs, and under his

---

Dos and Don'ts on the Longe Line

WHETHER YOU USE THE LONGE for behavior training or to help your horse develop a better gait, here are a few guidelines that produce the best results.

Do:

▶ Keep sessions short. Work no longer than 20 minutes total, or 10 minutes in each direction.

▶ Keep the longe line slack most of the time, avoiding a steady pull on the horse's head. Give him the free use of his head and neck as he works to prevent him from leaning on the line and developing a stiff neck and body.

▶ Vary the work. Change gait and speed in gait frequently. Once or twice around the circle in one gait without a change is enough.

▶ Stop and praise the horse frequently. Go to him and let him know he has done well, then return to the center and ask him to move out again.

▶ Ask the horse frequently to bend his head and neck toward you, helping him become flexible.

▶ Keep the horse focused on you. Remind him to pay attention to your cues with gentle tugs and releases on the line.

▶ Have a cheerful but firm attitude. Smile!

Don't:

▶ Overwork the horse. He should finish a lesson calm and confident, not worn out and mentally agitated. Don't work any horse longer than 20 minutes on the longe line.

▶ Drill constantly on one gait or one speed.

▶ Let the horse lean on the line and turn his head to the outside. Keep him slightly bent to the inside of the circle.

▶ Use strapwork to force his head into a particular position. Light tugs and releases on the line are more effective in the long run because they do not set up resistance in the head and neck. The horse needs freedom in his head and neck to develop a flowing gait.

▶ Allow the horse to meander around with his attention on other horses or things. He should concentrate on you and his work, not the grass outside the ring.

▶ Approach the lesson as a grim task, or a way to wear out or punish your horse. Longe work is just a teaching technique, and does not need to be stressful for you or your horse.

belly from both sides. Show him that you are not going to hurt him with it. He should not fear the whip, and you should think of it as an extension of your hand and arm, not an instrument for inflicting pain. If, because of previous training, he is afraid of the whip, do not carry it. Instead use your arm and snap your fingers to signal him. Do *not* twirl the end of the longe line to signal the horse to move. Although twirling the end of the longe does work to move a horse forward, it vibrates the horse's headgear and can confuse him. It also has major limitations in the signals it can give the horse. You can't use it very effectively to signal a horse to keep his distance, slow down, or bend his body. If you use a whip as an extension of your arm, you can cue a horse for all these things.

To begin:

• Stand at the horse's left shoulder, facing him, about 5 feet away from his body.
• Hold the longe line in your left hand. Carry the whip and lash together in your right hand, aimed down, close to your side.
• Gradually step away and to the rear of the horse, playing out several feet of line, lifting the whip so that it is even with his rump, holding the lash as well as the shaft of the whip.
• Say the word *walk* and gently tap the horse once on the buttock with the end of the whip shaft. (Do *not* whip him with it or crack the lash.) He may be confused and turn to face you.
• If he faces you, step back and to the side again, so that you are closer to his rump than his shoulder, but not so close that he could kick you. Repeat the tap with the whip shaft and issue the command to *walk*, being sure to leave the longe line slack as you do. He may take a step forward, and then turn toward you again. You may need to push your hand into his neck, or point the tip of the shaft of the whip toward his shoulder using the longe whip as a spacing device to convince him to stay at a distance from you.
• Push him away from you and, being careful to stand out of kicking range, repeat the tap of the whip on his buttock. Push him away if necessary by pointing the tip of the whip at his

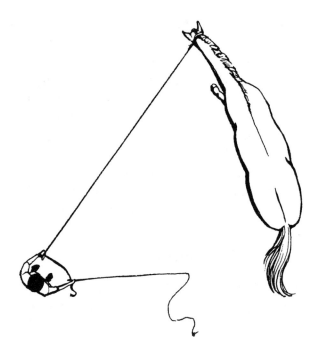

When your horse understands working on the longe, try to stay about even with the midpoint of his body. Point at his haunches with your whip to move him out; point at his shoulder to keep him from drifting too close to you.

shoulder, and keep maneuvering to stay almost behind the horse. Be sure to keep the longe line slack, with no tension in it, as you send your horse forward with the touch of the whip shaft. It may be necessary to increase the tap of the whip to a light spank, but eventually the horse will get the idea and start to walk around you.

Once he begins to move, don't stand still yourself. Keep maneuvering so that you are about 6 feet away from your horse, at first a little closer to his haunches than his midline. You will be moving in a kind of dance with your horse, constantly adjusting your position so that your body position will drive him around you. Keep the longe line slack most of the time, with only an occasional pull and release to keep the horse going in a circle. Think of the exercise as pushing your horse around you with your body and the longe whip, not leading him around you with the line.

Let him walk around you for a while, with occasional taps or touches from the whip as needed to keep him moving forward in a circle, which may be a wobbly oval at this point. Use the verbal command *walk* each time you touch him with the whip. In a few minutes he will walk around you in a small circle, moving forward as soon as you lift the whip and point it at his haunches, responding to your voice.

Teaching *Whoa* on the Longe

If your horse already understands the word *whoa* from round-pen work, you can just say it and he will stop automatically on the longe. For horses that have not had much ground work, you should teach the verbal command to stop on the longe. You can use some other word besides *whoa* if you want, but be consistent in the one you do use.

- As your horse circles you at a slow walk, give a light tug and slack on the longe line and say *whoa*. He may stop in response to the familiar verbal command plus the pull and slack, or he may keep going.
- Flick the longe line up and down if he continues to move. This may put enough pressure on his nose to get his attention and cause him to stop. If flicking the line is not enough to stop him, pull strongly on the line and instantly slack it, repeating the word *whoa* and continuing to pull and slack the line until he stops.
- Go to him instantly when he stops, keeping the line slack. Pet and praise him as he stands still on the slack line.
- Always stop him on the line of the circle, facing forward, not toward you. Avoid letting him take even one step toward you by flicking the longe line and walking to him as soon as he stops. Do not let him get into the annoying habit of turning to face you every time he stops. Later in his longe-line work, you will be asking for some exercises that require him to face forward and work from a stopped position. He can't do those very well if he turns toward you automatically every time he stops.
- Step back a couple of steps from the horse and start him circling again, still at a walk on a slack line, no farther than 6 feet away from you.
- Stop and start him a few times. Soon he will stop on the word *whoa*, and you can use only a

Whoa and Stand

IN ADDITION TO TEACHING YOUR HORSE to stop on the word *whoa* on the longe line, take a few extra moments to teach him the additional command *stand* after he has stopped. This word means "stay still" and is slightly different from the *whoa* command, which means "stop moving forward."

Once your horse has stopped in response to *whoa*, insist that he stand still on the end of the longe. If he tries to move even one hoof, flick the longe line in a light pull and slack motion and use the word *stand* until he stays motionless. Keep the line slack when he is still. You can let it sag to touch the ground between you and the horse as a preparation for later teaching him to ground tie. While he is standing still, praise him and reward him by going to him, taking up the line, and petting him. Practice the command *stand* whenever your horse has initially stopped but started to fidget.

Don't wear out the magic of the word *whoa* on small movements; reserve it for stopping the horse when he is moving in a walk or something faster.

light vibration on the longe line to reinforce the command.

- Go to the horse, reattach the longe line to change direction, and teach the whole lesson over again from the other side.

Because horses do not often translate things learned on one side to the other, it may be just as difficult for him to understand longeing in the other direction. Notice which side is more difficult for him, and in future lessons work him just a little bit more often on that side. You will improve his coordination by doing this and, with enough practice, help him become almost ambidextrous.

A Faster Walk on the Longe

Once your horse understands how to circle you in a small circle on the longe at a slow walk and how to stop on command on the circle, you can ask for more speed on the line.

• As the horse circles you in a slow walk, say *walk up* or *walk out* to ask for increased speed in the walk. Sound excited as you say it to encourage him to move out.

• If he fails to move out, let out the lash on your longe whip and crack it on the ground behind him. Do *not* hit a horse with the lash of the whip.

• If he still fails to move out tap him once on the haunch with the shaft of the longe whip; do not hit him with the lash to make him go. With practice, your horse will move out with more speed in response to the verbal cue *walk out* while you point with the shaft of the whip at his haunches.

• As the horse speeds up from the slow walk, play out the line until he is circling about 15 feet (approximately 4 meters) from you at a faster walk. Let him circle once or twice at a faster walk, then slow him back down to an ordinary slow walk, using the word *walk*, but drawing it out in a descending tone to sound more like *waaaaalk*.

• If he continues walking with too much speed, flick the longe line once to remind him to slow down, but be prepared to urge him forward again if he misunderstands and stops.

• Let him walk slowly, stop him with the word *whoa*, move him out in a slow walk again, then stop and repeat the whole process in the other direction.

With most horses, this lesson in beginning longe-line work takes one session of about 20 minutes from start to final *whoa*. Some learn more quickly, and others with previous training problems take several sessions. Once your horse understands the basics, you can begin to work on balance changes and flexibility in the walk that will carry over to more advanced work in his gait.

Longe-Line Exercises for Flexibility

When your horse is circling around you easily at a slow and slightly faster walk, stopping instantly on the command *whoa,* and keeping his head and neck straight ahead of him on a slack line as he goes, you can begin to work on lateral flexibility on the longe line.

Neck Bending

As a first, simple flexibility exercise, ask your horse to bend his head and neck slightly toward you as he circles. Use a light, elastic pull and slack on the longe line to draw his nose toward you. Don't pull strongly enough to stop him, but just enough to bend his neck slightly in on the circle. Point the tip of the longe whip at his shoulder to prevent him from moving his whole body toward you, if necessary. Walk him for a few steps with his head and neck curved toward you, then let him return to carrying them straight ahead of him. Repeat a few times, then stop the horse, reverse directions on the longe line, and repeat the exercise.

Spirals

As your horse becomes more accustomed to circling around you on the longe, start to vary the diameter of the circle. Play out line until he is walking in a very large circle, then gradually shorten the line until he is circling about 10 feet (or approximately 2 meters) away from you. Alternate large circles with smaller ones and ask him to bend his neck occasionally. Point your whip at his side as a spacing device to help him stay on an even circle, not an oval, around you. Vary the speed of his circles from a slow walk to a faster one, asking him to spiral frequently from a large to a smaller circle and then back out again. Working in these small spirals on the longe will help develop elasticity in his back and body and improve his overall flexibility.

Rating Speed and Stride Length

While working on the longe at a walk, ask your horse to move out with energy, preventing him from breaking into some other gait with light pull/releases on the longe line. As he speeds up in the walk, he will take longer steps than he does when he is walking slowly. Let him walk at a faster speed about halfway around you, then ask him to slow down using light tug/releases on the longe line and the word *easy*. Prevent him from stopping by pointing the tip of the whip at his haunches. Now ask him to walk as slowly as possible around you, taking shorter steps. Vibrate the longe line lightly to slow him and point the tip of the longe whip at his shoulder to enforce the slower speed, but be prepared to point the whip at his haunches to move him forward if he stops. After he has traveled about halfway around the circle at this very slow walk, speed him up to his fastest walk speed again. Practice varying speed in the walk from very slow to very energetic for three or four repetitions, then go on to spirals or stopping and standing.

This little exercise in controlling the speed of the walk will help your horse develop better balance because he will be constantly shifting his body weight forward and to the rear as he changes from the slow walk to the fast walk.

Longe-Line Work Over Poles

Longeing over poles at a walk is useful for developing muscle tone and agility in all horses, but for gaited horses that have a problem with an unwanted pace or stepping pace, it is an essential preliminary to work in gait on the longe and under saddle. Build on your horse's earlier experience of being led over poles at a walk by longeing him over poles of various heights. Set up a star pattern of four poles flat on the ground, one at each point of the compass, and longe your horse over them at the slow walk. With light, downward tugs on the longe line, ask him to lower his head to look at the poles, keeping the line slack when he lowers his head.

As soon as he is comfortable walking over four poles, raise alternate poles on the cement blocks, giving him a more difficult obstacle. Over time, as he masters walking over four poles, increase the number to eight, spaced at different distances and heights, and longe him over those. Vary his speed from an ordinary walk to a very slow walk as he negotiates the poles. As he practices longeing the poles, he will become more and more aware of the placement of his hooves and his coordination will improve as the muscles in his shoulders, haunches, and hind legs strengthen. Do not overdo this work, but practice some of it every time you longe your horse, especially if he has a tendency to pace.

Possible Problems on the Longe Line

Although most horses easily learn to work on the longe, a few find it difficult. Some will not move away from you, no matter what you do. Others start out well but then become bored and either turn and come to you or turn away and pull against the line. Others develop the habit of drifting in, cutting their circles smaller and smaller until they are right next to you. Some will go along nicely for a while, then throw a fit and start running or bucking on the line. If you have worked only with horses that were previously trained by someone else to circle on a longe, these little tricks can be a surprise, but they are not particularly unusual and can be overcome.

The Horse That Won't Move Away from You

One of the most common problems in longeing a horse is clingy behavior. Your horse refuses to move away from you. No matter how you try to move behind him, he turns so that his shoulder is closer to you than his hip. This behavior may be the result of previous poor training with a whip, insecurity, or simple confusion. You can help the clingy horse to understand that he is supposed to move away from you on the longe in two ways.

First, ask a friend to lead the horse from the far side in a circle around you to show him that he is expected to circle you at a distance. The helper should then slowly drop away from the horse and let him continue to circle on his own. This method is not always convenient, but with time and practice it does work.

Alternatively, use the fishing pole mentioned earlier as potentially useful longeing equipment. Attach it securely to the ring under the halter with a short piece of light cord and some duct tape. Keeping the longe line slack, push the horse's head away from you with the pole as you drop back toward his haunches, tapping him with the whip. This can be a little tricky, but it works well if you do not have a helper handy. Longe for a few lessons using the pole in addition to the longe line until the horse understands that he must circle at a distance from you, then discontinue using it.

The Horse That Turns and Comes Toward You

Sometimes horses circle for a little while, then decide they have done enough and turn and come to you without being invited. The fishing pole method also works for horses that turn in, but before you use it, first try pointing the tip of the whip shaft at your horse's shoulder or poking his shoulder with it as he turns toward you. Hold the lash and shaft together in your hand, and say *keep your distance* or *move over* when he tries to come in. You will probably alternate pointing the whip at his haunches to keep him moving and at his shoulder to keep him away from you for a while, but soon he will understand that he is expected to keep away from you when he is on the longe.

The Horse That Turns Around Away from You to the Outside of the Circle

This evasion doesn't appear until the horse has been working on the longe for several lessons, is getting a little tired of it, and decides that he would just as soon leave, thank you. Working inside a round pen may prevent this little maneuver, but some horses can turn away just as well into a rail or wall as in a more open setting. Horses with this habit need a little more leverage on the head to keep them aimed straight than that provided by a line snapped under the jaw on the halter, and they do better wearing a snaffle bit and bridle as longeing headgear. Here's how to prevent a horse from turning away from you on the longe.

- Clip the snap to the far ring of the snaffle bit, then run the line under his jaw and out through the near ring.
- Start the horse circling on the longe. When he tries to turn away, pull and release the line, turning his nose back toward you. Release pressure when he stops looking away from the circle and bends his neck toward you slightly. He may be a little upset that he could not evade your control by turning, and he may stop or even buck.
- Don't make a big deal out of his pique, just urge him forward with your voice and a tap

from the whip if necessary to remind him that you are in charge.
- To change directions on the longe, stop him, go to him, and reattach the line on the other side. Repeat in both directions, as needed.

Once a horse has figured out how to turn away from you, he will try it from time to time just to see whether it will work. In the future, longe a horse like this in a snaffle bridle or in a halter with the line run under his jaw rather than in a longeing cavesson or bosal.

The Horse That Drifts into the Circle

Some horses will gradually start making smaller and smaller circles on the longe, until they end up in your lap. You can prevent a horse from doing this by keeping him moving forward with some energy in a fast walk. Use the end of the shaft of the longeing whip to point at or tap his shoulder to keep him away, holding the lash in your hand.

The Horse That Runs or Bucks on the Longe

These evasions happen with young horses that do not get a lot of exercise, especially on cool, windy days. Respond by leaving the longe line as slack as possible, dropping the whip on the ground, letting the horse cavort for a while, and then calming him with your voice. Don't make a big deal out of this spirited behavior; don't yell *whoa* when it will obviously not mean a thing to the horse. Relax, be calm yourself, apply pulls and slacks to the longe line to slow him, and say *steady* or *easy* in a calm tone to settle him down. It can do physical damage to jerk down a horse that is running full tilt or bucking, so don't try to pull him suddenly to a stop; let him quiet down on his own.

Given time and calm tones of voice, even the silliest horse will eventually settle down. When he does, ask him to circle at the walk a few times, remind him that he is supposed to obey you by stopping and walking him out again, then work slowly and quietly until he is clearly relaxed and listening to you before you ask for more energetic gaits during that lesson.

To avoid bucking and running on the longe, make sure your horse has had some time to run out in the pasture or at least some free time in a large arena before you work with him. If he has a lot of energy, let him use some of it up running free before his lessons. The round pen and the longe line are not places for a horse to get exercise or wear off excess energy. They are training tools; reserve them for that purpose.

The Horse That Cocks His Head and Neck to the Outside of the Circle

This action usually doesn't occur until a horse is working at some speed on the longe, although it can appear at the walk. It is a very bad habit, because it allows the horse to brace against the turn of the circle and prevents him from stretching his back and neck correctly on the longe. One method of preventing this behavior is to constrain a horse's head with side reins, shortening the one to the inside of the circle. Sometimes this works, and sometimes it just sets up more resistance in the horse's neck and jaw. You can overcome this bad habit without using side reins that may limit the horse's neck movement.

• Attach the longe line under his jaw or use a snaffle bridle as you would for a horse that turns away from you. This will give you control of his head.
• Use light, elastic tugs and releases on the line as the horse walks around you to ask him to tip his head and bend his neck slightly toward you. Pull directly toward you so that he turns his nose toward the center of the circle.
• As you bring his head in, point the longe whip at his shoulder, preventing him from moving his body into the circle. This will also provide him with a focal point to bend around.
• Keep the line slack when he curves his neck toward the center of the circle. This will prevent him from leaning on the line and becoming stiff.
• Use light pulls and slacks on the line to remind him occasionally that he is expected pay attention and to bend along the line of the circle. He will soon learn to focus on you, not

on things outside the round pen or corral, and will travel with his head and neck curved on the line of the circle.

Longe-Line Work for Easy Gaits

Once your horse understands how to work on the longe at the walk, the meaning of *whoa*, and the various flexibility and coordination exercises on the longe at a walk, he has a good foundation for more specific longe-line exercises that can complement ridden work in the easy gaits. For gaited horses, however, beyond the basics of getting started at the walk and slightly faster walk, gait work on a longe line can be tricky. You may find that your horse does not automatically go into his easy gait on the longe line, working instead in a hard trot or even a pace or stepping pace. (Refer back to chapter 1 for gait identification tips.)

It is normal for gaited horses to have problems doing their easy gaits in smaller circles. If you help your horse adjust his head and neck position and start at slower speeds before you ask for his easy gait on the longe, he may be able to do some gait work as he

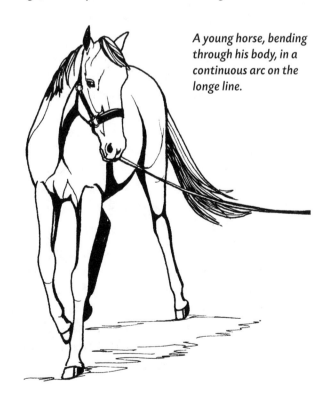

A young horse, bending through his body, in a continuous arc on the longe line.

[85]

develops increased flexibility and the ability to rate his speed in his gait. But as long as he can do basic exercises in the walk, don't worry if he does not work in gait on the longe. For horses that have trouble doing their gaits on the line, use longe-line work to complement ridden gait work, not to replace it.

Establishing the Flat Walk as the Foundation for the Fox Trot and Running Walk

If you have practiced speeding up and slowing down the ordinary walk, and your horse either fox trots or does a running walk as his easy gait, you can move him on up into a flat walk. This work on the longe will also help a Peruvian Paso begin to develop the slow paso llano, which is basically the same gait as the flat walk.

- Ask your horse to circle you at the fast ordinary walk. Play out a few feet of line until he is circling at about 20 feet from you. Keep some slack between your hand and his head.
- Release the lash of the longe whip from your hand and tell your horse to *walk out* while snapping the whip behind him to move him forward with some energy. Continue this until he moves out into a flat walk speed, about 5 or 6 miles per hour. He may continue going at an ordinary walk; he may move out in a flat walk; or he may get excited and start racing around in a hard trot, pace, or gallop.
- If he speeds up too much, pull and slack the line and calm him with the words *easy* or *settle down* until he returns to a walk. When you are sure he is calm, try again, pushing him gradually on for speed in the walk with less use of the whip.

Your horse will probably go for about a half circle in the faster walk, then either speed up or slow down to a slow walk. Be ready for this and try to keep his speed even all the way around you, driving him on when he slows by pointing the whip at his haunches, slowing him with light pulls and slacks on the longe line when he speeds up. Keep slack in the line. Prevent him from pulling on it by playing out line and give a strong pull and slack instantly if he tries to lug or lean on the line. Be sure to give his head and neck plenty of freedom on a slack line. Ask him to circle you three times in the flat walk, then return to the ordinary walk for a couple of rounds. Stop him, go to him, praise him, and then repeat the whole process going in the other direction.

Possible Gait Problems in the Flat Walk

With any luck, your horse will move out of the ordinary walk right into a flat walk or slow paso llano when you ask him for more speed. At this point, his flat walk should be a slightly fast, reaching version of an ordinary walk. Unfortunately, your horse may not flat walk easily just by being pushed out of the ordinary walk. He has a couple of gait choices that are faster than a slow walk but slower than his intermediate gait, and he has no reason to know which one you want him to do. Your job is to help him do the gait you want.

The Pace-Walk

Probably the most common gait your horse will offer in place of a flat walk is the pace-walk. This is a slow stepping pace with either long, sloppy, loose steps or with short, choppy, tight ones. Although the loose "swingy" walk is sometimes an indication of "gaitedness" in horses, if you don't want a stepping pace as your horse's preferred gait under saddle, it is a good idea to discourage it whenever it pops up. The slow sobreandando is considered desirable in Peruvian horses, and if your horse offers it, you may allow him to continue in it. However, it is a good idea to develop a true slow paso llano in addition to it for comfort on the trail. A horse that pace-walks at slow speed will probably give you only an unwanted stepping pace when you try to speed him up on the longe or under saddle. Here are a couple of strategies.

- Longe your horse about 20 feet away from you at the ordinary walk and, while observing the way he moves his legs and body, slowly speed him up. Notice at which speed he breaks from the walk into the pace-walk. Ask him to walk just below that speed.

• Curve his head and neck slightly toward the inside of the circle, preventing him from turning his nose to the outside by intermittent pulls and slacks on the line.

• Lower his head by making light downward tugs on the longe line, keeping your hand low and bending down a little from the waist if necessary, to ask the horse to travel with his head lower than his withers.

• Ask again for a faster walk, keeping your hand down. The pace-walk may disappear if the horse moves with a lowered head and neck.

Another strategy is:

• Place one ground pole in the path of his circle and longe him over it at a slow walk.

• Speed him up into the flat walk, keeping his head low with light, downward tugs on the line. As he steps over the pole, he will flat walk for a step or two.

• Place another pole on the circle, opposite the first one, and longe him over the two poles, keeping him relaxed on a slack line as he goes over the poles. If he tries to rush over them, stop him, go to him, and settle him down. Return to longeing him over the two poles.

• Add two more poles to the longeing circle, one at a time, until the horse has four obstacles to remind him to avoid the pace-walk.

Your horse should flat walk all the way around the circle if you keep his speed just above that of an ordinary walk, prevent him from raising his head, and do not push him too fast. Eventually, you can try removing the poles to see whether he can maintain the gait without them. As with all longe-line work, be sure to repeat this entire exercise in both directions.

Don't be worried if your horse continues to pace-walk despite the lowered head, larger circle, and poles. Some horses may have trouble doing a flat walk unless they first learn to hard trot on the longe, and others never do learn to do the gait on the longe. Even horses that have trouble with the gait on the longe can learn it under saddle.

The Fox Walk

Some horses skip over the flat walk and go into a more diagonal gait, either a slow fox trot or a fox walk when they are pushed out of an ordinary walk. Since the fox walk is a very nice trail gait and seems to be easier for some horses than a true flat walk, it is not a major fault if your horse prefers to do it on the longe. The flat walk

To help your horse develop better coordination and begin to break the timing of the pace, you can longe him at slower speeds over a single pole. Be sure to ask him to move on a slack line with his head in a relatively low position.

or slow paso llano, however, works better for building muscle and flexibility as well as thrust from the hindquarters, so it is a good idea to ask for it on the longe if possible.

Steps to discourage the fox walk on the longe are:

- With your horse at the end of about 15 feet of longe line, slow him to an ordinary walk.
- Very slightly raise his head by lifting your hand and giving upward pulls and slacks on the longe line.
- Push him gradually in the walk with the command *walk out* and a tap from the whip, if necessary.
- Prevent him from going into the fox walk by slowing him with a pull and slack or jiggle on the longe and keeping your hand and his head up just as he is about to break into the diagonal gait.

With practice, you can push his walk into a good flat walk, preventing the fox walk, but it will take careful timing in the way you use the longe to do it.

Longeing in the Fox Trot

Once your horse is working easily in a flat walk on the longe, it can be fairly simple to ask for a fox trot if you want to encourage that gait. Let out the longe line until your horse is circling at about 20 feet from you. As he moves in the flat walk, urge him on for more speed, tapping the whip on the ground behind him and saying *fox trot*. Say the words "fox trot" with a light upward lilt as he breaks into the gait and praise him lavishly when he does it. Let him go for a few steps in the gait, then return to the flat walk. Repeat in both directions, then gradually increase the number of steps he takes in the gait.

Unfortunately, your horse may not understand that you want the fox trot gait, and he has a lot of others to offer at speeds faster than the flat walk. He may offer the pace or stepping pace, even if he has stopped doing those gaits at flat-walk speed. You can help solve this problem by longeing him over poles, helping him break up the timing of the lateral gaits (see chapter 10 for more on longe-line work over poles to break up a

pace). He may hard trot, either on his own or in response to the work over the poles. You can help him convert that gait into a fox trot by slowing him down just a little with light pulls/slacks on the longe line while being prepared to increase his speed in tiny increments from the flat walk by pointing the whip at his haunches. Push his flat walk but restrain him from the hard trot and he will soon begin to diagonalize his steps in a slow fox walk. Praise him; build on that gait by increasing the time he spends in it and gradually asking for more speed.

Longeing in the Running Walk

Once you have established a good flat walk or slow paso llano, it is relatively easy to encourage a running walk or faster paso llano. First let out enough line so that your horse is circling at least 20 feet away from you, then ask him for a little more speed by pointing the whip at his haunches and saying *run walk* or some other verbal cue to indicate that you want him to go faster. Be prepared to check his speed if he goes too fast with light pulls and slacks on the longe line. Keep him moving forward with energy by pointing the whip at his haunches. You may also find that if you hold the longe line a little elevated, keeping the horse's head high with very light, constant contact on the line, you can prevent your horse from going into a trot or fox trot; if you keep his head low with a low hand, you can prevent the pace or stepping pace. If he is very trotty, you can also discourage that gait by using a series of light gives and takes on the line. To break up and lateralize his gait into a running walk, bring his head and neck toward the center of the circle, then let them return to a straight position. Again, work over poles to break up a stepping pace or hard pace can help, and working slowly to increase his speed from the flat walk will make it easier for him to go into the running walk.

When he can sustain the running walk for a complete circle around you, begin to alternate that gait with the walk and flat walk and with occasional halt/walk transitions. Build his ability in the gait slowly and don't expect a lot of speed in the gait on the longe. Don't be disappointed if he will not do the gait in a circle on the longe. Many horses that do not gait

Mixing Gaits on the Longe

IT CAN BE DISCONCERTING if your horse starts out in the easy gait you prefer and then suddenly switches to something else. A horse may start out in a fox trot, switch to a hard trot, switch back to a fox trot, throw in a few steps of a running walk, and then settle down into a pace. This tossed salad of gaits happens because he is learning how to balance in a circle on the longe and every slight change in the amount of bend in his back or in the terrain will throw him into a new body position and a different gait. Most horses eventually overcome this problem, but you can help by encouraging the gait you want and discouraging the others. This takes timing!

Watch your horse closely and, at the first sign that he is going to break out of the gait you want into another gait, slow him with a light tug and release on the longe line. Notice whether he habitually breaks into a pace at one place in the circle. Lower his head when he approaches that place to prevent the pace. Place one pole across his path in that location, encouraging him to hard trot a step over it. Bring him back from the hard trot to his easy gait with light jiggles upward on the longe line as soon as he goes over the pole. Notice whether he habitually hard trots in another place in the circle and anticipate that gait by raising your hand and the longe line slightly, supporting him with a higher head position.

It is perfectly normal for most gaited horses to switch gaits on the longe at first, so do not be discouraged if you can't keep your horse in his gait for very long. Be glad that he does it for even a few steps.

---

at all on the longe do a lovely job of their gaits under saddle once they can go in a straight line.

Longe-Line Work in the Racking Gaits

It is very difficult, and for most horses impossible, to rack or saddle rack with any speed on the longe line. There is no point in working on that gait in small circles on a line. The slow paso corto, or "show walk," however, is possible for some horses on the longe, and you can work to encourage the slower, tighter steps of that gait in a small circle.

To ask for that gait, once you have taught your horse to work in various speeds of the ordinary walk, shorten your line so that he is moving at a moderate walk on a small circle, no more than 15 feet away from you. Tighten the line so that you have a steady light contact on his head, then raise your hand to ask him to raise his head as you push him for speed out of the walk. It is very important to maintain this high head position and light tension on the line; without it the horse may fox trot or do a stepping pace. Keep his energy up by pointing at his haunches as he circles you. If he tends to go into a stepping pace, try lowering his head just a little but keep him moving with energy, while main-taining some tension on the line. Work at a moderate speed in the gait, then alternate a few slower steps with a few faster ones to change the length of your horse's step in the gait, using the same technique you used for that exercise in the ordinary walk.

You may find that your horse will not do the corto/show walk on the longe line in a circle but will do it easily when being driven in a straight line. If that is the case, don't waste your time asking for the gait on the longe; you can ground drive your horse in his gait instead. See chapter 13 for more details on ground driving.

Work on the longe line in gait is not for all horses or all people. There are a few things that you can teach on the line that will help your horse be more responsive and flexible under saddle, but the bulk of gait work is much easier for any horse in straight lines. If your horse has a lovely easy gait when he's free in the pasture and offers it to you under saddle but stiffens up and starts pacing on the longe line, don't continue to work him on the longe in that gait. Practice the basics on the longe in a walk and do your gait work under saddle. Help your horse do the gait you want. Avoid putting him in a position where the only gait he can do is one you *don't* want.

A Little Bit About Spooks and Desensitizing

Pleasure horses are only pleasant to ride if they are not shying and jumping sideways at every blowing leaf. There is no reason a gaited horse should be any different in this respect than a non-gaited one. There are plenty of methods for teaching horses to accept scary objects or activities. If you plan to follow the leadership method rather than the dictatorship method of horse training, however, the best way to desensitize the horse is to start with a small "spook." Reassure him that you won't let "it" hurt him no matter what "it" is, wait until the horse accepts and is calm about the spooky activity, and then gradually increase the fear factor of the spooky object. Teach your horse to accept scary things on a slack lead line with verbal or sometimes food rewards for quiet behavior, reminding him to stand if he moves without punishing him for showing fear.

Follow these simple steps, increasing the difficulty of the spooky encounter in small increments, and you

Fear or Pretense?

HORSES ARE USUALLY HONEST in their reactions to spooky things. Some are born brave, not bothered by anything that comes along, no matter how peculiar. Others are born timid and see every tall weed as a potential threat. As you practice ground work desensitizing your horse, you will soon discover which personality he has. Those that are especially fearful will respond best to slow, tactful exposure to scary objects and frequent repetition at their comfort level, however low that may be. Take time with these sensitive horses, and understand that they may never accept spooky objects or situations as well as their bold brothers. The brave ones, however, may startle once at something, and then ignore it from then on.

Be fair to your horse and accept his inborn personality for what it is. You can do a lot to help a timid horse overcome his fear, but his initial reaction to strange things will never be the same as that of a horse that was "born bold." Be patient with him, help him through his fear, and do *not* punish him just because his natural reactions are not those of a horse that is born with a different personality. Nurture can do only so much to overcome nature.

Some horses, however, perhaps from some peculiar equine sense of humor, will pretend to spook at something that they have previously accepted as a normal part of life. Although it would be nice to believe that horses could only show uncomplicated reactions to experiences in their lives, some of the more intelligent ones can be very inventive. What other explanation is there for a horse that walks quietly under a particular tree every day when being led from his stable and suddenly decides there is an invisible mountain lion hiding in the branches, and skitters sideways when you lead him by? Yes, there may be something in the tree, but often there is nothing different about it or the way you handle him.

If he does this "skittering" routine a couple of days in a row, even after being allowed to stop, look at the tree, and apparently accept it, the best explanation for the behavior is that he is trying to play a little game with you. To deal with this sort of playfulness, first make absolutely sure there *is* no mountain lion in the tree, then remind the horse verbally that his antics are not appreciated. Say "cut that out" or "behave" in a stern tone, and follow it up with a quick tug/release on the lead rope to remind him that you mean business. Walk him past the tree several times, insisting that he pay attention to you and not to the phantom predator in the branches. He should soon figure out that you really don't appreciate his joke.

If your horse is one of these creative thinkers, be prepared for him to react to objects while being ridden out on the trail with the same type of inventiveness that he displays at home on the ground. If he is not displaying real fear, verbally correct his antics and use leg pressure to drive him on past the pretend spook. You must be sure, however, that he is playing games and not actually afraid of something before you use this strategy. Practice reading his reactions to various things on the ground should give you a good idea of whether he is showing true fear or simply pretending.

can eventually teach a horse to stand still on a slack line while you fire a hunting rifle beside him. An example of how to help your horse overcome fear is desensitizing to a plastic bag.

• With your horse standing still on a slack line beside you, have a friend pick up and gently wave a plastic grocery bag about 15 feet from you.

• When the horse becomes alert, talk to him quietly, and reassure him that the bag will not hurt him. If he moves, repeat the word *stand* and give one pull/slack on the lead rope. Talk to him and keep him focused on you. As soon as he ignores the bag and is calm, praise and pet him, give him a treat if you wish, and ask your friend to move to within 10 feet.

• Repeat the process until the horse is quiet and accepting of the bag at that distance. Then have your friend hand you the bag.

• Repeat the process, moving closer to the horse in small increments until he is quiet with you holding the bag at arm's length. Bring the bag closer to the horse, letting him sniff and touch it. Let him touch it with his nose; don't push it into his face.

• Begin to slowly rub the bag over his neck and shoulders. Repeat until he is unconcerned about the bag touching his body. Begin to slowly rub the bag on his front legs and under his chest.

• Repeat until he is not concerned with the bag on his legs or under his belly. Hold the bag on the other side of your body from the horse, and begin to shake it.

• Repeat until the horse is not concerned about the bag being shaken at a distance from him. Gradually bring the bag closer to the horse until he accepts you shaking it around his neck, shoulders, and head, as well as under his belly and on both sides of his body.

• Reward him and praise him one last time for accepting the bag, then go on to something else.

There are obviously some spooky things you can't bring to the horse; you will need to take the horse to them. A good example is overcoming fear of the sound of a chain saw. If someone is sawing firewood, lead your horse to within a reasonable distance, where he can see the saw and the activity. When he shows discomfort, stop, reassure him, relax him by lowering his head with the neck-stretching cue, and praise him, keeping him on a slack lead but using a strong pull and slack on the line and the command *stand* if he tries to turn and leave.

As he becomes comfortable with the noise, slowly move closer. Stop again when he shows discomfort, reassure him, and go on as before, bringing him slowly closer to the scary activity and noise.

Using this method, by the time you have a full woodpile, you can probably have your horse standing, bored, within a foot of the saw. This is a lot less stressful on the horse than tying him up with a strong halter and rope to a stout pole and forcing him to stay there while you run a chain saw next to him. It is also a lot more useful for building a confident, trusting relationship with him under saddle.

Good Sense with Ground Work

Moderate amounts of ground work can help your horse develop good manners, flexibility, and muscle tone. Too much of it can make him resistant, sour, and uncooperative. Do a little of this work once in a while. Don't constantly drill your horse in any of these exercises. Establish his ability to walk beside you, back up when you ask, yield to pressure, and work on the longe, but don't practice these things every day, or even every week. Two or three times a week on the longe for no more than 20 minutes to practice walk flexibility and gait work is plenty for any horse. Once a month as a reminder for the other ground exercises is enough, once your horse understands them. If you constantly pick at your horse, doing exercises and other little tasks to excess, he may tune you out and act like an equine zombie or become so annoyed with the idea of working with you that he develops more overt resistance, pinning his ears, biting, and even kicking at you. Remember that one of the main purposes of ground work is to help your horse be more pleasant to ride. So ride him!

CHAPTER FIVE

Developing the Ordinary Walk

The Base Gait for All Easy-Gaited Horses

Calm, forward, straight.
— GENERAL L'HOTTE (1825–1904)

The calm, slow ordinary walk may not seem to have much in common with the faster, more exciting easy gaits, but it is the mother of them all in two ways. First, each easy gait follows the same footfall sequence, and most of them follow the same support pattern as the walk. Second, exercise and training in the walk will help a horse develop the strength and flexibility he needs to perform the faster easy gaits.

When a horse walks well his back muscles work with elasticity and each of his legs works independently. Each step he takes exercises his entire body in a gentle but effective way that helps him build endurance without stress. Over time, work in the ordinary walk will pay off in a well-conditioned, athletic horse that can perform his easy gait with less exertion.

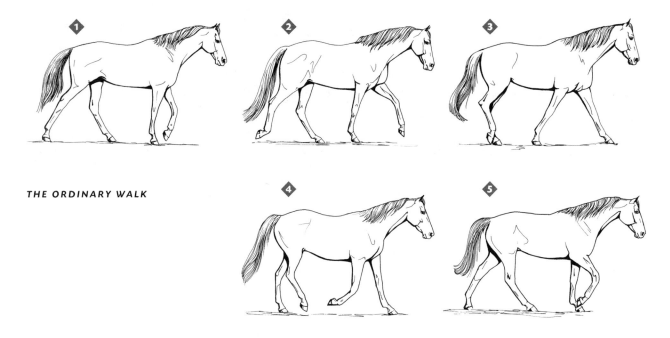

THE ORDINARY WALK

Why Walk?

Horses learn easily at the ordinary walk because they are generally relaxed and calm at that gait. If you take advantage of this to teach your horse to respond to the aids and to learn the basics of adjusting tension in his ligament system, he will be able to use his body better when you do speed him up into an easy gait. Practicing exercises at the walk will also help your horse learn to control his balance and speed, making him more

agile and safer to ride on the trail. Finally, once he develops a good easy gait, work in the walk can provide "rest and relaxation" for your horse, allowing him to stretch his back and preventing his vertebrae from becoming cramped together.

All horses walk, but not all horses walk well. Your job as his rider is to help your horse work in a good ordinary walk in which he is calm, focused on what he is doing, and moving straight without slewing his neck or haunches to one side. Through learning to respond to the aids, and practicing simple ridden exercises, your horse can develop an outstanding ordinary walk while preparing the way for a good, consistent easy gait.

What Are the Aids?

THE TERM MAY BE INTIMIDATING, but the *aids* are simply ways of communicating with your horse. The *natural aids* are specific patterns of pressure and release from your hands through the reins to the bit or noseband, from your legs against the horse's sides, and from your weight in the saddle. All of these help the horse understand what you want him to do. In addition to physical aids, your voice works as another type of natural aid, reinforcing what you tell your horse through touch. Spurs and whips are *artificial aids* that can sometimes be used to reinforce the action of the natural aids when necessary.

Basic Skills at the Walk

You can help your horse develop a good ordinary walk in an enclosed area or out on the trail, but at first it is best to practice this gait and all the exercises that go with it on flat terrain, away from the distractions of other horses. For riding, fit your horse with a simple, non-leverage snaffle that is comfortable for him, or if you and your horse are accustomed to working without a bit, use a sidepull or noseband jaquima. Don't use a curb bit unless your horse has such a hard mouth that you absolutely can't control him without it, in which case you should use the mildest curb possible. A Kimberwicke/Uxeter may be the best option for a horse with a very hard mouth. Since you will have the best results teaching your horse many of the exercises that will improve his gait in either a snaffle bit or bitless headgear, you may want to take time to "step him down" from the curb to teach him to respond to a bit with no leverage while he is learning the basics at the walk. Avoid mechanical hackamores. Because they clamp around the horse's jaw with curb action, mechanical hackamores do not give good, clear signals for the exercises you will be practicing.

Basic Control in the Snaffle Bit

If you choose to retrain your horse from a curb to a snaffle, take some time to get control of him in the non-leverage bit before you try any serious riding in it. Don't just put on a snaffle bit and expect that your horse will slow or stop from a fast gait the first time you ask him. Gaited horses that have been ridden with heavy contact in a curb bit often have numb mouths and can't feel the milder action of the snaffle. If you try to stop or slow them without leverage by using a direct, simultaneous pull from both hands on the reins, they may just keep moving or even speed up. *Don't try to stop a horse like this by pulling back on both reins at once in a snaffle bit.*

One-Rein Stops
Try riding in the snaffle bit in a controlled area, never out on the trail at this stage. To stop and slow your horse in a snaffle, instead of pulling back with both reins simultaneously, say the word *whoa* (assuming you have taught him that command on the longe or in a round pen first) and squeeze/release with first one hand, then the other, to signal the horse that he is expected to respond somehow to the bit. Reinforce the bit cue by tipping your pelvis backward into the heavy seat; breathe out to settle your weight on his back. If he ignores these cues, try turning his head to one side with your left rein, until you can see his entire eye on that side, releasing the other rein to allow the bend. As he turns his head, press against his side with your left leg, asking him to yield his haunches away from your leg pressure. (He should understand yielding away

from pressure if you have practiced this during the ground work phase of his training.) This *one-rein stop* will unbalance him a little and may be enough to get him to stop on command. Practice it at the walk and at slightly faster speeds, alternating left and right side cues, so that he learns to stop easily with the use of either rein. Use this cue to ask for a stop instead of pulling straight back.

Doubling a Horse
If the one-rein stop is not enough to slow or stop your horse, you may need to try a stronger control measure. Learn to *double* your horse to stop him. This approach should be used only in emergencies or when all other attempts have failed and should be done in a full-cheek snaffle or bitless headgear to prevent the bit from being pulled through the horse's mouth. *Never double a horse in a curb bit of any kind.*

The one-rein stop. *Ask the horse to stop by yielding his hindquarters over one step to the right in response to pressure from your left leg while tipping his head to the left in response to pressure on the left rein.*

PHASE 1 *PHASE 2*

Double your horse to stop him by turning his head sharply and kicking him strongly through a tight turn with the opposite leg. This is an emergency brake; don't overuse it!

Phase 1: *Beginning the turn, left leg strongly on the horse, right rein pulling his head around.*
Phase 2: *Horse follows through the turn, bending sharply. Always follow this with a moment on a slack rein, allowing the horse to settle from the turn.*

Steps for doubling a horse to the right:

• Shorten the right rein a few inches to begin to bend your horse's head and neck to the right.
• Lower your right hand well below the swells on a Western saddle.
• Quickly, pull back and to the side, outside, away from the horse with the right rein, turning the horse's head and neck sharply and bringing his nose almost to his side while allowing your left hand to yield forward to allow him to turn his neck.
• Boot/kick with your **opposite** or left leg to push the horse through the turn to the right.
• Turn 180 or at most 360 degrees very quickly, then slack off all rein and leg pressure to allow your horse to settle in place.

Double your horse quickly so that your rein and leg action are simultaneous and your horse "swaps ends" in one sharp turn. Follow it with a few seconds' grace period to allow him to settle down and relax, then move him forward again, slowly. If he again ignores a milder cue to stop, repeat the double, this time turning him to the opposite side. Repeat the exercise until he will walk forward quietly and stop in response to light squeeze/releases on the reins and seat cues.

Don't overuse this tool! It is a rough-and-ready method for dealing with a horse's failure to stop and should only be used if he is "deaf" to milder cues. It will get the attention of even the most numb-mouthed horse, allowing you to stop him in most circumstances.

Riding Forward in the Walk

Once your horse responds to a snaffle or will work in bitless headgear, inside a small arena, you can start to help him develop his ordinary walk. With your hands in the base position, take up your reins so that you have light contact with your horse's mouth or nose, about the weight of a small plum in each hand, and ask your horse with a single squeeze/release of your calves to go straight forward, relaxing your fingers on the reins at the instant you give the signal with your legs, to allow and encourage him to move forward. He should move out in a slow, relaxed walk.

If he does not respond to this light leg signal, don't kick him or constantly flap your lower legs against his side. Instead, reinforce your squeeze/release with a tap from a dressage whip on his side, behind your leg. Use a long dressage whip, not a crop, so that your hand can stay in the base position without moving as you give the tap. Reinforce your single squeeze/release leg signal with the whip, using your legs *first*, until your horse moves off easily in a walk from a light leg signal alone. Your horse should walk forward in a more or less straight line.

Assessing Your Horse

Notice how your horse is walking. Does he walk "drunkenly," meandering around, not going in a straight line? Is he crooked in the way he walks, cocking his head and neck to one side and perhaps slewing his body sideways as he goes forward? Is he strung out in the walk, undulating his back and slopping you from front to back in the saddle? Is he nervous in the walk, taking jigging steps and prancing, wanting to go faster? Is he uneven in his speed at the walk, slowing down to almost a stop and then moving on in bursts of speed? Is he lateral in the walk, swaying you from side to side in the saddle? Is he diagonal in the walk, perhaps bouncing up and down a little in the croup as he walks? Your goal in the ordinary walk is for your horse to walk calmly forward, holding his body straight and concentrating on where he is going at a relatively slow speed. How close is he to achieving it? Most gaited horses have a lot of work to do before they are calm, forward, and straight in the ordinary walk.

Because horses are living creatures, none of them is born exactly symmetrical with a completely straight body, but most of them can learn to move with their hind hooves on the same track as their front, their shoulders and hips in line, and their necks and heads held straight in front of them. Traveling with a straight body is especially important for easy-gaited horses because a crooked horse is usually a pacey horse, and not many people want to ride a pace for pleasure. At slow speeds, crooked horses often pace-walk instead of working in a good four-beat ordinary walk.

Before starting work to help straighten your horse, check to see whether his spine is permanently curved to one side or the other (scoliosis) or whether he has more muscle development on one side than the other. Stand on a block behind him as someone holds his head and look down at his back. How does he line up from tail to poll when he is standing still? Just like people, horses are left- or right-handed. Your horse will probably show a little more muscle development on one side than the other. Remember this when you work with him, and ask him to work a little more frequently in the direction of his less developed side. If he shows just a little more muscle development on one side of an otherwise straight back, correct riding and an exercise program to strengthen his weaker side will definitely help his ability to move straight. If his body has a great deal more muscle on one side than the other, while his spine appears relatively straight, he may have dental issues that will respond to equine dentistry or muscle blocks that can be helped by chiropractic care. If his back is noticeably twisted, however, he may have skeletal limitations that keep him from moving straight, and you may not be able to help him correct the problem.

Assessing Yourself

In addition to looking at your horse, have a friend observe how you look when you sit in the saddle. Ask your friend to walk behind you as you ride forward at a slow walk and tell you what she sees. Is your spine aligned over the center of the horse's back? Are your hips and shoulders parallel to one another? If you sit crooked, with one hip lower than the other, or your back twisted to one side, you can cause your otherwise straight horse to travel crooked as a result. Try to sit straight and balanced with your weight evenly distributed over your seat bones as you ride your horse forward. When you sit straight in the saddle, you can help him travel straight. Maybe you could do with some physical therapy, yourself!

Steering

A horse that wanders and can't move in a straight line at a walk is annoying and dangerous on the trail. If your horse is clumsy or absentminded at the slow walk there are some very simple aids that will help him go where you aim him.

About Contact

CONTACT IS THE FEEL you have of your horse's mouth or nose and the feel he has of your hands through the reins. It can be as light as a single grape or as heavy as a jumbo grapefruit. During a single riding session, the amount of contact you have with your horse will often vary widely from heavy to light and back again, depending on the exercise you are teaching and the way your horse responds to your aids. Some easy-gaited horses are so accustomed to feeling a heavy pull on the reins that they become confused if they are ridden with less contact, and a few are so sensitive that any contact at all is too much for them. Try for a middle ground with your horse, spending most of your time riding with contact about the weight of a small plum in your hands. Try to ride with your wrists relaxed and your fingers elastic and fluid on the reins, not with stiff hands tightened into fists. Don't attempt to follow your horse's head movement with your hands and arms. Use elastic fingers to give and take on the reins while keeping your hands steady in the base position. This will not be easy to do on horses with tough mouths, but over time, if you ride with soft hands, even horses that at first respond to nothing less than 10 pounds of pressure on their mouths will lighten up and work with much less. Learn the feel of elastic and light contact at the ordinary walk before you try to use it at other gaits.

- Set up two cones, one at each end of your arena or ring, or pick out two landmarks along a straight stretch of trail. Starting beside one cone, take even, light, "plum-feel" contact with your horse's mouth or nose through both your reins, making sure that they are equal in length between his mouth and your hands. Ask your horse to walk toward the opposite cone.
- Sitting balanced and straight in your saddle, let your weight fall evenly on your seat bones as he walks. To help yourself sit in the middle of your horse, think of your body melting around your horse's back, with your weight dripping down evenly on both sides of his body through your legs to the ground. Keep your head and chest up and eyes forward as the rest of you melts around your horse.
- Hold your legs close to your horse's side, not pressing on him.
- Keep your chin or lower jaw level and focus straight ahead on the cone. Squeeze/release once with your calves to signal your horse to walk forward.
- If your horse wanders over to the right, press your *right leg* from the thigh to the calf very gently straight into his side while taking slightly stronger contact with your *left rein*, not pulling back or to the side but simply tightening your fingers, to keep his head aimed straight. In this way you support and channel your horse to help him keep his body straight. If he wanders to the left, use the opposite aids (left leg, right rein).
- Practice walking straight to the cone, then turn around it and walk back to the opposite end of the arena, trying to keep your horse as straight as possible. Look at the tracks he leaves to assess how straight he is traveling.

Think of your horse's body as flexible thread that you are aiming through the eye of a needle with your seat, hands, and legs. A nudge here and a nudge there will keep him straight, until he learns to go where you guide him and you do not need to remind him with obvious nudges. He will then keep straight if you simply sit straight and balanced in the saddle, keep your legs draped down his sides, and maintain light, even

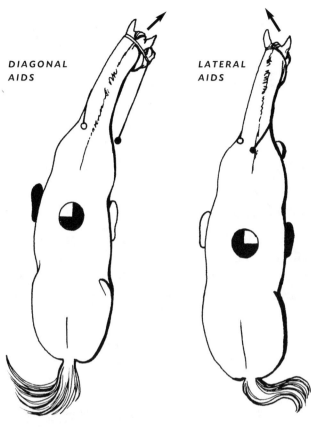

DIAGONAL
AIDS

LATERAL
AIDS

Diagonal aids: Right hand leads the horse into the turn, left hand is passive but maintains contact; the left leg presses against his side, urging him into the turn, and the seat shifts right to encourage him to adjust his balance to the right. Horse moves right.

Lateral aids: Right hand presses the rein against the horse's neck in front of the withers, left hand stays passive but maintains light contact; right leg presses into the horse's side, left leg is passive, and the seat shifts left to encourage him to adjust his balance to the left. Horse moves left.

around. To develop his flexibility, teach him to respond to basic aids for turning.

The elementary turning signals most horses learn are the *diagonal aids*. Don't be intimidated by the name! Diagonal aids simply mean that you apply pressure primarily with the leg on one side of the horse while you increase contact with the rein on the opposite (diagonal) side to direct his energy in a specific way. If you get confused about these signals to your horse, remind yourself that you always use the leg on the side of the horse away from the direction you are turning him to nudge him through the turn. Right leg=left turn, left leg=right turn. You already used these aids to help your horse move forward in a straight line. Now use them to help him develop flexibility and strength in his back, as well as for improving his ability to turn. Be sure to practice all exercises in both directions, but work a little more often in the direction that is more difficult for your horse.

- Set up a couple of cones at opposite ends of your arena or pick out a couple of bushes or shrubs on the trail to give you a visual focal point for riding a turn. Sitting in the base position, ride your horse forward at an ordinary slow walk, aiming for a place about 10 feet (approximately 2.5 meters) to the left of the cone or bush.
- As you near the cone, adjust your pelvis just a little so that you are sitting very slightly more heavily on your right seat bone, keeping your hips parallel with your horse's hips and keeping your upper body straight.
- Gently turn your upper body to the right while taking slightly more contact with your right rein and holding your hand out about 8 inches to the right side of your horse's withers, "leading" the horse into the right turn.
- At the same time, press lightly with your left leg, just slightly behind the girth, to urge your horse into the turn, keeping your right leg still and quiet, draped against your horse's side.
- Ride through the turn. Release all leg and rein pressure, and ride forward at a walk straight to the other cone. Turn again, this time in the opposite direction. Praise your horse.

contact on your reins. Practice riding in straight lines on the trail and in your arena, checking to see how you are doing by looking at the tracks your horse makes in the dirt. With practice and guidance, he should be able to walk straight.

Elementary Turning and Response to Legs and Hands

Your gaited horse may not understand how to bend his body in a simple turn, may resist by throwing his head in the air if you ask him to change directions quickly, and may take the area of half a football field to turn

Practice riding your horse with diagonal aids every time you change directions or make a sharper turn, giving clear signals that you want him to bend his body, following the lead rein and moving away from the pressure of your opposite leg. He will soon begin to bend his body through turns rather than slewing through them like a tank. Practice sharper turns as he learns to bend through the more gradual ones, keeping your lead rein closer to his withers, until he can turn very sharply at the walk with only a light twitch of your fingers on the rein and a touch from the opposite leg.

Beginning Lateral Aids

The basic diagonal leg and rein aids for a turn are the easiest for a horse to understand. Once he learns to bend and turn in response to them, you can teach him the more difficult (from his point of view) *lateral aids* for a turn. Learning to respond to these signals will make your horse more maneuverable on the trail and prepare him for more advanced suppling exercises. These aids are lateral because to do them you will be using pressure from your leg and rein on the same side of the horse. To begin, teach your horse to turn away from an indirect, or bearing, rein, while maintaining contact with his mouth through both reins. This is easiest for a horse to understand in a snaffle bit.

- Ride forward at a walk, with even, light contact on the reins.
- Slightly increase weight on your right seat bone, keeping your upper body straight. Do not lean over toward the right.
- Begin the turn by "opening the door" with your right hand, taking it a few inches out to the side of the base position, maintaining contact with the bit.
- Follow the right hand with the left, bringing the rein across the horse's neck a couple of inches, just in front of his withers. Maintain contact with the left rein, but do not pull back on the rein. Try to maintain the horse's head and neck straight in front of him, or at most slightly bent to the left.
- Simultaneously, press straight into your

horse's side with your left leg, just where it falls in the stirrup, to urge him over to the right. The horse will turn to the right, in response to the use of the left rein and leg.

Practice in both directions until your horse will move in a wide turn in either direction in response to your leg against his side and the bearing rein against his neck, with only a little support from the direct rein.

Learning to Neck Rein

For trail riding, most people enjoy being able to ride with slack reins held in one hand, directing the horse by neck reining. Believe it or not, horses are not born knowing how to do this! Actually, the term "neck rein"

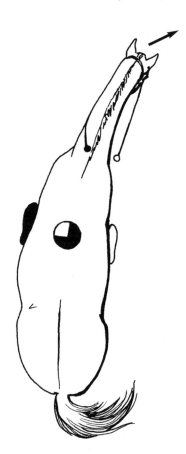

Beginning neck reining. Left leg presses into the horse's side, right leg is passive, left rein is draped but not pressed across his neck, right rein maintains very light contact, and the seat shifts to the right to encourage him to adjust his balance to the right. Horse moves right.

is a little misleading, because horses that turn correctly from a rein placed against the side of the neck usually respond mostly to the leg and seat aids that accompany the rein signal for the turn. This is not the same as the turn you taught your horse with the more English-style bearing rein or lateral aids; it takes a little more finesse in the way you use the reins.

The basics of neck reining are not very difficult to teach. With a little practice horses can be neck reining within a week or two, at least sufficiently for pleasure riding at slow speeds in the walk.

- Holding one rein in each hand, sitting in the base position, ride forward at a walk.
- Hold the right rein low and away from the horse's neck, "opening the door" to the right.
- Lightly increase contact with the right rein, using it as a direct rein to begin the turn.
- Lay the left rein (neck or indirect rein) across the horse's neck, in front of the withers. Release all contact with that rein. Do not pull back on the left rein, and do not press into the horse's neck with the left rein. Simply drape it across the horse's neck about halfway between the poll and withers. Allow the right rein to tip the horse's nose and neck slightly to the right.
- Press straight into the horse's side with your left leg from thigh to ankle.
- Simultaneously shift your weight slightly to your right seat bone, while looking to the right.
- As the horse turns to the right, discontinue the direct (right) rein aid, but continue the seat and leg aids and the drape of the left rein against his neck. Ride forward, then repeat in the opposite direction.

Remember that the most important aids for a turn are leg and weight cues. Never pull back or across the horse's neck with the neck rein. Do not try to push him to the right with that rein, but instead add it to the clear cue of the direct rein, leg, and weight aids. Keep your reins slack most of the time as you practice neck reining, using only intermittent tension or contact through them to the horse's nose or mouth.

Practice this sequence of aids each time you change direction. Soon your horse will respond to them easily,

What Are Slack Reins?

A REIN IS SLACK when there is no tension on it between your hand and your horse's mouth. A rein can be slack without drooping into a loose loop. Lack of tension and a slight swing in the rein is sufficient to qualify as slack.

turning with just the touch of the neck rein on his neck. You can gradually discontinue the use of the direct rein for turns, eventually holding the reins in one hand and neck reining the horse around the arena. Neck rein at a slow walk for part of each riding session but continue to do most of your riding with two hands. Your horse will probably need more training in gait and flexibility before he is ready to be neck reined all the time.

Circles, Spirals, Figure Eights, and Serpentines

Most horses are crooked under saddle because they are naturally more flexible to one side than the other. Once your horse has had some practice with both diagonal and lateral aids to help him move straight, you can start working on ridden exercises to strengthen his weak side and stretch his strong side. You may have done some of this with ground work on the longe, using circles and spirals to the horse's stiffer side (the side he has more trouble bending toward) to strengthen him. Riding at the ordinary walk, continue with those exercises and add figure eights and serpentines. The bending will supple him and help him develop equal muscle tone on both sides.

Don't drill your horse in any of these exercises, but try to include a few of them each time you ride him. Several repetitions in each riding session will stretch your horse without boring you and him. Don't be frustrated if your figures are not perfect the first few times you try them, but don't settle for sloppy, odd-shaped ones, either.

The point of these exercises is not just getting around the circle or other figure, but bending the horse's body so that he develops the elasticity and flexibility he needs so he can do them well. When he can bend well, to either direction, he can walk straight well, too.

Circles

Start with a simple, large circle, about 60 feet (or approximately 20 meters) in diameter. If it helps you focus on the size of the circle, put one of your cones at the center and another just outside the track or rim. You can also take a 30-foot (approximately 10-meter) length of rope, anchor it at the intended circle's center, and scribe a line around the circumference with chalk or flour to provide a path to follow.

- Start at a walk, with your hands and legs in the base position, sitting balanced and straight in the center of the saddle. Do not lean toward the center of the circle.
- Take even contact on the reins, about the weight of a plum in each hand.

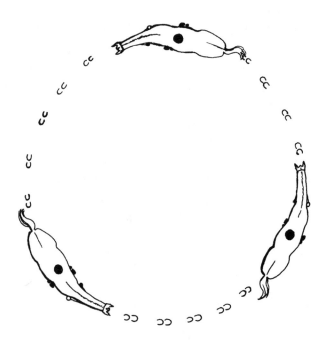

Aids for riding a circle. Outside leg back from the girth and inside leg at the girth, channeling the horse's body through the turn.

- Lower your right hand (the inside hand, or the one toward the center of the circle) about 2 inches, and allow your left hand (your outside hand, the one toward the outside of the circle) to give forward about an inch, flexing the horse's neck just enough so that you can see his inside eye. Take a fraction more contact with your right hand and press the left rein into the horse's neck as a very gentle bearing rein. Do not try to neck rein the horse, and do not bring your left hand across the horse's withers. Simply support the bend you have created with the right hand by the action of the left.
- At the same time, press lightly straight against your horse's side with the right leg, directly over the girth, while keeping your left leg solidly along his side with slightly less pressure, just behind the girth. This will offer him the right leg as a focal point to bend around and remind him with the left leg that he is to bend. Keep up his forward momentum with gentle pressure/release from both legs, as needed.
- Ride at a walk around the circle. If your horse starts to drift toward the center, press a little more with your inside leg. If he starts to drift outside the track, press a little more with your outside leg. Your legs keep his body slightly bent to the curve of the circle while your reins keep his head and neck on the same curve. Practice circling in both directions, changing directions through the circle in a curved path.

At first, you may ride oval shapes or even amoeba shapes. But if you practice and pay attention to your aids and your horse's response, you will be able to ride a good, round circle fairly soon. Practice large circles for several lessons; when you have mastered the large circle, reduce the circumference by several feet until you are riding a circle with about a 50-foot (or approximately 15-meter) diameter. Practice that size circle for several lessons, until your horse bends easily in either direction and maintains a round circle without prompting from your legs or hands. Then reduce the size to a 40-foot (or approximately 10-meter) diameter. At this smallest circle, your horse will be bending in a pronounced arc from head to tail. As your horse becomes more flexible, vary the size of your circles often. Ride a large circle, then a small one, then a medium one. Change directions often and ride slightly more often in the direction that is more difficult for your horse.

Spirals

A spiral is simply a number of circles of increasingly smaller diameter strung together. Do not attempt to ride spirals until your horse can work easily in a truly round 10-meter circle. To ride a spiral, start with your largest circle, then gradually reduce the size of the circle a couple of feet at a time, adjusting the horse's bend as you ride the smaller circles.

To ride spirals:

- Start at an ordinary walk on a 20-meter circle.
- Slightly increase the pressure of your left leg just behind the girth, pressing straight into the horse's side.

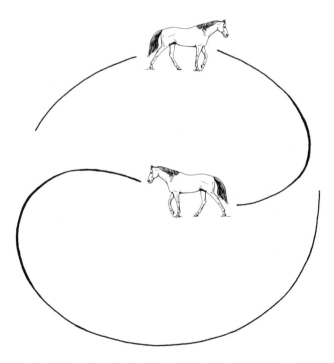

To change directions in the circle, *make a sinuous path through the center of the circle, similar to the yin/yang symbol, gradually reversing your aids as you make the turn. This bends your horse as he changes direction so that he stretches muscles on both sides of his body.*

Reversing the Circle Aids from Right to Left

RAISE YOUR RIGHT HAND, lower your left hand, take a fraction more contact with the left hand than with the right, press your right rein slightly into the horse's neck as a bearing rein, and move your right leg slightly behind the girth, pressing very slightly more with it than the left leg, which moves forward to even with the girth. Your right hand has now become the outside hand on the circle, and your horse has changed directions to start circling to the left.

- At the same time, take very slightly stronger contact with your right rein, asking the horse to bend his neck and head a fraction more toward the center.
- Support the contact of the right hand with the left hand, keeping it just a fraction higher than the right, preventing the horse from bending too far to the right.
- Reduce the circumference of the circle to 17 meters, then 15, then 12, then 10, increasing your bending aids from left leg and right rein as you ride smaller and smaller circles. Ride only one circle of each size, then reduce the diameter to the next smallest.
- Ride one small 10-meter-diameter circle, then begin to reverse the process, making the circles larger at each trip around. Reverse the aids. Press a little more with the right leg straight into the horse's side at the girth and reduce pressure from the left leg. Reduce contact with the right rein and take up just a slight bit more contact with the left, still maintaining some bend in the horse's neck but reducing the amount of curve in his body as the circles increase in size.
- When you are back to riding a 20-meter circle, change directions through the circle and repeat the exercise in the other direction.

Practice spirals occasionally to help your horse develop more lateral flexibility and to break up the monotony of repeated work in circles.

Spirals, figure eights, and serpentines: Useful exercises for bending a stiff horse.

SPIRAL

FIGURE EIGHT

SERPENTINE

Figure Eights

A figure eight is simply two circles connected to one another at one side. Riding figure eights is valuable because the horse has a very short period to change from bending in one direction to bending in the other. This bending exercises his back and neck muscles and develops flexibility. If you have a large arena, you can start with two 20-meter circles and connect them into a figure eight. If your work area is smaller, try two 15-meter circles instead. Of course, don't start that size figure eight until your horse has mastered walking in a 15-meter circle in both directions.

- Start with an ordinary walk in a large circle to the right using the aids for a circle.
- Walk halfway around the circle, then instantly reverse your aids, as you do when you change directions through a circle.
- Remember to raise your right hand, lower your left hand, and move your right leg slightly back from the girth while shifting the left so that it hangs at the girth. Your right hand has now become the outside hand, your right leg is now the outside leg, and your horse has changed directions to start circling to the left.
- Ride around the circle to the left, then, back at the point where you originally changed from a right to a left circle, reverse your aids again, and ride a circle to the right. This time your left hand will rise, your right hand will drop and take up a bit more contact, and your left leg will move back behind the girth with slightly more pressure to bend the horse.
- Practice several figure eights at the walk, then go on to something else.

With practice, you will become increasingly coordinated at reversing your aids and your horse will respond quickly to the change in direction of the bend.

Serpentines

Serpentines are somewhat pear-shaped half circles strung together. The horse changes direction at each half. If your horse can work a good round 15-meter circle, he can do a triple-loop serpentine. When he can walk a 10-meter circle, he can do a good four-loop serpentine. Don't be tempted to work tight serpentines until your horse can walk a small circle without cocking his head, leaning to the outside, or otherwise showing stiffness in his body. You ride serpentines the same way you do a figure eight, except that you reverse your aids more frequently in each pattern. You may want to place a cone at the center point for each loop of the serpentine to give you a focal point for the turns.

Dealing with the Pace-Walk

While most gaited horses will do an ordinary walk with even four-beat timing, some walk with lateral timing, doing a slow stepping pace instead of a true walk. If your horse pace-walks at slow speed, he will also have trouble doing most of the faster easy gaits. Try to correct his timing at this slow speed so he will have fewer problems when you ask him to speed up and work in gait.

The exercises for staying straight and developing lateral flexibility are very useful for a pace-walking horse. Sometimes all it takes to help a horse develop an even walk is keeping him aimed straight, riding him with light contact on the bit, and increasing his lateral flexibility so that he bends easily to each side. If your horse has learned to respond to both lateral and diagonal aids and has begun to work circles but is still pace-walking, practice a few more simple exercises and riding techniques to help him develop a square, ordinary walk.

Pole Work

One of the best techniques for teaching a horse that does a pace-walk to walk squarely is to work him over a series of poles. You may have already done some longeing over poles with your ground work, but now your horse should be ready for you to increase the number of poles, change their spacing, and ride him over them.

Set out a row of four poles spaced about 3 feet (or slightly less than 1 meter) apart and ride your horse over them at a slow walk. Practice walking over them a couple of times to see whether you need to adjust the spacing; they should be spaced so that your horse can walk over them without hitting them with his hooves. When he has mastered the line of four poles, set out another row of four poles about 10 feet (or about 2 meters) away from the first set. Walk him over the two sets of poles, in both directions, two or three times each riding session. Keep him focused on his work by not overdoing the exercise. The poles will encourage him to pick up his feet a little higher from the ground and may change the timing of his walk.

Flexing at the Poll and Lowering the Head

Occasionally a horse will pace-walk if he is allowed to carry himself strung out, head high, with his nose stuck out in front of him, despite light contact on the bit or noseband. If you teach a horse like this with slightly increased contact on the reins to flex slightly at the poll and bring his forehead toward vertical while lowering his head just a little, that position may be enough to stretch his ligament system and help him walk evenly. To teach a horse correct flexion at the poll, first start on the ground with a reminder of the direct flexions he learned during his earlier ground work, using a snaffle bit or jaquima noseband. Then mount up and ask him to move forward at slow speed while asking for some direct flexion from the saddle.

• Ride the horse forward in a walk, or pace-walk, if that is what he offers.
• Lower your hands to either side of his withers (below the swells on a Western saddle, at the "button" on an English saddle).
• Take light, "plum-feel" contact on the reins. The horse will go as before, nosing out.
• Keeping your hands fixed in position, squeeze/release with your fingers on first one hand, then the other, asking the horse to relax his jaw and "give" his head to you, bringing the forehead toward vertical. Alternate these squeezes with leg pressure from your calves to keep the horse moving forward. Do not try to pull his head into position and do not squeeze with your legs at the exact instant you are squeezing with your hands. (Don't ride with

the brake and accelerator on at the same time!) Do not pull with your whole arm to seesaw strong pressure on the reins. Squeeze/release with your *fingers* until he relaxes tension at the poll and flexes. He should bend his neck only at the poll, not in the middle; the highest part of his neck will be between his ears. This will take time. Be patient and reward only when he gives his head.

• The *instant* he relaxes tension in his jaw and flexes at the poll, release pressure on the reins by relaxing your fingers and return light, consistent contact. This release is his reward for bringing his head into a more vertical position. Without the reward, he will simply become tense in the new position; you will have replaced a lazy use of his body with a stiff use of it, and he will continue to pace-walk. Of course, he will probably return to a nose-out position as soon as you release pressure. Just let him walk a few steps with his nose out, and then take up slightly increased contact to ask again for flexion at the poll. Alternate between light contact and slightly increased contact until he maintains poll flexion for a few steps with light normal contact.
• Allow him to walk a few steps with some flexion at the poll and notice how his back feels under you. He should be walking squarely, not slopping you from side to side. If he is still pace-walking, he may need more work on relaxation and reaching down and forward into the bit or noseband before he is ready to work with a flexed poll.

All of these techniques can help turn a pace-walk into a square walk. If your horse is still pace-walking at slow speed after you have tried them, refer to chapter 9 for more solutions.

Half Halts

One of the best tools for controlling the speed and body position of a horse is the momentary checking motion called a half halt. Although you will not be using this technique very often in an ordinary walk, it is a good skill to learn at slow speed so that your horse will understand the signal at his faster gaits. The half halt is a quick tightening and release of the fingers of both hands on the reins accompanied by a slight deepening or shift to the rear of your seat and a squeeze/release of your calves and upper thighs. This technique can be used to rebalance and prepare a horse for gait changes and to change his body position in his gait.

- Ride forward at an ordinary walk. Squeeze/release with your calves to ask him for some energy in his walk, then prepare him for the half halt by tipping your pelvis back into a slightly heavier seat. Keep your upper body straight: shoulders over hips, hips over heels.
- Follow this seat adjustment with a slight tightening of your upper thighs against the horse.
- Simultaneously breathe out and squeeze/release your fingers on the reins. If you are holding your hands properly, thumbs uppermost, wrists relaxed and in a straight line with your forearms, the squeezing motion will cause the heels of your hands to retract very slightly towards your body. Then return to the original position as you release the tension in your fingers.

This action momentarily increases your contact with the bit and reduces the horse's forward momentum, shifting his balance to the rear. Remember the order of the half halt: squeeze with the *calves,* adjust the *seat,* tighten the *thighs,* squeeze with the *fingers, release* all aids.

Later, when you try half halts at faster gaits, your horse may not respond as easily as he does in an ordinary walk. If the horse does not respond by a rebalancing to the rear at faster speeds, repeat the half halt with a little stronger squeeze from your fingers. Use a series of three half halts, each with progressively stronger squeezes on the reins. Repeat until the horse responds by shifting his weight to the rear and reducing speed. Then release all aids.

Besides working to slow down a horse, half halts also can work as a "wake-up call." Each time you transition from a slower to a faster gait, or from a faster to a slower, prepare the horse for the coming change of

speed with a light half halt. This will help him improve his balance and make smoother transitions, and prevent him from stringing out into a fast gait or "plopping" down into a slower one. When you use a half halt, you will need to use your legs twice during the exercise. Continue to use your thighs in conjunction with your seat as you check the horse, but then follow up by squeezing/releasing with your entire leg just a split second after the squeeze of your fingers so that you are never "riding with the brakes on," but instead are catching your horse's forward momentum with the checking action of the reins, legs, and seat and encouraging the horse to move forward before he slows too much.

Lateral Half Halts

In addition to the regular half halt in which your fingers squeeze both reins, another useful tool is the lateral half halt, in which you squeeze/release one rein alone while maintaining consistent contact with the other. Lateral half halts are very useful with horses that have a tendency to shy, as well as with horses that string out into a stepping pace.

To prevent a shy, apply a lateral half halt by squeezing/releasing repeatedly on the rein on the opposite side from the object the horse is likely to shy at, while pressing slightly into his side with the leg on the same side. This keeps the horse straight, parallel to the "spook," and prevents the horse from dodging sideways.

Riding into a Halt

Helping your horse stop in balance is a little more complicated than just stopping all forward movement. Although you can certainly stop a horse by just pulling back on the reins for a moment, sitting back in the saddle, or saying *whoa,* to halt him in balance you will need to use your seat, leg, and rein aids together to guide his body so that he comes to a stop with his hind hooves parallel to one another and his weight distributed very slightly toward his hindquarters. You can ride into a halt in a snaffle, curb, or bitless headgear, although a snaffle is best for starting this exercise.

• Riding forward in an ordinary walk, sit straight in the saddle with your hands in the base position. Squeeze/release with your calves to ask your horse to move forward with energy into the halt.

• Squeeze/release with your upper thighs to slow the flow of energy through his back while tipping your pelvis slightly so that your weight is shifted into the heavy seat, tightening your buttocks just a little. This will tell him to slow down.

• Exhale to let your weight fall deeply into the saddle. This will tell him to stop walking.

• Squeeze/release the reins as soon as you have exhaled. This will reinforce the seat and leg aids, send his balance a little to the rear, and help him stop in a balanced position. Don't pull back on the reins or move your arms. Let your fingers tell your horse to stop.

• Allow your horse to stand, with slack in your reins, while you praise him for a good halt. Then move forward, taking up light contact again.

Repeat the halt aids every time you stop your horse and soon he will come to a balanced halt with only the slight shift of your seat and tightening of your thighs. Remember the sequence: *calves* to ask for forward movement, *thighs* to begin the halt, *seat* to reinforce the action of the thighs, and, finally, *hands* to bring the whole thing together. It may take some time for him to stop completely square on all four legs, but if you keep practicing, his balance will improve and he will stop with his hind and front legs even.

Backing Up

Many gaited horses do not know how to back up under saddle. This basic skill, in addition to being very useful on the trail, is also a good exercise for conditioning your horse's back, making adjustments in his ligament system, and improving his balance. As your horse is learning a balanced halt, begin to teach him to back straight. Remind him how to back from the ground, then mount up and help him learn to back in balance, in response to seat, leg, and rein aids. You can do this in a snaffle, curb, or bitless headgear.

• Sitting straight and balanced in the saddle, ride your horse into a halt. Glance briefly over your shoulder to make sure nothing is behind you.

• Take light contact with the bit, your hands a little below the base position.

• Tilt your pelvis into the light, "allowing" seat. This will help your horse's back to lift just a little more easily than if you sit a more centered seat.

• Maintaining contact with the bit, squeeze/release or vibrate with your lower leg from knee to ankle against his side, well behind the girth. Repeat the word *back* as you do this, if your horse has learned the verbal cue on the ground.

• Squeeze/release on the reins to reinforce the action of your legs, if necessary. Do not pull back with a steady pull. Vibrate the reins as you vibrate your legs. Your horse should take one step back. Praise him as he backs up.

• Immediately stop vibrating the reins and relax your calves, taking them off your horse's side and returning them to the base leg position. Adjust your pelvis back to the centered, base position. Your horse should stop and stand still. Praise him, reward him, then walk forward quietly in an ordinary walk. Repeat this sequence several times in each riding session until your horse backs one step easily without rooting or lugging on the bit. Then ask for a few more steps back, building until he can back easily four or five steps without twisting his body or pulling on the bit.

Halt, Back, and Walk

Once your horse has mastered coming to a balanced halt and backing up, add the next part of the exercise and ask him to walk forward as soon as he has taken his last step back.

Walk, come to a halt, and back two steps. As he is taking his last step back, move your legs to the base position, quickly adjust your seat to the centered position, lighten contact with the reins while maintaining low hands, and use your calves with a strong squeeze/release at the girth to ask him to move forward in a walk. If he seems confused at first, reinforce the leg aid with a light tap from a dressage whip behind your leg. Practice until he moves forward instantly when he feels the change in your seat and legs. In time he should be able to step right out of the back into a forward, energetic flat walk. In the process, he will develop better balance and a stronger back.

Mounted Rotations

If you neglected to teach him the turn on the forehand and turn on the haunches as part of your ground work, review those exercises in chapter 4 and teach him now, before you try these maneuvers from the saddle. The rotations are the mounted form of these two ground exercises, and they are the foundation for the more complex exercises that will help him develop lateral flexibility. These exercises must be taught in a snaffle bit, noseband jaquima, or sidepull. A curb bit will put too much pressure on the horse's jaw as he learns these turns and may cause him to become stiff and resistant to the aids.

Turn on the Forehand

The mounted turn on the forehand is a fairly simple exercise if you approach it a step at a time. Practice it first a couple of times in both directions from the ground, then mount up and, with your horse standing squarely (all four feet lined up under him), ask him to move his haunches away from your leg.

Here are the aids for a turn on the forehand to the left (reverse aids for a turn to the right):

• Ride your horse from a walk into a square, balanced halt. Sit straight and balanced, holding your reins in the low base position, one on each side of his withers, with very light feel of his mouth through the reins.

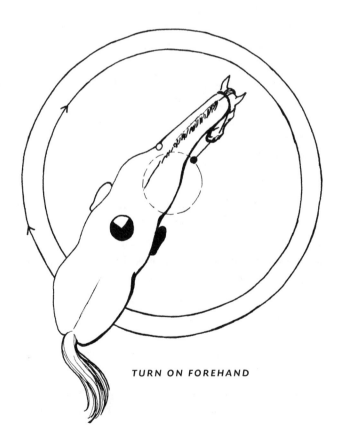

TURN ON FOREHAND

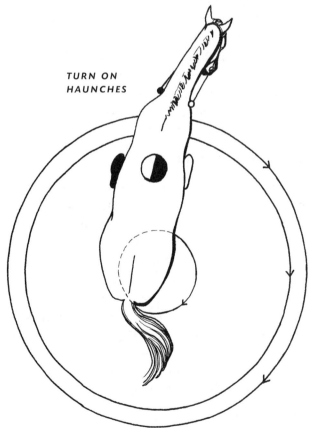

TURN ON HAUNCHES

Mounted turns on the forehand and haunches will increase your horse's responsiveness and flexibility.

• Tighten your right rein very slightly to tip his nose to the right, just enough to see his eye. If necessary, take light contact with your left rein to remind him not to move forward. Adjust your seat to the rear and right, freeing the horse's left shoulder.

• Simultaneously, press straight into your horse's side with your right calf, just behind the girth. Do not kick and do not use a squeeze/release. Maintain steady, even pressure with your right calf. If necessary, press lightly with your left calf at the girth to prevent your horse from backing up.

• Sitting balanced slightly to the right, ask your horse to move his hindquarters over one step. Stop him and praise him, ride him forward one step, then reverse your aids, asking him to move his hindquarters over in the other direction.

Build on this exercise slowly, a step at a time, until after several lessons you can ask your horse to move his hindquarters over a quarter turn in each direction. Don't try to make him pivot on his front feet or move quickly away from your leg. The point of this exercise is to gain quiet control of the placement of his hind hooves, teaching him to yield his hindquarters over calmly from leg pressure when asked.

Turn on the Haunches

The mounted turn on the haunches is more complicated than the turn on the forehand. Horses seem to prefer to turn on their front legs, probably because when they are carrying weight on their backs they must shift more of their balance to the rear before they can move their forequarters. It takes time for a horse to learn to do this, so there is no point in teaching this exercise before your horse can easily back up and work good, even circles and curves. The point of the exercise is to teach him to make a small circle with his hind feet and a larger one with his front. This has the benefit of avoiding the torque in the hocks of a pivot spin while still turning the horse in a small space, his weight balanced to the rear.

Practice the turn on the haunches a few times on

the ground, then mount up and ask your horse to back up. Next, work a few small circles and curves, using both the direct and indirect rein. You can then follow one of two approaches to this exercise.

You can continue to ride circles, making them smaller and smaller, using the indirect rein strongly against the side of his neck just in front of his withers while using your leg on the same side with strong pressure straight into his side, just in front of the girth. This use of lateral aids will encourage the horse to do very tight circles, his hind feet taking small steps to the side as his front ones take longer steps.

You can also teach your horse to move his forequarters directly away from leg and rein pressure. This may be easier to teach because it builds on the ground work you have already done. The aids for this type of turn on the haunches are:

• Halt your horse as squarely as possible.
• Back one step to move his hindquarters under his body.
• For a turn to the right (shoulders move to the right), press lightly with your left rein just in front of the withers.
• Tip your horse's nose to the right with light vibrations from your right rein.
• Shift your weight slightly to the right.
• Press strongly with your left leg, just behind the girth, pressure angled toward the right shoulder.

Your horse will probably be confused by these cues initially and may back a step or two. This is normal. Take advantage of the fact that he is moving and push strongly with the left rein against his neck, as a bearing rein just in front of the withers, this time increasing contact with the right rein to the equivalent of the weight of a medium orange. Your horse will take one step to the side with his front legs, usually crossing his left over his right. He may also move his hind legs to the left. This is not a problem. You are not trying to teach him to pivot on his hind legs, but to step quietly to the side with them while taking larger steps to the side with the front legs.

Again, build on this exercise, a step at a time, until your horse can move his forequarters over a quarter turn in each direction. This exercise will help your horse develop strength in his hindquarters, flexibility through his body, and better balance for trail riding, as well as making him more maneuverable and responsive to an indirect or a neck rein.

Controlling Speed and Step Length in the Walk

Under saddle, many gaited horses walk at a very fast clip and appear unable to slow down or take shorter steps. A few others take very short, restricted steps, with no reach. Oddly enough, out in the pasture, these same horses can walk very slowly from one clump of grass to another, can modify the length of their steps to pick their way over logs or through boulders, and can head back to the barn with long, reaching strides in the walk. Although it is true that some horses are built to take longer steps than others, they all have the ability to control how far they reach and how fast they move in the walk. If you cue him correctly, your gaited horse can walk slowly and take smaller steps, or walk quickly and take longer steps, under saddle as well as he does when free in a pasture. The secret to controlling the speed and step of your horse's walk lies in the way you use your leg, seat, and rein aids.

Slowing Down the Walk

How do you ask your long-stepping, fast-moving horse to slow down, and why would you want to?

One reason to control your horse's walk is safety. If you have a horse that rushes along taking huge steps and he is suddenly confronted with rough ground or downed timber on a trail, he is most likely going to stumble and trip. Another reason to control your horse's walk is for companionship on the trail. If you ride with folks who have horses that are not gaited, they may not take such long steps, and you will end up either rushing ahead and waiting for them or forcing their horses to jog to keep up with your horse's walk. Neither makes for a very pleasant trail ride! Perhaps the best reason to slow the walk, however, is that most horses that take very long steps at a fast ordinary walk also slop you from front to back in the saddle, producing the dreaded "camel walk" and dragging their hind

legs behind them instead of using their hindquarters to push them forward. If they are taught to take shorter, slower steps at the ordinary walk, they also learn to use their backs more efficiently and are much more pleasant to ride.

You can use a curb bit for this exercise if your horse is accustomed to one, but a snaffle or even a bitless sidepull or jaquima will work just as well.

- Ride in a straight line in an ordinary walk, sitting in the base position with no pressure from your legs or hands, maintaining the plum feel of contact with your horse's mouth.
- Feel the rhythm of your horse's walk. Now, sit very still in the saddle, tightening your abdominal muscles between your belly button and rib cage, firming your lower back muscles as you do. This will prevent you from moving in the saddle and will keep you still. Envision your seat bones as heavy weights, with gravity pulling them straight down into the seat of the saddle.
- Continue to resist the front-to-back motion of the horse by tightening your buttocks slightly and sitting in the heavy seat.
- Slightly tighten your upper thighs, keeping your calves away from the side of the horse. This will also resist the forward motion of the horse.
- Use light squeeze/releases with your fingers on the reins to reinforce your back, weight, and leg aids. Do not pull back on the reins; instead, take and release pressure at every other step, keeping your hands low and quiet.
- In response to all these cues, your horse will slow down and take shorter steps for a stride or two. Praise him, then allow him to go for a few strides in the faster walk.
- Practice slowing a few steps every four or five strides. Gradually increase the number of slower and shorter steps you ask for until your horse can walk slowly in small steps several times around your ring on a light rein, with no more contact than the feel of that elusive plum in your hands. It will take time to reach this goal. Do not expect your horse to do this after only a lesson or two, or even after a month or

two of practice. But, if you are persistent and tactful in the way you work on this, even a very long-strided, high-energy horse will eventually be able to walk slowly and quietly when you ask.

As your horse learns to slow and shorten his steps in his ordinary walk, you will begin to feel a change in his back. His muscles will feel a little more full under your seat, and the push from his hindquarters will be more controlled and tighter. The "camel walk" will disappear, and his hind legs will come under him more strongly, although in a shorter step. Your horse will have begun to semi-collect himself at the ordinary walk.

Speeding Up the Ordinary Walk

Occasionally, a gaited horse walks as if he is a tightly wound toy. He may take very short, slow steps, or a great number of short, fast steps. Although it is much more difficult for a horse that is not built to take long steps to increase his stride than it is for one that has the conformation for longer steps to shorten them, you can help even the tightest horse walk a little faster and take slightly longer steps.

You can use the same techniques to encourage more reach from a horse that has an average ordinary walk, improving the way he responds to your aids and building a foundation for longer strides in the faster gaits. Think of this as playing the other end of the scales in the walk from those you played to slow your horse down. Again, you can work in a curb or snaffle bit as well as without a bit, if that suits your horse.

- Start in the ordinary walk, again sitting in the base position, hands low, reins held with the light plum-feel contact.
- Feel the horse's back under you and try to determine when the right hind leg is moving forward. (It may help to have a spotter on the ground tell you when this happens until you can feel it from the saddle.)
- Sit relaxed in the base position, with no tension in your back, buttocks, or upper thighs. Let your legs drape down over the horse's sides.
- Keep your fingers relaxed on the reins with elastic feel of the horse's mouth or nose, but do

not row or pump your hands back and forth with the motion of the horse's head; keep them still and let your fingers open and close slightly on the reins instead. Allow the horse to carry his head somewhat lower as you ride, releasing tension in his neck.
- Begin to squeeze/release with your lower calves each time you feel his right hind leg move forward. This will cause the left hind leg to start pushing off from the ground a bit more strongly, increasing the horse's step length.
- Give the leg squeeze/release aids every other step for about halfway around your arena, preventing your horse from breaking into anything but a fast walk with a light squeeze/release on your reins. His strides will begin to lengthen, and his walk will speed up.
- Praise him, let him return to his previous walk on a loose rein, then repeat, going in the other direction.

If you practice asking your horse to lengthen his stride and walk faster for a short while every time you ride, his walk will become more relaxed and he will cover more ground with less effort than he did in the short, choppy walk he originally used.

Playing the Scales

One of the better exercises you can practice with any gaited horse is increasing and decreasing step length and speed in the ordinary walk. This will help strengthen his back and improve his responsiveness to your aids while he works calmly in a gait that is not stressful to his body. After you have taught your horse to lengthen and shorten his steps at the walk, ask him to put those skills to work in an exercise that lengthens and shortens his body as well as his steps.

- Sit straight in the saddle, balanced in the base position. Ask your horse to start out in an ordinary walk, taking light contact with the bit or noseband. Go at whatever speed and step length your horse offers.
- Ask him to increase his stride length very gradually, squeezing/releasing with your calves

at every other step and relaxing your fingers on the reins. Don't allow them to become totally slack, but open your fingers just a little to lighten contact with his mouth. Follow his motion with a soft, but not sloppy, seat in the saddle, relaxing your back and abdominal muscles.

• When your horse has reached the longest step he can take, begin to bring him back to a shorter step. Tighten your back muscles slightly, breathe in and up to tighten your abdominal muscles, and slowly tighten your upper thighs to resist the motion of his back. Gently increase contact on the bit by closing your fingers on the reins. He will begin to take a slower, shorter step. Continue these restraining aids until he is taking the shortest step

possible, then release them and ask again for a longer step.

• Alternate asking for a longer and shorter step several times whenever you ride your horse.

If you practice riding in an ordinary walk to teach your horse the skills he needs to respond to your aids, straighten his body, rate his speed, and begin to develop flexibility, he will be more responsive and sure-footed on the trail and more consistent in his easy gait. Every time you ride, try to practice an ordinary walk using aids to keep your horse's body straight, working circles and other figures to help him develop flexibility while keeping his walk even and energetic. If you help him improve his muscle tone and ability to use his body in the walk, he will be a much more pleasant horse to ride on the trail in any gait.

CHAPTER SIX

The Flat Walk, or Slow Paso Llano

It is vital for a horse to have a good, reaching, even, free walk.
— JAMES FILLIS (1834–1913)

While all horses can walk, not all of them can do the faster, longer-striding flat walk. The slow paso llano is the same gait as the flat walk, done with termino instead of head nod. The methods for establishing the flat walk will work equally well to develop a good slow paso llano, and for simplicity in this book the term "flat walk" applies to both for training purposes.

This gait is great for trail riding because it is comfortable to ride and easy for the horse. It is a balanced gait with no wasted motion and plenty of drive from the hindquarters for hill work. It is also one of the gaits that gaited horses do not share with their non-gaited cousins.

Flat Walk First

If you expect your easy-gaited horse to do a running walk, a paso llano, or a fox trot as his intermediate gait, it is important for him to develop a good, consistent flat walk first. Old-timers used to say a horse should be ridden for at least three months in the flat walk to build his rhythm and strength before he even attempted to do a running walk or fox trot. Although you may not want to ride exclusively in the flat walk for that long, moderate work in the gait will improve your horse's overall condition and help him do most of the faster easy gaits with less effort. If your horse is expected to work in a saddle rack or true rack, you will probably not need to bother trying to work on the flat walk. Your horse will have other gait options at flat-walk speed.

The easiest way to ask for a flat walk is to speed a horse up from the fastest ordinary walk, adding an upper register to "playing the scales," as discussed in chapter 5. Before you can do this, however, make sure you can recognize the gait when your horse does it. If you have never experienced a flat walk or are unsure about how it feels, try to borrow a horse that does the

gait well and memorize the way he moves under you in the gait. It is very difficult to help a horse do the gait if you are not familiar with it yourself.

How the Gait Feels

When he flat walks or does a slow paso llano, a horse's body feels energetic and balanced under your seat, with both his shoulders and his hindquarters working equally. You will hear and feel each hoof contact the ground individually, with no side-to-side or up-and-down motion, although you may feel a slight front-to-back rock in the saddle. In a flat walk you may also notice that your horse's up-and-down head nod is more pronounced as his speed increases from the ordinary walk, although in the slow paso llano your horse's head and neck will remain stable, while his termino may increase.

There are other gaits that feel similar to the flat walk.

Fox Walk

Because it is done at about the same speed and is comfortable to ride, the fox walk or slow fox trot is sometimes mistaken for the true flat walk. The main differ-

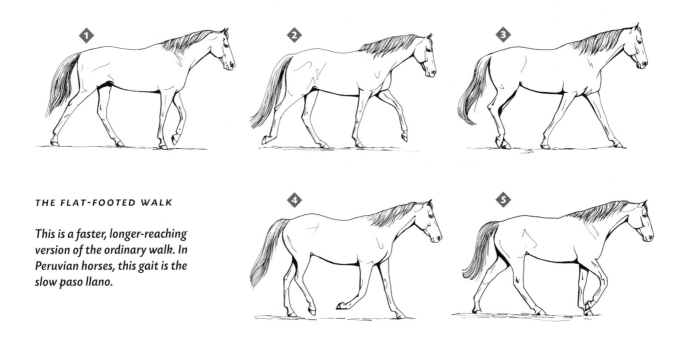

THE FLAT-FOOTED WALK

This is a faster, longer-reaching version of the ordinary walk. In Peruvian horses, this gait is the slow paso llano.

ences between this gait and the flat walk are a slight bounce in the hindquarters and a definite 1-2, 3-4 beat.

Stepping Pace/Amble/Sobreandando

Another gait that is sometimes mistaken for a flat walk is the stepping pace, amble, or sobreandando. The main differences between this gait and the flat walk are a slight side-to-side sway in the saddle and a definite 1-2-3-4 beat sound. If you can't tell from the feel of his back, you may be able to tell whether your horse is doing a stepping pace by looking at the front of your saddle. If the pommel or horn appears to move from one side of the horse's withers to the other, he is most likely doing a stepping pace.

The flat walk is natural for many horses as they speed up from an ordinary walk.

- Start in a fast ordinary walk on flat ground in a straight line. Sit straight in the saddle with your lower back and abdominal muscles firm but elastic. Arch your back slightly into the position you would use to back float while swimming.
- As your horse moves forward, keep your hands low, slightly below the base position, with light "plum-feel" contact on the reins.
- Squeeze/release with your calves, using both legs, urging your horse to increase his speed.
- If your horse tries to pop into something faster than a flat walk, release all leg pressure. Check his speed with a squeeze/release from your fingers on both reins and resist his motion slightly with your lower back. Move into the heavy seat to prevent him from speeding up into a faster intermediate gait.
- Your horse should go into a medium-speed, four-beat flat walk. Ride in that gait for a few steps, then relax in the saddle. Return to an ordinary walk and pet and praise your horse. Gradually increase the number of steps he takes in a flat walk until he can go all the way around your arena work area or for a moderate distance on a flat section of trail. If you are working in an arena, be sure to work in both directions. Practice a little more often in the direction in which your horse is normally less flexible.

Solving Simple Problems in the Flat Walk

If your horse does a flat walk in response to these aids, you can concentrate on improving the rhythm and consistency of the gait. You can help your horse with any problems by working him at a fairly slow speed at first and learning to time your leg and rein aids to encourage or check him in his gait.

Keeping Speed Even

It is easiest to work on consistent speed in a large arena or ring with a firm, level surface, where you don't have to worry about changes in footing or other distractions. Try to get the basics established before you trail ride on uneven ground in a flat walk.

To rate speed in the flat walk:

- Starting with light "plum-feel" contact on the reins, push your horse on for speed from an ordinary walk with one squeeze/release from your calves. Sit upright, with your back and abdominal muscles from belly button to rib cage holding your body erect.
- Your horse should flat walk a few steps and then may speed up into a running walk or fox trot.
- Check his speed with a light squeeze/release vibration on the reins and a slight resistance from your back muscles. Do not tighten or push with your back into the full heavy seat, but change the tension in your back about as much as you would to breathe in a half a breath.
- Your horse may slow down to an ordinary walk. That is a sign that you have relaxed your back too much and may have squeezed too hard on the reins.
- If this happens, ride for a few steps in the ordinary walk, then ask again for the flat walk, this time checking your horse's speed just before he starts to string out into a faster gait by lightly squeezing/releasing on only *one* rein. Keep your body erect but not stiff. The rein you use will depend on your horse. If he is stiff to the right (does not bend easily to the right) use

the right rein. If he is stiff to the left, use the left rein. Using the rein on his stiff side will help straighten his body, and as it straightens, slow him.

• As your horse slows down, use a very light touch straight into his side with the calf of your opposite leg to remind him to keep moving (right rein, left leg; left rein, right leg). This use of the rein and leg should be familiar as the diagonal aids you used in various exercises in the ordinary walk.

• If your horse ignores these aids and continues to slow down too much into an ordinary walk, ask him to move out again. Use both calves to squeeze/release pressure on his sides and keep your fingers soft and elastic on the reins.

With practice, you should be able to regulate your horse's speed at the flat walk , catching him just before he speeds up into another gait and preventing him from falling back into an ordinary walk. For particularly laid-back horses, you might need to carry a dressage whip to reinforce your leg cues. If you do use the whip, carry it so that it touches the horse's flank *behind* your leg and tap him with it only *after* you have used your legs in a squeeze/release. Do *not* develop the habit of using the whip as a crutch in place of your legs; *never* tap with the whip before you ask the horse to move out with your legs.

Alternate squeezes on the reins and from your legs until your horse settles into a steady, medium speed at the flat walk, then stop using these aids, allowing him to maintain the gait on his own. He will be moving faster than his fast ordinary walk, but not so fast that he becomes rushed or strung out. Reward him for a good performance by relaxing in the saddle; follow his motion with your lower body by flexing at your waist but not rocking on your seat bones or "belly dancing" in the saddle. Pay attention to your horse. If he changes speed or starts to change gait, touch him with your calf or resist his motion by stiffening your lower back slightly to bring him back to a flat walk.

Practice a moderate speed in the flat walk every time you ride until it becomes very comfortable for your horse. He will start to develop a good, even

rhythm in the gait as a result of working at consistent speed. Do not worry if he does not take long reaching steps in the gait at first. They will come later when he has developed more muscle strength. Work on consistency in the gait at a controlled speed first.

Uneven Gait on Uneven Ground

Horses that have a good flat walk on flat ground will sometimes have trouble in the gait when they start to work over uneven terrain on the trail; they often become trotty going uphill and pacey going downhill on even the slightest of inclines. This happens because going uphill, your horse shifts his weight a bit to the rear and his back becomes a little more round than it would be on flat ground. Going downhill, his weight shifts to his shoulders, and his back may become slightly more hollow than it would be on level ground. These changes in his back position are reflected in the gait he uses.

To teach your horse to flat walk consistently on slightly uneven ground, you need to help him maintain his back position as close as possible to the one he uses on the flat. To work on this, find a stretch of trail or part of your pasture that has a very gentle slant. You can also grade your ring so that one end is slightly lower than the other. The slope should be gentle, no more than a few degrees. Don't try to solve this problem on a steep bank.

You have two tools to help your horse stay balanced in the flat walk. You can use your weight to affect the way his back is carried, and you can use your hands on the bit or noseband to help him adjust tension in his ligament system, which will also change his back position. Your horse should do his flat walk with his back in a mostly neutral position: not too rounded or he will trot, and not too hollow or he will pace.

Using Your Weight

If you move your weight toward your horse's loin, his back will hollow a little. If you move it forward, he will be more likely to round a little. So, when facing a slight incline, instead of sitting with your balance forward as

Riding Transitions

TRANSITIONS IN SPEED IN A SINGLE GAIT, or between gaits, help a horse develop balance and elasticity in his muscles. To ride a good transition, you need to do a little more than just speed your horse up with a shove from your legs or slow him down by a pull on the reins. A balanced transition includes weight, leg, and rein cues that help the horse prepare his body for the coming change in speed.

Upward transitions in speed are the easiest to ride. With your horse in an ordinary walk, prepare him for a speed increase by using the *activating aids*. You activate your horse through a series of cues from your weight, legs, and reins that encourages him to move out with energy.

Start by lifting and opening your chest by slightly arching your back, then put some active tension into your lower back muscles. Think of the way your back works when you pump a swing into the air, and use a similar but softer push with your lower back to energize your horse.

Follow this light push from your back with a squeeze/release from your calves and a gentle opening of your fingers on the reins. Don't allow the reins to become totally slack, but lighten your contact just a tiny bit as you ask your horse for more forward energy. Relax your back as soon as your horse has moved out in a slightly faster gait; don't keep pushing, or he may end up going faster than you intend.

Downward transitions in speed can be a little more difficult to ride well. If your horse is flat walking, ask him to slow to an ordinary walk by first sitting deeply in the saddle, relaxing, and letting your weight sink onto his back without leaning backward or forward, but releasing all active tension in your lower back muscles. At the same time, tighten and release your buttocks and your upper thighs and very gently squeeze and release your fingers on the reins. Breathe out. As you do this, be prepared to keep your horse moving by using your activating aids, or he may skip over the ordinary walk and simply halt.

you normally would for riding up a hill, to help a horse that tends to trot going uphill remain in a flat walk, sit straight in the saddle with your pelvis tipped into the heavy seat. Don't sit slumped back in the saddle or in a chair seat that will put your weight far behind your horse's balance point. Sit just slightly less forward than you normally would for riding up a hill. This will shift your horse's balance a little to the rear and will encourage him to stay in gait rather than trot.

Facing a slight decline with a horse that tends to become pacey going downhill, sit straight in the saddle, this time tilting your pelvis just a little toward the light, allowing seat, not leaning forward or back, with your weight balanced straight over the strongest part of his back. This position will encourage your horse to shift his balance to the center, may help him raise his back, and can help him flat walk rather than pace.

Combining Weight and Rein Aids

In addition to using these simple weight shifts to affect your horse's balance, ask him to change his head and neck position to adjust his ligament system as you work up and down the slight hill. If he prefers to trot uphill, take light, "plum-feel" contact with his mouth or nose and gently ask him to raise his head while bringing his nose toward vertical. To do this, raise your hands an inch or two above the base position, so that they are waist high, and shorten your reins just enough to bring his nose in a couple of inches. Use light, repeated squeeze/releases on the reins, not a steady pull, to change his head position. Shift your weight into the heavy seat as you do this.

For the horse that prefers to pace going downhill, along with a weight shift and sitting lightly in the saddle, lower your hands to ask him to lower his head and neck. Keep your hands below the swells of a Western saddle, or at the buttons on an English one, well below your waist level. Use light, alternating squeeze/releases on the reins to encourage your horse to keep his head and neck as low as possible, stretching his neck, and bringing his nose just a little toward vertical, changing his balance so that he stays in a walk.

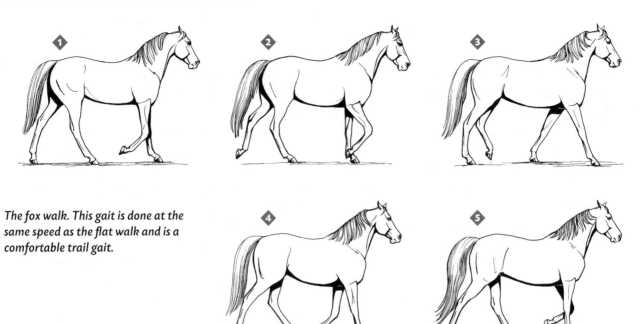

The fox walk. This gait is done at the same speed as the flat walk and is a comfortable trail gait.

If you find that these simple techniques do not work to keep your horse in a good flat walk on a small incline, don't just give up and allow your horse to do whatever he feels like up and down hills. Rate his speed so that he is doing an ordinary walk downhill and a slower but still energetic flat walk uphill. It is better to drop back to an ordinary walk than to allow him to develop the bad habits of pacing downhill or trotting uphill. See chapter 9 for more methods on helping your horse avoid a pace.

Fox Walk

Horses with a strong inclination to fox trot will often go into the slower diagonal fox walk when pushed out of the ordinary walk.

The fox walk is pleasant to ride and can be very surefooted for your horse on the trail, but it is not quite as effective for developing the condition of your horse's back and hindquarters as the flat walk. Teach your horse the flat walk to help him develop his body so that he can do his faster gaits with less effort. There is nothing "wrong" with the fox walk, you can certainly continue to ride your horse in this gait if you prefer, but try to develop a flat walk in addition to it.

To correct the fox walk:

• Return to the ordinary walk. Sit straight in the saddle with your abdominal and back muscles holding you erect but not stiff. Arch your back very slightly, as you would to back float. Maintain the "plum-feel" on your reins.
• Push your horse out of the ordinary walk with strong, intermittent leg squeezes, remembering to open your fingers and relax tension on the reins every time you squeeze with your legs.
• The instant he starts to lose the even, four-beat rhythm of the walk, check his speed with a light squeeze/release on the reins, holding your hands low.
• He may slow to an ordinary walk when you check him.
• Move him on with a squeeze/release from both calves, just as he starts to slow down.

With a series of squeezes with your legs and light checks with your hands, regulate the gait, encouraging the flat walk and checking before he breaks into a fox walk. The flat walk that results will not be very fast or refined, but it will be faster than an ordinary walk and not a diagonal fox walk. The quality and consistency of the gait will improve gradually as the horse develops strength and rhythm. Over time, increase the distance you ride in this gait, and gradually start to push it for speed as you would an ordinary walk.

Sometimes a fox-walking horse may slip into a stepping pace as you slow him from the fox walk. If the stepping pace is not a gait you prefer to do with your horse, it can be a difficult problem to deal with. It is a good idea to let a horse with this problem work in the fox walk instead of the flat walk for a month or two, building his muscle strength in that gait. You may even want to work in the fox trot or hard trot for a while. Then try the flat walk again. If he still pops into a stepping pace, use the techniques in chapter 9 that deal with the pace to help him develop the flat walk.

Exercises in the Flat Walk or Slow Paso Llano

As your horse begins to develop some consistency in the flat walk , start to integrate some work in that gait into the exercises you started in the ordinary walk. Practice walking slowly, then making the transition up the scales through a medium-speed ordinary walk, to a fast, long-striding ordinary walk, and then into the flat walk. Stay in the flat walk for several strides, then begin the transition back down the scales, ending with a slow, shorter-stepping ordinary walk. This practice in transitions will help your horse develop elasticity from poll to tail as well as increase his overall muscle tone and responsiveness to your aids.

In addition to making simple transitions in speed, you can try riding some large circles, figure eights, and serpentines in the flat walk. You may find your horse can walk straighter lines and work rounder circles in the more forward-moving flat walk than he could in the ordinary walk. If he seems to have trouble staying consistent, however, don't work on them until he has had some more advanced training. It is not unusual for a horse to need more work on flexibility before he can do a good round circle in a flat walk without hopping or breaking into a stepping pace. Ride in straight lines and practice transitions to develop his flat walk before you worry too much about how well he can do more complicated patterns.

The Results

After working consistently in the flat walk, your horse should have a good foundation for understanding your aids, and his physical condition should be strong enough to allow him to work in a faster gait without tiring. He may not have spent three whole months working exclusively in a flat walk, but even a few weeks devoted to that gait will enhance his ability to do his easy gait. Practice in a consistent, rhythmic flat walk will improve all of his faster gaits by improving his muscle tone and stamina.

CHAPTER SEVEN
The Stepping Pace, Amble, or Sobreandando

The amble is a lower gait than the walk, but infinitely longer strided.
— FRANÇOIS ROBICHON DE LA GUÉRINIÈRE (1687–1751)

Many gaited horses, when asked to speed up from an ordinary walk, immediately go into the stepping pace, or amble. This laterally timed, uneven, four-beat gait can be done with low sweeping action or some animation at a variety of speeds, from as slow as the slowest walk to as fast as some horses can gallop. There are almost as many names for this gait as there are human languages because it is the most common of the easy gaits, done by many breeds of the world's gaited horses. In English, it has often been called the *amble*. Because the word "'amble" also carries the connotation of a slow, aimless walk and the gait is much more than that, the term "stepping pace" is perhaps more accurate.

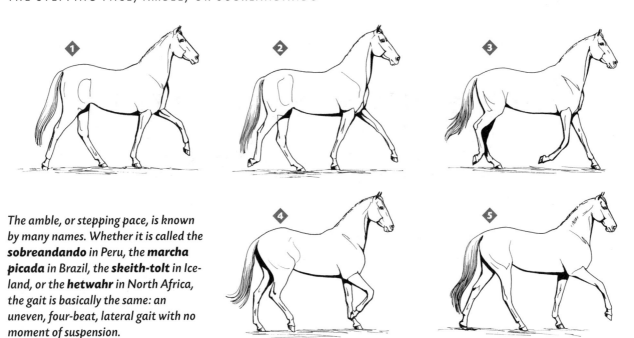

*The amble, or stepping pace, is known by many names. Whether it is called the **sobreandando** in Peru, the **marcha picada** in Brazil, the **skeith-tolt** in Iceland, or the **hetwahr** in North Africa, the gait is basically the same: an uneven, four-beat, lateral gait with no moment of suspension.*

The accepted gait of some easy-gaited breeds, the stepping pace is usually comfortable to ride and relatively energy-efficient for the horse. It is considered undesirable in many breeds, however, and because it can be stressful for a horse's back to ride for long periods in the gait, too much work in the stepping pace can be a problem for the long-term soundness of pleasure horses. If your horse naturally does the stepping pace and it is considered acceptable for his breed, or if he simply will not do any other easy gait despite training and conditioning to help him use his body in a different way, try to balance the time you spend in this gait with work in the ordinary walk. The different use of his body in the walk will give his ligament system a chance to stretch and help keep his back healthy by preserving the spacing between vertebrae that is so important for his future soundness.

How the Gait Feels

The stepping pace is usually comfortable to ride at slower speeds. It rocks you gently from side to side in the saddle, swaying you along with the motion of the horse's back. You may be able to feel one side of the horse's back, then the other, tighten under your seat as each lateral pair of legs advances in turn. Some horses swing their heads and necks from side to side away from each advancing pair of legs as well, but others either maintain a steady head and neck carriage or nod slightly up and down. You should be able to hear four distinct, uneven beats when the horse travels in a slow stepping pace.

At faster speeds, the stepping pace may become rougher to ride, although it is never as jarring as a true pace or trot. In this quicker gait, you will feel a distinct shift from side to side in the saddle, but not the strong bounce that is typical of the true pace. Horses that stay smooth in the fast stepping pace will continue to rock you gently from side to side as they speed up. At top speed, the beats of the gait blur together, and the head and neck motion of the horse diminishes. The horse may appear to hold his head higher at faster speeds, and his croup may begin to bounce up and down as he moves his hind legs more rapidly, although you will probably not feel this motion in the saddle.

Similar Gaits

At a slow speed, the stepping pace might be confused with the flat walk, slow paso llano, or fox walk. At a faster speed, it might be mistaken for a saddle rack. There is nothing "wrong" with your horse doing any of those gaits in place of a stepping pace as long as

THE STEPPING PACE, AMBLE, OR SOBREANDANDO

you find them pleasant to ride and he seems relaxed doing them.

The Flat Walk or Slow Paso Llano

Not many horses will prefer to flat walk in place of a stepping pace if they have been bred to do the more lateral gait. Occasionally, however, one will seem to "stick" in a fast walk instead of doing a stepping pace. Both gaits are smooth, but they feel quite different from the saddle. When you are trying to tell which gait the horse is doing, it may help to close your eyes and concentrate on feeling his motion with your seat. While the flat walk offers a solid feel of the horse's back staying steady under your seat as each hoof hits the ground at equal intervals, in the stepping pace you will feel his back filling on one side, then the other, as you sway very subtly from side to side in the saddle.

The Fox Walk

Although it has a similar speed and sound, the fox walk does not feel the same as the stepping pace. The fox walk has a slight bobble, or up-and-down bounce in the hindquarters that moves you from front to back in the saddle in a push/pull motion. Remember that in a stepping pace, your movement in the saddle will be a side-to-side sway. If you feel a bobble and front-to-back motion in the saddle, your horse is most likely doing a fox walk.

Saddle Rack

This gait can be just as smooth as the stepping pace and can be done at the same speeds. The saddle rack, however, has a 1-2-3-4 sound, gives more of an up-and-down action in the hindquarters, and has more of a roll or climbing feel in the shoulders. If you feel a lot of motion from your horse's hindquarters and it seems as if he is climbing in front while you sit calmly in the center, he is probably doing a saddle rack, not a stepping pace.

Developing the No-Problem Stepping Pace

Many horses prefer to go in a stepping pace at speeds above an ordinary walk. You can work in this gait in a snaffle, curb bit, sidepull, Peruvian bozal, or noseband-type jaquima and any saddle that fits your horse and you and allows you to sit balanced and straight. Mount up and sit in the base position with your body relaxed and your weight centered over your seat bones. Try to use a light, "plum-feel" on the reins. Hold your hands a couple of inches above the normal base position to encourage your horse to carry his head and neck slightly elevated. Don't pull up or back as you raise your hands, just use the same light feel of the reins you normally keep at the ordinary walk. Move your horse out in an ordinary walk. Push him up into the stepping pace by asking for a little speed with a squeeze/release from both your calves while simultaneously relaxing your fingers on the reins. Your horse may automatically go into a stepping pace with virtually no work on your part.

Rating Speed in the Stepping Pace

Even though the gait is natural to your horse, you will probably need to help him travel at consistent speeds in it. Some horses will start out in a bold stepping pace but over time dwindle down to a slow crawl in the gait, while others seem to have a gait-inflation problem, starting at a moderate speed stepping pace and ending up going faster and faster in the gait. For trail and pleasure riding, you will want to be able to control how fast your horse is going and to maintain him at that speed until it is your idea to change. The same aids that work to control speed in other gaits will work for the stepping pace, although you may find that they will work better if you use slightly different hand and body positions.

- Start out in a stepping pace from the ordinary walk, sitting centered in the saddle with your hands slightly above the base position. Use a single squeeze/release from your legs to ask the horse to move out and relax your contact on the reins just a little as he speeds up. He should travel at about five to six miles per hour, noticeably faster than his ordinary walk.
- Ride for a few strides and notice whether your horse stays at a moderate speed in the stepping pace, speeds up, or slows down.

• If he tries to speed up, lower your hands an inch or two to the base position and tilt your pelvis into the heavy seat position. Breathe out and simultaneously squeeze/release your hands on both reins. Continue to sit "heavy" and squeeze/release on the reins until he slows down to his original, moderate speed. Be prepared to speed him back up if he slows down too much.

• If he tries to slow down from his original flat walk speed, raise your hands an inch or two from the base position, maintaining lighter than "plum-feel" on the reins. You should not try to lift and hold the horse's head up with your hands; simply ask him to carry it higher on his own by raising your hands to give him a different base at the other end of the contact he feels through the reins. Arch your back as if you were back floating in a pool, holding your shoulders over your hips with energetic tension in your lower back muscles and abdominal muscles. Squeeze/release with both calves straight into your horse's sides, urging him forward. Be prepared to slow him down if he speeds up too much in response to these aids.

These aids are basically the same ones you would use to rate speed in any gait, except that in this case you raise your hands slightly if your horse slows down and lower them slightly if he speeds up. Adjusting your hands adjusts his head and neck positions, changing the tension in his ligament system and helping him slow down or speed up while continuing to work in the stepping pace. A lower hand slightly tightens the tension in the system, encouraging the horse to slow down; an elevated hand loosens tension in the system, encouraging a horse to speed up.

Improving Reach and Smoothness in the Stepping Pace

Very often, horses that take longer steps in the stepping pace are also smoother to ride. Some horses naturally take longer steps in the gait than others, but as you discovered while working with the ordinary walk, you can always help your horse take longer steps, within the limits of his conformation. To make the most of his natural ability and produce longer steps in the stepping pace, a gait that has no moments of suspension where he can bounce from hoof to hoof, your horse needs to reach with his shoulders and his hind legs. A good way to help him reach and stretch is to practice riding him on a very slight downhill grade, asking him to lower and extend his head and neck. This will shift his center of gravity forward in his body and can help loosen tight shoulder muscles as he reaches forward with his front legs to stay in balance.

• Ride in an ordinary walk, then push your horse into a stepping pace.

• Lower your hands to each side of his withers, feeding slack into each rein until your horse lowers his head slightly from his usual position. Do *not* increase contact on the reins. Keep your fingers soft and relaxed and avoid putting pressure on your horse's mouth.

• Very lightly squeeze/release on each rein, alternating hands until your horse responds by lowering his head and nosing out a little from his usual position. This will shift his center of gravity forward and cause him to take slightly longer steps with his front legs. To ask him to match those steps with his hind legs, practice the second part of the exercise that follows, using your seat and legs to energize his hindquarters.

• As your horse lowers his head a little and begins to reach more in front, tilt your pelvis into the heavy seat position.

• Feel the rhythm of your horse's gait and, as he swings his back from side to side, gently shift your weight from side to side along with his motion, going with the swing. Each time you sway in the saddle, you will be weighting one of his hind legs a little more than the other.

• As your weight is over a hind leg, squeeze/release with your legs to ask him to push off a little more strongly with that leg.

• Your horse will start to take longer steps both in response to your weight and leg aids and in response to the natural weight shift produced by lowering his head and neck on a downhill slant.

• Praise him and pet him, then allow him to return to an ordinary walk.

Practice this exercise a little each day on a slight downhill and also on flat ground, asking your horse for longer steps in the gait. **Caution:** Do not continue the exercise if he starts to do some other gait or becomes rushed in his stepping pace. Return to an ordinary walk and a slower, tighter stride in the stepping pace if he starts to hop or mix gaits.

Another exercise that is very useful for developing longer stride in the stepping pace is work in serpentines. Your horse should be familiar with these exercises from work you did to develop flexibility in the ordinary walk. To work in the stepping pace, increase the number of loops in the serpentine, make them tighter, and modify the aids you used for the walking exercises. This time, you are not asking your horse to bend his body in a gradual curve as you did in the walk. You want him to bend sharply, using his shoulders and haunches more than his body to make the turns. To benefit from working serpentines in a stepping pace, your horse needs to maintain a higher head carriage and bend less through his body. This use of his body will preserve the tension he needs in his back to allow him to do the gait while working around the curves of the serpentine. You may want to set out four or five cones to provide turning points for the figure before you start. Do this on flat, smooth ground at first. When your horse is comfortable with the exercise, you can practice on a fairly wide trail or in the pasture.

• Start out in the stepping pace, sitting in the center of your saddle.
• Tip your pelvis into the heavy seat position.
• Raise your hands a couple of inches above the base position to help your horse elevate his head and neck. Do not increase contact on the reins or pull back. Just lift your hands a little with the same contact through the reins you normally use, preferably the "plum-feel."
• As you start around the first cone to the left, raise your left hand a fraction more, increasing your contact momentarily with that rein. At the same time, press lightly straight into your horse's side with your left leg, giving him a fulcrum to bend around. Keep your right leg

draped against his side just behind the girth to prevent him from swinging his haunches outside on the turn.
• Immediately reverse these aids as you start around the next cone. Remember to keep your horse's head and neck slightly elevated with a slightly higher hand position as you work this type of serpentine to prevent him from breaking into a different gait.

With some practice in these two exercises, your horse's stepping pace should become smoother and show more overstride in the track of hoof prints. Try both of these exercises in slow and moderate speeds of the stepping pace as your horse's gait develops. They may help his fastest speed in the gait become more consistent and pleasant to ride.

Solving Problems in the Stepping Pace

Some horses that automatically go into a slow stepping pace from a walk have trouble maintaining the gait at faster speeds. Others seem to have trouble doing the gait even at slow speeds. Horses have the same problems doing the stepping pace that they have in performing all the other easy gaits: They may be too diagonal or trotty, or too lateral or pacey, or they are inconsistent and mix gaits. If your horse has these problems, it does not mean that he is not "natural" in his gait; it only means that he may need a little help to achieve the balance and tension in his dorsal ligament system that will allow him to do his gait and carry you at the same time. If your goal is a good stepping pace at any speed, you can help your horse develop the gait through some basic riding techniques that will adjust the tension in his ligament system and change his rhythm.

How to Solve Problems with the Fox Trot or Trot

A horse that goes into a diagonal gait when shifting up from the slower stepping pace or the ordinary walk has a little too much tension in his ligament system to do the stepping pace and not enough tension in his back muscles. His timing and rhythm are also different from the lateral, swinging motion of the gait. To help him become more lateral, change the tension in his back by changing his head and neck position and adjust the rhythm and timing of his diagonal gait by changing the way he carries his weight. Start changing his balance and back tension in the ordinary walk before he speeds up into a more diagonal gait. Then, once he understands your cues, you can use the same aids to help him modify his body use if he speeds up into an unwanted diagonal gait. This exercise may work best on a slight downhill slope, but you can also practice on flat, firm ground.

• Sitting straight and holding your hands in the base position, one rein in each hand, with even "plum-feel" contact, ask your horse to move out in an ordinary walk in a straight line with a squeeze/release from your legs.
• Tilt your pelvis into the heavy seat, and raise your hands a few inches above the base position to encourage your horse to lift his head and neck, putting a little slack in his ligament system.
• Begin gently to alternate tension on the reins, moving your horse's head and neck from side to side as he goes forward. This will interfere with his normal walking rhythm and cause him to begin shifting his weight from side to side.
• At the same time, begin to press down with one seat bone, then the other, shifting your weight from side to side in the saddle in rhythm with the alternating pressure on your reins. This will also encourage your horse to shift his weight a little from side to side and to tighten alternating sides of his back.
• Keep your horse moving forward with squeeze/releases from both legs as necessary. He will begin to go "off square" in his walk and start to do a stepping pace.
• Encourage the gait by relaxing in the saddle, breathing out a half breath, and relaxing contact on the reins. Be prepared to return to the side-to-side weight shift and rein use if he goes back to an ordinary walk.

Practice this exercise until your horse will automatically go into a stepping pace whenever you lift your hands a little bit and shift your weight subtly from side to side. Even non-gaited horses can learn to do a stepping pace from this technique, if you practice often enough. For your gaited horse, it should not take more than a few tries for him to understand the cues to go into the lateral stepping pace from the square walk. You can then speed him up and use the same aids to modify a fox trot or trot.

• On a slight downhill grade or on flat ground, speed your horse up from an ordinary walk into a fox trot or hard trot.
• Sit back slightly in the saddle, tilting your pelvis into the heavy seat position, or even into the chair seat.
• Raise your hands a few inches above waist level, maintaining steady "plum-feel" contact with the bit, to raise the horse's head and neck. Gently alternate pressure in the reins if necessary to interfere with the diagonal rhythm of the fox trot or hard trot, but do not take stronger contact with the bit.
• Your horse should break from the diagonal gait and return to the lateral stepping pace.

If this does not work, start over at the ordinary walk, put the horse in a slow stepping pace, then very gradually increase his speed, maintaining the lateral gait with your rein and weight aids. Prevent him from breaking into a diagonal gait as he speeds up; at the first hint of a fox trot or fox walk, slow back down to the slower stepping pace and start over.

If your horse has this much trouble working in the stepping pace, consider letting him fox trot instead. Both gaits are comfortable to ride, and if you are trail riding, the "gait police" won't arrest you for using the gait the horse prefers.

How to Solve Problems with a Hard Pace

A horse that automatically speeds up into a hard, true pace, has a little excess slack in his ligament system, the opposite problem of the horse that hard trots. The solution is to tighten the ligament system just a little bit, but not so much that the horse starts to fox trot. You can help your horse make these adjustments by riding him in footing that changes the way he uses his back and changing the way he uses his head and neck and his back muscles.

Using Terrain

Horses are more inclined to do a hard pace going downhill on hard surfaces. To help your horse use his body differently, try asking him to speed up his gait only on flat ground or on a slight uphill grade. Practice asking for speed going up the grade, then walking slowly back down again. Ride him on soft grass or dirt, not on pavement or hard packed gravel, when you ask for the stepping pace. To help him use his legs and back better, you can also set out poles in a pattern of two, then one, then two, and practice riding over them at the stepping pace. Your horse may hard trot or fox trot over the poles, but he will most likely do a stepping pace and not a hard pace between them.

Changing His Neck, Head, and Back Use

It is a little tricky to help a horse just enough for him to stop hard pacing and start doing a stepping pace without going overboard and asking for so much change in his body that he becomes too diagonal in his gait. Because horses are less likely to hard pace going uphill, practice this exercise on a slight uphill grade if at all possible.

- If your horse speeds up into a hard pace, slow him down until he is doing a good, square, ordinary walk.
- Tilt your pelvis slightly into the light, allowing seat. Hold your upper body steady, chest raised, shoulders and arms relaxed. This will relieve some of the tension in your horse's back muscles and increase the elasticity of his back.
- Lower your hands to either side of your horse's withers, below the swells of a Western saddle and about even with the buttons on an English saddle. With light, alternating downward pressure on first one hand and then the other, ask him to lower his head and neck. Keep your basic "plum-feel" while asking him to lower his neck.

- As the horse lowers his neck and maintains contact with the bit, ask him to bring his nose just slightly toward vertical, flexing a little at the poll. This will slightly increase the tension in your horse's ligament system and raise his back a tiny bit.
- His hard pace should begin to break into a smoother stepping pace. If he continues to do a hard pace, change your seat position into the forward or hunt seat, leaning forward in the saddle. This abrupt balance change may be enough to break up his hard pace, and may cause him to start trotting. You will then be able to modify the trot into the stepping pace by slightly raising his head and neck as you sit in the center of the saddle. Experiment alternating the forward seat with the straight seat to find the one that works best for keeping your horse in the stepping pace.

Use these aids along with work on soft ground and over scattered poles to help your horse learn the body position and timing of the stepping pace.

Mixed Gaits

Your horse may start out in a nice stepping pace, speed up into a hard pace, slow down into a fox trot, and then at the next turn in the path, start hard trotting. Such inconsistency can be normal for a young horse that has not been set in his gait and can also show up in an older horse if you become a passenger instead of an active rider on his back. As a rider, you have the job of reminding your horse which gait you want and encouraging him to do it. Use weight, leg, and rein aids to solve the problem of mixed gaits.

You can wait until your horse changes gait and then remind him either to lower his head (if he is pacing, using aids to convert that to a stepping pace) or to raise it (if he is trotting, using aids to convert that to a stepping pace) and keep changing him back to the stepping pace every time he goes into another gait. Over time, he will get the message and stay in the gait you want. This method, however, can produce a jerky, uneven gait, even if it *is* the one you want.

A better method, and the secret to a smooth, flowing performance, is to *anticipate* changes in gait before they happen so that you can prevent them. Be aware of the terrain. If at a certain place in your arena or on the trail your horse always starts to hard trot because the ground slants uphill, be ready before you get there to reinforce the aids that prevent the trot. If he always goes into a hard pace around a certain turn, be ready the next time you ride through it and reinforce the aids to prevent the pace before he starts to break gait.

In addition to paying attention to obvious terrain changes that will change your horse's balance and gait, learn to think with your seat and feel when your horse starts to become a little less solid in his gait. His back muscles will change a little just before he changes gait. If he is about to break into a hard trot, they will seem to loosen and rise a little. If he is about to break into a hard pace, they will sink a little under your seat and feel more rigid. The instant you feel these changes in his back, respond by either raising or lowering his head and adjusting your seat in the saddle. It takes practice and time, but if you are aware of your horse, you can learn to anticipate any changes in gait and prevent them with only minor adjustments to your aids.

Appreciating the Stepping Pace

The stepping pace, amble, or sobreandando can be a pleasant gait to ride, energy-efficient for most horses, and enjoyable on the trail. Many horses do the gait with little or no help from their riders, although others may need just a little work to find and maintain it. Because horses can do this gait at a variety of speeds, from very slow to very fast, horses that prefer it can provide a smooth ride for long trail rides over varied terrain, without changing gears. If you want to sit back and enjoy the scenery without much movement in the saddle, you may discover that you prefer a horse that does a stepping pace.

Remember that there is a downside to the gait, however. The slightly hollow position of the horse's body required to produce the gait can lead to muscle atrophy in his back and may cause his vertebrae to impinge on one another, contributing to later unsoundness. It is possible to balance this body position and keep your horse's back healthy by riding him frequently in an ordinary walk while practicing the stretching and bending exercises to keep his back fit and supple. If you choose to ride in the stepping pace, be sure to spend at least a third of your time in the saddle in the ordinary walk to keep your horse's back as sound as possible.

Practice the stretching exercises frequently, whether on the trail or in an arena. Keep an eye on the muscles in your horse's back, and if they seem to be losing tone or atrophying, work him on the longe at a trot, if possible, using cavalletti or pole exercises to help rebuild them. Pay special attention to saddle fit. If his saddle originally fit well and suddenly appears to "bridge" on his back, leaving dry spots at the shoulders and loin, he may be losing muscle mass in his back. Use pads or shims to make the saddle more comfortable for him, and redouble your efforts at keeping his back strong through exercises in the walk.

Look at his belly muscles, as well. If he starts to look "potbellied," it is a sign that he may have been spending too much time in the stepping pace, and not enough time doing belly lifts or other exercises to keep up the tone of his abdominal muscles. Practice hill climbing at a walk to encourage him to tighten that belly, along with more cavalletti work on the longe.

The effect the stepping pace often has on the back of horses that do it, and the lack of strong push from the hindquarters in the gait, may be the principle reasons it is not considered desirable in many gaited breeds. It is also possible that the gait is unpopular with some because it somehow carries the taint of being "too common" or not stylish enough for show purposes. Since the gait is found in all gaited breeds all over the world, it is indeed "common," but it can also be very stylish, as performed by Peruvian Paso horses with speed and termino, or by Brazilian Mangalarga horses with naturally high knee and hock action. In addition to horses in those breeds, where the gait is considered acceptable and desirable, it is also interesting to note the number of show horses that are represented to be doing a running walk or a rack but are in truth doing a very flashy version of the stepping pace. The gait may not be considered desirable for them, but it is certainly present in many breeds of horses that are not "supposed" to do it.

Historically, of course, the stepping pace or amble

has been the most prevalent of the easy gaits. It is the stepping pace that is pictured on the cave walls in southern France. It is an ambling horse that appears carved in stone among Hittite artifacts, on Egyptian tombs, on Pictish relics in Great Britain, and on ancient Chinese art. It is the ambling horse that is portrayed again and again in Roman wall paintings, woven into medieval tapestries in France and England, and depicted in antique Scandinavian woodcuts. Obviously the gait was useful as well as beautiful to all those generations of horsemen who bred horses that preferred it and to the artists who celebrated it. It would seem very peculiar to them that the gait they prized is sometimes considered "second class" in modern gaited breeds.

The stepping pace continues to be found in all breeds of horses that do the easy gaits. It is only human preference that has caused it to be scorned in some of those breeds. The horses don't particularly care what humans think they should do; they choose the gait that is easiest for them and leave us to deal with the results. If your horse has a strong preference for this gait, and you enjoy riding it, don't worry whether it is the appropriate gait for his breed. Use the terrain available and basic weight, leg, and rein aids to ask your horse for the gait when you want it, and enjoy the ride. You will be in the good company of riders — from all parts of the world and from all eras of equestrian culture — who appreciated the comfort and style of the stepping pace.

CHAPTER EIGHT

Introducing the Easy Gaits

The Fox Trot/Trocha, Running Walk/Paso Llano, and Rack Family of Gaits

It all depends on the horse.
— OLD HORSEMAN'S SAYING

In the best of all possible worlds, your gaited horse ought to move out directly into the gait specialty of his breed when he is pushed for speed from an ordinary or a flat walk. In the real world, however, your horse may not know what gait you think he should do. The gait he chooses will depend on his breeding, conformation, physical condition, and previous training, and the way you sit in the saddle and use your hands on the reins. If you are riding for pleasure, your horse's choice of gait is not as important as it would be in the show ring. It is a good idea to try at least to help him develop the gait his breed is supposed to do rather than allow him to switch into a different gait every time the terrain or his mood changes. If he strongly prefers a gait that is not the one associated with his breed, you enjoy it, and he seems comfortable in it, there are no gait police to arrest you if you allow him to do it, even if his papers say he should be doing something else. Before you become resigned to doing only that gait, however, see how he responds to different riding techniques for developing other gaits.

The Fox Trot
(Trocha/Marcha Batida)

The fox trot is the only diagonally timed easy gait. Due to this timing, it is a very stable gait that provides good support for quick turns. On the trail, a horse doing the fox trot can be very surefooted. In the American West, cowboys often preferred horses that did this gait because they covered ground well, were smooth to ride, and retained good balance for working cattle. The moderate-speed fox trot, from six to eight miles per hour, has been described as being "easy on the horse and easy on the man" because it is an energy-efficient gait with no wasted motion or extreme speed. There is no suspension or leaping motion in the gait, so there is less concussion to the horse's legs than in some other gaits, and this can contribute to long-term soundness. Because most horses fox trot with a neutral back position, work in the gait can also preserve healthy spacing between the vertebrae, another factor in soundness.

While the gait is the specialty of the Missouri Fox Trotter, it is also accepted and used by the Brazilian Mangalarga Marchadores (marcha batida) and some strains of Colombian Paso (trocha) horses. In addition to horses that are officially encouraged to do the gait, many gaited horses of other breeds will also fox trot. It is one of the few easy gaits that can be taught to non-gaited horses, although horses "man made" in the gait do not have the range of speed or reach of those born to do it.

How the Gait Feels

The fox trot is the only easy gait that both pushes you from back to front in the saddle and offers a slight bobble or stutter-step bounce in the hindquarters. In some horses you may feel a pull or rolling motion in the shoulders in addition to this bobble in the hindquarters. The sound is always an uneven four-beat *ka-chunk, ka-chunk,* with the beats closest together coming from the set-down of the diagonal hooves. The gait may or may not be accompanied by noticeable up-and-down head and neck nod, depending on the horse and the way he uses his shoulders. Missouri Fox Trotters will usually nod their heads a fair amount; Colombian trocha horses do not nod theirs at any time.

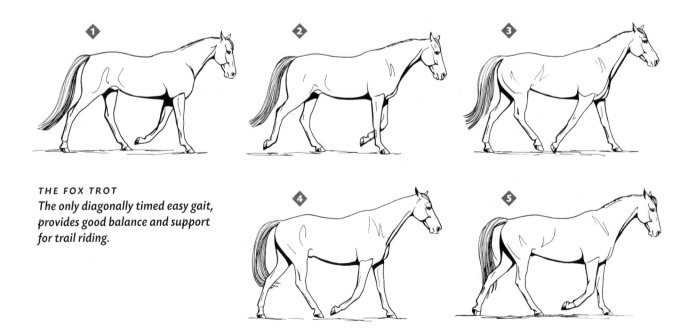

THE FOX TROT
The only diagonally timed easy gait, provides good balance and support for trail riding.

Possible Variations

At slow speeds, the fox trot becomes a *fox walk*. This comfortable gait has the same diagonal paring and timing as the fox trot, but with less action in the hocks and drive from the hindquarters. It may lose some of the bobble or stutter-step feel of the faster gait and can be smoother to ride. It is a surefooted, low-concussion gait that is probably used by more trail and pleasure riders than the faster fox trot. The speed of the fox walk is between five and six miles per hour, in the same range as the flat walk.

At speeds faster than eight miles per hour, the fox trot can be very similar to a diagonally timed rack. This version of the gait has a short moment of suspension as weight is shifted from one hoof to the other and, as a result, has intervals with only one hoof in contact with the ground. It takes much more energy to do this fast *fox rack* and can be hard on the horse because it increases concussion to his legs. It is also not as smooth to ride as the more moderate-speed fox trot. Because this version of the gait is tiring to the horse and often rough to ride, it is not the best choice for long-distance trail riding. Because it is fast and flashy, it is often seen in the show ring.

The final variation in the fox trot is the compressed, short-stepping *trocha* gait that is sometimes exhibited by Colombian Paso trocha horses. This gait retains and sometimes exaggerates the hock action and upward drive from the hind legs of the regular fox trot, but is done with shorter steps. It is comfortable, about the same speed as the corto gait of the Paso Fino, and can be very pleasant to ride on the trail.

Developing the No-Problem Fox Trot

Most horses that are bred to fox trot will go into the gait when they are sped up from the fast ordinary walk or the flat walk. To begin work in this gait, tack your horse up in a snaffle bit, curb bit (if he is accustomed to it), sidepull, or noseband jaquima. Don't use a California bosal for much work in the fox trot; it can inhibit your horse's head nod and affect his rhythm in the gait.

- Ride forward in the flat walk in the base position, one rein in each hand, with light "plumfeel" contact on the reins.
- Ask for more speed with a squeeze/release from your calves. Relax your fingers on the reins each time you squeeze with your calves.
- Continue to push your horse for speed until you feel his rhythm change and he breaks into a slow fox trot. Discontinue leg cues and breathe out and relax while sitting straight in the saddle.
- Be prepared to squeeze/release your fingers on the reins and adjust your seat to a slightly heavy position to check his speed if he tries to move too fast, and gently touch him with your calves and adjust your seat into the lighter, allowing position to speed him up if he starts to slow down into a walk. Do not freeze on the reins or pull on them to slow him down or kick him in the flanks to increase his speed. Allow him freedom to move his head and neck in rhythm with his gait.
- Ride for a short distance in the fox trot, and then return to the flat walk or ordinary walk, using a light squeeze/release on the reins and simultaneously breathing out to relax your abdominal and lower back muscles. Praise your horse!
- Return to the fox trot, this time traveling farther in the gait. Alternate the slow fox trot, the flat walk, and the ordinary walk, spending about a third of your riding time in each gait. This will help your horse develop stamina and condition for more advanced work in the fox trot.

Your horse may be a little unbalanced and awkward in his fox trot. This is not unusual and may be a result of lack of support from the bit or noseband. If you are riding in a bit, maintain light, even contact with your horse's mouth. Don't alternately pull hard and let the reins go slack, or pull so hard he lugs against the bit with a stiff neck and jaw. Keep your hands steady and separate in the base position and use pressure and release from your fingers along with adjustments in your seat to rate your horse's speed. If you are riding with bitless headgear, you can also help his gait by reminding him with squeeze/releases from your hands to rate his speed and head position. Squeeze on the reins when he starts to string out and lose balance in the fox trot and release when he returns to a more desirable gait. Don't ride with a heavy, steady pull on the noseband because that will dull his response to it and can eventually lead to him ignoring signals from it entirely. It may also make him lug against the noseband, nose out, and fall into a hard trot.

To help develop your horse's balance in the fox trot, practice the exercises that work to improve balance in the ordinary walk and flat walk. Ride frequent transitions between the flat walk or ordinary walk and the fox trot, using the same weight, leg, and rein aids that you used when teaching these exercises in the flat walk. Work in large, 60-foot circles in a relatively slow fox trot or fox walk, helping your horse bend his body with diagonal leg and rein aids. Practice large figure eights and serpentines in the fox trot, helping him adjust to bending his body in both directions in the gait. To develop better balance in the fox trot, try to ride your horse in the gait as often as possible on a slight uphill grade on firm, but not hard, footing. Don't ask him to fox trot on uneven ground or on a downhill grade until he is very balanced and consistent in his gait. If you do, he may start to do a stepping pace downhill or a hard trot on broken ground.

Solving Simple Problems in the Fox Trot

Unfortunately, not all horses that are expected to fox trot go directly into the gait when they speed up from an ordinary walk or a flat walk. Your horse may skip right over the fox trot and start doing a hard trot. He may simply increase speed in his flat walk and start doing a running walk, or he may become excited and edge into a rack when he is asked for more speed. He may be inconsistent, doing all these gaits, a few steps at a time, switching back and forth among them so quickly you can barely recognize one gait before he is doing something else. And, of course, your horse may have a more complicated problem in the fox trot and slip into the pace or stepping pace as soon as you push him out of a slow ordinary walk. All of these unexpected gaits except the pace are relatively easy to deal with using seat, leg, and rein aids.

The Trot

Remember the hard trot? The gait you thought you would never feel again when you started riding a gaited horse? Most gaited horses will do it, even if they are not expected to. While work in the hard trot is very useful for developing better easy gaits for some horses, when the gait pops up unasked for in a horse that is expected to fox trot, it can be a problem. Fortunately, it is relatively easy to modify a hard trot into a smooth fox trot.

To convert a hard trot into a fox trot, adjust your seat and hands to change the way your horse is using his back. Because you will be asking your horse to change his head and neck position, tack him up in a snaffle, non-leverage bit. You can work in a curb bit if your horse is accustomed to one, or in a sidepull or jaquima, but it is better to use a non-leverage bit for this exercise, if at all possible. The snaffle will give clearer cues than other headgear.

There are two effective ways to encourage a horse that hard trots to modify his gait into a fox trot. The first one to try is to "catch" your horse in the fox trot between the flat walk and the hard trot. This method of pushing the walk and restricting the trot will work on non-gaited as well as gaited horses; at first it produces a slow, fox-walk type of gait.

- Sitting in the base position, one rein in each hand, with light contact on the horse's mouth, push your horse into a flat walk.
- Tilt your pelvis into the heavy seat position.
- Squeeze/release pressure with both calves to push your horse faster in the flat walk, until he is just about to break into a trot.
- Instantly squeeze/release with both hands on the reins to slow him. Be prepared to squeeze with your legs as he slows down to keep him moving with energy.
- Continue to push the flat walk, but restrain the trot until your horse finds the middle ground of the fox walk. Relax in the saddle and return to the base position as a reward as soon as he starts to fox walk. Praise him, and repeat.

You can also convert a trot directly into a fox trot. This method works best with horses that are basically well gaited but get a little too enthusiastic when asked for speed from the walk. It is a little harder than the first method on the rider who must be able to sit a hard trot to follow it effectively.

- Sitting straight, speed your horse up from a flat walk into a trot. Tilt your pelvis into the heavy seat position. Sit down to the trot; do not try to post it or stand in your stirrups.
- As your horse trots and you sit the gait, raise your hands from the base position a few inches, keeping light contact with his mouth and asking him to raise his head and neck slightly. Squeeze/release on both reins to ask him to check his speed a little. He may slow into a fox trot in response.
- If he continues to hard trot, use light vibrations upward on first one rein, then the other, to raise his head and neck. As his head rises, bring his forehead toward vertical with steady, slightly stronger contact on the reins. This is a direct flexion, an exercise he should understand from your earlier ground work, if he has not already been trained to do it from the saddle. This use of your reins will change the tension in his back and begin to slow the set-down of his hind hooves.
- Continue to ride him forward with your weight slightly back in the saddle and his forehead brought toward vertical, being ready to push him on with squeeze/releases from your calves if he slows down to a walk or restrain his speed with squeeze/releases on the reins if he speeds up in the trot.
- Discontinue active leg and rein actions but maintain your slightly higher hand position as soon as he goes into a fox trot. Relax in the saddle by breathing out and reward him for doing the gait you want by praising him.

If you remember to slow your horse just a little, sit slightly behind the straight position with a heavy seat, and raise his head a little while bringing his forehead in toward vertical whenever he begins to stretch out into a trot, he will soon fox trot consistently when you speed him up from the flat walk. Your horse will soon learn to prefer the energy-efficient trot.

The Running Walk

It is difficult to think of this easy gait as a problem. It is very comfortable to ride and pleasant on the trail for both the horse and the rider. There is nothing "wrong" with the running walk, and if your horse chooses to do it, you can certainly ride him in that gait if he prefers it. If he is from a breed that is expected to fox trot, however, you can probably teach him to do that gait. It is usually not too difficult to modify a running walk into a fox trot.

Start out with your horse in a snaffle bit or curb bit (only if he is accustomed to one). You can try this exercise with a sidepull or jaquima, but neither will be as effective as the snaffle bit. Ride with two hands on the reins in the straight, base position. Push your horse up from the flat walk until he is moving in a running walk.

- As your horse moves in the running walk, shift your weight slightly in the saddle into the light, allowing seat.
- Lower your hands to either side of his withers, feed some slack into your reins, and, using light downward pressure with one hand, then the other, ask him to lower his head and bring his nose toward vertical.
- Push him on for some speed with squeeze/releases from both calves straight into his side.
- He may start to fox trot. If he does, praise him, relax your back and abdominal muscles in the saddle as a reward, and gradually return to the base seat position.
- He may also start to hard trot. If he does, shift your weight back to the center of the saddle, raise your hands an inch or so, and allow his head to rise, encouraging him to nose-out just a little.
- If he continues to do a running walk, try adjusting your weight toward the back of the saddle by tilting your pelvis into the heavy seat position. This can sometimes work to help the horse change the tension in his back. Experiment to see which method works best for your horse.

As a final resort, if your horse persists in doing a running walk and you truly feel that you prefer a fox trot, set out a few poles spaced about 3 feet apart. Sit in the forward seat, give with your hands until the reins are completely slack and you have no contact with his mouth, and move him out over the poles. He may fox trot over the poles or skip past the fox trot into a hard trot, and you can then work on modifying that gait back into a fox trot.

The Rack

Some horses become excited and high-headed when they are asked for more speed from a flat walk and will rack or saddle rack in place of the fox trot. Although this is a comfortable gait that is a lot of fun to ride, it can be hard on the horse's back and legs, and it is not as energy-efficient for trail riding as the fox trot. The rack is relatively easy to convert into a fox trot by helping the horse to relax and lower his head, changing the essential tension in his neck and over his shoulders that always accompanies the rack.

If possible, tack your horse up in a snaffle bit. It is very difficult to ask a horse to relax and stretch in a curb bit, and it is also difficult to do this in a sidepull or jaquima. If you do ride bitless, try to attach your reins in a position that encourages your horse to lower his head. For some horses this will be the upper set of rings on a noseband jaquima, for others it will be the lower set on the barbada.

- Start in the flat walk, sitting straight with your hands lowered a few inches from the base position.
- Ask your horse to lower his head and neck with light, alternating squeeze/releases down and to the side on the reins. One squeeze/release should instantly follow another from the opposite hand. Do not seesaw with strong alternating pressure on the reins. Squeeze/release with your fingers; don't pull or tug.
- Keeping your hands and his head as low as possible, gradually push your horse out of the flat walk with a light touch from your calves. Continue to use light squeeze/releases to ask him to maintain a moderate speed and relax your back and abdominal muscles so that you are not pushing him with your seat. You may find that tilting your pelvis into the light, allow-

ing seat will also help your horse fox trot in place of the rack.
- Practice alternating between the flat walk and the faster gait until he relaxes and goes into a fox trot. If you have trouble getting him to relax and stretch his neck, follow the more complete directions for the neck stretching exercise in chapter 9.

It is usually possible to help a horse stop racking and start fox trotting by slowing him down and lowering his head and neck. You can also modify the gait by riding uphill as you ask for speed from the flat walk. The change in balance required to go up the hill will also change the tension in your horse's back and may be enough to get him started in the fox trot. If all else fails, you can also ride a racking horse over poles to break up his gait, as described for those that do an unwanted running walk. Be prepared to work him from a hard trot into a fox trot if you use poles to break up the rack.

The Running Walk/Paso Llano

The true running walk and the paso llano are two slightly different versions of the same gait. They are evenly timed in both the pick-up and set-down of the hooves, with no moments of suspension when more than two hooves are off the ground. There is some overstride by the hind hoof over the track of the front in the track or trail. This gait is very comfortable to ride, relatively energy-efficient for the horse, and a pleasure on the trail. It was developed to cover ground smoothly at moderate speeds between six and ten miles per hour as a traveling gait and a working gait for supervising large plantations. For simplicity, the term running walk is used here for both gaits.

There is little concussion to the horse's legs in the gait when it is performed at moderate speed with the hind hoof sliding into place; this can contribute to the long-term soundness of horses that use the gait. Because most horses do this gait with a neutral back position, correct work in the gait will also preserve healthy spacing between the vertebrae, another factor

THE RUNNING WALK

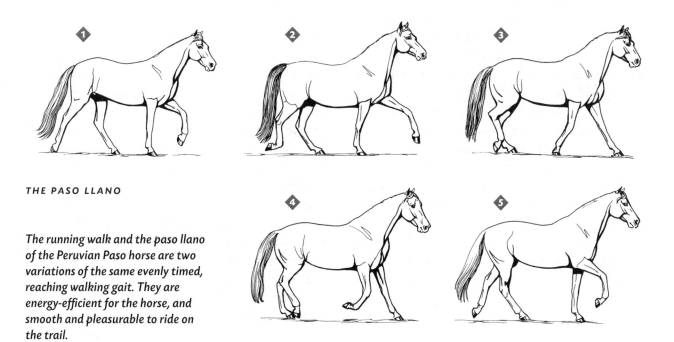

THE PASO LLANO

The running walk and the paso llano of the Peruvian Paso horse are two variations of the same evenly timed, reaching walking gait. They are energy-efficient for the horse, and smooth and pleasurable to ride on the trail.

in helping horses stay sound. Although the breeds most identified with the running walk (paso llano) are the Tennessee Walking Horse and the Peruvian Paso, some individuals in other breeds around the world choose to do the gait. It is not as common as the other easy gaits, however, a fact that is reflected in the very few languages that have words to describe it. It is not a gait that can be easily taught to a non-gaited horse. A horse must be born with a special elastic quality in his back that allows him to do this gait. A horse can, however, be encouraged to use his inborn flexibility to do the running walk rather than some other easy gait.

How the Gait Feels

The running walk or paso llano feels very similar to the flat walk or slow paso llano, but with more energy from the hindquarters. The gait rocks you gently from front to back in the saddle, with the feeling of drive and push from the hindquarters balanced by a rolling, reaching motion in the shoulders. It feels very stable, and the sound is always an even four beat, with no hoof beats sounding paired in time.

In Walking Horses and most other horses that do the gait, the running walk is accompanied by a deep, even, up-and-down head nod that is timed with the advance of each front leg. This allows free motion in the advancing shoulder by shifting the weight of the head and neck up and away from it. Because there are four legs moving completely separately in the gait and the hind on one side is at the farthest back part of its contact with the ground just as the front on the same side is vertical (or halfway through its support phase), it may appear that the head and neck move in time with the hind legs. However, the motion of the head and neck and the movement of the front and hind legs work together as a cycle, with the tension of the ligament system, which is directly connected to the hind legs, playing a part in the movement of the neck. The muscles that have the most effect on the position of the head and neck, however, are connected more directly to the shoulder than they are to the hind legs.

In Peruvian Paso horses, this head nod is mostly absent or greatly reduced. It is replaced by the outward rotation of the front legs from the shoulder, called *termino*. This rotation is the result of a slightly different muscle use in the neck and over the shoulder blades than occurs in other horses as they do the running walk. It is not the result of conformation flaws in the front legs or a lack of connection between the hind legs and the neck, but results from extra elasticity in the joints and tightened muscles over the shoulders and at the base of the neck.

Possible Variations

At slower speeds, the running walk can become a flat walk, with the transfer of weight between the front hooves happening when both are flat on the ground. At faster speeds, those greater than eight miles per hour in most horses, the gait begins to resemble the rack, with the transfer of weight between the front hooves occurring when both are off the ground. At even faster speeds, the gait becomes even closer to the rack, with the transfer of weight in both the front *and* the hind hooves occurring with both hooves off the ground. These variations are all done with even timing and are not very far removed from the true running walk. When the gait becomes lateral in timing, however, it is no longer a running walk and has become either a stepping pace or a rack. Many horses change into those two gaits when they are pushed for speed in a true running walk.

Developing the No-Problem Running Walk

Your horse has a good foundation for this gait if he has been working in a consistent flat walk or slow paso llano.

Tack him up in a snaffle bit that is comfortable for him, or a sidepull, Peruvian bozal, or jaquima. Try to avoid using a curb bit if possible, at least for beginning work in this gait. You will be able to give clearer aids with the snaffle bit if you need to adjust your horse's head and neck position to modify the way he uses his back and encourage the running walk. Later, of course, when he is set in the gait, you can use a mild curb effectively in the gait. Don't use a California bosal for much work in this gait; it can inhibit the way a horse uses his head and neck in the gait.

If possible, find a slight incline or a flat area with soft ground to start work on this gait. Do not ask for it on a downhill grade or on very hard footing. Remember that most horses are more likely to go into an even four beat or a diagonal gait uphill and more likely to go into a pace or stepping pace downhill. Take advantage of this when you work in the running walk.

- Ride forward in the flat walk or fast ordinary walk with your hands in the base position, with one rein held in each hand and light contact on the reins if you are riding in a bit or only the weight of the reins in your hands if you are riding bitless. Sit straight and balanced in the saddle.

• Squeeze and release with your calves, asking your horse to speed up his walk.

• As you ask for more speed, lower your hands a few inches from the base position, asking the horse to flex a little at the poll with light squeeze/releases on both reins. Do not use pressure from the reins at the exact moment you ask for speed with your legs. Squeeze with your calves, release leg pressure, and then squeeze/release with your fingers to avoid riding with the brake and accelerator at the same time.

• Gradually increase your horse's speed until he is moving out at a fast, even, four-beat running walk or paso llano. Relax your weight in the saddle by breathing out and sitting softly, following the motion of the gait with an elastic but not sloppy lower back.

• The instant your horse starts to change his rhythm or gait, slow down and return to a flat walk; do **not** let him string out into a pace, stepping pace, fox trot, or rack.

Build your horse's ability in the running walk on the foundation of his correct four-beat flat walk; don't expect it just to happen by accident. If he tends to become inconsistent at faster speeds, keep his speed relatively slow and his gait even until he develops the strength and elasticity in his back to maintain the correct position for the running walk at faster speeds.

Balance and Support

Give your horse an advantage for developing good balance by remembering to work on the running walk only on flat ground or a slight incline on soft, but not deep, footing. Gentle hills will help your horse stay evenly balanced under your seat by naturally shifting his weight just a little toward the rear, while soft footing will delay the breakover of the hooves as they lift from the ground, which can encourage even timing.

The uphill grade will also help the horse round his back a little and push more effectively with his hindquarters in his gait; a decline will shift his weight forward onto his shoulders, hollowing his back a little and encouraging a stepping pace.

Your horse may be somewhat uneven and awkward in his gait. Keep his speed even in the gait by alternating squeeze/releases from your calves to speed him up and squeeze/releases from your fingers to slow him down and adjusting your seat from "allowing" to heavy, as you did in the flat walk. Once his speed is even, help him develop better balance by riding with steady, light contact on the bit to support him in the gait. Keep your hands and fingers quiet on the reins; don't alternate between tight reins that pull on his mouth and floating reins that leave his head and neck without guidance. Eventually, you will be able to ride with slack reins, one-handed, but at the beginning of gait work, for most horses that have been trained in a bit, it is better to give the horse all the help you can by riding with some contact on his mouth. If you are riding bitless, you can ride with just a little contact on the noseband as you start out. Remind the horse to stay in gait with a stronger squeeze/release on the noseband reins and be ready to give this aid the instant you feel his back or rhythm start to change.

Practice riding frequent transitions between the flat walk and the running walk. These exercises will contribute to good balance in the gait and improved poll-to-tail flexibility. Unless your horse is very well set in the running walk, however, do not try to ride circles or other figures with him in that gait to improve his flexibility. It is very difficult for a horse to bend his body on a curve and still maintain the elastic use of his back that is necessary for the running walk. Instead, work circles of various sizes, figure eights, and serpentines in the flat walk to help him build the flexibility necessary for bending in the faster running walk. Do not try to ride a 20-meter circle in the running walk until your horse is able to work a 10-meter circle in the flat walk without losing the timing and form of the gait. On the trail, use the running walk when you have a nice long, flat stretch ahead of you or a gradual hill. Return to the flat walk when you go down the other side of that grade.

Solving Simple Problems in the Running Walk

Although some horses will go directly into a running walk when they are pushed in speed from a flat walk, yours may not be among them. He may fox trot or hard trot or he may do some type of rack when you speed him up. He may be inconsistent, switching gaits frequently as you go along. He may also pace or do a stepping pace. All of these gait problems, except the pace, are relatively easy to deal with by using your seat, leg, and rein aids. If the pace is a problem for you and your horse, refer to chapter 9 for help.

The Trot

There is nothing wrong with riding your horse in the trot, but you probably didn't choose a gaited horse because you preferred trotting to riding a smooth running walk. Fortunately, most horses that are expected to do a running walk do not trot very often under saddle. A horse may slip into the trot, however, if he is pushed for too much speed on the flat or on a relatively steep uphill grade while his head and neck are low and stretched out and his rider has slipped into a forward seat. If your horse has a good flat walk, first try avoiding the trot and going directly into the running walk. Sometimes you can prevent your horse from going into a trot by sitting a little straighter in the saddle, keeping even contact on the reins, and bringing your horse's forehead in toward vertical while very slowly edging up his speed in the flat walk. You can also try to modify the trot into the running walk by altering his body position and rhythm with your seat and hands as he trots. If he doesn't respond to those methods, you may need to follow a two-step process, first breaking the diagonal trot into the slightly less diagonal fox trot, then modifying the fox trot into the square, even running walk.

Fit your horse in a snaffle or curb bit for this exercise. Although it is possible to change your horse's gait from a trot into a running walk in a sidepull, Peruvian bozal, or jaquima, it is usually easier to do it in a bit. Try to work on a slight downhill grade or a level stretch of ground with firm footing, if you can. This will help change the tension in your horse's back and loosen up his gait a little.

- Ride your horse forward in the trot, sitting straight, your hands in the base position, with even, light contact on the reins. Sit down to the trot; do not post or stand in your stirrups.
- Gradually raise your hands a couple of inches above base position, as you rotate your pelvis into the heavy seat position.
- With your weight back and your hands a little higher than normal, gently alternate squeeze/ releases on the reins to bring your horse's forehead toward vertical and to encourage his head to swing a little from side to side. At the same time, shift your weight gently from one seat bone to the other. This will begin to throw your horse's rhythm off in the trot and change the timing of his legs so that it is closer to even.
- The instant your horse shows hesitation in the trot and starts to do an even, four-beat gait, **stop** all side-to-side motion with your seat and hands. If you don't stop at just the right second, you may end up throwing your horse into a stepping pace instead of the running walk. Sit centered and still in the saddle, with your hands quiet in the base position, and let him go for a few steps in the running walk. Relax, return to the flat walk, and praise your horse. Gradually increase the steps your horse takes in the running walk until he maintains the gait easily, avoiding the trot as much as possible.

The other method for dealing with the hard trot is to work your horse into a fox trot first, and then convert that gait into the running walk. Follow the steps in the section on the fox trot (pages 136–137) for converting the trot into a fox trot. Then go on and modify that gait into a running walk or paso llano.

The Fox Trot

Some horses naturally go into a fox trot from a flat walk, even if they are bred to do a running walk. For others, the fox trot is a stepping-stone to the running walk from the hard trot. If your horse is working in a fox trot instead of a running walk, whether he chose the gait on his own or you have already changed his gait from a hard trot to this easy gait, you will need to help him change his body position from the more rounded, low-headed one that encourages the fox trot to a higher headed, slightly less rounded one that allows the running walk.

• First, ride your horse in a flat walk, with light, even contact on the reins. Push that walk for speed while restraining or checking him just as he tries to break into the hard trot, using squeeze/releases from your calves to push him for speed and squeeze/releases from your fingers on the reins to check him until he breaks into a fox trot.

• Your horse's back will feel tighter and fuller under your seat than it does at the flat walk. Relax in the saddle and follow the motion of his back for a few steps, then raise your hands just a little from the base position to raise his head. Tilt your pelvis into the heavy seat position and squeeze/release on the reins to prevent him from speeding up into a hard trot. Breathe out and relax your lower back and abdominal muscles.

• Tighten first one side of your lower back, then the other, to interfere very slightly with his rhythm in the fox trot. Do not shift weight from side to side as you would to break up a trot, but instead tighten and resist his motion, without moving your upper body. You will feel his back begin to change, to soften a little under your seat, and his rhythm will change from the uneven, four-beat fox trot to an even, slow, four-beat running walk.

• Relax tension in your back, but maintain your seat and hand position, encouraging your horse to continue on in the running walk. Praise him for doing the gait, relax in the saddle, slow to a flat walk, then repeat.

• Gradually increase the number of steps he takes in the running walk and reduce the time he spends in the fox trot until he automatically goes into a running walk when you ask for speed from the flat walk with your hands slightly above the base position and your weight shifted toward your tailbone.

Some horses may discover that they like to work in a fox trot and become stuck in that gait on the way to developing a running walk. This is not a major problem for pleasure or trail riding, and if your horse is one that started out in a hard trot, finds he prefers to fox trot, and will not go easily into the running walk, you can continue to ride him most of the time in the fox trot. Allow him to fox trot, but every few rides, on a nice downhill grade, experiment to see whether he will do a running walk. After several months of work in the fox trot, he may surprise you by shifting into the running walk when you ask.

The Rack

Most horses that do a rack instead of the running walk are being pushed for too much speed and carrying their heads too high. This combination creates the tension at the base of their necks and over their shoulders that produces the saddle rack or true rack, characterized by the lateral pick-up and even set-down of their hooves. Although the rack is fun to ride and can sometimes be a useful training tool for wearing off excess energy in high-strung horses, it is a good idea to teach your horse to develop a running walk for long rides when you want him to conserve energy but still cover ground. Converting a true rack or any of the other gaits in the rack family into a running walk is not a very difficult process.

If possible, fit your horse with a snaffle bit for this exercise because you will be lowering his head. You can try it in a curb if you need that bit to control your horse, but a curb bit may not be the most effective tool because it tends to promote a high head. You can, of course, use a sidepull or jaquima with the reins attached so that you can lower the horse's head easily. Ride on flat ground or a slight uphill grade in soft, but not deep, footing, if possible. Start out in a flat walk, sitting in the base position with light even contact on the reins, then ask your horse for speed with a squeeze/release from your calves on his sides.

• As your horse speeds up into a rack, check his speed with repeated squeeze/releases from your hands on the reins, while resisting some of his forward motion by tightening your lower back.

• Lower your hands from the base position so that they are below your horse's withers as far as they will go without causing you to lean forward. Keep them separated, about a foot apart.

Use light, alternating squeeze/releases to ask your horse to lower his head a little while he is slowing down.

• Shift your weight in the saddle so that you are sitting in the light, allowing seat, but do not move your upper body forward into a forward seat.

• With your horse's head somewhat lowered, ask him to bring his forehead in toward vertical, flexing slightly at the poll. He should slow down, and you should notice his back change under your seat, becoming slightly full and more elastic.

• Breathe out, relax, and follow the new motion of his back. Be ready to move him up with a little more speed if he slows down to a flat walk, touching him lightly with your calves to urge him gently on instead of squeezing him into a faster gait.

• Return to the flat walk, relax, and praise your horse. Then urge him on into the faster gait, this time shifting your seat and lowering your hands before he moves up from the flat walk. This should prevent him from going back into the unwanted rack.

The Rack Family of Gaits

This family includes corto, largo, slow tolt, fast tolt, singlefoot, saddle rack, and true rack. Although they range from the very slow forward progress, rapid step, and high action of the fino fino to the flashy speed of the fast tolt or speed rack, the members of the rack family of gaits are very closely related to one another. Alternating two-foot, one-foot support patterns differentiate the fast, true rack from the slower versions, which most frequently offer a two-foot, three-foot support sequence. The timing of these gaits is unique because they are all slightly lateral in pick-up and even in set-down. Racks are all very comfortable to ride and can be exhilarating for short or longer stretches on the trail. The true rack can reach speeds above 25 miles per hour, is very energy intensive, and can create a significant amount of concussion for the horse's legs, especially if done with high action. The saddle rack, at eight to ten miles per hour, is a pleasant trail gait, not as tiring to a horse as the true rack, and, because of the two-foot, three-foot support of the gait, is not as hard on the horse's legs. The corto, which is the slowest version of the gait that can reasonably be used for trail riding, is even less

THE PASO CORTO

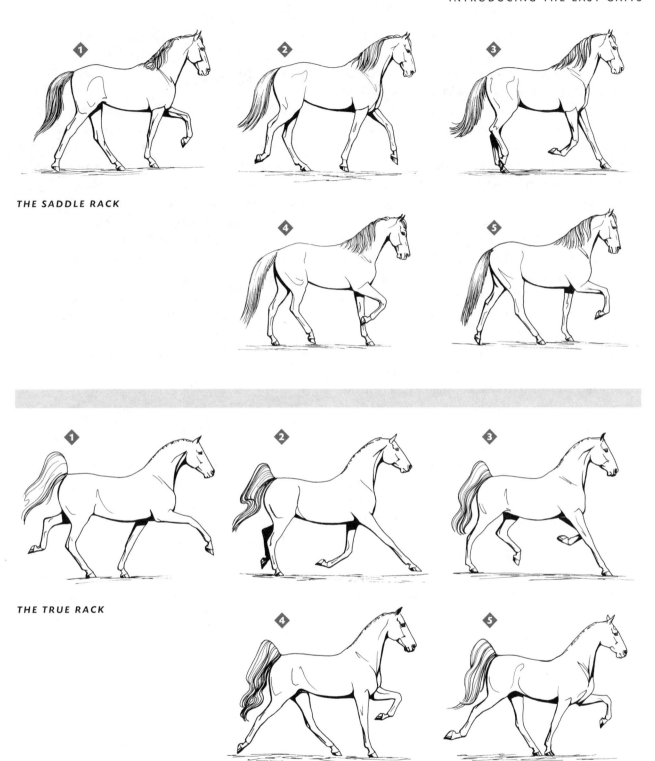

THE SADDLE RACK

THE TRUE RACK

The rack family of gaits includes the very slow and short-stepping paso corto, the longer-stepping saddle rack (which is also known as the paso largo or slow tolt), and the true rack (or fast tolt). These gaits are all laterally timed in pick-up and evenly timed in set-down, four-beat gaits. The slower gaits have a two-foot, three-foot support sequence, but at faster speeds, the weight transfers between hooves are achieved with a moment of suspension, giving the gait a two-foot, one-foot support.

tiring to a horse and, if performed with low action, not particularly hard on his legs.

All of these gaits, however, require the "essential tension" (see Essential Tension and the Racking Gaits at right) of the neck and shoulders, which is accompanied by a slightly hollow carriage of the spine. This position, if maintained for long periods, can cause a narrowing of the intervertebral spaces of the spine and may, in the long run, cause the vertebrae to begin to impinge on one another, leading to back problems and sometimes to stumbling with the hind legs. It is very important to ride horses that prefer to do one of the rack family of gaits in the walk, and, if possible, the trot in addition to their easy gait. The walk and trot allow horses to stretch their backs and maintain healthy spacing between the vertebrae to counteract the compression that may occur in the rack.

The rack and its close relatives are second to the stepping pace as the most common easy gaits in the world. There are words for rack or saddle rack in many languages, and horses all over the world, from Kirghiz in Asia to Boerperds in South Africa to the Tongan Singlefooter, do this gait or a slower version of it. The gait is natural to most of these horses, but because it is also possible to train a non-gaited horse to rack, the gait has often been considered artificial by people who are not familiar with the types of horses that do it from birth.

Many gaited horses of any breed will easily go into a saddle rack, in addition to or in place of their other easy gaits when their riders use weight, leg, and rein aids to support the essential tension in their necks and the tightening of their back muscles to produce the gait.

How the Gait Feels

All of the gaits in the rack family feel essentially the same; speed is the only variable. As your horse moves in a rack or saddle rack, you will feel his shoulders roll and climb and his hindquarters bob up and down, but you will be sitting still in the eye of this storm of energy on his back. The sound of his hoofbeats will be an even 1-2-3-4, and his head and neck will be carried high and upright, with no nodding or swinging from side to side.

Essential Tension and the Racking Gaits

IN THE RACK, a horse travels in a unique body position. His back and body are carried in a slight inversion that lowers the back, but with less slack in the ligament system than is evident in the pace. This inverted position is accompanied by contracted muscles that pull the base of the neck back toward the chest at the junction of the first and second thoracic vertebrae, deep within the neck at the center of the chest. Tension at the base of the neck, contracting muscles over the tops of the shoulders and over the loins, and strong use of the muscles along both the underside and the top of the neck elevate the horse's head and neck in the gait. The result is the essential tension in the neck that allows the horse to rack rather than pace or stepping pace. Without this specific use of the neck, a horse carrying his head elevated and forehead vertical with contact on the bit will pace or even trot instead of rack. For this reason, it is not enough just to elevate the head of a horse to help him rack; you must also help him achieve that essential tension as he raises it.

Rack Variations

The slowest gait in the rack family is the fino fino of the Paso Fino horse. It is characterized by very rapid, but very short, steps, in which the horse may seem almost to do the gait in place and may at any given moment have three hooves on the ground. This is not a trail gait! It is a particular art form that is unique to the Paso Fino horse and should be appreciated as an interesting, if not practical, movement of the horse. Horses that do this variation of the gait frequently become stuck in it and do not willingly take longer steps or move out with much forward speed.

The paso corto is a more forward-moving version of the gait, not as slow as the fino, but often retaining the rapid, short step of the fino. Most trail and pleasure horses do a longer-striding paso corto that is about the same speed as a flat walk. This gait can be speeded up to the point where it blends into the speed of the paso largo, or saddle rack. The so-called show walk of many American racking horses and of the various Mountain Horse breeds is the same gait as the trail-type paso corto, a slower but forward-moving saddle rack.

The saddle rack, the singlefoot, the paso largo, and the slow tolt are the most familiar names for the racking gait that is done at eight to ten miles per hour with a three-foot, two-foot support sequence. This gait is characterized by ground-covering speed, reach in the steps, and extreme comfort for the rider.

In the true rack, the fastest of the rack family of gaits, a couple of timing variations are sometimes seen. Neither fits the complete definition of the rack, but both do have the one-foot, two-foot support sequence of that gait. Some horses, when pushed for extreme speed, do a lateral rack with lateral timing in both the pick-up and set-down of the hooves. This gait is sometimes mistaken for the true rack in the show ring or in speed-racking contests, but is actually a form of a stepping or broken pace. Other horses, when pushed for extreme speed, become more diagonal in the timing of their racking gait. This gait is also sometimes mistaken for the true rack or for the fast paso largo, but it is actually a type of fox trot or fox rack.

Developing the No-Problem Saddle Rack

Most gaited horses go willingly and easily into a saddle rack if you modify your seat a little bit from the base position and ask them to work with the essential tension over their withers and shoulders that goes along with the gait. Frequently, all you need to do is ask for some speed and enjoy the ride.

You can work in this gait in a snaffle bit, but a sidepull or other bitless headgear or a mild curb may be more effective in helping a horse use his body in the saddle rack. If you use a snaffle, you may find that it is difficult to keep your contact light and your hands quiet. If you do not like the idea of riding in a typical curb, a low-port Kimberwicke/Uxeter bit with reins attached on the lowest slot can be very effective and almost as mild as a mullen snaffle. Ride with one rein in each hand as you start work in this gait.

Work on flat ground with a firm surface as you and your horse become familiar with the gait. Don't start out in deep footing or uphill because that may cause your horse to trot; avoid starting on a downhill grade as well, because that may cause your horse to pace or do a stepping pace.

- Start in an ordinary walk, sitting in the base position with light, even contact on the bit.
- Modify your seat by tilting your pelvis into the heavy seat position. Press straight down with your backbone toward the saddle. This change in your pelvic position will cause your legs to hang just slightly in front of vertical with your heels a little in front of your hips. Don't lean back with your feet on the "dashboard," but do modify the normal, straight seat so that you are sitting heavier in the saddle.
- Raise your hands a couple of inches above the base position, until they are waist high, maintaining light but constant contact on the bit or noseband and raising the horse's head a little. This will help develop the essential tension in the base of the neck that must accompany the saddle rack. Don't pull back hard, just maintain the same even contact you normally use at the walk; don't hold your hands at your chin, just raise them to waist height from the original lower base position.
- Push your horse on for more speed with a strong squeeze/release from your calves. The saddle rack is an energetic gait, so you must insist that your horse move out with speed and energy from the walk. Squeeze and release with your hands held in the higher position if he starts to hop or tries to canter or gallop.
- If you keep his energy level high but prevent him from breaking into another gait, your horse should do a relatively slow, even, four-beat saddle rack, show walk, or paso corto. Because he is a trail or pleasure horse, you will want him to cover some ground in the gait, so do not try to hold him back or shorten his step. Relax your fingers a little on the reins, still holding your hands waist high, to avoid inhibiting his reach in the gait.

• Go for a short distance in the saddle rack, then lower your hands and return to the walk. Praise and pet your horse and repeat, gradually increasing the distance he goes in the gait.

At first, work in the slower, more contained show walk, or paso corto. When you are certain that your horse is solid in that gait and can maintain his rhythm without either slowing to a walk, hopping with his front legs, or skipping beats, gradually increase his speed, first to a saddle rack, then to a true rack, if your horse can do that gait. For trail riding, the true rack takes so much energy that you may want to ride it for only very short periods. As you ask for more speed, sit relaxed but still slightly toward the back of the saddle, and squeeze/release strongly with your legs while keeping your fingers relaxed on the reins, maintaining your horse's higher head position. Keep his rhythm even by checking with light rein pressure and maintaining a little stronger contact with the bit if he starts to lose form, or tries to half canter or otherwise mix gaits. Be ready to ask for more speed with your legs if he slows down and to check his speed with your hands if he starts to string out into another gait. Maintain some tension in your lower back muscles to brace and push against the saddle as a reminder to him that he is expected to tighten and push with his own back muscles.

Your horse may be more comfortable in this gait at first if you allow him to nose out, with no visible flexion at the poll. This permits him to maintain the correct tension in his ligament system for the gait with less stress than trying to keep a "pretty" head set. It is also easier for a horse to develop the essential tension over his shoulders and at the base of his neck if he is not asked to bring his forehead toward vertical. Once he is very comfortable in his gait, you can of course bring his nose to a more vertical position through light, intermittent squeeze/releases on the reins, if you prefer. Be careful, however, not to cram him into the position, so much that he starts to pace.

Don't try to ride small circles or other figures in the saddle rack with any speed. You can certainly work small circles, figure eights, and serpentines in a slow paso corto or show walk if you wish, but because of the way a horse uses his body to work in one of the racking gaits, he will not be able to bend very well through his body as he does them. He will most likely turn tightly, with no arc through his body, and may try to go with his head and neck bent to the outside of the curve on a circle. This is a normal result of the way his ligament system and muscles work in the gait. Don't force him to bend too much or he may lose the racking gait and start doing something else. If you need to help your horse overcome problems with one-sidedness or lack of flexibility, practice the circles and other bending exercises at an ordinary walk.

The saddle rack is so much fun to ride, you may become addicted to it or to the even faster rack and lose track of how long your horse has been working in the gait. Try to remember that this gait can be tiring and hard on your horse's legs and back. Balance time spent in it with equal or more time in the ordinary walk, trot, or other easy gait, if your horse offers to do one. If you don't overdo the amount of time you spend in the gait, your horse will be more willing and able to do it.

Solving Simple Problems in the Racking Gaits

Of all the easy gaits, the saddle rack is perhaps the easiest to develop, even in horses that are not born to do it. Some horses, however, need to be reminded that they can do it in place of, or in addition to, a hard trot, fox trot, or running walk. It is not difficult to help horses that do these gaits develop a good saddle rack for trail riding through the use of leg, seat, and rein aids. Horses that prefer to do a stepping pace or pace at speeds above a walk are more tricky to help into gear and are discussed in chapter 9.

The Trot

Although some breeds of gaited horses are expected to trot in addition to a racking gait, for others the hard trot is regarded as a major fault. Unless your horse shows no sign of gait at all either under saddle or in the pasture, it is not difficult to convert his hard trot into a slow rack. It is even possible to teach some horses that do not exhibit any gait other than a walk, trot, and canter to saddle rack.

Although you can work on changing the trot into a saddle rack in a snaffle bit or go bitless with a nose-

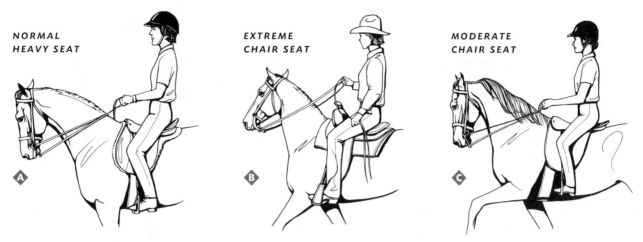

NORMAL HEAVY SEAT

EXTREME CHAIR SEAT

MODERATE CHAIR SEAT

The normal and exaggerated seats for riding a rack.
A. *You can ride most horses at a rack in a normal, heavy seat, with a slight tilting of your pelvis and your hands at waist level.*
B. *If your horse is strongly inclined to hard trot, however, you may need to sit in an extreme chair seat with your feet ahead of your hips, your weight pushed back toward the cantle of the saddle, and your hands held higher than normal. This position can help the horse use his body to rack.*
C. *You should try to return to a more moderate, chair seat as soon as he develops consistency in the gait.*

band jaquima, it is easier to do it in either a curb bit, a Pelham with both curb and snaffle functions, or a true double bridle with both a snaffle and a curb bit. Try to find a slight downhill grade with firm footing to work on, as this will automatically encourage him to hold his back in the slightly hollow position favorable for the saddle rack.

There are two options for developing a saddle rack in a horse that seems to prefer to trot. The first, and probably the easiest, is to prevent the trot from showing up at all by working the horse up in speed gradually from the walk, developing his timing and essential tension from that gait. The second is to convert the trot directly into a saddle rack once the horse has already started moving at speed in that diagonal gait.

• Start in an ordinary walk, sitting in the base position, with light, even contact on the bit.
• As your horse starts down the slight incline, change your position in the saddle to the heavy or chair seat, pushing down into the saddle with your tailbone, with your legs forward of the base position, feet in front of your hips.
• Raise your hands to the high position and, while pushing the horse on for speed with **strong** squeeze/releases from your calves, begin

to alternate tension on your reins, strongly increasing contact on first one, then the other, swaying the horse's head and neck slightly from side to side. This will begin to break up the even lift off of his hooves at the walk.

• Push your horse on for faster speed while keeping his head high and your weight pressed into the cantle area of your saddle. He will begin to do a very slow, saddle rack (at this speed, it is a stepped rack). Go on for a few steps in this gait, then praise him, return to the walk, and start over.

• Build on the stepped rack gradually, increasing leg pressure to ask for more speed while preventing your horse from breaking into a trot by keeping his head and neck elevated and continuing the strong alternating tension on the reins. Over time, the gait will gain speed and become first a saddle rack, then, with some horses, a true rack. Be careful not to turn the gait into a stepping pace.

This technique will work even for some horses that do not show any signs of an inborn saddle rack. It is an old method for training trotty Saddlebred horses to rack that predates the use of weighted shoes and wedges by about 100 years and is very similar to the methods used in England in the 1600s to train trotting horses to rack. Although this process will not work for all non-gaited horses, it can work for many of them and will almost always work in a couple of sessions for horses that are bred to be gaited.

To convert a trot directly to a saddle rack, you will need to change the timing of your horse's footfalls so that the diagonals hit separately, either speeding up or slowing down the timing of the set-down of a front or hind hoof in the pair. By changing the muscle use of his shoulders, you can slow down the set-down of a front hoof, and by changing his overall balance, you can alter the pattern of set-down of all of his hooves. To do this, you will need to adjust the tension in the horse's dorsal ligament system and create the essential tension in his neck and shoulders that in turn causes changes in the timing of his front legs. Very simply, if a horse is trotting, to get him to rack you need to raise his head and neck, put some tension into the base of his neck and over his shoulders, and shift your weight so that you cause him to tighten his back muscles.

• On a slight downhill grade, start out in the trot, using a chair seat with your hands well above the base position, raising the horse's head and neck, and maintaining even contact with the bit. *Sit down* to the gait; do not try to post or stand in your stirrups.
• Begin to alternate light tension on the reins with pulsing vibrations from one hand, then the other, just enough to shift your horse's head slightly from side to side.
• Simultaneously, shift your weight very slightly from one seat bone to the other, timed to the use of your hands. Shift your weight to your right seat bone as you squeeze your right rein, to the left as you squeeze your left rein. Your horse will begin to hesitate in the trot, skipping a beat here and there.
• Continue using your hands and weight to adjust your horse's balance until he changes from the diagonal trot to an even or slightly lateral gait. Praise him, reward him with a short walk on a slack rein, then repeat the exercise, building a few steps at a time in the saddle rack.

Move to flat ground and repeat.
• As soon as possible, when your horse is able to sustain the gait for a good distance on flat ground, return your hands to slightly above the base position and discontinue alternating tension on the reins and shifting your weight. Gradually return to a straight position in the saddle, but continue to use the heavy seat position.

When your horse understands these aids for the saddle rack, you should be able to shift him back and forth between the trot and that gait by simply lowering your hands and sitting a more forward seat for the trot and raising them while sitting in a slight chair seat for the saddle rack.

The Fox Trot/Trocha

Many horses from breeds that are expected to perform a gait from the rack family may prefer a fox trot or trocha. For trail or pleasure riding, this preference is not a big problem, but it is nice to be able to ask a horse for the gait his breed is famous for and actually get it. Keep the fox trot if you want it as another option for your horse, but see whether you can help him do his saddle rack as well.

It is easier to change a fox trot into a saddle rack than it is to modify a hard trot into that gait because the fox trot is a four-beat gait like all the racking gaits. Again, the secret to changing the gait is to raise your horse's head and create the essential tension at the base of his neck that is required for the racking gaits. You can use a snaffle if that is what your horse is accustomed to wearing, although a mild curb bit, Kimberwicke/Uxeter, or noseband jaquima may work better for encouraging him to lift his head. Use the same technique for converting a fox trot into a saddle rack as you would use to change a hard trot into it. If your horse continues to insist on fox trotting, and you are only interested in trail riding, there is no harm in allowing him to do the gait he prefers if you enjoy riding it.

The Running Walk

Because the saddle rack is only one step away from the running walk in timing and support, it is relatively easy to develop it from an even running walk. Not many horses that are expected to rack will prefer the running walk, although often horses that are expected to do a running walk will rack by mistake if their riders ask for speeds that make it impossible for them to maintain the even, four-beat running walk.

Start on flat ground with firm footing, in any headgear your horse prefers. Sitting in the heavy seat position, raise your horse's head slightly from his running walk position by raising your hands, maintaining light contact through the reins to support his head and neck. Push him on for speed, while keeping his head and neck high. He should go directly into a saddle rack or rack.

Consistency in Gait

If your horse presents you with "extra" gaits from time to time, you can probably get him back into the gear you want after a few steps. If he is like many gaited horses, however, he may continue to switch gaits whenever he goes up or down a hill, or when the footing changes from firm to soft and back again, or if you sneeze at the wrong moment. You may seem to be doing a lot of gait adjustment, achieving only a few steps of his gait in between the corrections. To help him become consistent in one gait, you need to *anticipate* when he is about to change out of it and *prevent* him from switching gaits instead of reacting after he has moved out of the one you want. This is where you start really riding your horse, not just "passengering" him.

Your Seat and Hands

Because the slightest shift in your weight can be enough to change the balance of any horse, to help keep a horse with "extra gaits" consistent, you'll need to develop a strong but flexible seat, independent use of your hands, and a thorough knowledge of how each gait feels. Remember that if your horse is moving into a more lateral gait, you can remind him to tighten his ligament system by lowering your hands and shifting your weight into the light, allowing seat. If he is moving into a more diagonal gait, you can change the tension in his ligament system by raising

your hands, bringing his nose in toward vertical, and shifting your weight into the heavy seat. If he is correct in his gait, sit quietly, centered in your saddle in the base position with light, even contact on the reins. Go with the flow!

Dealing with Terrain

If your horse is going into a more lateral gait on a downhill slant and into a more diagonal one on an uphill slant, most, but not all, horses' backs anticipate these changes. Before you get to a dip in the road, use your allowing seat and lower hands to tighten his ligament system just a little. As you come to a slight uphill, use the heavy seat and higher hands to create a little more slack in his ligament system. If you anticipate changes in the grade of trails you ride, you can prevent your horse from changing gaits on slight hills.

Learn the Feel of Gaits

Before you can successfully anticipate gait changes, you need to become so familiar with the feel of your preferred gait that you can identify it without thinking. To "learn" a gait, ride other horses that are set in it, if yours is not. Ride your own horse in a place with just the right footing and terrain so he does the gait without effort. Close your eyes and memorize every little wiggle and glide of the way he moves in gait. If he does his gait on the longe line, have someone longe him in it while you sit on him, "surrendering" yourself to the feel of the gait without the distraction of steering your horse or controlling his speed.

Make the feel of his gait a part of your body and an extension of your breathing! When you know his gait that intimately, you will be able to tell when he is thinking about changing because just before he changes gait, he will start to adjust his rhythm and the muscle use in his back. His back will start to change before his legs shift into a different gait. **Feel** his back and his rhythm in his easy gait and respond to **any** change the instant it starts.

- If his back suddenly feels more stiff and tight under your seat, he is probably about to move into a more lateral gait. Instantly shift your weight into the light seat, lower his head and neck by lowering your hands, and check his speed to prevent the gait change.

• If his back feels very full and elastic under your seat, he may be about to go into a more diagonal gait. Instantly shift your weight slightly toward the heavy seat and raise his head and neck by lifting your hands, and ask him to bring his forehead slightly more toward vertical with light vibrations on the reins.

• If you feel the rhythm of his gait fading, he is about to change into some other gait. Adjust his body *before* he falls into a completely different rhythm.

Resist your horse's attempts to change out of his gait by first engaging your abdominal muscles between your belly button and your rib cage and tightening your lower back. Reward the correct gait by relaxing those muscles and softly following the motion of the gait. If you consistently use these body aids to prevent a gait change, soon the feel of resistance from your tightened back may be enough to keep your horse in gear.

Transitions Between Gaits for Multi-Gaited Horses

Once your horse is "set" in the easy gait you want, you may want to experiment with some of the others in his repertoire. Although most gaited horses have a strong preference for one single easy gait, a number of them are able to do several easy gaits consistently, and some combine this talent with the ability to perform a good hard trot in addition to their smoother gaits. Although this ability to do a number of gaits is officially encouraged in Icelandic and Saddlebred horses, if yours is one of these talented individuals in some other breed, don't be afraid to encourage him to do more than one intermediate speed gait **after** he has learned to do the gait you want when you ask for it. If you take advantage of his extra gears, you can help him go for longer rides with less fatigue. Because each gait exercises a different set of muscles in a horse's body, changing from one gait to another allows the horse to

rest one set of muscles while another group is working. If you are happy riding in one easy gait, however, don't worry about finding others in your horse. Maintaining one consistent easy gait is enough for most people and most horses; finding others is entirely optional!

By now you should have a fairly good idea of how to go about helping your horse change his body position to change his gait. Remember that if you want to change his gait to a more lateral one, you should sit slightly heavier in the saddle with your hands a little higher than the usual base position to support his head and neck in a higher position. If you want to ask him to do a more diagonal gait, sit in the lighter seat with your hands below the base position to lower his head and neck.

A Typical Multi-Gaited Ride

Sitting straight in the saddle with your hands in the base position, maintaining light, even contact on your reins in a snaffle, curb, or bitless headgear, move your horse out in an *ordinary walk*. Squeeze/release with both of your calves against his sides to ask him to move. He should move out in an ordinary walk, nodding his head rhythmically in time to the movement of his shoulders and hind legs. He will be traveling 3½ to 4 miles per hour.

From the ordinary walk, ask your horse for a *flat walk* or *slow paso llano*. Sit straight in the saddle, keeping your hands at the base position or perhaps a bit below it, squeezing/releasing with your calves to ask for more speed. Limit his increased speed with squeeze/releases on the reins if he tries to go too fast or into another gait. He may raise his head a little and bring his forehead toward vertical, flexing at the poll. The action of your legs and reins will not be simultaneous, but by closely coordinating them, you can increase his speed in the walk while preventing him from breaking into some other gait. Your speed will be between 4½ and 6 miles per hour in the flat walk.

To move out of the flat walk into a *trot*, you will again need to adjust the frame or body position of the horse. To trot, your gaited horse needs a longer, more stretched outline than for the flat walk. Maintaining light contact with the bit, lower your hands and yield them forward so that they are on either side of the horse's withers, no higher than the pommel of the saddle. This hand position will help the horse stretch his neck forward and down and "nose out" a little in front. At the same time you yield your hands forward, tilt your pelvis in the saddle into the light, allowing seat, or perhaps the forward seat. Squeeze and release with your calves to ask him to move forward with energy. Your horse should stretch his neck down into the light pressure of the bit, at the same time taking longer strides, and start to trot. He may maintain this gait better if you post it or stand in the stirrups rather than sitting in the saddle as he does it. Although he can probably go faster, your horse's speed will be 6 to 8 miles per hour in the trot.

To change from the trot into the easy gait closest to it, the *fox trot*, ask your horse to modify his body position and shift his balance a little toward the rear. Change your own body position by rotating your pelvis into the base seat with your hands in the base position. Squeeze/release pressure on the reins, asking your horse to raise his head and tuck his nose a little, at the same time keeping up his speed with intermittent squeeze/releases from your calves. By alternating the use of your legs and your hands, you can help your horse change his rhythm in the gait, alter the exact synchronization in his diagonal legs that's required for the trot, and begin to fox trot. Your speed will be between 6 and 8 miles per hour in the fox trot.

The next step on the scale away from the fox trot is the *running walk*, or *paso llano*. To change into that gait from a fox trot, you will again need to modify the body position of both your horse and yourself. Shift your weight into the heavy seat. At the same time, maintain contact with the bit and raise your hands slightly above the base position to ask your horse to bring his nose in slightly toward vertical. This will shift the horse from the neutral/round position of the fox trot to the neutral/hollow position necessary for the running walk. For a horse that can readily do a fox trot and a running walk, this change in position should be enough to shift him from the diagonal fox trot to the more square running walk. For a less confirmed horse,

it may also be necessary to shift your own weight slightly from side to side, resisting the motion of the fox trot and helping the horse change to the more lateral running walk.

As soon as he has picked up the desired gait, stop any side-to-side weight shifting to prevent him from going overboard and moving into a pace. The horse is now doing a running walk, or paso llano. You will feel a strong driving motion from his hindquarters as each hind leg moves forward with a long, gliding step and a pulling or rolling motion in his shoulders. Your speed will be in the same range or slightly faster than that of the fox trot.

The next gait on the list is the *saddle rack* or *rack*. To shift to this gait from the running walk, the horse changes from a neutral/hollow frame to a more contained position, creating the essential tension at the base of his neck and the tightness in his back that must accompany any gait of the racking family. To help him achieve this, first modify your seat to help him tighten the muscles in his back, using a slight chair seat so your legs and feet hang in front of the straight, base position. Your shoulders may be a little behind your hips, and your hips will be slightly behind your heels in this position. At the same time, raise your hands slightly above your waist, maintaining light tension on the reins and allowing the horse to nose out just a bit from his position in the running walk, but supporting him as he raises his head. This will encourage the tension at the base of his neck that is necessary for the rack. Increase the horse's speed from a moderate running walk with a strong squeeze/release from your calves. Your horse will start to rack or saddle rack, going much faster than the running walk.

You may want to change from the saddle rack into a running walk or into a trot or fox trot. If you return to the straight or slightly forward position in the saddle, lower your hands and yield them forward, your horse should change into running walk, or with a slightly more forward seat position, into a fox trot or trot.

Of course, not all horses will change gaits this easily, and many of them will not shift at all from the one easy gait that is their preference. You may find that you prefer to stay in a single easy gait. The choice is yours.

CHAPTER NINE

The Pace Problem and How to Solve It

These kind of horses are called "natural pacers," and it is a matter of utmost difficulty to make them move in any other manner.
— Isaac Weld, Jr., *Travels Through the States of North America*, 1800

What can you do if every time you push your horse for a little speed from an ordinary walk he immediately goes into a stepping pace, or, with a little more speed, moves into an unwanted hard pace? Because the flexibility and bone structure that make it possible for a horse to do the easy gaits are closely connected to those that produce the most lateral gait, it's not surprising that the pace seems to lurk in the background, just waiting to interfere with the smooth ride you expect from your easy-gaited horse. (The flying pace of Icelandic horses is not all that rough to ride, but it is also not a very good trail gait, so for your Icelandic pleasure horse, even that pace may not be desirable.) Fortunately, even if your horse is strongly inclined to pace or stepping pace, you can help him change the way he uses his body and convert him into a less lateral gait. This is a little more challenging than the body work your horse might have needed to deal with other gait problems. Eventually, however, through consistent work to strengthen his muscles and adjust his ligament system, even a horse that seems to prefer a hard pace can learn to do a more comfortable easy gait. Both the stepping pace and the hard pace present the same training issues and respond to the same solutions.

How Does a Horse Do a Pace or Stepping Pace?

A horse moves in a *pace* by advancing his lateral, or same-side legs, at almost exactly the same time, jumping from one set to the other with a moment when all four hooves are clear of the ground. In the *stepping pace*, there is no moment when all four hooves are clear of

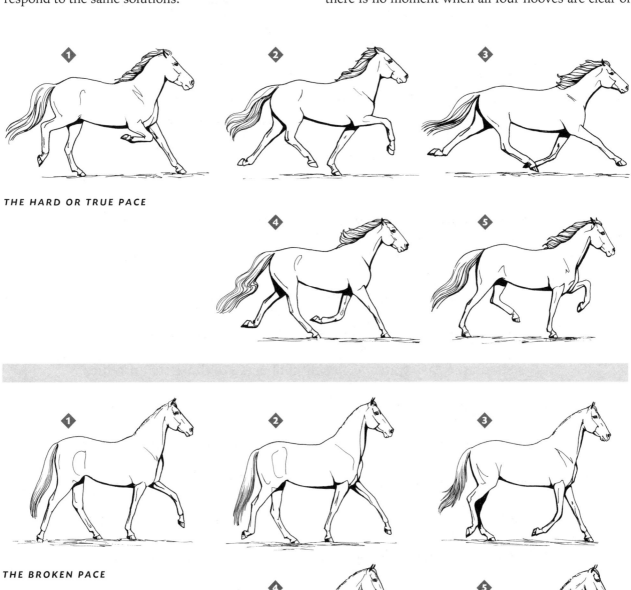

THE HARD OR TRUE PACE

THE BROKEN PACE

Lazy Pacers and Nervous Pacers

A HORSE THAT IS EXTREMELY LAID-BACK, with little energy and no impulsion or thrust working forward from his hindquarters, will often do a stepping pace. A horse like this is sometimes called a lazy pacer or leg pacer. He will often travel with a low head but no stretch in his neck or back muscles and, as a result, he will have too much slack in his ligament system. His abdominal muscles are also slack, failing to support his spine and position his pelvis to generate efficiently the pushing power of his hind legs. A lazy pacer often lacks muscle tone because he has not had sufficient exercise. To help a lazy pacer find a less lateral gait, it is important to wake him up first and teach him to develop impulsion, or the pushing power of his hindquarters.

A horse that is nervous, high-headed, and tense will also do a stepping pace, or may even do a hard pace. A horse that does this is sometimes called a nervous pacer or body pacer. He will have a stiff neck and high head, reflecting an overactive flight reflex, and may have clamped muscles in his back that prevent him from developing efficient thrust from his hind legs. His high head position increases the slack in his ligament system and prevents the efficient use of his abdominal muscles. To help a nervous pacer find a less lateral gait, it is important to relax him first and teach him to stretch his body. Then you should begin work to recondition his muscles so that he can carry his body in a more rounded frame.

the ground, and the hind hoof noticeably sets down before the front hoof on the same side. Most horses with an inclination to pace will first do a stepping pace, with two or three hooves in contact with the ground at all times, then move into a true pace when pushed for more speed.

Back Position

Horses that pace always do so with "hollow" or slightly swayed backs. This happens either because the horse is high-headed and stiff, clamping the muscles along the back and at the withers, with inadequate tension in his ligament system, or because he is strung out and traveling with a low head, slack neck, and drooping abdominal muscles that do not support his spine and allow the ligament system to develop excessive slack.

Muscle Use

Pacers tighten alternating sides of their backs as they sway their barrels away from each advancing set of lateral legs. This can contribute to the visible "wagging" in their hindquarters and the side-to-side swing of their heads and necks. Their haunches are often less developed than those of trotting horses, and they have

slack belly muscles, reflecting the weak use of their back muscles. They frequently look ewe-necked, with bulging muscle on the underside of their necks and sometimes a false crest about halfway between the poll and withers.

Why Does a Horse Pace?

Your horse does not pace just to irritate you. He uses the gait because for some reason his body is in the physical position that produces the pace. His back is hollow, his neck is stiff, and his body does not have the essential tension that produces the racking gaits. His hind legs trail behind him as he moves, and he is using the muscle groups that cause him to shift his weight from side to side. There are several possible reasons for this body use.

Basic Conformation

Your gaited horse may have a physical conformation that inclines him to travel in a hollow position. A long back, a short, upright neck, and hind legs that are "camped out" with the hocks behind the buttocks and so long from hip to fetlock that he is rump high can almost guarantee a pace or stepping pace in a gaited horse. These conformational liabilities can be overcome to some extent through exercise, but a horse that is strongly built to pace will usually revert to it if he is not **consistently** exercised in a different gait. Know your horse's conformation and be realistic about what he can be expected to do with it. If he is built to pace, he may never do anything but a stepping pace as an easy gait.

Condition

A horse that has weak neck, back, abdominal, and haunch muscles will be inclined to pace. A young, immature horse, or an older one that has not had much exercise, may not have the strength to move with any speed while carrying weight. His back will sag down, and he will pace under your weight, even if he never shows the gait at liberty in a pasture. If you let a younger horse mature before you ride him he may avoid the stepping pace. If you develop the body of an older horse through consistent exercise designed specifically to strengthen his back, he may later move easily into his easy gait with no hint of a pace. He may, however, revert to a pace if his exercise and fitness level are decreased. Horses that have had a long winter vacation in pasture frequently offer only a stepping pace for the first few rides in the spring, but return to their easy gait with exercise.

Mental Attitude

Some horses pace because they are tense due to fear. Exercises to stretch the neck and back will often relax mental and physical tension for these horses, helping them develop a calmer attitude. As they learn to relax through stretching exercises, they will also learn to use their bodies more effectively, avoiding the pace.

Other horses pace because they see no point in expending the muscular effort it takes to support their backs under your weight. These horses pace with a low head and neck carriage, bumbling along half awake, dragging their hooves close to the ground with as little exertion as possible. Exercises to develop energy and willingness to go forward into bit contact and to build muscle strength can help overcome this lackadaisical attitude.

Pain

The pace can be an early warning system that there is something physically wrong with your horse. **Pay attention,** especially if your horse has been working nicely in gait and suddenly starts pacing. If your saddle digs into his back; if he is sore from a long ride over rough ground the day before; if his hooves are worn down to the quick; or if he has strained a muscle while running in the pasture, your horse may pace. Sometimes a young horse that has worked well in his easy gait one day will start out the next by pacing because he is sore from working his immature or unconditioned muscles the day before. If you build your horse up gradually with consistent but slow work, you should be able to avoid the "sore muscle" pace. Avoid other causes of the "pain pace" by making sure that your saddle fits and your horse is sound for riding before you put him to work.

Wiring

Some horses pace because the gait is so ingrained in their nervous systems that they will do nothing else, either when ridden or free in a pasture. These horses will pace at a slow walk or at the speed of a fast gallop over rough or smooth ground, up- or downhill. Such horses are very challenging to work with and, fortunately, very rare in most gaited breeds. Most can be "rewired" to do some gait other than a pace, if only a slightly more comfortable stepping pace. If your horse refuses to do any gait but a hard pace at liberty or over poles, he may be one that is "wired" for that gait.

Discouraging the Pace

How you deal with a pace or stepping pace depends partly on which other gait you are trying to help your horse perform. If you expect his gait to be a flat walk, fox trot, running walk, or paso llano, he will respond best to exercises that strengthen his body to allow him to carry himself with a more rounded back and neck, eliminating the position that causes the stepping pace or hard pace. If he is expected to go into one of the racking gaits, he will respond to a slightly different technique for changing the tension in his ligament system and developing the "essential tension" at the base of the neck that accompanies those gaits.

Changing the Pace or Stepping Pace into a Fox Trot, Running Walk, or Paso Llano

If your horse is expected to fox trot or running walk/paso llano, start the process of eliminating the pace by teaching him to do a solid flat walk or slow paso llano in place of the stepping pace when he speeds up from an ordinary walk.

Finding the Flat Walk or Slow Paso Llano

If your horse goes immediately into a pace from an ordinary slow walk, first teach him to achieve a solid, reaching flat walk. Although developing the flat walk will not guarantee a perfect easy gait, it will help your horse begin to improve the fitness level of his body and learn to use his neck and back more effectively.

Although the following techniques discourage a pace and encourage a flat walk by changing the timing of a horse's footfalls, they also work to condition his back and neck so that he can use his entire body more effectively. They are not a complete cure for the pace, but they are a good place to begin. Most gaited horses will do a flat walk at least part of the time: over poles, up hills, and in soft footing.

Poles and Cavalletti

Working over poles or low cavalletti interferes with the flight path of a horse's hooves, forcing him to stop pacing to keep from tripping. This exercise can also help him develop the muscles of his back and hindquarters while they are working harder to lift his legs over the poles. By encouraging a gait besides a pace, work over poles helps to "reprogram" the horse's nervous system through habituation, making him more likely to choose a flat walk or other gait in place of the pace when the poles are removed. This combination of building muscle tone and changing hoof flight patterns will help most horses begin to lose the pace habit.

Longe-Line Work Over Poles

You may have done some longe-line work when you were teaching your horse ground manners and coordination at the walk. If you also spent some time working on his gait on the longe, he ought to be familiar with trotting over poles. If you haven't been doing much ground work, return to it and reacquaint your horse with the idea of trotting over poles on the line (see chapter 4).

Start by setting out pairs of poles on the ground, about 3 feet apart, at intervals around your longe circle. You will need to adjust the pole spacing for your particular horse, keeping in mind that a long-legged, long-stepping horse will work better with wider spacing than a short-legged, short-stepping one.

Walk with your horse around the circle, showing him where the poles are set, then longe him over them, pushing his speed in the ordinary walk until, just before each pair of poles, he breaks into a slow stepping pace. Keep the longe line slack, allowing him the free use of his head and neck. Just before he reaches the poles, use a light, downward tug on the longe line to ask him to lower his head. He may tick the poles with his hooves and might stumble at first. Slow him down and let him "find his feet" over them, then ask again for the flat walk over the poles. If he continues to stumble, change the spacing of the poles to accommodate his step length. If your horse persists in pacing over the poles, raise them on cement blocks to about 8 inches off the ground so that he will have to pick up his feet a little higher to go over them. This will cause him to use his back more strongly to lift his legs and will also change the timing of each step.

Practice longe work over poles for 10 to 15 minutes total, several times a week, working the horse in both directions, but practicing a little longer to your horse's stiff side. He may flat walk over the poles, then return to a stepping pace or pace in between them. If so, add a single pole between the pairs of poles as a reminder to help him keep lifting his hooves and increase the number of steps he takes in a flat walk.

Ridden Pole Work

As your horse begins to develop a flat walk on the longe over a few poles, start to ride him over a series of poles. Set poles out in groups of two or three in various places around your arena, using the same posts or rails you used while doing ground work. Set poles within the groups at about 5 feet apart to begin with.

Avoid flimsy plastic poles; they will shatter if your horse steps on them. You can use solid lengths of old telephone poles or railroad ties so that you won't need to reset them constantly if he ticks them with a hoof. You can also use manufactured cavalletti, or build some homemade ones consisting of poles between pairs of cement blocks. Do not set up a long row of solid, thick poles to try to force your horse to stop pacing. Too many poles in a row will only make him resentful of the obstacles and may cause him to rush over them. You will have better results if you keep the exercise nonthreatening by limiting the height and number of poles.

Carrying your weight will affect the position of your horse's back. He may flat walk very nicely over the poles on the longe, but change back into a pace when you get on him. You can help him elevate his back somewhat by sitting lightly, with your crotch out of the saddle, leaning slightly forward as you start riding over the poles.

- Hold your hands well below the pommel of your saddle, low on either side of your horse's withers and at least a foot apart, with a slack, relaxed feel in the reins. Your reins should be adjusted so that you can take light contact if you close your fingers, without being so loose that they swing and flop against his neck.
- Walk your horse slowly over the poles a few times so he knows where they are, encouraging him to examine them with a lowered head and neck.
- Keeping your reins slack, gradually urge your horse into flat-walk speed (which for him will be a pace).
- Ride him over the poles at this fast walking speed with slack but not flopping reins. Be prepared for him to trip and stumble a few times.
- He will probably flat walk slowly over the poles, then return to a pace between groups of poles. If he becomes excited and starts to hard trot over the poles, reduce the number of poles in a row, and relax him by riding for a little while in an ordinary walk. Then try again, keeping him slowed to a flat-walk speed with light squeeze/releases on the reins.

Practice this work over the poles for a short time, then work on something else to prevent your horse from souring on the exercise. Go outside the arena and take him on a trail ride at an ordinary walk to give him something else to think about.

The Role of the Trot

YOUR HORSE MAY SHIFT IMMEDIATELY from the pace into a hard trot over poles on the longe. Don't worry. This will not interfere with his ability to do his easy gait. Work in the trot will help condition his muscles, habituate his nervous system to moving in a gait besides a pace, and create more flexibility in his body so that he can eventually do his easy gait more effortlessly. It is a good idea to *encourage* a pacey horse to trot over poles until he develops the strength to maintain a flat walk.

Allow him to trot over the poles for at least half of each longe-line session, over a period of several months to build his back and leg strength. Once he has learned to trot consistently over the poles, you can then slow him back down to a flat walk from the trot with a light tug/release on the longe line, holding your hand low to encourage him to maintain a lower head and neck position. Prevent him from slowing to an ordinary walk by pointing at his haunches with your longe whip. Between the trot and the ordinary walk, you may be able to "catch" him in the flat walk. Praise him for flat walking, encourage him with your voice, and try to keep him in the gait for as long as possible. At first he may do only a few steps, but in time he should be able to flat walk in a large circle around you, at first over the poles, then without them.

The flat walk over a set of poles. Don't put more than a few in a line, and space them for your horse's natural stride.

After a few sessions of working over the poles under saddle, your horse will start to take a couple of steps in the flat walk in between groups of poles. Sit relaxed in the light, allowing seat, keeping your hands low and quiet as he takes these beginning steps in the flat walk. Reward him by staying with his movement in the gait, keeping your upper body quiet and your legs still against his sides. If he starts to pace, resist the movement by sitting straight, tightening your abdominal muscles, breathing in and up, and stabilizing your lower back. At the same time you resist with your seat, slightly increase contact with one rein on the horse's stiff side, usually the right, to check his speed and keep his neck straight and relatively still. Don't pull back on the rein, but close your fingers around it until you feel about as much weight as a small orange in your hand. Hold that contact for a second, then return to the lighter, "plum-feel" on the rein. This use of one rein is a light, lateral half halt. It will help straighten his body just a little. Reminding him to keep his neck straight and slowing him down just a little may be enough to prevent him from swaying his body from side to side in the pace.

If necessary, place one pole about halfway between your groupings of poles as a reminder for your horse to continue in the flat walk. Eventually, after several weeks of practice, he should go all the way around your arena in the flat walk. When he does that, reduce the number of poles in a group to two and continue to ride him over them for several more lessons. Your goal should be to reduce gradually the poles in the arena to a few "reminder" poles at places he seems inclined to break into a pace. In time, even they can be removed and he may flat walk easily around the arena.

Success with poles does not mean that your horse will never do a pace again. Most horses that are trained away from the pace using poles will revert to it when ridden downhill or on hard ground or in pain. Because it takes a little more than pole work to "cure" the pace completely by helping your horse develop a different body position, avoid riding him downhill at anything but an ordinary walk until you can teach him to rebalance his body through other exercises.

Hills

Most horses will work in some gait other than a pace if they are going up a hill. To work easily uphill, a horse must push with his hindquarters, slightly round his back, and push with his hind legs. This body use makes a pace difficult. Take advantage of this when teaching your horse to flat walk. Push him out of the ordinary walk on a gradual uphill grade, asking for an even, energetic flat walk, about five miles per hour. Encourage him to move with light squeeze/release of your legs, timed at each forward step he makes with his hind legs to ask for the energetic walk. Return to an ordinary walk on level ground, and, of course, avoid asking for any speed at all going downhill. This type of exercise will help build the horse's back and hind-quarters and improve his performance on flat ground.

Footing

Many horses that pace or stepping pace will change to a flat walk, running walk, or fox trot when ridden in soft footing. This happens for two reasons: first, because the footing surface delays the lift off of the hooves, and second, because to work in deeper footing, a horse needs a more active use of his back to lift his legs. Riding a horse with a pace problem in a recently plowed field or deep grass is an old technique that works, at least during the time the horse is being ridden in that environment. If you have access to a sandy stream bed, some loamy but not slippery mud, or even a flat field with six or seven inches of new-fallen snow, you can use this footing to help your horse break the pacing habit. You can also arrange your arena or ring so that you have a firm path near the rail and a slightly softer, deeper track just inside the firm path, allowing you to move from firm to soft footing and back again as your horse's gait indicates. Deep or soft footing works best to discourage a pace if you can ride in it for a short stretch between longer stretches of work on firmer ground, preferably on a slight uphill grade. Be careful not to overdo this work; deep footing is tiring to negotiate and can be harmful to the tendons in your horse's legs. A minute or so of work in deep footing out of every 15 minutes you ride is plenty.

Conditioning to Cure the Pace and Improve the Gaits

People have used poles, hills, and footing to cure the pace for generations. These methods work, but they do not always last. To avoid the body position that causes the pace and to improve his overall condition,

a horse also needs work in specific exercises to increase his lateral and poll-to-tail flexibility and strengthen his neck and back. These exercises should be done at first in an ordinary walk in the snaffle bit, jaquima, or sidepull. You can also do some of this work in a Kimberwicke if your horse is not responsive in a snaffle.

The All-Important Neck-Stretching Exercise

Your horse's ability to work well in a flat walk and eliminate the pace depends on a strong, stretched, semi-rounded back working as a "connection" from his hindquarters to his poll and jaw. You can help him develop that connection by improving the strength and elasticity of his neck and back muscles. The first step in improving the tone of those muscles is teaching him to lower and extend his head and neck on cue. This exercise goes by many names: "long and low," "showing the horse the way to the ground," and "head down and out." It is used in many forms of training, and it is **vital** to teaching any horse to stop pacing. You can practice the neck stretching exercise either in an arena or out on the trail. It should become a regular part of your riding routine as soon as your horse understands it.

Phase 1: Reach and Relaxation
Before you mount up, practice lowering your horse's head and neck from the ground, reminding him of what he learned during earlier ground work. Massage his neck just behind the poll, encouraging him to relax and reach forward. With your hands on each side of his nose, on either the sidepull or the rings of the snaffle bit, gently press forward and down, first to one side, then the other, asking him to lower his head. He should remember this exercise and relax down and forward easily.

Next, while you are in the saddle, teach your horse to lower his head and relax in motion. The aids for this exercise are fairly simple.

- Mount up and ride at the ordinary walk in a 60-foot circle or a straight line.
- Hold your hands low, below the swells of the

Phase 1. Asking your horse to reach down and forward is the first step in creating the connection through his body that will help him stop pacing. Keep your hands low and separate, but continue to sit straight in the saddle as you teach this exercise.

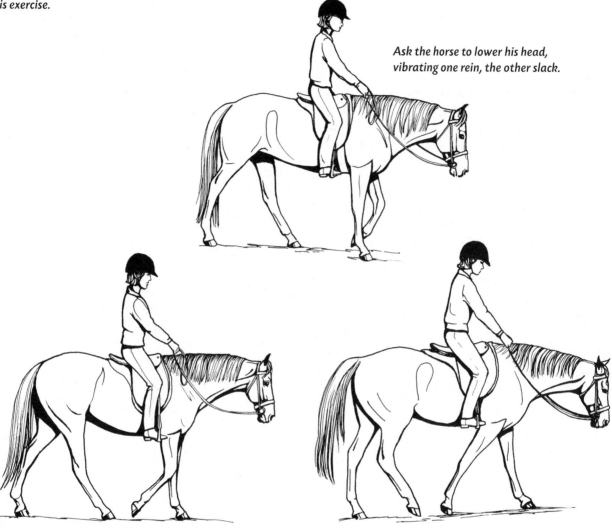

Ask the horse to lower his head, vibrating one rein, the other slack.

The horse is beginning to reach down, with slack in both reins.

The horse is totally relaxed on loose reins.

saddle and at least two feet apart, with only the weight of the reins as contact. Do not ride with normal "plum-feel" contact to begin this exercise. Your horse must have no constraint on his mouth or neck at first as he learns to relax down and forward.

• Vibrate the right rein lightly down and to the side, with a squeeze/release motion on the rein, then allow that rein to go slack. As soon as the right rein is slack, vibrate the left rein lightly

down and to the side. Do not alternate strong pressure on the reins. Allow all tension to leave one rein before you squeeze/release the other. Keep your horse moving forward with occasional light squeeze/releases from your calves.

• Your horse will eventually begin tentatively to reach forward and down just a little with his head and neck. Allow your reins to slip slowly through your fingers, so that there is no restriction on your horse's head. Let the weight of the reins hang in a heavy loop between his mouth and your hands, encouraging him to lower his head. Ride for a few steps in the neck-stretched position, then take up your reins and return to the starting position. Repeat, going around the arena or circle in the other direction.

After some initial confusion, your horse will start to reach forward and lower his head and neck as soon as you give alternating vibrations down and to the side with the reins. Be sure to reward him by riding with complete slack in the reins when he lowers his head, encouraging him to move with his head and neck as low as possible, stretched out in front of him. Since the purpose of this early stage of the exercise is to relieve tension in your horse's neck muscles and to begin to stretch his ligament system, avoid any pressure on the reins that might bring his forehead toward vertical. Keep your hands low and your reins slack; use only occasional vibrations on the reins to remind him to maintain a lowered head position. Be sure to keep him moving forward in the walk with occasional squeeze/releases from your calves. Although it may take you several lessons to teach your horse to lower his head very far in response to your cues, eventually he will relax and reach forward and down when you vibrate one rein to the side and down.

The point of this exercise is not just to get your horse to lower his head! While it is relatively easy to teach a horse to drop his head as a conditioned response, the point of this exercise is to teach him to reach forward toward the bit as he relaxes his neck, developing his confidence in the bit and your hands on the reins. Practice asking your horse to lower his head and stretch his neck, asking for more steps and a lower head each lesson, until he can easily carry his poll well below his withers on a slack rein when asked. This relaxation phase of the exercise may be easy for a lazy pacer to learn, but expect it to take time with a nervous pacer or one that has been trained with the use of bitting rigs or other head-setting devices. If your horse has been taught to carry a high head, it is a physical challenge for him to lower his neck and reach forward. It can take several months of practice before a very stiff, high-headed horse can lower his

neck and relax on cue with a rider. Give your horse the time he needs to stretch those muscles and ligaments.

When your horse has learned to respond to the neck-lowering aids, practice frequent transitions between the lower, neck-stretched position and a more normal position. This will alternately stretch and contract the muscles in his neck and back and develop elasticity. This exercise will begin to eliminate some of the poll-to-tail stiffness that contributes to the pace and will also prepare your horse's body for later work in a more balanced position in the flat walk.

- Sitting straight in the saddle, ride in the lowest neck-stretched position at an ordinary walk with loose reins.
- Gradually shorten the reins a couple of inches until they are no longer loose, but are still slack. You should feel no tension between your hands and the horse's mouth, only the weight of the reins in your hands with no feeling of contact.
- Bring your hands closer together so that they are no more than eight inches apart.
- Slowly return to light contact on the reins, allowing the horse's head to lift so that the poll is above the withers. Do not try to set his head with your hands. Simply return to light, even contact on the reins in place of the longer, slack feel you used for lowering his head.
- Ride for several steps with the new, higher head position, then return to the neck-stretched position on slack reins. Praise your horse!

Repeat several times in both directions. Practice frequent transitions in the ordinary walk between the neck-stretched position, with slack reins, and the "normal" position, with light contact, when you ride.

Phase 2: Reaching into Contact with the Bit
Once your horse understands the basics of reaching down and forward and does it easily whenever you ask with alternating light downward and outward vibrations on the reins, you can teach him the next phase of the exercise: reaching down and forward into the bit. This exercise begins to stretch the ligament system, connecting the energy from his hindquarters to his jaw through his body. With it, you start the process of

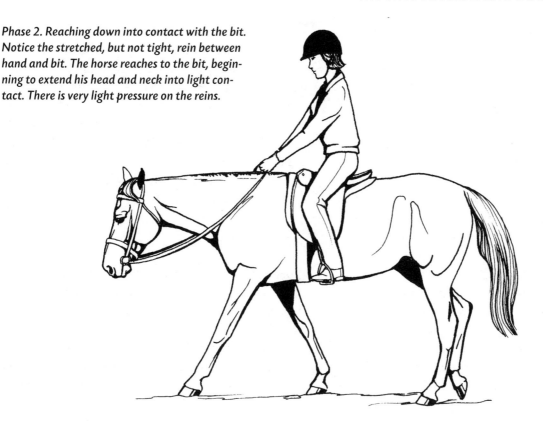

Phase 2. Reaching down into contact with the bit. Notice the stretched, but not tight, rein between hand and bit. The horse reaches to the bit, beginning to extend his head and neck into light contact. There is very light pressure on the reins.

elevating your horse's spine away from the hollow, pacing position. It is the basis for later advanced work in accepting the bit and working "on the bit" that prepares a well-trained horse for the curb. This exercise should be done in a non-leverage snaffle bit; do not expect to succeed in bitless headgear. You can, however, try it with a Kimberwicke/Uxeter if your horse absolutely will not respond to a non-leverage bit.

• Sit straight in the saddle, with your hands low on either side of your horse's withers. If your hands are above the swells on a Western saddle, they are too high.

• Squeeze/release with your calves to ask your horse to move forward in an energetic ordinary walk.

• Gather your reins so that you feel very light contact with the horse's mouth, with no more weight in your fingers than that of a small plum.

• Begin to ask your horse to lower his head. Squeeze/release with first one hand, then the other, using light pressure down and to the side. Begin to separate your hands, first a foot,

then two feet, apart. Lighten contact after each squeeze on the reins, but do not completely release your feel of his mouth.

• Let your reins lengthen a fraction at a time as he reaches down, but rather than allowing total slack as your horse reaches forward, maintain the "plum-feel" in your fingers as he lowers his head. Think of your hands as forming the wide base of a triangle and your horse's mouth as the apex of that triangle. As you widen the base, his head will lower; don't blunt the apex by pulling back with your hands. Encourage him to chew his way to the ground by maintaining light, vibrating contact with his mouth, slacking by opening your fingers, one hand at a time, as he lowers his head, then reestablishing contact when his head and neck are at a lower position.

• Squeeze/release with your legs, reinforcing the leg aid with a tap from the dressage whip, if necessary, to keep your horse moving forward with energy in his walk, reaching for contact with the bit. He should continue moving forward into contact, not stopping or hesitating in response to the feel of the bit. (Remember: Avoid the habit of nagging him with constant leg pressure or kicking. He must learn to go forward with little work on your part. It is better to give him a tap with the dressage whip to keep him moving than to kick at him or constantly "hug" his sides with leg pressure, which will only dull him to leg cues.)

• Keep your hands low and separate to prevent him from raising his head. If he tries to raise his head, simply separate your hands a little wider instead of pulling down. His head will drop lower again.

• Maintain consistent, light, "plum" contact in both reins. Separate your hands if necessary to keep his head and neck lowered. Keep your hands steady so that he moves into the contact of the bit. **Never pull back** on the reins to maintain the contact. Ride in the faster walk, keeping the horse moving with alternating squeeze/releases from your calves, maintaining his head and neck in the lowered position with light, even contact with the bit. Return to an ordinary walk with loose reins, keeping his head lowered. Reverse directions and repeat. Praise your horse!

As you practice this exercise, sit straight in the saddle, balanced over your seat bones in the base seat position, while squeezing/releasing with your legs to push your horse into the feel of the bit at an energetic ordinary walk. Don't pull back on the reins and squeeze with your legs at the same time. Squeeze him "into" your hands, taking contact only when you have stopped urging him forward. Don't be afraid to use your legs to remind him to move. The action of your legs on his sides will help him tighten his abdominal muscles and increase the lift of his back. Within a few lessons, you should begin to feel a slight fullness in his back under your seat as he begins to use his back muscles in a more elastic way and as his back rises as a result of improved muscle tone. That is a sign that he has begun to lift his back under your seat and to develop elastic strength in his neck.

There are no shortcuts. Do not try to force your horse into a low position through continuous strong rein pressure, martingales, tight cavessons, or other gimmicks. That strategy will only destroy the tentative connection you should be building between his back, his mouth, and your hands. Work slowly and ask for a little at a time, and your horse will eventually accept the bit and stretch into it, through his back. Be sure to let him relax on a slack rein, and trail ride at a walk for relaxation in between sessions of work accepting the bit. Keep your horse mentally alert so that he will want to work for you.

Finally, a Flat Walk

When your horse is moving easily in this low position on light contact in the ordinary walk, push him more strongly forward with your legs, asking for the flat walk. If you ask him to move forward with energy while he is accepting contact with a lowered head and neck, he should start to flat walk with consistency and drive from his hindquarters. His back will rise. He will be unable to pace in this position.

Be careful not to overdo this work on contact in the flat walk; it takes time for a horse to build the muscle necessary to maintain this position. Ask for a few steps at a time, and return instantly to a slower walk at the first hint of a stepping pace. Build his ability in the gait slowly, gradually increasing the number of steps until your horse is easily maintaining the stretch and roundness in his back for several circuits of your arena. You can then go on to teach him to work on the bit.

Phase 3: Raising the Head and Neck with Elastic Contact

To establish the flat walk with contact and a lowered head and neck, be prepared to work with a very pacey horse for several months. Condition your horse to stretch down into the bit and increase elasticity in his back and neck.

• Practice riding with a lowered head on slack reins.
• Make frequent transitions between that position and a more normal head position with light contact in an ordinary walk.
• Increase the amount of work with contact and a lowered head and neck in the flat walk.

Phase 3. In the final phase of the neck-stretching exercise, the connection is made between hindquarters and mouth, and the horse moves forward on elastic contact with the bit in a flat walk, first with a more normal head position, then with semi-collection.

The base of his neck rises as the horse begins to lift his head from the lowered position.

His head and neck elevate as his hindquarters lower, maintaining the lift at the base of the neck.

The goal: semi-collection on a light rein. The horse flexes at the poll and stretches his entire ligament system in the flat walk.

As he gains strength, ask him to maintain engaged back and neck muscles with a slightly higher head and neck while working on contact with the bit. This is similar to bringing his head back up from the relaxed neck-stretching exercise, but it increases tone in the neck and back muscles and stretch in the ligament system.

While practicing this exercise, be careful to avoid pulling your horse's forehead in toward vertical. His head position must result from the stretching of his muscles in his neck and his ligament system as he reaches toward the feel of your hands through the bit. At first his nose will extend outward, as it did in the early stages of learning this exercise on a slack rein. As he develops his neck, the muscles will stretch and curve into a smooth arc from withers to poll. His forehead may then begin to come more toward vertical on the same light contact he searched for when reaching out and down.

- Sitting straight in the saddle, ride forward with good momentum in the flat walk in the neck-stretched position, with contact on the bit.
- Maintaining light, even contact through both reins, bring your hands closer together until they are about 8 inches apart. Your horse's head and neck will begin to lift as the feel through the reins changes.
- Allow your hands to rise along with the horse's head and neck until your hands are even with his withers.
- Ride for several steps and then return to the lower position on contact by lowering and separating your hands. Praise and reward your horse by riding at a relaxed ordinary walk on slack reins.

This exercise will encourage the horse to raise his head and neck slightly and perhaps to bring his forehead in just a bit toward vertical. This is not a high "head-set" position and is not as elevated as your horse will eventually carry his head, once he develops more strength in his back and hindquarters. It is a gradual step up from the very low head and neck position he has been using. If you are careful when you allow his head to rise, he will continue to use the same stretched and elastic muscles he has developed by working into contact with a lowered head, and his flat

walk will become more balanced. The base of his neck will rise, and he will be well on his way to banishing the pace from his list of gaits.

The Halt, Back, and Go

Working on the neck-stretching exercise and teaching your horse to move into contact will increase his poll-to-tail strength and elasticity. You can also help him raise his back and overcome the pace position by practicing the halt, back, and go exercise you taught him in the ordinary walk (see chapter 5). Practice this first in the ordinary walk, then in the flat walk. If you did not bother to teach him this exercise earlier, do it now as part of strengthening his body to cure the pace. Practice the exercise, several times, each time you ride him.

Developing the Running Walk/Paso Llano or Fox Trot from the Flat Walk

Once your horse has developed his flat walk as a result of working through his back and into contact with the bit and has started to become more flexible from side to side, you can begin to speed him up from the flat walk, asking for his faster easy gait. He should go easily into a running walk or fox trot from the flat walk as you squeeze/release with your calves, maintaining light contact with the reins.

The Running Walk/Paso Llano

The running walk is simply a faster, longer-reaching version of the flat walk. Help your horse find this gait by pushing him on for speed very gradually from the flat walk while sitting straight and balanced in the saddle. This can be a delicate process because most horses, if pushed abruptly for too much speed, will skip over the running walk and return to the pace. Avoid this by keeping his head and neck low while maintaining light contact with his mouth and asking for increased speed with only a touch from one calf. Check your horse's momentum with a very light touch/release on the diagonal rein: If touching with your left leg, use your right rein. To lower his head and neck and to reestablish the connection through his back to your hands if he starts to pace, **immediately** lower and separate your hands while maintaining contact. Check his speed with a squeeze/release on both reins; return to the flat walk, and, keeping your hands low, ask again for a very tiny increase in speed. Work at that speed, avoiding the pace, and build on his ability to maintain it over time.

To help your horse develop muscle tone and elasticity in his back, practice transitions between the ordinary walk, flat walk, and running walk, playing the scales both up and down in speed. Help your horse find his gait by using hills or other favorable terrain to encourage the body use that enables him to achieve it. Over time, you can increase your horse's speed in his running walk until he can maintain a slow version of the gait both up slight grades and on flat ground. This may take several months of work for a horse that was very pacey to begin with, but if you avoid riding in the pace by returning to an energetic flat walk and gradually push for a slow increase in speed, his body will develop the strength required to sustain the running walk. You can then build on that foundation to improve the gait and his ability to do it on varied terrain.

The Fox Trot

The fox trot presents a slightly different challenge for the pacey horse. Many of them will automatically go into a fox trot once they have learned to make the connection through their bodies in the flat walk. Some, however, may work very well in a flat walk, but go directly into a running walk, or slip back into the pace, when you ask for more speed. To move up from the flat walk with a horse like this, start by sitting a slightly more forward seat in the saddle while you ask for more speed with a gentle squeeze/release from your calves. At the first hint of a pace, lower your hands and separate them, very slightly increasing contact on the bit. This may be enough to cause your horse to move into the diagonal fox trot.

Using the Trot

If lowering the head and neck with increased contact does not persuade your horse to fox trot, move into a true forward seat and push him on for more speed,

encouraging him to hard trot, over poles if necessary. Do not post this gait, but don't try to sit it, either. Use a two-point forward seat or stand in your stirrups to keep your weight off the saddle and allow his back to rise. When he is moving in a rhythmic trot, sit down in the saddle, in the straight, base position, and gradually check your horse's speed by gently squeezing/ releasing on the reins with low hands until he is just about to lose the trot and return to a flat walk. Relax in the saddle by breathing out and softening the muscles in your lower back, keeping his head low with just enough contact to bring his forehead slightly toward vertical. Check his forward speed with a very light vibration of both hands on the reins, but be ready to maintain his momentum with a touch from your calves in between the vibrations. You should be able to find his "sweet spot" for the fox trot just above the speed of his flat walk and below his trotting speed. Praise and reward him for doing the gait, return to the flat walk, and start over.

The next time you ask your horse for more speed, try to find the fox trot without going into the hard trot first. It may take some time and practice, but even a very pacey horse will fox trot if you maintain low hands, help him raise both his back and the base of his neck with alternate use of light leg and rein pressure, and keep your seat light on his back. Remember to make the fox trot easier for your horse by taking advantage of soft footing and slight uphill grades to help him maintain the gait. With time and exercise, his back should develop the strength to carry you in a fox trot on flat ground as easily as he does up a slight grade.

From Pace to Rack

Raising the base of your horse's neck and teaching him to stretch his entire ligament system is good exercise and beneficial for any horse. If you expect your horse to rack, however, once you have followed that method for discouraging the pace, you may find that he will prefer to do a running walk or fox trot to any of the rack family of gaits. If your horse is pacey and you expect him to do some type of rack, although it will be very good for his body to teach him to stretch and raise his back, he must also learn to develop the special tension in his neck and back that goes with the rack. Teach him the neck-stretching exercises and to work with contact in a walk, then let him return to his normal, higher head position before you start developing the rack. You can work on the racking gaits in a mild curb bit, jaquima, or other bitless headgear. You may also use a snaffle bit, although the snaffle may not be the most effective tool for teaching the head position that accompanies the racking gaits.

Developing the Corto, Slow Tolt, or Saddle Rack from the Fast Walk

If you have established an even, fast, ordinary walk and taught your horse to maintain light contact on the bit, you can often go directly from that gait into a slow rack, avoiding the pace. To accomplish this, change contact with the bit by raising your hands very gradually to waist height, supporting your horse's head in a higher position with light, upward vibrations on the reins, while at the same time tipping your pelvis from the base position into the "heavy" seat. The tension on your reins will be more up and back than the level, elastic feel you maintained when allowing your horse's head to rise with contact in the walk. This requires a very subtle elevation of your horse's head, without jerking or holding it up with heavy contact or pulling his nose in with traction on the reins. Your fingers, not your fists or arms, ask for this change in head and neck position.

Developing the Corto, Slow Tolt, or Saddle Rack Directly from the Stepping Pace

Some horses will not be able to go directly from the fast walk into the racking gaits, but will instead return to the stepping pace as soon as you try to lift their heads to encourage the rack. You can try teaching these horses to hard trot over poles and then change to a slow saddle rack through that gait, although you may not have much success with that method. You can also try to convert the stepping pace directly into a saddle rack. This will take some finesse in the way you use your seat and hands, but with many horses it

is possible. A horse that is doing a stepping pace, while usually moving with tightened back muscles, lacks the essential tension at the base of his neck and over his shoulders that produces the saddle rack. He also carries his back in a slightly more hollow position, with less tightening of the muscles over the loin than is required for the saddle rack. Use seat, leg, and rein aids to help him raise his back, tighten the muscles over his loin, and develop tension at the base of his neck.

- Sitting in the base position, ride your horse forward with speed in the walk until he breaks into a stepping pace.
- As you feel him break into the stepping pace, tilt your pelvis slightly forward so that your weight is just in front of your seat bones, in the light, allowing seat. This will help your horse lift his back slightly from the hollow position of the stepping pace. (**Note:** With some horses, it may work better to shift your weight back into the heavy seat to cause them to tighten the loin muscles instead of forward to encourage the back to rise. Experiment with both seat positions to see which is more effective for your horse.)
- Raise your hands a few inches above the waist-high position and, with upward vibrations from your fingers, ask your horse to raise his head. At the same time, bring his nose slightly toward vertical with very gently increased contact. Don't try to develop a vertical head set with traction. Ask him to bring his neck and head slightly back toward his withers while maintaining his high head position with continued upward vibrations on the reins to elevate his head and neck.

With this support of his head and neck and the change of weight on his back, your horse should begin to do a few steps in a slow saddle rack. Ride for a short distance in the gait, praise him, then return to the ordinary walk. Repeat several times, asking for a few more steps in gait each time. Gradually increase the number of steps he takes in the saddle rack, until he is able to do it easily for longer distances. You may find that your horse responds better to this technique on hard footing while rounding a slight curve, or on a slight uphill grade. Experiment to find the best terrain and position for your horse.

How Long Will It Take?

After a couple of months of consistent work, with little or no change to your horse's "default pace gait," you will probably wonder whether what you are doing is worth the effort. The siren call of the quick fix of shoeing or other mechanical means of obtaining a specific gait, or a facsimile of that gait, may begin to appeal to you. Consider your horse's overall, long-term soundness, and resist the temptation. It can take over a year of consistent, correct work to overcome the strong body habits of a horse that is stuck in an unwanted pace or stepping pace.

Whether you keep working to eliminate the gait that long or decide to settle for an amble from your horse is up to you. Give yourself and your horse a chance before you give up on trying to change his gait.

After a fair trial, you may certainly decide that you can be happy riding a stepping pace if that is what your horse truly prefers. Just don't assume that he can't do anything but pace if he doesn't start doing the gait you want after only a month or two of work.

You Can Do It!

While it may take some time, you **can** help your horse recondition his body so he works in his easy gait and stops pacing or stepping pacing at speeds above a walk. Help him develop his muscular strength with consistent, moderate work in his gait alternated with longer periods of work in the walk and flat walk in the stretched neck and elastic contact positions. If you avoid overdoing the gait work, remember not to ask for gait on downhill grades or very hard footing, and build your horse's strength and flexibility while avoiding the pace, he will eventually become so comfortable in his gait that he will do it without constant reminders of how to carry his body. He may even start doing it on his own, out free in the pasture.

CHAPTER TEN

Improving the Flat Walk and Intermediate Gaits

Ask often; expect little; reward greatly.
— GENERAL FAVEROT DE KERBRECH (1837–1905)

By now your horse should be working in both a fairly consistent flat walk and his preferred intermediate gait on flat ground, with light contact on the bit or noseband. He may still lose form going up or down a slight grade or around a curve, and although he can work nice circles in the ordinary walk, he may lose his gait if you try circles or turns at a faster speed. He may offer you only one speed in his gait and take steps that are either shorter than you would like or longer than those practical for trail riding. It is time to refine his gaits, improve his ability to control his step length and speed, and develop his flexibility in gait.

First Things First

NOTE: If your horse is not yet working well in both an ordinary walk and his intermediate gait, moving forward easily in response to your aids with even contact on the bit, do not start work yet on stride shortening or lengthening, or the lateral flexions. He needs to have a good base level of fitness and responsiveness before he can improve his gaits.

Semi-Collection and Shorter Strides

If you have practiced the neck-stretching exercise in chapter 9 and taught your horse to accept and work into the bit, shifting his balance slightly toward the rear, he is ready to move on to the next phase: developing the elastic and effective use of his back. If he did not have a pace problem to begin with, and you have not yet taught him the neck-stretching exercise, teach all three phases now in the walk or flat walk to develop the muscle tone in his back and neck, as well as his acceptance of the bit. Then proceed on to the next stage of physical fitness.

Developing Semi-Collection

While gaited horses do not work in true collection in their easy gaits, those that do the fox trot, running walk, or paso llano can learn to carry their bodies in a semi-collected position. They can slightly raise their backs and shift their weight a little toward their hindquarters, moving with impulsion into a slightly rounded but still neutral position from the flatter neutral position of their ordinary gait. This semi-collected position improves your horse's balance under your weight and provides more stability on the trail. It also allows him to use his entire body more effectively in his gait. When you taught him to work on the bit with light contact in the third phase of the neck-stretching exercise, that began the process of semi-collection; continue the exercise as he develops more strength in his back and neck.

The process of developing semi-collection will take time; there are no shortcuts. Don't try to ride your horse into a more "collected-appearing" position by pulling back on the reins to bring his nose in while kicking or spurring him forward to cram him into a shorter body frame. That type of "push/pull" riding will make his back stiff and his mouth dull and may cause him to revert to a pace. Instead, develop his forward motion with your legs, allow it with your seat, and catch it with your fingers, without ever giving the rein and leg aids at the same moment. If you follow that technique your horse will be light, balanced, and able to move in semi-collection without constant pressure from your legs or pulling from your hands.

This exercise works best in a snaffle bit, but you can also use a mild, short-shanked curb bit or a noseband to develop the same feel. Do not try this with a California bosal if you have not had a lot of experience using one.

- Sitting balanced in the base position as your horse moves forward in an ordinary walk, adjust your reins so that you have light, "plum-feel" contact with the bit or your horse's nose through a noseband.
- Ask your horse to move forward with energy in a flat walk or slow paso llano using light squeeze/releases from both calves.
- Adjust your pelvis into the light, allowing seat position. Gently squeeze/release on the reins, just enough to check his forward speed a little, not enough to slow him down into an ordinary walk. Be ready to squeeze/release with your calves if he loses energy or tries to return to an ordinary walk.
- Alternate your leg and hand aids, channeling the energy from his back through his legs to create a slightly higher step with less reach forward. You will feel his back rise under your seat and his hindquarters push a little more strongly with each step. His head and neck will rise a little, and his forehead will begin to come more toward vertical without any change in your hand position or contact on the reins.
- Go a short distance in the semi-collected flat

walk, then return to an ordinary flat walk by relaxing your fingers on the reins, releasing the tension in your upper legs, and giving a stronger squeeze/release with your calves.

Practice semi-collecting the flat walk for short intervals, alternating with time spent in the normal, or working, flat walk and in your horse's easy gait. Be sure to practice the first and second parts of the neck-stretching exercise in between periods of semi-collection to keep your horse from either becoming tight, bringing his forehead behind vertical, or "sucking back" in his neck. Alternating his body position will help your horse's back muscles develop elasticity and strength so that he can work in a more even and fluid gait. As your horse becomes more fit and able to carry himself in the semi-collected flat walk, you can gradually increase the distance he travels in that gait.

When your horse has mastered semi-collection in the flat walk, you can use the same aids to semi-collect his fox trot or running walk. Start by pushing him into a moderate-speed fox trot or running walk. Again, use your seat and alternating rein and leg cues to ask him to bring his body together, slightly shortening his steps and channeling his energy into a light, upward carriage of his body rather than into long forward steps. Practice for short periods, with plenty of work in the ordinary speed of his gait and relaxation on a slack rein to keep him from developing a tight neck or choppy gait.

Shortening Strides

Most people who ride gaited horses concentrate on increasing stride length, not shortening it. Obviously, for moving at speed on flat ground, long strides are a desirable trait. For riding down hills or just picking his way through tricky footing on the flat while in gait, however, your horse will be more surefooted if he learns to move with slightly shorter strides. When you were working on playing the scales, you may have practiced shortening his steps in the ordinary walk. You can now apply the same technique to ask him for shorter strides in both the flat walk and his intermediate gait. As he learns to modify his step length in his gait, his body will develop more strength and agility.

Be careful! If your horse has any tendency to pace, this exercise may cause him to revert to that gait. Do not push him for shorter steps until you are certain the pace has been eradicated. Even if he was not pacey to begin with, this exercise can cause his back to stiffen; a stepping pace or hard pace can result from tight back muscles. Alternate shorter steps with longer steps, incorporating frequent circles and other bending exercises along with free work on a slack rein to keep your horse relaxed and willing. Ask for only a few shorter steps at a time, and then let your horse relax and stretch.

- Sitting straight in the base position with light contact on the reins, use one strong squeeze/release with your calves to ask your horse to move forward in an energetic flat walk.
- Adjust your pelvis so that you are sitting in the heavy seat. Push down with your back to press your seat into the saddle.
- Raise your hands an inch or two above the base position. As your horse moves along in the flat walk, begin to catch his forward energy with light, vibrating squeeze/releases from your fingers on the reins. Don't pull back or use stronger steady contact, but finger the reins to ask your horse to bring his forehead toward the vertical and check his speed.
- As you squeeze/release with the reins, very slightly tighten your inner thighs. Do not squeeze hard or try to grip with your upper legs; make your thigh muscles firm against the saddle, with a gentle lifting motion. This will resist the forward flow of energy in his back and channel it slightly upward.
- Your horse will begin to take slightly shorter steps. Ride him for a few steps, then praise him and reward him by breathing out and returning to the ordinary flat walk on a slack rein. Repeat, alternating short with more ordinary steps in the flat walk.

Practice this exercise until you can reduce your horse's stride length in the flat walk to about half what it is in his ordinary speed of the gait. You can then go on to try slightly reducing his stride length in his intermediate gait, using the same aids.

Staying in Gait Down Small Hills

If you ride in the hills, you have probably noticed that your horse seems to lose his gait as soon as the trail takes the slightest downhill slant. This happens because going downhill encourages a hollow body position even in horses that do not carry themselves that way on flat ground. To retain his gait downhill, a horse needs even more help to prevent his back position from becoming hollow than he does on the flat. Once your horse has developed the strength to use his back and body in semi-collection on flat ground, you can begin to ask him to avoid the pace at speeds faster than an ordinary walk on slight downhill slants. When you come to a slight downhill grade during a ride, ask your horse to semi-collect, using upper leg cues to help him hold his body together, and add frequent, very light squeeze/release reminders from the reins to bring his forehead toward vertical. Do not try to hold his nose in as he goes downhill; squeeze/release on the reins to ask him to balance a little to the rear, semi-collect his body, and avoid the pace.

An oblong arena, graded on a slant, can be a useful teaching tool for this work in semi-collection. When you can keep your horse in the same gait all the way around the arena, semi-collecting him for the downhill slants and allowing him to work in a more neutral body position on the flat stretches, you can be sure that he is set in his gait. Practice first in the flat walk/slow paso llano. When your horse is able to maintain that gait, go on to a slow fox trot or running walk/paso llano.

Continue to avoid riding down **steep** hills in gait, however, because this will put a lot of unnecessary stress on your horse's legs. Practice staying in gait on slight grades of no more than five degrees and continue to do an ordinary walk on steeper inclines. When your horse can stay in his gait on these slopes, you can try riding down slightly steeper hills in gait, but be ready to return to the flat walk at the first hint of a pace. When you do ride down steep hills, use the aids for semi-collection to help your horse maintain his balance toward the rear in an ordinary walk. He will be less likely to trip or rush if he goes down steeper hills with his balance shifted slightly toward his hindquarters.

Increasing Stride Length

Your horse's basic easy gait may be smooth and a little faster than his flat walk, but it might not be very long-strided. Now that he has learned to semi-collect, you can teach him to semi-extend his gait with longer strides as well. The driving force for a longer step comes from the same back and haunch muscles that combine to produce the shorter, lighter step in semi-collection. Think of your horse's back as a kind of spring: Coils get tighter as he semi-collects, then expand with energy as he goes into an extended gait.

To develop a longer stride, start first in the flat walk on level ground. You can practice this exercise in a snaffle bit, a mild curb, or bitless headgear, although it will be most effective in a snaffle.

- Sitting straight and still in the saddle, with your hands in the base position, squeeze/release with your calves to move your horse forward in a flat walk, maintaining light contact with the bit.
- Ask the horse to semi-collect, shortening his steps as much as he is able while still moving in the flat walk. Keep your upper thighs firmly against his sides to maintain him in the shortened flat walk, with light squeeze/release vibrations from your hands to remind him to keep his steps shorter but slightly elevated.
- Shift your pelvis to the light, allowing seat and simultaneously relax your fingers on the reins, release all pressure from your upper thighs, and squeeze strongly with your calves to ask your horse to move forward with energy. Allow his head and neck to reach forward. He will move ahead with energy and take a few longer steps. Praise and reward him, return to a base flat walk, then repeat the entire exercise. If your horse has trouble increasing his stride length with these cues, try shifting your pelvis into the heavier, pushing seat to encourage him to move forward with more energy. Some horses respond better to this position than to the lighter seat. Because it can be hard on your horse's back, return to the base position as soon as possible if you use the pushing seat.

Over time, your horse will develop the strength to respond with sustained, longer strides in the flat walk to your change of seat, the relaxation of your fingers on the reins, and a strong push with your calves. When he has learned to reach farther in the flat walk, go on to teach him the same technique in his easy gait.

In addition to using these techniques for increasing his stride on level ground, you can also increase his ability to take longer steps and move in a faster version of his gait by practicing on a slight downhill grade **after** he has completely conquered any tendency to pace. Ride him in a moderate speed in his easy gait and, as you come to a small grade, ask him to speed up with a strong squeeze/release from your calves at the same time that you shift your pelvis into the heavy or pushing seat, while maintaining even contact with the bit with low hands, bringing his forehead slightly toward the vertical. He will take longer, faster steps in his gait as he goes down the incline. Be ready to slow him back down to a more moderate speed the instant before he starts to pace or otherwise break gait. With some practice, the slight downhill grade you once avoided because it always caused your horse to pace can become a useful tool in teaching him to reach out and work with long steps in his gait.

The Value of the Trot

Although gaited horses are not generally encouraged to trot, that gait can be a valuable part of the training program to enhance the easy gaits. If your horse is working well in his gait and you see no need to try to change his stride length or back use, don't bother with the trot. If he was originally pacey and continues to be tight and choppy in his gait, however, don't be afraid to use the trot to stretch and condition his back, shoulder, and chest muscles. Trot work won't ruin his easy gait as long as you continue to spend most of your time working in the gait you prefer and you use clear aids to tell your horse which gait you want.

Asking for the Trot

Review asking your horse for the trot on the longe line, using poles or cavalletti if necessary to help him

do the gait, then see whether he will trot under saddle. He may not. Don't press the matter if he will not do the gait! You probably didn't buy an easy-gaited horse to ride him in a trot, and longe-line work in a trot is plenty for most horses. The trot can be an effective addition to his overall physical fitness program, but it is not mandatory for performance of his easy gait. If he won't trot, don't worry about it.

To find your horse's trot under saddle, first sit in a forward seat, weight off the saddle, with your hands yielding the reins down and forward. This seat and hand position will allow his back to rise and swing a little more than it does when you are seated in the saddle and will be so different from the position you use to ride his easy gait that he will not be confused by it. Encourage the gait either by staying in the two-point position or posting, but don't try to sit the gait unless your horse is a very strong trotter to begin with. Trot him on flat ground or up a slight incline for a short distance, then settle back down in the saddle and return him to his easy gait by sitting straight and bringing your hands back to the base position. Alternate the two gaits and positions, encouraging him to reach forward as he moves into the trot. With practice, he will begin to carry the longer, more elastic strides of the trot with him when he returns to his easy gait. He won't forget how to do his easy gait if you trot him occasionally to help him stretch his muscles, and you may find you enjoy a chance to post once in a while.

Increasing Flexibility

As you are teaching your horse the beginnings of semi-collection and to increase his stride length, you can also help him develop more lateral flexibility. This will enhance his ability to take longer steps by strengthening his back and will also prepare him for later work in the canter. While the following exercises are frequently taught in a trot, for your gaited horse they will work best in an ordinary walk and eventually in a flat walk or slow paso llano. Do not try these exercises in a running walk, fast fox trot, or in any of the racking gaits. The body use and support of those gaits will not allow your horse to flex correctly in the back and loin, and they could cause him more harm than good.

The Lateral Flexions

These exercises expand the flexibility your horse began to develop with the rotation exercises. If your horse reverts to a pace in a large circle or around the ends of your arena, practice in the haunches-in and its companion exercise, the shoulder-in, will help him develop the muscular strength he needs to carry him-self through a curve while maintaining first a flat walk, and then his easy gait. If you practice these exercises often, they will also help your horse develop equally on both sides of his body, making it easier for him to go straight down the trail in his gait. Teach your horse the lateral flexions in a snaffle bit or bitless headgear. Do not try to teach a horse to bend through his body in a curb or gag bit of any kind.

Beginning Haunches-in

This exercise builds on the aids your horse learned for the turn on the forehand. In addition to increasing his ability to bend and respond to your aids, the haunches-in is also very useful preparation for later work at the canter.

In a correct haunches-in, a horse travels with his head, neck, and shoulders parallel to the rail and his hindquarters shifted over one half step, so that the outside hind hoof steps into the track of the inside front hoof. To teach this exercise to your horse, first ride a small circle at the walk in one corner of your arena. Then, as you are coming out of the circle with his shoulders and neck parallel to the rail, maintain the bend in your horse's body, but ask him to travel straight, keeping his neck and shoulders parallel to the rail while his hindquarters yield over to the side.

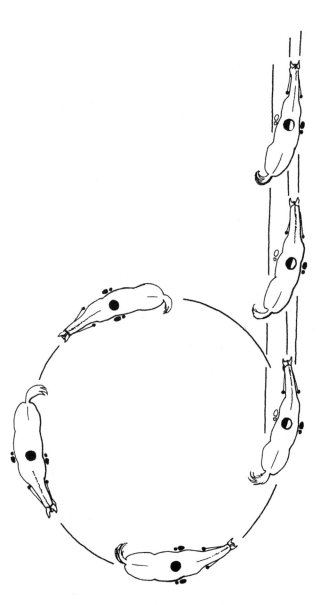

Riding a haunches-in to the left from a small circle. This exercise builds your horse's flexibility and prepares him for later canter work. After the small circle is complete, press straight into your horse's side with your right leg, behind the girth, and shift your weight to the left side of your seat.

• Ride a 10-meter-diameter (approximately 40-foot) circle in an ordinary walk, left leg pressing lightly at the girth to keep the circle from becoming too small, right leg pressing lightly behind the girth to keep the horse bent on the circle, left hand maintaining contact and keeping the horse bent on the circle, right hand supporting the left with light contact, preventing the horse from bending his neck too far in the curve.

• As you reach the point in the circle where your horse's head, neck, and shoulders are parallel with the rail, adjust your seat so that you are carrying more weight on your left seat-bone. Press with your right leg, pushing strongly with your calf just behind the girth to keep the horse's hindquarters yielded over one step from the track of the front hooves.

• Adjust your left rein with very light contact to maintain the bend in his neck that he had on the circle while increasing contact slightly on the right rein to keep him from continuing on in a circle off the rail.

• Press lightly with your left calf at the girth to keep the horse moving forward.

• Ride a couple of steps with your horse's haunches moved over from the rail, then finish the exercise by returning to a small 10-meter circle. Praise your horse, reverse directions and aids, and repeat on the other side.

Gradually increase the number of steps your horse takes in the haunches-in until he is able to do the exercise along the entire short side of your arena. Do not try to go through the corners in this exercise yet. Eventually your horse may be able to maintain the bend through the corners, but that takes a lot of flexibility and strength, and he won't be ready for that step for some time.

Don't perform this exercise with your horse's body in a straight line, his nose over the fence while he steps sideways with both front and back legs. The point of the exercise is the curve in the horse's back as he does it; without that curve there is no stretching or conditioning of the back muscles. Done correctly, with a bend in his body, the haunches-in works to supple your horse's loin and hindquarters and improve the strength of his hind legs. Done incorrectly, all it accomplishes is moving his hindquarters away from pressure.

You can practice the haunches-in on the trail as well as in an arena. All you need is a reference point (for example, the rail) and relatively level, even footing.

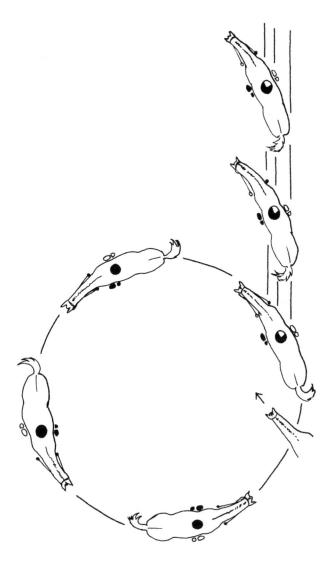

The shoulder-in will help your horse develop flexibility in his shoulders and power in his hindquarters. Be sure to ride it with your horse bent equally through his body, not just bending his neck to the inside while his back stays parallel to the rail.

Shoulder-in (Shoulder-fore)

Once your horse has begun working good 10-meter circles in the ordinary walk and learned the beginning haunches-in, you can teach him the shoulder-in, or, at the beginning stage, the shoulder-fore. This is the only exercise you will practice in which your horse does not look directly in the direction he is going. The exercise stretches the shoulder and chest muscles and supples the back, neck, and hindquarters, as well as beginning to help the horse shift his weight toward the hindquarters. It can be a very good warm-up exercise for a pacey horse because it stretches stiff muscles. Sometimes a few minutes at a shoulder-fore will be enough to help a stiff horse avoid the pace for his whole lesson. Although it is traditionally taught in the trot, your horse will get plenty of benefit from this exercise in the ordinary walk and eventually the flat walk.

At a beginning stage, the exercise is a shoulder-fore, with minimal bend in your horse's body. His tracks will show that his front hooves are moved off the rail a little bit, but there will be four distinct tracks from each hoof on the ground. As a horse develops more flexibility, he will eventually be able to bend a little more into a true shoulder-in, and his right hind track will fall on his left front track. While that more difficult exercise is extremely useful for horses that work in collection and can be very beneficial in loosening the shoulders and chest to produce longer reach in the front legs, it takes time for a horse to develop the strength to maintain that much bend through his body correctly. There is no point in attempting that version of the exercise until your horse is able to work in semi-collection with light contact in gait in a 10-meter (approximately 40-foot) circle.

• Sitting in the base position, with light contact on the bit in an ordinary walk, ride a 10-meter circle to the left in a corner of your arena. Ride the circle with your usual aids: left hand slightly lowered with enough contact so that you can see the corner of your horse's left eye, right hand supporting by maintaining contact, left leg pressed lightly to the horse's side at the girth, right leg pressing slightly behind the girth.

• As you come out of the circle with your horse's haunches parallel to the rail, adjust your aids so that your left leg from thigh to calf presses strongly through your horse's body at an angle from the girth toward his right shoulder. Shift your weight very slightly onto your left seat bone, lightening the horse's right shoulder as you change your leg pressure, freeing the horse's back so that he moves forward while bent to the left side.

• Simultaneously, increase contact with your left rein slightly, and bend your horse's neck just enough to see his entire left eye. Convert your right rein from the supporting position you used in the circle to an indirect rein. Maintaining contact with his mouth, press the right rein against his neck just in front of the withers to signal him to move his shoulders over. Keep your right calf softly against your horse's side, just behind the girth, to prevent him from moving his haunches too far toward the rail.

• Maintain your shoulders parallel to your horse's shoulders and your hips parallel to his hips, twisting very slightly at your waist as he does this exercise.

• The horse should move forward with a slight curve in his body, his hindquarters parallel to the rail, and his shoulders and neck curved away to the inside, away from the rail. He gently bends his body around your left leg as he moves forward. Practice a few steps of the shoulder-fore and then finish by returning to the 10-meter circle. Praise your horse, reverse directions, and practice the exercise in the other direction.

After several months of practice with just a slight bend in his body in the shoulder-fore, go on to teach him the true shoulder-in. Use the same aids that produce the shoulder-fore, but ask him to bend a little more in his neck and body while bringing his shoulders farther away from the rail, until he is stepping in his right front track with his left hind hoof. Use the indirect, right bearing rein more strongly than the direct left rein to move his shoulders away from the rail, creating an even arc from his poll to tail. Be careful to avoid doing a "neck-in," with a stronger bend in his neck than in his body. A "neck-in" will do nothing to help supple your horse's body, and is a major fault in the exercise.

Practice a little in each of these lateral exercises every time you ride your horse. Try combining them, moving from haunches-in to shoulder-in on one side, making a small circle, and then practicing the exercises on the other side. Don't drill in these exercises! A few steps here and there of the haunches-in and shoulder-in will help your horse become more flexible without making him sour. If you do nothing but these exercises for an entire session, your horse will most likely detest working in them, will become stiff and resistant, and will not gain one bit of flexibility from them. Instead of concentrating on flexions alone, string them together with the things he already knows, such as large circles, serpentines, and straight lines. These exercises don't have to be repetitive work; they can be fun for both you and your horse. Do some smaller circles and then larger ones, as your horse becomes more flexible. Mix things up. Practice out on the trail in between periods of moving along with a long-strided, relaxed gait, just to see whether your horse is paying attention to you.

Sidepass

Although it doesn't have the suppling value of the lateral flexions, the sidepass, or side step, can be very useful for trail horses and for developing responsiveness to leg and rein aids. If you taught your horse to do a side step from the ground, he should be able to learn it easily from the saddle.

By now your horse should be familiar with the turns on the forehand and haunches from the saddle and should have practiced them enough to move easily away from your leg pressure. Practice a few quarter turns both on the forehand and the haunches to remind him of the aids for these maneuvers. This refresher will make it easier for him to learn the side step, or sidepass. Again, you can teach this exercise in a snaffle bit or bitless headgear, but it is better not to try it in a curb bit unless your horse absolutely will not respond to any other bit.

While you can teach your horse to side step by heading him into a wall or fence so he can't go forward and then applying the aids to move him to the side, this really is not necessary. If your horse is responsive to your leg and rein aids and understands the turn on the forehand and turn on the haunches, you will not need a wall to force him to step to the side.

- Sitting in the balanced, base position, ride your horse from a walk into a halt. Maintain light contact with his mouth after the halt. Do not allow the reins to go completely slack. Slightly weight your right seat bone, but continue to sit straight and balanced.
- Press directly into the horse's side with your left leg, just behind the girth, to move his haunches over one step, while simultaneously pressing with the left bearing rein against his neck just in front of the withers, to reinforce the leg aid. Open your right rein, moving your hand slightly to the side from the base position. This will move his shoulders over one step.

- If necessary, prevent him from moving forward with slightly increased contact from your right rein. Praise him, and walk forward a couple of steps. Halt. Repeat in the other direction.

Gradually add steps to the side as your horse learns to perform the exercise, until he will go five or six steps easily to the right or left.

At first your horse's response will be a little awkward. Remember that the point of this exercise is not only to move him to the side but also to refine his response to your leg and rein aids. You could easily force him to move to the side with a visual cue or a few taps from a whip, but that would not necessarily teach him much about responding to your aids or improving his balance under saddle. Don't become rushed or impatient while you teach this exercise; take it slow and easy to help your horse understand what you want.

Once your horse is working the side step easily, you can combine it with the rein back to form a square. That will give you a good idea of how responsive your horse has become to your seat, leg, and rein aids, and can serve as a little test of your progress. To ride a square, first ride your horse straight into a halt, then ask him to side step three steps to the right, back three steps, side step three steps to the left, then go forward three steps back to the starting point. At first he will probably be uneven and heavy on your hands as he works the square, but with time and practice he should move into the pattern smoothly.

Leg-Yield and Half-Pass

Because the horse moves in the same general way for both of them, these two exercises are sometimes confused with one another. In the leg-yield, the horse moves forward and to the side while maintaining a straight body or a slight bend away from the direction of travel. Because it doesn't require much lateral flexibility, the leg-yield is fairly easy for a horse to learn. It can be very useful on the trail if you want to get out of the way of someone else's fractious horse while still moving forward. In a half-pass, the horse moves forward and to the side while bending his body in the direction in which he is traveling. It requires a level of lateral flexibility and strength in the hindquarters that

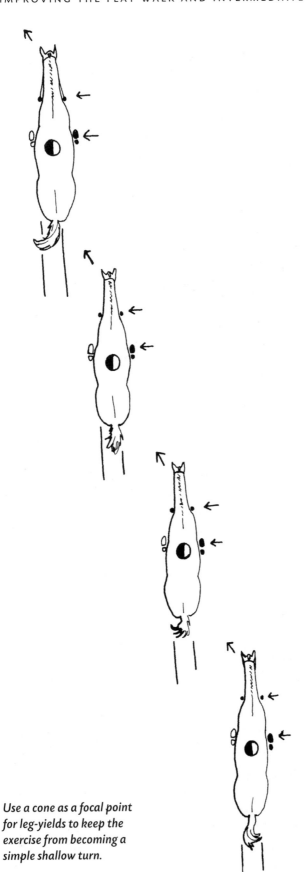

Use a cone as a focal point for leg-yields to keep the exercise from becoming a simple shallow turn.

may take several years of work for many gaited horses to develop. It is a good exercise for building a horse's body and ability to work in true collection, but it is not really necessary for pleasure riding.

Although it does not work as well to supple and develop a horse's body as the half-pass, the leg-yield can help loosen stiff shoulders and hindquarters a little because the horse crosses his legs as he performs it. To practice good leg-yields, it helps to have a visual point to aim toward. A few highway cones or rocks work for marking points in an arena.

You can also practice this exercise out on a wide trail, using brush or trees as visual targets.

Sitting in the base position, ride in an ordinary walk around your arena, and then turn down the center line.

- Ride in a walk, about 10 feet away from the rail of your arena.
- Slightly shift your weight onto the *right* seat bone, and simultaneously press with your *left* calf, as it hangs at the girth, angling the pressure toward your horse's right shoulder.
- Press your *left* rein lightly against your horse's neck, just in front of the withers, to ask him to move over toward the right.
- Squeeze/release lightly with your right leg, just behind the girth, to keep the horse moving forward.
- Keep just enough contact on your right rein to support the action of the left, maintaining a straight head and neck carriage. Do not try to turn his head to the right in the direction of the yield and do not allow him to go forward with his head and neck cocked toward the left. He must maintain a straight body for this exercise to be correct; otherwise he will execute a stiff, cramped sideways movement, not a fluid yield from the pressure of your aids.
- When you reach the marker you set at the rail, about 10 feet from the corner of your arena, change your aids. Send your horse straight forward: Relax your seat into the base position, return your hands to the base position with even, light contact on the reins, press lightly with the left leg against the horse's side where

it hangs at the girth, and press strongly with your right leg at the girth. Both leg and seat aids work to encourage the horse to move straight forward.

This exercise is not as complicated as it sounds. It takes some practice and coordination, but with time you should have no trouble doing a leg-yield for several yards in each direction in an ordinary walk. While the exercise will not help your horse develop much lateral flexibility, it will help him develop better responsiveness to your aids and will make him much more pleasant to ride on the trail. A quick leg-yield is a welcome tool out on the trail when you need to move away from an oncoming mountain bike or ATV or to avoid a hole in the ground.

The half-pass is a bit more complicated to teach, but you may want to try it as an additional suppling exercise. Don't try to do this exercise from a leg-yield; start it from a shoulder-in to create the bend in the horse's body that is the most valuable part of the exercise.

- Ride a 10-meter circle in an ordinary walk, coming out at the rail in a shoulder-in position to the left.
- Shift your weight onto the left side of your seat while increasing pressure from your right leg, behind the girth, to urge your horse to the left, away from the rail. Maintain light contact with your left leg, just in front of the girth, to preserve the curve in his body.
- Slightly increase contact with the left rein, to help create a left curve in the horse's neck. Bend his neck just enough for you to see his left eye. Maintain light contact with the right rein, using it as an indirect rein, just in front of the withers, to encourage the horse to move to the left and to limit his neck from bending too far.
- Ride forward and to the side for a few steps, then return to a 10-meter circle.
- Praise your horse, reverse directions, reverse aids, and repeat.

You can practice this exercise occasionally, at an ordinary walk, to see how well your horse is learning to respond to your aids and to improve his flexibility. It is not necessary for trail or pleasure riding, but it can be an interesting challenge if you enjoy doing arena exercises.

Working in Contained Gaits

If your horse prefers one of the racking gaits or a stepping pace, he will not be able to do that gait in true semi-collection, but he will be able to change the degree of containment in his body. (See chapter 2 for an illustration of containment.) He will be able to take shorter or longer strides by adjusting the tension in his ligament cable system. He can work in a very short body frame or a longer one while still maintaining his gait. He can also learn to negotiate very small circles and turns in his gait, while responding to your seat, leg, and rein aids.

Developing the Contained Gaits

A horse achieves the slower, shorter-stepping paso corto, "show walk," or slow tolt by shifting his balance a little toward the rear while maintaining and sometimes increasing the essential tension at the base of his neck and tightening the muscles over his loin. This position provides him with more stability on the trail and a different balance under the rider than he has in the faster, less-contained version of his gait.

Once your horse has started working consistently in a moderate speed at his gait, develop this shorter frame by teaching him to respond to seat, leg, and rein aids that ask him for a higher, tighter neck position and increased tension in his back muscles. You can work on all of these gaits in a mild curb bit or a noseband jaquima. Sidepulls or California bosals do not work effectively for these exercises, and the snaffle bit, although it can work for some horses, is not designed to produce the head and neck position that accompanies containment.

- Ride your horse forward in an ordinary walk, then ask him to move into his easy gait, sitting in the base position, hands at waist height.
- Begin to ask your horse to shorten his step by tightening your lower back muscles, tilting your pelvis into the heavy seat.

• At the same time, increase your contact on the reins to that of a heavy plum, bringing your horse's nose in toward vertical, while angling the pressure of your contact slightly upward. Do not let your hands freeze on the reins; take and release contact with small vibrations of your fingers on the reins, never using a steady pull. Persuade, don't force, your horse to raise his head and neck and bring his forehead in toward vertical.

• Your horse may try to slow down to a walk. Prevent this with light squeeze/releases with your calves to keep him moving forward with energy.

• Ask for a few short steps in his gait, praise him for them, then relax your aids and let him move out with more speed on a looser rein. Practice again, this time increasing the number of steps he takes in the shortened form of his gait. Don't overdo this. Build gradually, a few steps at a time, until he can go halfway around your arena in the shortened gait without any signs of resentment for the contained position.

When practicing containment, you will notice immediately whether your horse has been carrying his body straight. The tightened frame will accentuate any crookedness in his back. A crooked horse will often try to move with his hindquarters off to one side as he develops the shortened gait. Check again to make sure your saddle fits him and that you are riding straight and centered on his back. Make sure that his bit fits him correctly and that you are not inadvertently tightening one rein more than the other.

To offset this crookedness, return to the ordinary walk, practice some of the lateral flexions in that gait to stretch his muscles on the stiff side, and work some circles and spirals in the walk in both directions. Increase his exercise program in the flexions and circles in the ordinary walk, and then try shortening his gait again.

Practice riding up hills in a shorter-strided ordinary walk to build more strength in his back. When his body is stronger, he should be able to move in a fairly straight direction with increased containment in his body.

Stride and Speed

In addition to teaching your horse to achieve a shorter, more contained gait, you may also want to increase his stride and speed in his racking gait. Because a fast rack is a lot of fun to ride and can really cover ground, it is nice to be able to use it on the trail when there is a long stretch of good footing. Just remember not to overdo this gait because it can be very stressful to your horse. It may be easier to try this for the first time on a slight downhill grade on firm footing.

• Start out in a moderate speed of your horse's gait, rather than the tightly contained, shortened version of it. Ride sitting straight in the saddle, hands at waist height, with light, even contact on the reins.

• Tilt your pelvis into the heavy position and press down with your back muscles into the saddle. Your lower back should feel about the way it does when you pump forward on a swing. This action with your seat will tighten your horse's back muscles over his loin and urge him forward.

• Simultaneously squeeze/release strongly with your calves while gradually reducing contact on the reins until you have about the weight of a strawberry instead of the base plum-feel in your fingers. Maintain support for his head and neck: Don't allow your reins to go totally slack, but relax your fingers just a little on the reins to encourage him to move forward with more speed.

• Your horse should drive forward with his legs, taking longer steps and increasing his speed. Praise and reward him, then continue for a short distance driving with your back as he increases his stride length. Return to the base position to ask him to slow to a more moderate speed of his gait.

Practice increasing and decreasing stride length each time you ride. Be patient. Don't expect top speed and extension in the first week or month or even two months. Over time, your horse will develop more strength and endurance in his gait and be able to sustain the faster, longer-strided gait.

Develop the Ability to Work at Several Speeds in Each Gait

IN PERUVIAN HORSES, the ability to perform a gait at a variety of speeds is called "thread." A horse is said to have a wide thread if he can perform the same gait at a slow walking speed or at the speed of a moderate gallop, and a narrow thread if he can do the gait only at one speed. Your horse is probably capable of a variety of speeds and styles in his easy gait that you have never explored. If you practiced "playing the scales" in the ordinary walk to reduce and increase your horse's speed and step length in that gait and have worked a little to teach him semi-collection or containment and longer stride, you can apply the same techniques to discover the other versions of his easy gait.

As you explore this, be careful not to push him up into a different gait or slow him down into a walk. Be ready to adjust your seat and hands if he starts to break gait. At speed, the instant you feel his rhythm in his easy gait begin to change, use a light squeeze/release on the reins to slow him while adjusting your seat to shift your weight into the heavy seat while breathing out to relax your lower back. If he starts to slow into a walk, instantly release contact on your reins and tilt your pelvis to the "allowing" position while giving a light squeeze/release with your calves to keep his energy level up. Return to his ordinary speed in gait and the base position for your seat, then start over to ask for more or less speed.

Ask for only tiny changes in speed over several weeks of lessons and you will be surprised at what your horse can give you. Of course, not all horses have the same ability in gait. Some will excel at faster speeds; some will be better at semi-collection or containment. Experiment with your horse to see what he can do, but don't be disappointed if he does not have a very wide thread. As long as he will do a comfortable slow, moderate, and faster version of his gait, he has plenty of thread for trail and pleasure riding.

Riding through Curves and Circles in Gait

Once your horse has developed more lateral flexibility and strength through work in the haunches-in and shoulder-in, as well as through practicing circles, spirals, and serpentines of all sizes in the ordinary walk, he should be able to work through a curve or on a large circle first in a flat walk and then in his easy gait. The best way to help him stay in gear while negotiating a bend is to first ask him to semi-collect or contain his gait, bringing his balance closer toward his hindquarters, then ride through the curve while supporting his head and neck with light, consistent contact.

Curves and Circles in Semi-Collection

To help a horse maintain a fox trot or running walk through a curve and later a circle, start by practicing these exercises in the flat walk. You can work in a snaffle bit or bitless headgear, although the snaffle will be more effective in asking the horse both to semi-collect and to bend through his body. Don't use a curb bit for this exercise, because the action of a curb does not help a horse bend laterally.

- Sit straight and balanced with even, light contact on the bit in an energetic flat walk.
- As you approach the bend for the curve or start on the circle, ask your horse to semi-collect his gait. Use light squeeze/releases on the reins, tilt your pelvis into the heavy seat, slow his speed just a fraction, and shorten his stride so that his balance is brought toward his hindquarters just a little.
- Ride into the curve or circle using the same aids you used in the ordinary walk: Lower your left hand to ask for the bend in his neck, support the left hand with consistent contact from the right, press gently into his side with your left calf, and maintain pressure behind the girth with your right calf.
- Ride your horse through the curve or circle, keeping his body semi-collected as he bends.

He should be flexible enough by now to avoid stiffening into the pace position with your seat, leg, and rein aids to help him bend while semi-collected. If he reverts to a pace as he makes the curve or circle, slow down to an ordinary walk, ride through the curve or circle again, and practice semi-collection on straight lines until he begins to lift his back and the root of his neck a bit in response to your alternating leg and rein aids. Then try again, following a slightly more gradual curve or a larger circle. Don't expect to do a small 10-meter circle in a running walk or fox trot, but do try larger 15-meter and 20-meter circles in those gaits once your horse can work the smaller ones in the flat walk.

As with all the flexibility exercises, practice will develop muscle tone and increase your horse's ability to bend his body and maintain his gait. Don't drill him constantly in semi-collected curves or circles; practice two or three in each direction and then go on to something else. For most trail riding, it doesn't matter whether your horse can take a curve in gait. The ability to use his body effectively, however (which results from practice in curves and circles in gait), will make him less likely to break into an unwanted stepping pace or pace on the trail.

Curves and Circles in Containment

In the faster gaits of the rack family, horses do not bend through their bodies well on tight curves or circles. The tension in their backs and loins that accompanies those gaits makes it impossible for them to bend the same way horses do in the other easy gaits. They can, however, work curves and tight circles in slow, contained versions of their gait.

Horses do not bend through curves in a continuous arc in the slower gaits in the rack family. Instead, they make a tighter and sharper turn, keeping their bodies straight between withers and tail, but bending in the neck. While turning, it can be difficult to maintain the essential tension at the root of the neck that allows your horse to use these gaits. Sometimes horses that do the racking gaits will lower their heads and necks and fall into a fox trot/trocha or a pace when they are asked to negotiate curves or small circles. You can help your horse overcome this tendency by reminding him to tighten the root of his neck and to maintain a relatively high neck carriage, bending his neck but not his entire body to the side as he turns.

- As you start into a circle or curve on your horse, increase his containment by maintaining your hands at waist height.
- Very slightly increase your contact with his mouth or nose with light pressure on the reins while tightening your upper thigh muscles against the saddle and tilting your pelvis into the heavy seat.
- Keeping his head and neck high, ask him to negotiate a circle to the right. Slightly increase contact with your right rein, increase weight on your right seat bone, and press into the girth with your right leg from thigh to calf, maintaining light pressure just behind the girth with your left calf.
- Start with a wide curve or larger circle. As he becomes able to negotiate the gradual turn in gait, make smaller and smaller turns and, eventually, circles. Praise and reward your horse, then go on to work in a straight line to prevent him from becoming sour from too many tight turns in gait.

If you ride only for pleasure or on the trail, you may never need to ask your horse to negotiate a tight curve or circle in one of the slower racking gaits. If you have worked a little on this skill, however, he will be more responsive and easier to keep in gait on any type of trail.

Using Circles to Improve the Racking Gaits

Horses that do the slower racking gaits, in particular the paso corto and show walk, sometimes lose form in their gait as they slow down. They may tend toward a trocha or fox trot or, occasionally, toward a more lateral stepping pace. A very useful technique for tightening the gait and keeping timing correct is to work these horses in tight circles and figure eights in their gait. By asking a horse to keep a bend in his neck on a circle, while maintaining a relatively high head, the essential tension at the root of his neck can be strengthened, and his gait will be strengthened.

Start the exercise by riding at a slow corto or show walk in a relatively large circle, about 15 meters in diameter, using the aids mentioned above. Then, tighten the circle, until he is working at about a 10-meter diameter. Keep his head and neck high, with contact even on both reins, *not* asking him to curve his neck into the turn. Keep his head and neck straight to begin this smaller circle. Gradually ask for a slight bend in his neck so that you can see his entire inside eye. Make the circle smaller, until he is working at about a 9-meter diameter.

Be sure to keep his head and neck elevated by maintaining consistent contact with his nose or mouth, and keep him moving with some energy with light squeeze/releases from your lower legs. This exercise will not work if you allow him to lose forward momentum or lower his head.

When he works well at the 9-meter diameter, make the circle smaller, until he is going around at about a 7-meter diameter. Continue decreasing the size of the circle, until he is working at a 2 to 3-meter diameter, then spiral back out again.

Practice spiraling in and out of these circles in the corto or show walk in both directions, then combine them into figure eights. At the first sign of a trocha, fox trot, or stepping pace, immediately return to a larger circle and start again. Practice these exercises sparingly, maybe once or twice a week at most, to prevent the horse from souring on them. After a couple of months of occasionally practicing these exercises, you should see an improvement in the consistency of your horse's gait at slower speeds.

The Results

After this work teaching your horse to extend and semi-collect or contain his gaits and helping him improve his flexibility and responsiveness to leg and rein aids, he will start to bloom. His neck and back will appear more muscular and full, especially along the topline of his neck and on either side of his spine. His hindquarters will fill out and develop definition along the buttocks. His shoulders and chest should begin to fill out, as well. His abdominal muscles may become more defined if he has been working in semi-collection, and his gaskins and forearms may also develop more muscle tone.

Along with these physical changes, and as a direct result of them, his gait will become more consistent. He should be able to stay in gear through most changes in terrain, and the hills you may have dreaded because they once brought out a pace or a hard trot will no longer present a challenge. As his gait improves due to the work in semi-collection or containment, his maneuverability and surefootedness on the trail will also increase.

With this foundation of physical and mental development, your horse is finally ready to canter. He is also a candidate for some finishing touches that will make him even more enjoyable to ride on the trail or in an arena. He is almost to that magical point where his gait and his ease of handling make him an ideal pleasure horse.

CHAPTER ELEVEN

The Canter

All good riders know, from experience, that a horse's canter
is dependent on his training before he starts the gait.
— GUSTAVE LE BON (1841–1931)

There is a persistent myth that the canter is not natural to any of the gaited breeds and that training a gaited horse to canter will ruin his easy gaits. Although it is true that a few gaited horses do not seem to be able to canter no matter how much effort goes into training them for that gait, many gaited horses can canter easily and naturally while maintaining the ability to perform beautifully in their easy gaits. Some gaited horses, especially those that prefer the more lateral gaits, may find the canter difficult, but most of them can be trained to do it.

Developing the Canter

Your easy-gaited pleasure horse may be a natural at the canter, or he may be one of those horses that can't do the gait either under saddle or free in a pasture. If he naturally prefers to fox trot or work in a square running walk, it is likely that he will canter easily or need just a little help developing the coordination and strength to perform the gait. If his preferred gait is a rack or stepping pace, unless your horse shows no inclination to canter or gallop at liberty, he can be helped to develop the gait in addition to his intermediate gait through exercises to improve his coordination, strength, balance, and responsiveness to your aids. Far from ruining his easy gait, becoming fit enough for canter work may improve the way he travels in all his gaits.

You will soon discover whether your horse has difficulty with the canter, and you can decide for yourself whether it is worthwhile to ask him to develop it. If you ride for pleasure, you may not want to bother teaching him to canter because you can enjoy riding his smooth easy gait at canter speed, but don't be intimidated by the idea of helping your horse develop the gait. It is not a particularly complicated process for most horses.

What Is the Canter?

The canter is a three-beat gait done at a moderate speed, no faster than 10 miles per hour. The footfall sequence of the canter on a left lead is as follows. The right hind hoof sets down: the first beat of the gait. The left hind hoof and the right front hoof (the diagonal front) set down simultaneously: the second beat of the gait. The left front hoof sets down: the third beat of the gait. Then all four hooves clear the ground for a split second. The lead of the canter is determined by which front hoof sets down last in the sequence. If a horse "canters" with any variation of this footfall pattern or timing, he is not doing a true canter.

A good pleasure canter is not defined by slow speed, although it should not be very fast, or by high action in the front, although it should not be done

with heavy, low steps as the horse struggles along with his weight over his shoulders. For trail riding, you should try to develop a semi-collected gait, with the horse moving forward easily, his back muscles elastic, and his hindquarters lowering in proportion to the rise of his forequarters. He should have no stiffness or hitching in his hind legs and should work in a true three-beat gait, retaining a moment of suspension in the gait when all four hooves are free of the ground. This allows him to round his back and concentrate his energy so that he can thrust himself forward and upward efficiently with his non-leading hind leg in the first phase of the gait. The concentration of energy produces a gait that is rhythmic, fluid, and graceful to watch, as well as a pleasure to ride.

Problems in the Canter

To canter smoothly, a horse needs a strong back, strong hindquarters, well-developed stifles, and elasticity in his body. His legs must work together in a coordinated way to produce the specific and complex footfall of the gait. His back must round slightly to allow him to push off with his outside hind leg, hindquarters tucked under his body, flexed downward at the lumbosacral junction. If his back is stiff and his coordination and timing are off as he sets down his hooves, he may do a faulty variation of the canter. If he is not very strong and balanced to begin with, he may be so stiff and uncoordinated with a rider that he does a faulty canter under saddle, even though at liberty he canters correctly. There are several potential problems for gaited horses in the canter.

The Disunited Canter

A horse "goes disunited" when his hindquarters completely lose coordination with the front and he leads with one leg in front and the diagonal one in back. This creates a rough, awkward motion and can cause a horse to fall, particularly if he catches a front heel with a hind hoof. A disunited canter is almost always caused by lack of condition in the back muscles and weak thrust from the hindquarters. It doesn't happen very often in horses that are at liberty, but it can happen all too easily if the weight of a rider interferes with a horse's balance.

Another extremely rough type of disunited canter occurs when both hind hooves set down at the same time, close together, without a "hind lead" in the gait. This sometimes happens when a stiff horse is changing leads or when his hind legs and back lack muscle tone.

The Four-Beat Canter

This gait is probably the most common faulty canter. It is sometimes mistakenly called a lope, although a true lope is really just a less elevated or collected canter that has the correct three-beat sequence. Although horses do use the four-beat gallop at speed, the correct, slow canter is always a three-beat gait.

The four-beat canter happens for two reasons. The first is that the horse carries too much weight on his shoulders, either from poor balance or due to excessive pull on the reins, which causes the front hoof of the diagonal pair in the canter to set down before the hind. The second is that the horse's hindquarters are inhibited by a lack of flexibility in the back and weak use of the stifles, causing the hind hoof of the diagonal pair to set down before the front. This second type of faulty canter may happen with very low-headed,

FOOTFALL SEQUENCE OF THE CANTER — RIGHT LEAD

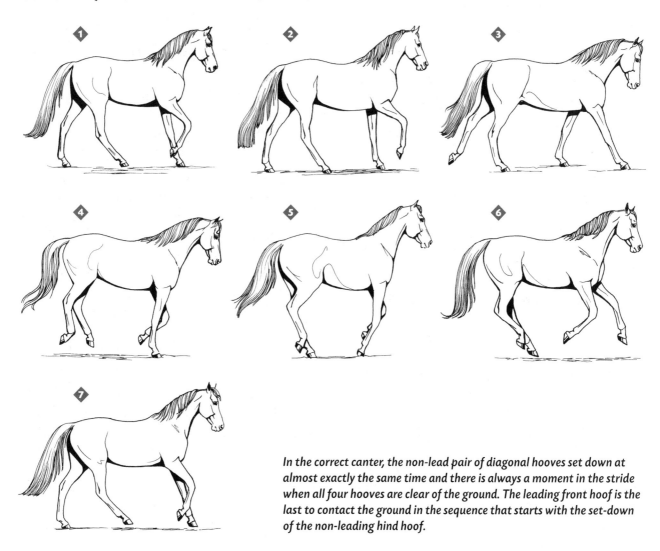

In the correct canter, the non-lead pair of diagonal hooves set down at almost exactly the same time and there is always a moment in the stride when all four hooves are clear of the ground. The leading front hoof is the last to contact the ground in the sequence that starts with the set-down of the non-leading hind hoof.

strung-out horses, but it can also happen along with high action in front if the horse is not working with elastic back muscles and strong stifles.

The Mixed Canter

A horse may also exhibit trotting or walking motion in either his front or hind legs along with a cantering motion from the other pair, producing an odd half canter, half something else. This peculiar "gait" sometimes happens if you ask for the canter without helping the horse carry his body so that he can push off with his hindquarters. It can also happen if you try to slow a horse down without helping him maintain a slightly rounded back. This gait is so common in gaited horses that it has a specific name in some languages, although the closest term for it in English is "wicky wack."

Why Do Gaited Horses Have Problems in the Canter?

Gaited horses have two physical conditions that may make it hard for them to canter smoothly.

"Wiring"

Gaited horses frequently move in lateral gaits. If your horse had a problem with the pace or stepping pace when you first asked him for his easy gait, even if he now works in a different easy gait, he may have trouble with the canter because of the wiring, or strong neural pathways, that contributed to those lateral gaits. Like the pace or stepping pace, the canter has a lateral element in the way legs move on the leading side of the horse. The leading front and the hind on the same side move forward slightly together in time, although the non-leading front and hind do not move forward together. It can be difficult for a horse that has the habit of moving lateral legs forward in pairs to change the timing of one pair only slightly while completely separating the movement of the other pair. His neural pathways may be so strongly developed for the lateral pairing of his legs that he is not able to change the timing of his leg movements.

Back and Spine Use

In addition to the above coordination challenge, many gaited horses have very stiff backs, either from incomplete training or from the natural inclination to work in a hollow position connected with the ability to do lateral gaits. Those that work in the racking gaits have also developed the essential tension at the root of the neck that further reduces their flexibility. Because a horse with a stiff back has trouble lowering and pushing off from his haunches, he will have difficulty with the canter. He may also have poor balance, making the canter truly difficult. A gaited horse with these physical problems often will not canter free in a pasture, let alone with a rider.

Working with the Horse's Body to Develop the Canter

Most gaited horses can be trained to canter if they are taught to be supple and responsive to the aids, and helped to develop their overall fitness, **before** they are asked for the gait from the saddle.

There are two ways a horse can move into a canter.

- The horse's forward momentum in a trot builds speed to a point where he loses his balance and must catch himself by switching into the canter or lope. This method is often used with non-gaited horses.
- The horse shifts his balance and weight to the rear in a slow speed at a trot or walk. He is asked to move into the canter just as his outside hind hoof touches down, building on the impulsion and thrust of that hind leg to push his forequarters upward into the first phase of the canter.

Even horses that have been trained to canter by chasing their balance in the first method are retrained into taking the canter from the second, balanced position after they have developed enough strength to achieve it.

The support sequence of most of the easy gaits makes it very difficult for a horse to chase his balance into a canter from those gaits. Because of this support problem, most gaited horses that are trained to canter go into the gait from the walk or flat walk, very rarely from their easy gait. Cantering from a walk takes a lot of strength in the hindquarters, and not all gaited horses can accomplish it. Because it requires a lot less effort for a horse to canter by "chasing his balance" in the trot, it is often easier to teach a gaited horse to canter by initially encouraging him to hard trot at liberty or on a longe line and then asking for the canter from the trot.

If you have worked to develop a good ordinary and flat walk and taught your horse to semi-collect, however, you can ask him to canter under saddle from the flat walk. He may go into the gait in response to very strong leg aids pushing him for speed.

Sit straight in the saddle, feel when one of his hind legs starts to move forward in the walk, rock your seat slightly from back to front, as if pumping a swing, and squeeze strongly with both legs while gently lifting the reins. See what happens. Your horse may go directly into the canter. Then again, he may be confused by the whole exercise. If that is the case, try teaching him the canter on the ground, first from a hard trot, then from the walk.

Gaited horses usually respond well to learning the canter through ground work. They discover that they **can** canter, while simultaneously developing body condition and balance for the gait. After they have learned to do the gait without a rider, they are much more likely to do it under saddle. By following up basic ground work in the canter with continued practice in the lateral flexions and other ridden exercises, your horse will gradually develop the ability to do a flowing three-beat canter under saddle.

Ground Work for the Canter

The amount of ground work you do to prepare your horse to canter under saddle will depend on how well he canters without a rider. If he has a fluid, well-balanced canter when free in pasture and trots more than he paces at liberty, you may only need to practice a few times on the ground in order to teach him the verbal cue for the gait. If he has an awkward, strung-out canter in the pasture, a little more ground work will help him develop better balance in the gait so that he can retain that balance under saddle. If he doesn't

canter very often when he is free in a pasture, you will need to devote a lot of time to ground work to improve his coordination and strength so that he can do the gait while carrying your weight.

Be careful not to practice canter work on the longe or in a round pen for more than 20 minutes total every other day. If you can't keep track of the time, set a kitchen timer to remind you when to stop! Work in small circles at speed is very hard on your horse's legs, and it can be especially difficult for gaited horses that have long hind legs. If your horse needs a lot of work to develop a canter, spread it out over several months rather than trying to accomplish everything he needs in a week. It takes time to condition and reeducate muscles and build your horse's ability to canter.

If your horse canters well in the pasture and will trot easily on the longe line or in a round pen, ground work for the canter can consist of teaching him the verbal cue for the gait and letting him practice it in both directions, bending his body and taking both leads. You can do this work either at liberty in the round pen, if you are accustomed to using that method, or on the longe line in a corner of your arena if you do not have a round pen.

Longe-Line Method for Horses That Canter Easily

After some warm-up on the longe practicing the walk, his intermediate gait, and a medium-speed trot, encourage your horse to move up into a fast trot by pointing the shaft of the whip at his haunches and repeating the phrase *trot OUT*. Allow him to trot at speed once around the circle. Then, keeping the line slack, push him out of the trot into the canter, repeating the word *canter* and cracking the whip behind him to encourage him to move out. If he is startled into a gallop, drop the whip and relax him, using the word *easy* accompanied by light pulls and slacks on the longe line until he slows down. Start over, this time just tapping the ground with the tip of the whip to urge him into the canter.

If he seems stuck in the trot, repeat the verbal command and the crack of the whip until he moves into the canter. He may be confused at first, but if you are persistent he will break into a clumsy, fast, loping canter. Praise him, allow him to canter halfway around the circle, and then return him to the slower trot. Repeat several times, until he goes into the canter when you ask for it from the fast trot. Return to a walk, stop him, pet him, then change directions and repeat. Practice a couple of times in each direction, then go on to a pleasant trail ride or some other quiet activity.

The next time you work with your horse, ask for the canter from the fast trot again several times, until he goes into the gait every time you say the word *canter* and you are certain he understands the verbal cue. Then ask him to work in a slower, less forward-reaching trot. Use light vibrations on the longe line to ask him to slow down a little and semi-collect in the trot while pointing the end of the whip at his haunches to keep him moving forward. Watch his legs. When his outside hind hoof is about to set down, tell him to *canter* and urge him forward by tapping the whip on the ground. He should move out into a slightly more balanced canter for a few strides. Let him canter halfway around the circle, then return him to a walk. Praise him, let him walk at least halfway around the circle, then return him to the slow trot and ask for the canter again. Repeat this exercise three or four times, then reverse him, and practice in the other direction. Praise him for every effort. Keep him calm and balanced by allowing him to canter only part of the way around the circle.

As you practice asking your horse for transitions up to the canter from a slow trot and back down from it into a walk, he will begin to develop better balance in the gait as his back becomes more elastic. After several sessions of asking for the canter from the slow trot, you can ask for it from a flat walk, using the word *canter* at the same time he sets down his outside hind hoof. Practice asking for the canter from the flat walk several times during each session until your horse goes easily into a relatively slow, controlled canter from the flat walk. At that point, your longe-line preparation will be done, and you can go on to riding the canter. Under saddle, your horse will probably take the gait from a flat walk or walk at the verbal cue to *canter*, when added to basic diagonal leg aids for the gait (see below).

Unfortunately, not all gaited horses canter in the pasture or work easily in a trot on the longe line. For horses like this, some time free-longeing to establish a gait other than a pace at fast speed will help begin to adjust the body habits that produce faulty canters. If you don't have a round pen, you can bring your horse to about the same stage by working him on a slack longe line in a large circle. Once the initial exercise of learning the verbal command to canter and beginning to change the coordination of his legs is done, you can go on to more precise longe-line work to develop a more supple and balanced body.

Free-Longeing for Horses That Have Difficulty Cantering

Begin free-longeing for a canter by turning the horse loose in a round pen with good, soft footing. Position yourself toward his hindquarters and start him circling in a walk. After he has walked around the pen a couple of times, move him on into a canter or gallop, using the word *canter* and waving a hat or lead rope or cracking a whip behind him until he moves out with speed around you. Ask for a lot of speed instantly, instead of allowing him to speed up gradually out of the walk.

Pay attention to the type of gait he chooses at canter speed. He may switch leads, front and back, pace, rack, or mix the pace with the gallop. Allow him to circle a few times in both directions in this fast, mixed gait, then stop him. Help his coordination by setting out a couple of poles at opposite sides of the pen to break up his gait into a trot for a few steps, then ask again for the canter. He may trot over the poles and then revert to his pace-canter or other faulty gait. Let him work over them for a while to see whether he develops better coordination with practice. If he continues to have trouble, set up a low cavalletti next to the rail, urging him to jump over it in whatever gait he is doing. Jumping will require him to push off with his hindquarters and change the timing of his hind legs, converting his gait into a canter for a couple of strides after he has gone over the jump. Say the word *canter* as he takes the gait and praise him when he does, even if it is only for a step or two.

Be sure to circle him in both directions in the round pen, encouraging him to bend and canter on both leads. Don't expect a good canter from this type of round-pen work, but use it to diagnose what his problems are likely to be and to let him know that you want him to move out faster than he is accustomed to going.

Longe-Line Work for Horses That Have Difficulty Cantering

After a few sessions of free-longeing, your horse may begin to work in a fast, strung-out lope or slow gallop. His coordination will begin to improve slowly, but he will probably be stiff, high-headed, and awkward. For more advanced work to develop the canter, switch him to working on the longe line, either inside the round pen or in the corner of your arena. With the line attached you can adjust his head and neck position, control his speed, and ask him to bend his body into the canter position more easily than you can while free-longeing. You can also guide him over poles or cavalletti a little more effectively with the longe line and whip to cue him.

Begin longe-line work for the horse that has trouble cantering by helping him get in shape physically for the canter. Longe him at a walk, then trot him over a row of cavalletti set at a low, then medium, height to build strength in his stifles and back. Alternate this with regular longe-line work, asking him to circle around you at the end of the longe line in an ordinary walk over four poles set in a star pattern. Keep the line slack, but with light, intermittent downward tugs, ask him to keep his head and neck low. Encourage him to speed up from the walk into a slow trot, still main-

taining a low head and neck. Follow the same procedure you would use for a horse that is more natural in the trot, controlling his speed with your voice and tugs on the longe line, and by pointing the longe whip at his hindquarters. When he is working in a consistent, rhythmic trot over the low poles, ask him to canter just as he approaches one of the ground poles, paying out line so that he is cantering at the end of the longe, in a large circle. As he goes into the fast canter or lope, very gently tug and release downward on the longe line, and tighten it with a gentle pulsing motion just enough to bend his head very slightly toward the inside of the circle. Pull and slack the line very gently to slow and bend your horse on the circle, being ready to ask him to keep moving in the canter if he tries to slow down. Let him go about halfway around the circle, then return him to a walk to keep him from getting excited and to help him change his balance toward the rear. Practice a few more times asking him to canter from the trot and returning him to the walk, and praise him when he does a few steps of a slower, less strung-out canter. Stop him, pet him, and then repeat the exercise in the other direction.

Practice longeing your horse at the canter several times a week, gradually discontinuing the use of the poles as he responds to the cue for the gait. If he seems to have trouble striking off into the canter on a particular lead, use a single cavalletti to help him lift into the first phase of the gait in that direction and work a little more to that side in the gait. Once he is cantering

Trotting over a set of cavalletti is very useful for strengthening the stifle joints of any horse. Practice it to help your horse develop a stronger canter or for general physical fitness.

Standard and Non-Standard Canter Aids Under Saddle

MOST HORSES ARE TRAINED to go into the canter under saddle from a specific set of weight, leg, and rein aids. To ask for a canter on a right lead, the **standard cues** are:

▸ Sit slightly more heavily on your left seat bone.

▸ Press your left leg straight into the horse's side just behind the girth.

▸ Keeping your right leg at the girth, squeeze strongly with both legs to urge the horse forward with energy.

▸ Maintain slightly more contact on the right rein as you lift it a fraction to raise your horse's head and tip his nose very slightly toward the right.

▸ Relax pressure from your legs and reins to reward your horse as he canters.

Note that these are diagonal aids, your leg on the opposite side from the desired lead asking the horse to move into it, and your rein on the same side as the desired lead helping to guide him into it.

Many gaited horses are taught to canter in response to **non-standard aids**. The most common nontraditional canter aids (for a right lead) are:

▸ Turn your horse's head to the left, away from the leading leg, by tightening your left rein.

▸ Shift your weight slightly over his right shoulder and push him into the gait with your left leg, tilting his body sideways and forcing him to catch his balance with his right front leg as he speeds up, throwing him into a right lead.

OR

▸ Kick or poke him on the right shoulder or elbow with your right toe while pushing him up into speed with your left heel.

Horses that have been trained with these cues will not respond to more traditional aids and may lead you to believe that they don't know how to canter under saddle until you ask them in a way they understand. If your horse does not canter in response to standard cues, try one of the non-standard ones.

consistently, if slightly awkwardly, gradually reduce the size of the longeing circle. Over the next several sessions shorten the longe line, until he is cantering in a 10-meter (or approximately 40-foot) circle. This smaller circle will encourage him to bend his body a little more in the canter and will begin to change his balance so that he slows down and shifts his weight back toward his hindquarters. Practice transitions between the canter and the trot or walk, avoiding cantering him entirely around the circle more than once or twice a session. The frequent changes of balance from these transitions will help him develop the canter better than constant work in the gait. A horse learns to canter well not by cantering, but by making frequent transitions into and out of the gait.

Beginning the Canter Under Saddle

Once your horse is cantering well and consistently on the longe, you can add some ridden work in the gait.

Because it will help your horse continue to develop strength and flexibility, continue to longe him occasionally over poles and cavalletti to help condition his legs and back and to develop strength in his stifles.

To ride at the canter you can use a snaffle bit, mild curb, or bitless headgear. Try to find a slight incline to work on because working uphill will help your horse push with his hindquarters and round his back. Do not try to start a horse in a canter on uneven ground or any noticeable downhill slant. Avoid cantering down even the slightest dip, as this will throw your horse's weight onto his shoulders and interfere with his coordination. Horses that have trouble with a disunited canter or a four-beat canter will be much less coordinated if cantered on a downhill slant.

• Sitting in the base position with slack reins, ride your horse in a walk or flat walk up a small hill outside your arena.

• As you ride up the hill, adjust your pelvis into the full forward seat, leaning your upper body slightly forward.

- Rock your pelvis gently once from back to front in the saddle by pumping your lower back forward.
- Squeeze hard with both legs, while repeating the word *canter*.
- Tap your horse sharply on the haunches with the dressage whip to reinforce your pushing leg and seat aids.
- Your horse should go into a fast, loping canter. Release your leg aids, but continue to follow his motion with your seat.
- Gradually slow him by sitting a bit more upright, using light squeeze/releases or vibrations of your fingers on the reins to bring him to a flat walk.

Repeat several times in each riding session. Do not worry about leads, leg action, speed, or other niceties of the gait. At this point, you are working on teaching the horse to perform a gait that is at least close to a canter. Perfecting that gait comes later.

If your horse does not canter at once, repeat the tap with the whip and squeeze with your legs until he takes off into a three-beat gait. He may try to go into a rack or some other gait, but if you relax him, return to the walk, and ask again while keeping his head and neck lowered with light contact, he should eventually go into the canter. Do not try to pop him into a canter from the rack or pace; he will generally pace or rack faster instead of cantering. If your horse persists in taking some other gait than the canter when you try this exercise, stop, start over from a walk, and ask for the canter again.

If he continues to choose the pace or some disunited hopping gait, return to longe-line work until he is more solid in a lope or canter without a rider, then try again. Try the "hill technique" several times to see whether your horse will canter in response to your aids and the familiar verbal cue. If he does not seem to understand what you want, return him to the longe line, work him at the canter for a few circles, then ask a friend to longe him at a canter while you sit in the saddle. This can be a very useful technique for horses that are unsure about cantering under the weight of a rider, but do respond well on the longe line.

Practice cantering up the hill for several lessons,

until your horse instantly goes into a forward, three-beat gait when you use the word *canter*. Gently rock your hips and squeeze/release with your legs. Ride with slack reins and maintain your horse's forward motion by following his motion with your seat, but try to avoid a flat-out gallop. If he accelerates, stop following his motion and resist his speed by tightening your lower back muscles and tilting your pelvis into the heavy seat, slowing him with light vibrations on the reins. Your goal is to teach him to move out in a canter with some energy, not to run away with you!

Once your horse understands that he can canter with you on a slight hill (this may take a month or so of work), you can start working on the gait on flat ground. Still riding in the forward seat in a large, smooth arena, practice asking for the canter as you ride over one pole in the middle of the riding area, encouraging him to lift his front legs and push off with his hindquarters. Canter a few steps, then return to the straight seat and the flat walk. Practice frequent flat walk-to-canter and canter-to-flat walk transitions down the center of the arena. This will teach the horse to canter more slowly without inhibiting his forward movement.

He will still be cantering fairly fast at this stage in training. *Don't* try to slow the canter below a fast, slightly strung-out lope for some time. He must be confident and willing to move forward correctly in the three-beat gait before he can learn to slow down in it. While you are practicing, notice which lead your horse seems to prefer in the canter. Most horses have a preference; many canter more easily on the left lead, a few prefer the right.

At about this stage in canter training, your horse may surprise you with a canter or a half canter/half hop when you ask him to increase speed in his easy gait. This is fairly common because it takes less energy to canter than it does to extend his intermediate gait. If your horse does this, discontinue canter training for a week or so, and reestablish his extended easy gait. Ride in a straight seat as you work on his easy gait, checking him the instant he tries to hop into a canter with a light squeeze/release on the reins. Sit still and balanced in the saddle, using only leg aids to ask for speed in his easy gait. When you return to working on the canter, use a forward seat and the verbal cue *canter* to differentiate between it and his extended easy gait. If you use different aids to ask for the canter than the ones you use to ask for speed in his easy gait, your horse will understand that he can continue to work in an extended easy gait as well as the canter.

Basic Leads

Once your horse is comfortable cantering up a gentle slope and across the center of the arena in a straight line, you can begin to teach him to canter on the flat in a specific lead. Generally, horses have better balance if they canter on the inside lead, the lead toward the center of the circle or arena, or the uphill lead if cantering across a slope. For general trail riding, you may not want to worry about leads, but if you plan to ride in turns or along hills in the gait, it is a good idea to teach him to take a specific lead in the canter on cue to keep your horse in balance. It is also less tiring for your horse if you ask him to change leads from time to time when cantering on the trail.

Start by riding at a walk. Pay attention as each of his hind hooves hits the ground, until you can tell which one is setting down. If you have not practiced doing this while working on your horse's ordinary walk, you may need a ground coach to tell you when a specific hoof sets down until you develop a feel for the placement of each hoof. Next, practice the lateral flexions in both directions to loosen any tension in your horse's body. Practice both the shoulder-in and the haunches-in, but spend a little more time in the haunches-in the in both directions. Ride your horse on the rail in a walk or flat walk in the direction in which he seems to prefer to canter. Take light contact with the reins, but do not pull on his mouth or interfere with his natural head position. Then ask him to canter, using the lead he prefers. All directions are given for a horse that prefers the right lead. Reverse them for horses that prefer the left.

- As you come to a corner of the arena, feel the movement of his hind legs with your seat.
- Just as the left hind leg comes forward in a walking step (this will feel full under your right seat bone), gently rock your pelvis from back to front in the saddle.
- Give a strong upward squeeze with both your thighs and calves.
- Say the word *canter*.
- Tap your horse on the left haunch with the dressage whip.
- Your horse should pick up a fairly fast canter on the right lead.

Praise him and allow him to canter down the long side of the arena, then slow him with half-halts into a flat walk. To slow him, be sure to shift your weight into the heavy seat in addition to taking light, vibrating contact with the reins. Praise him, pet him, then walk him in a slow walk for a few steps in the neck-stretched position, encouraging him to relax. Repeat twice, asking for the canter in a corner of the arena, going only halfway around the ring, then returning to a slow walk. Your horse will be doing a fast, strung-out, lope-type canter on his favored lead, not a very difficult task for him. Practice cantering on his preferred lead for several lessons, until he goes into the canter easily when you ask for it in a corner of the ring.

Standard Canter Aids for the Leads

For the right lead, you allowed your horse to move into the canter on his own, without asking for a particular

Identifying Leads

THERE ARE SEVERAL METHODS for telling which lead a horse is using at the canter. A common one is to lean forward and look down at his forelegs to see which is reaching more to the front. This method can backfire by throwing the horse off balance and interfering with his gait. Another less disruptive method is to glance down quickly at the horse's shoulders to see which is in front. A much less obvious method for determining leads is to sit still in the saddle, looking forward, and feel which of your own legs is moving more. Your leg on the "lead" side will move more than that on the other. Finally, you can eventually tell which lead your horse is using by feeling the way his back fills and pushes under your seat. His back will often feel slightly more full on the non-lead side.

Diagonal canter aids, asking for the right lead, with left leg and right rein cueing the horse.

lead, just as he cantered up the hill. Now that he knows what a canter is and can do the gait on his preferred (in this case, the right) lead in the arena, teach him to take the other lead in response to the standard diagonal leg, weight, and rein aids. To do this, reverse directions in the arena so that you are traveling to the left. Change the dressage whip to your right hand. Practice a few steps at the haunches-in to the left, being sure to keep your horse's shoulders and neck parallel to the rail, his head facing in the direction in which he is traveling.

• Ride your horse straight along the rail, in a flat walk.
• Press your right leg against his side, just behind the girth, asking for a very slight haunches-in to the left.
• As you start through a corner of the arena, feel with your seat for the moment when his right hind leg starts to move forward.

• Very slightly weight your right seat bone and signal your horse for the canter. Gently rock your pelvis, squeeze and lift with both your thighs; very gently raise the **left rein** to keep your horse's head and neck straight, and push strongly with your **right leg** just behind the girth to keep him in a slight haunches-in position.

Your horse should go into a canter on the left lead. If he does, praise him, canter along one side of your arena, then return to a walk. If your horse fails to take the correct lead, return to a walk and ask again at the next corner, pushing him as far as possible into the curve to bend him into a shallow C to help him take the correct position for the left lead. If he still fails to take the left lead, try putting him into a pronounced haunches-in to the left as he starts into the corner of the arena, keeping his head and neck bent very slightly to the left and then asking for the left lead. This will curve his body so that he **must** take the left lead. Canter down one side of the arena, return to a walk, then praise and relax your horse. Practice a couple of times, then reverse directions. Practice his preferred lead a couple of times, then go for a relaxing trail ride as a reward.

Canter at the semi-lope several times during each riding session, being sure to work on both leads, with perhaps a little more work on the lead he has trouble with. Because the canter can be exciting for your horse, keep him relaxed and calm in the gait by asking for only short periods in it. Don't get into the habit of letting him canter at top speed around the arena until he tires as a way to slow him down in the gait. The best way to slow and perfect the canter is not to keep cantering, but to practice short bursts in that gait with many transitions between it and the flat walk or ordinary walk. Continue to use a corner of the arena as a starting point for the gait if your horse is having trouble consistently taking his leads. This will help him bend and incline him to take the preferred inside lead.

Stay at this level of a fast, strung-out loping canter for several weeks while perfecting the correct leads in response to your cues, first in the corners of your arena, later along the rail in a straight line. This will preserve your horse's impulsion or forward movement in the gait and prevent some of the faults that can develop in the gait if it is slowed down too soon. It is a good plan to canter during a few lessons in the arena, then return to the slope or trail and practice there for a couple of rides before returning to arena work again. Your goal at this point is to develop a controlled, fast canter in a straight line on the correct lead, for a short distance, whenever you ask for it.

Possible Canter Problems Under Saddle

Your horse should canter in a three-beat gait with the inside legs leading both in the front and rear. Unfortunately, many gaited horses do not do this automatically. Although he may canter very well on the longe line, under your weight in the saddle your horse may canter disunited, may switch leads in back, or may revert to a pace. These faults in the canter are all signs of poor coordination and a lack of muscle strength. You can help overcome them with more work in conditioning exercises.

The Disunited Canter

This dangerous movement often happens because a horse is weak in his stifle joints and needs to build strength in his back. It can also happen because a rider bends over to see what lead he is on, disrupting his horse's balance and throwing a perfectly good canter off-stride. To avoid this, sit **straight** in the saddle as you canter without leaning to one side or the other.

Help the horse develop coordination by spending more time practicing the canter uphill, then return to arena work to see whether he has improved. Practice shoulder-in and haunches-in exercises to help strengthen his hindquarters. Ride over a series of poles or cavalletti at a walk or hard trot to help strengthen his stifles. Practice going over a 1-foot-high jump several times during each riding session to teach your horse to push with his hindquarters.

A horse may also canter disunited as a result of an injury or other physical problem. If your horse persists in cantering this way, have him checked out by a veterinarian and/or chiropractor. There is usually a physical reason for a horse to canter disunited, and it is always a good idea to get a professional opinion when the problem persists after the horse's strength and conditioning have been improved.

Lead Switching

Some horses will start out in a beautiful canter, then, after about four strides, bobble a step or two and start to go disunited or on the "wrong" lead. Again, this is a result of lack of strength in the stifles and back. To avoid the lead-switching problem while riding in the canter, keep your outside leg ready against the horse's side to return him to a stronger haunches-in position the instant you feel him begin to lose the C-curve in the direction of the desired lead. To help your horse stop switching leads, return to cantering uphill to improve his condition, and practice more shoulder-in work and work over cavalletti to improve his flexibility.

The "Pace Canter"

This "gait" develops when a horse lacks strength in his back and loses impulsion or forward momentum as he is cantering. He fails to bring his hindquarters under him, loses any roundness in his body, and falls into something that is not a canter or a pace, but a combination of the two. To overcome this problem, go back to work uphill, then reestablish a semi-collected position in the flat walk and intermediate gait. Spend some time building strength in the horse's back, practicing the walk/halt/back transition and transitions in speed in each gait, as well as between gaits. Then, being sure to use the haunches-in position to start the canter, push the horse forward with strong leg aids into a fast lope, perhaps even a gallop. Very gradually slow him to a canter with light vibrations on the reins, keeping your seat quiet in the saddle to resist forward motion. Be ready to squeeze with your calves to push him for more energy if he starts to pace, keeping his back rounded by keeping your hands low with light bit contact.

Remember that a very pacey horse may not be able to canter well due to his wiring and habitual body use. If you have not established a good flat walk and intermediate gait, you will not develop a good canter in a horse of this type.

The Four-Beat Canter

A rider who interferes with the impulsion or forward motion of the canter in order to slow it down can often create a four-beat gait. This is the reason it is so important to do early canter training on a slack rein and to slow the gait gradually by checking it with your seat and weight action rather than by restricting or inhibiting the forward motion of the gait through the reins.

In some horses, however, the four-beat canter can be a result of the lack of physical condition in the back and stifle joints. The basic flexibility exercises such as the shoulder-in and haunches-in, as well as stride shortening and lengthening, will work to strengthen the back. Work, either ridden or on the longe, over cavalletti and climbing hills, in a walk and a trot if possible, will also help. Gradually increase the steepness of the hills until your horse is able to power up a fairly steep bank, working his hind legs and stifles as he does. Remember to ride up hills in the faster flat walk but come down them slowly, in a very short-stepping ordinary walk.

Leads on Command

You may have been taking leads in the canter by using the corners of your arena. You should now start to cue your horse into either lead on the straight of way or out on a trail. This is not very difficult, if you remember that to take a lead at the canter, a horse must be slightly bent in the direction of the lead and must start with the non-leading hind leg. Horsemen have been taking advantage of this nature of the canter almost since leads were discovered.

The Diagonal Aids and Leads

You and your horse are now familiar with the idea of using the left leg and right rein to cue into a right lead and the opposite cues for the left lead. If you started cantering from a haunches-in position because your horse had trouble with a lead, you have been using strong diagonal aids every time you asked for that lead, even in a corner of the arena. You can now practice using them along the rail, away from the curves.

To take a left lead on the rail on a straight line, as your horse moves along the flat walk to the left in the arena, press with your right calf just behind the girth. Use less pressure than you would for a haunches-in to shift his balance over very slightly. Barely increase contact with your left rein to keep his head pointed forward. Do not allow him to point his nose over the rail and slew his body sideways without a bend. Shift your weight slightly to the right and to the rear and give the lifting canter signal with your thighs and seat, at the same time giving a very slight upward twitch with your left rein. Your horse should take off into the canter on the left lead.

If he does not, go back to a walk and repeat, this time giving a stronger signal to produce haunches-in. Practice taking the lead on the straight of way of your arena a few times, then repeat in the other direction, using the reversed signals for the left lead. Praise your horse!

Lead Changes

It should not take many lessons before your horse easily takes the lead you request with your diagonal aids. You can then try a *simple change of lead* down the center of your arena. To do this, canter in the left lead on a straight line well away from the rail, using a slight haunches-in to the left to ask for the lead. Return to a flat walk for a few steps, then reverse your aids, change to a slight haunches-in to the right, and pick up the right lead, finishing at the far rail. This may take some practice because you will not have the rail to guide you for the haunches-in cue, but soon your horse should take the lead you indicate. Praise him when he does what you ask. After several lessons, when he has mastered a simple change with a few steps of the flat walk between each lead, try gradually reducing the number of walking steps between lead changes. It will take time and practice, but eventually your horse will develop his condition and responsiveness to your aids so that he can take just a couple of walking steps between lead changes.

In time, you can cue a *flying change of lead* by quickly reversing your aids at the moment of suspension between the three beats of the canter, when your horse has all of his hooves clear of the ground. In this type of change, the horse switches his hind legs into the new lead before his front legs, maintaining good balance. This takes very good timing of the aids on your part and lots of practice feeling the different phases of the canter from the saddle. Flying changes are useful for jumping, games on horseback, and some cattle work, but most pleasure horses (and pleasure riders) don't really need to use them very often. Don't worry if you have trouble with flying changes, and don't become impatient or try to force your horse into them. To do them well, your horse must be very fit, and have a well-developed back and hindquarters, good coordination, and a complete understanding of your aids. He will probably not be ready to perform them correctly for at least a year after he has learned the simple changes of lead.

Advanced Canter Aids

As long as you are satisfied with your horse's response to diagonal canter aids, you should continue to use them. After several years of riding with the diagonal aids at the canter, however, you might eventually want to go on to the next step in refinement and teach him a more delicate response. You can teach your horse to respond to *lateral aids* for the canter once he is very supple and light in hand and when he has overcome any problem he might have with being one-sided. Do not confuse these aids with the jerk on the leading rein and toe in the leading shoulder cue used by some gaited trainers.

To cue for leads using lateral aids, discontinue the use of the leg on the opposite side of the horse from the desired lead. Use only a slight weight shift in that direction to remind the horse to plant the outside hoof first in the canter and a very light upward vibration on your "leading" rein to cue the gait. Reinforce weight and rein cues with a light rock forward from your seat, a lifting squeeze and release from your inner thighs, and a light touch from your leg on the lead side at **(not behind)** the girth to urge your horse on. He should take the desired lead with his body traveling straight, not bent in the shallow C. Only a very strong and fit horse is able to do this! Don't worry if yours does not take the desired lead the first time you try this method of cuing the canter. He may not be ready for lateral aids, and you should return to diago-

nal ones until he is more flexible and responsive to seat cues for the gait.

Slowing and Semi-Collecting the Canter

After several weeks to several months of practice in the canter on both leads, you can begin to teach your horse to slow his gait and semi-collect it. You can do this without ruining the rhythm and footfall sequence of the gait if you use your legs, seat, and hands to cue the horse. If you try to slow the canter by pulling on the reins, you will interfere with your horse's forward momentum and he will probably respond with a stiff, four-beat canter.

Slowing the Canter by Practicing Transitions

A common method for converting a fast lope into a collected canter is to put the horse into a small circle and force him to slow down by making sharp curves. This may work with some horses, but it tends to make gaited horses lose balance, fall into a mixed gait, or speed up due to nervousness rather than slow down. A better method that both helps a horse find his own balance and increases the power of his hindquarters is to practice transitions into and out of the canter/lope. Your horse should have had some practice doing this on the longe line before you started asking for the gait from the saddle.

- Ride your horse forward in a flat walk with light, even contact on the reins.
- Give the canter aids as you go through one curve of your arena.
- Canter halfway down the side of the arena or about four complete strides.
- Shift your weight into the heavy seat, asking him to slow down with your weight by tightening your back and abdominal muscles to resist forward motion.
- Lightly vibrate the reins, taking slightly stronger contact with the inside rein to slow your horse. Say the word *walk*.

Asking for Semi-Collection in the Canter

Practice making transitions into and down from the canter in the flat walk and ordinary walk will help your horse develop better balance and stronger hindquarters. As he becomes more physically fit, you can ask him to work in a more collected canter, rounding his back and working with his balance shifted more to the rear.

• Ride forward in a flat walk with light contact on the reins.
• Ask for a canter at the corner of your arena.
• Squeeze and lift with your thighs and calves and squeeze/release your fingers on the reins, holding your hands low on either side of the withers.
• Gradually ask your horse to bring his forehead toward the vertical with continued light vibrations on the reins. Alternate the vibrations of your fingers with squeeze/releases from your calves to keep your horse moving forward, as needed.

These aids will increase the energy of his hindquarters, while preventing him from moving out in a fast lope. The result will be that he lifts his forequarters a bit higher than usual, raising his head and neck as well, just as he thrusts forward with his hind legs. If you are careful to avoid a steady pull on the reins he will go into a naturally rolling, semi-collected canter with no stiffness in his neck or back. Ride at this gait for a few steps, then return to a flat walk. Repeat a couple of times in each direction, praise him for his work, and go for a relaxing trail ride in his easy gait to relax.

Practice this type of canter for several weeks, a few steps at a time, until your horse is comfortable in it. Then ask him to do it all the way around the arena, first in his favorite direction, then in the other. If he starts to string out into the lope, shift your weight a bit more to the heavy seat and use light vibrations on the rein on the leading side to slow him, supported by contact from the opposite rein to prevent him from turning.

Be sure to keep your horse moving forward freely, using squeeze/releases from your calves to keep his

Advanced aids for the canter, using the lateral aids to cue the horse for a right lead.

• Return to the flat walk. Praise your horse.
• Ride at the flat walk a few steps, then again ask for several strides of the canter.

Repeat flat walk/canter/flat walk transitions several times, in each direction, then ride at the flat walk in large circles and serpentines. Return to the canter a couple of times during your lesson, asking for only a few steps of the gait in between periods at the flat walk. Work on this both in your arena and out on the trail on a gradual slope to keep your horse from becoming sour on the gait. After he has spent at least a couple of months mastering the flat walk/canter transitions, begin to ask him for transitions from the ordinary walk to the canter and from the canter to the ordinary walk. This work will help him find better balance and natural collection in his gait and develop the strength required to do a slower, less strung-out canter when you ask for that gait.

haunches active. If you forget to ride with your seat and start to pull on the reins to slow the canter, you will soon convert it to a four-beat gait and lose the impulsion that makes the gait flow. Keep up the forward motion in the canter to prevent your horse from losing form and becoming stiff.

If you want to do more with your horse's canter, you can help him develop a higher, very slow gait by opposing the action of your seat and hands, "pumping" with your seat by rocking your pelvis from back to front in the saddle while keeping your hands fixed, restricting your horse's head motion in the gait. This will produce a canter with higher lift in the front legs, but it is not the rearing, flailing type of show canter that is sometimes associated with gaited horses. It is a balanced, flowing, and highly energetic canter. You probably will not want to do this gait on the trail, but it can be fun to develop for riding on the flat once in a while. A horse must have a very strong back and well-developed hindquarters to canter in this style.

- While riding in the canter, set your hands on either side of the horse's withers, at waist height maintaining light, even contact on the bit.
- Rock your pelvis from back to front at each stride while lifting very strongly with your inner thighs. Keep your hands steady.
- Restrain your horse's forward speed by increased vibrations on the reins with your fingers, keeping your hand stationary, as you push your seat foward.

Without lifting your hands or pulling on his mouth, you will invite your horse to come up higher with his shoulders and front legs through the use of your legs and seat in opposition to the vibrations from your fingers on the bit. Do not do this unless your horse is light and responsive to the bit and has developed a good ordinary canter. Avoid trying to force or physically lift your horse's head and neck with your hands to put him into a high, rolling canter. He must have good balance and strength in his back and hindquarters to do this correctly, and it takes work and conditioning developed at a less showy gait to achieve this.

With time and the correct use of your hands and seat aids, you can eventually refine the canter down to a very slow rolling gait. Although there is no point in going this far with a pleasure horse, people with the skill and time to work on it have eventually taught horses to canter in place and in reverse, using only their weight, legs, and fingers as cues. Obviously, it takes several years of work before a horse is physically ready to attempt that type of movement!

Cantering Directly from the Easy Gaits

Although it is not always possible to move into a canter directly from an easy gait, once your horse has mastered cantering from the flat walk or ordinary walk, you can begin to introduce him to the idea of doing it from his easy gait. This will be easiest to do from the fox trot, but you can also develop a decent canter-depart from a running walk. Taking the gait from the stepping pace or one of the racking gaits may be a little trickier, and you may not want to spend a lot of time on cantering directly from one of those gaits if your horse canters easily from a walk.

To canter from a fox trot or running walk, start by reviewing the feel of your horse's footfalls in his gait. Ride at a moderate speed while noticing which hind hoof is on the ground in each phase of a stride. Notice when the right hind hoof hits the ground. If necessary, close your eyes and feel with only your seat as your horse's right hind leg moves forward and his hoof hits the ground. If you have trouble with this because the movement is faster than it was when you tried it at a walk or flat walk, ask a friend with quick eyes to watch you ride again so she can tell you when that hind hoof hits the ground. Memorize that feel in your horse's gait.

Next, ride your horse in his easy gait at a moderate speed, with light semi-collection or containment, and as the right hind hoof hits the ground, use strong diagonal aids to ask him to strike off into the canter. Reinforce them with the verbal cue canter, if necessary. Maintain the "plum-feel" contact with his mouth as you do this, lifting lightly with the inside rein and gently rocking your seat in the canter cue to prevent him from simply speeding up in gait. He should take off into the canter directly from his gait or, at most, with a couple of steps of a mixed gait in between the easy gait and the canter. Canter him for a few strides, praise him, then return to his gait. Practice on both leads, until he is able to maintain his balance and strike off into a true canter in either lead directly after he has set his opposite hind hoof on the ground. It may take several weeks of lessons, but with consistent practice, the bobbled steps will gradually be reduced, and he will strike off cleanly into the canter from his gait.

Obviously, the key to a good canter-depart from an easy gait is timing the canter cues on your part. If you have a lot of trouble working this out, you can return your horse to longe-line work and ask for the canter that way, while you watch his hooves yourself. If you just can't seem to time the cue correctly, try setting up a low jump or pole on the longe circle, and ask your horse to do his gait up to the pole, then canter as he jumps over it. The pole will help him push off from his hind hoof into the motion of the canter by encouraging him to lift his front legs off the ground while still using his hind legs in his gait.

Cantering from the rack or stepping pace can be a challenge, especially if your horse did not canter easily under saddle in the first place. First, ask for the canter directly from a contained saddle rack or stepping pace, timing your cues to the set-down of the non-leading hind hoof. For some horses, that method will work well, but others will hop or skip a step or two when asked to canter from either of these two gaits. Other horses, because the stepping pace and rack can be done at a number of speeds, will simply go faster in their easy gait when you try to ask for a canter.

The option of teaching your horse to canter directly from his gait on the longe may not be available, since it is not always possible to work a horse in a stepping pace or rack at speed on the longe. You may find that the best method for making a direct transition from one of those gaits to a canter is to ride your horse over a small jump, giving the canter cues as he approaches the jump, and reinforcing them with a verbal cue to *canter*.

This may work, or it may produce a very uncoordinated jumble of gaits that is not quite what you had in mind. Practice for a few lessons to see whether your horse can learn to overcome this coordination problem, and if he just doesn't seem to be able to do it, you may want to abandon the project and simply allow him to canter from the walk or flat walk as he has been doing. Appreciate your horse's fast easy gait, and his ability to canter from a walk, while sparing him and yourself the aggravation of trying to do something that may not be natural for him.

Pleasure Riding at the Canter

It takes time to develop a solid, collected, forward canter. Dressage riders spend years perfecting the gait, developing the strength and flexibility of their horses to the point that they can easily change leads at every other step while moving forward with rhythm and grace. Although you will not be expecting this type of movement from your gaited pleasure horse, you can reasonably expect to spend a year or so polishing and improving his gait before he will canter at moderate speed in a semi-collected, flowing gait. Don't try to rush him or take shortcuts to force him to move in an artificial way. Take your time and his gait will reflect your hard work.

By avoiding gimmicks in his training and using specific aids for the canter, you will have trained your horse to do both a forward-moving, comfortable loping canter and a slower, more rolling, semi-collected one while avoiding confusion with his easy gait. With practice, he should have no trouble taking whatever lead you ask for after a light cue from your seat and legs. He should stay calm while he canters and be versatile and pleasant to ride in the gait, semi-collecting or speeding up at your will.

You **can** have the best of both worlds: a canter that is slow and rolling when you ask for it; one with plenty of impulsion when you want to make good time on the trail; and a smooth easy gait for the rest of your pleasure riding.

CHAPTER TWELVE

Finishing Touches

Hands without legs, legs without hands.
— FRANÇOIS BAUCHER (1796–1873)

Remember your original goal? You wanted to help your horse become a pleasure to ride down the trail in his easy gait, on slack reins held in one hand. So far, it seems as if everything you have done to develop his gait has required contact and two hands on the reins. Now that the hard work is done and your horse has developed the strength and flexibility he needs to carry his body in his gait with some support from contact on the reins, you can take him to the next level. He is now ready to carry himself in gait without your support and to make the transition to a curb bit if you want to ride him in one.

Staying in Gait on Slack Reins

If you want to ride with one hand on slack reins and stay in gait on the trail, your horse needs to carry himself without the constant support of the reins to remind him of the body position necessary for his gait. Some horses do this easily, and some never quite learn to work without at least some light contact on the bit. Yours should be able to carry himself in his gait if he has been worked consistently in it and learned to respond to your seat, leg, and very light rein aids. With his body in shape for his gait, see whether he can do it on his own.

Releasing Contact

Start this process in the snaffle bit or bitless headgear, then continue it in the curb bit, if you are making the transition into that bit. Sitting in the base position, ride your horse forward in an energetic walk with light, plum-feel on the reins. As he moves, gently slack off that feel by letting the reins slip a little though your fingers until you have only the weight of the reins in your hands. If he falters in his walk, either speeding up or attempting to change gait, momentarily retake contact by closing your fingers, remind him to walk, then release again. Ride on slack reins alternating with occasional contact as a reminder until he understands that you want him to carry himself in the walk without being held there with contact. You will need to support him from time to time, especially as he heads up or down hills, but with practice, he should begin to work with fewer and fewer reminders to stay in the walk.

Follow the same procedure in his easy gaits. Start slowly in the flat walk or his easy gait, and then gradually build speed as he is able to remain in gait. Be careful not to push for too much speed because he will probably not be able to go as fast in gait *without* the support of the reins as he can *with* it. Ride with mostly slack reins, reminding him to stay in gait with occasional squeeze/releases of contact but letting him do most of the work for maintaining the gait on his own.

Remember to change your seat position according to his gait. For the stepping pace and the rack family of gaits, sit in the heavy seat and lift your hands to the high position while keeping the reins slack most of the time. Sit straight or in the allowing seat for the fox trot or running walk, keeping your hands in the base or low position. Pay attention to the way your horse's back feels and, at the first sign that he is about to break gait, reestablish some contact and remind him to stay in gear. If you feel his back tighten or sink under you, anticipate a pace and instantly take contact to ask him to lower his head. If you feel his back rise under you, anticipate a hard trot and take contact to bring his nose in a little and return him to a slower easy gait.

If you ask and remind your horse, he can learn to do his gait on a slack "honesty rein" without constant contact to maintain his gait. Just make sure that he is working consistently in his gait with light support from the bit before you ask him to do it without contact.

Using the Curb Bit

You can ride your horse in a snaffle bit or in bitless headgear all of his life. If you are riding in a snaffle because you prefer that bit or riding bitless because your horse is uncomfortable in a bit, by all means continue to do so. There is no rule of horsemanship that says that any horse **must** be ridden in a curb bit. When it is used correctly, however, a curb bit can be more effective for relaxing his jaw and helping him carry himself in gait than a non-leverage bit or bitless headgear. Because a trained horse responds quickly and with little pressure on the reins in a curb, you can often ride in that bit with less physical effort than it takes to use a snaffle. This lightness of response is the main reason to use the bit. Curbs should never be used for stronger control through pain.

If your horse was originally trained in a curb and you "stepped down" to the snaffle or bitless headgear to work on his gait and flexibility, you might consider returning to a mild curb once his gaits are set and he is supple and responsive to the milder pressure of non-leverage headgear. If he has never been ridden with a curb bit, you may want to make the transition to that bit for trail riding.

When Is a Horse Ready for a Curb Bit?

Although many gaited horses are rushed into a curb at the beginning of their training under saddle, a horse is not truly ready for this bit until he is calm, forward moving, straight, supple, and balanced in a snaffle or bitless headgear. If he still has trouble maintaining a specific gait for more than a few steps or falls into a pace from time to time, he is also not ready to be ridden in a curb alone. Consider using the curb only if your horse does not act silly on the trail, does not nose out and run off at the canter, and does not toss his head or in other ways show resistance in a snaffle bit or bitless headgear. A curb bit will cause more pain than necessary if used to correct this type of behavior, dulling your horse's mouth and limiting his ability to respond to lighter bit cues. Using a curb for simple control or to "set" a horse's head is like using a bullhorn to talk to a person with normal hearing in a small room; while it gets the message across crudely, it hurts his ears and can eventually make him deaf.

If you have laid a good foundation for responsiveness by riding with light, plum-feel contact with the snaffle or bitless headgear, your horse should be ready for the transition to the curb.

Making the Transition from a Snaffle to the Curb

By now your horse should understand what you are asking for when he feels light pressure from a snaffle on his tongue, bars, and lips. He will not, however, be accustomed to feeling pressure on his poll or jaw from a curb strap or chain, and he has no idea what kind of response you expect with that pressure. If you abruptly substitute a curb for the familiar snaffle, he will be confused. He may resist the bit, lug on it, tuck his nose "behind" it, throw his head and nose in the air, and forget all the light responsiveness you have taken so long to teach him. Instead of suddenly substituting one bit for the other, it is often better to add the curb to the familiar snaffle, then gradually phase out the use of the snaffle.

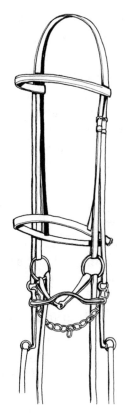

A Weymouth bridle, with two bits, can be a very useful tool for training a horse to work in the curb alone.

The Weymouth or Double Bridle

The oldest method of bitting that permits a slow introduction to the curb is the Weymouth, or double bridle, which consists of a thin snaffle (bridoon) and a short-shanked, thick-mouthed, low-port curb. This allows very precise use of both bits and is one of the most useful of all methods devised for communicating with the mouth of a horse. Using a double bridle requires skill from the rider and a horse with a fairly large, deep mouth. If you ride for pleasure, you probably will not want to bother with the complexities of a double bridle, and because many gaited horses have small, shallow mouths, the Weymouth may not be the first choice for making the transition to the curb for your horse.

The Pelham

The Pelham bit, while not as precise as the double bridle, can be a good alternative for making the transition to the curb. It is a combination bit consisting of a single mouthpiece with shanks, fitted with two sets of reins. One set of reins acts as a non-leverage snaffle on the upper part of the bit while the other set is attached to the shank and works as a curb. Pelhams are not particularly difficult to use and come in many styles, both English and Western. They have the advantage of attaching to any simple headstall. (The Weymouth requires an investment in a special bridle.) If you try one for the transition to the curb, you may find that you like the bit so much that you continue to use it after your horse works well in the curb alone!

Using the Pelham

Adjust the bit in the horse's mouth so that there is a small fold (not wrinkle) at each corner of the lips. Use a flat leather curb strap with the Western Pelham and a flat, interlocking link chain curb with the English type. Remove any twists in the curb chain so that it will lie flat against the horse's jaw. Attach the curb chain by running it through the snaffle loop on both sides of the bit, keeping it away from the lips. This will prevent the bit from pinching the horse's lips between the shank and snaffle loop. Adjust the chain or strap so that it is just tight enough to allow one finger to pass between it and the horse's jaw. This should allow the shank to pull back approximately 35 degrees before the chain is tight under the horse's jaw.

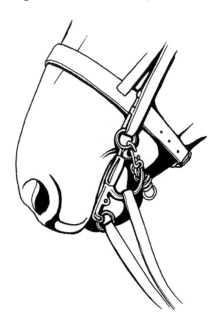

A Pelham bit, with curb chain adjusted in the United States Cavalry style that avoids pinching the horse's lips between bit and chain.

Reins

To use a Pelham, you will need two sets of leather reins. Attach the extra set of ⅝-inch-wide smooth leather reins at the shank end of the bit. It may be useful for these to be a contrasting color to the reins attached at the snaffle position near the mouthpiece so that you can instantly tell the two apart. Avoid riding with gloves while you are training your horse in the Pelham. They can make it difficult to adjust your rein length instantly, and they can also deaden the light feel you should have on the curb rein. If it is so cold that you must ride in gloves, perhaps your horse would be happier without a bit in his mouth. The delicate work of making the transition to the curb can wait until warmer weather!

How to Hold the Reins

Double reins can be a little intimidating at first. We all have images of "great riders" who work in two sets of reins and are so skilled with them that they leave the rest of us ignoramuses in the dust. There is nothing mystical about double reins; they are simply tools for training a horse. It takes much less dexterity to work with them than you need to type on a keyboard, play a musical instrument, or operate a touch-tone phone. You can use double reins like a pro if you think about what you are doing when you use them and spend a little time practicing with them.

One way to use double reins is to carry the snaffle reins in one hand and the curb reins in the other. Although this is an easy way to hold the reins, it will limit your ability to use the snaffle reins for lateral work and may cause you to overuse the curb in the transition period. The transition to the curb is easier if you ride with one snaffle and one curb rein in each hand, the method most commonly used with hunter/jumpers and park horses.

Some people prefer to ride with the snaffle rein above the curb in each hand. This can certainly work, but because most people have a stronger use of the heel of their hand than they do of the top two fingers, it makes sense to cross the reins, so that the snaffle is lower in the hand. That way the stronger contact of your whole hand will be on the milder snaffle part of the bit and the lighter contact of the upper two fingers will be on the more severe curb part of the bit.

This arrangement works best for making the transition to the curb because at first you will do most of your riding with contact on the snaffle rein. If you hold the reins this way, you can avoid taking strong contact with the curb by mistake, and when you do take contact with it, that contact will be intentional.

Most people who show in double reins separate them on either side of the little finger, curb above, snaffle below. You may find that it is more comfortable to use two fingers on each rein, in the utility method. You can use whichever method is most comfortable, as long as you know that if you ever wish to show a horse in double reins you must use the equitation method.

Riding with Double Reins

Because it may take a while for you to become accustomed to double reins, start out using them in a small ring or arena. This will leave you free to concentrate on what you are doing with your hands without the distraction of paying much attention to guiding or controlling your horse. Starting from the base position, adjust your reins so that the curb rein is slack, just hanging from your fingers, and the snaffle rein is short enough for you to take light, "plum-feel" contact with your horse's mouth if you close your hand and flex your wrist very slightly toward your body.

Ride at the ordinary walk and flat walk, at first with slack in both reins, then with light contact through the snaffle rein. Turn and stop the horse frequently, using leg and weight aids and the snaffle rein. When you are confident that you can use the snaffle rein while keeping the curb rein slack, move into a good flat walk, practicing figure eights and other maneuvers. Stop and back up frequently, being sure to use only the snaffle rein. Remember to avoid taking a strong, steady pull on the snaffle rein; use vibrations to ask your horse to flex at the poll and relax on the bit.

Aids for Transition to the Curb

After a couple of lessons with the snaffle rein alone, take up the slack in the curb rein so that you can put light pressure on it by closing your index and middle fingers, or release that pressure by opening those two fingers. Ride with those "curb" fingers open, then gradually start to close them while reducing your use of the snaffle rein by opening the fingers lower in your hand.

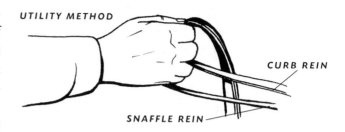

UTILITY METHOD

CURB REIN

SNAFFLE REIN

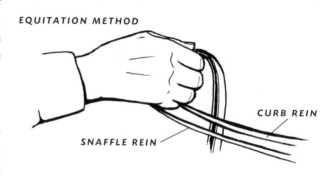

EQUITATION METHOD

CURB REIN

SNAFFLE REIN

Two ways of holding two sets of reins.

• Holding both reins in both hands, ride forward at the flat walk. Check the horse's speed with light vibration on the curb rein. He will flex his neck at the poll in response to this light use of the curb and may mouth the bit gently.

• Ride him forward with his neck arched at the poll for a few steps, keeping very light contact on the curb rein and dropping all contact with the snaffle rein. Do not ride with contact on both reins at once. If you do this in a Pelham, the curb will override the snaffle and you will be riding with only curb contact.

• Ask your horse to halt using leg and weight aids and following up with a light squeeze/release on the curb rein.

• Move him forward again with a squeeze/release from your calves.

• As he walks forward in an energetic walk, maintain very light contact on the curb to remind him to maintain his head and neck position. There should be barely more than the weight of the reins in your "curb" fingers.

• Ride for a few more steps, then return to light contact on the snaffle rein, slacking off on the curb as you push your horse on into gait.

You will find that it takes much less contact with the curb rein to ask the horse to tuck his nose, flex his jaw, or stop than it takes to accomplish the same thing on the snaffle rein. Remember this, and be aware which rein you are using at all times. Gradually increase the number of steps your horse takes while you maintain **very light** contact on the curb rein until, after a couple of weeks, you can ride him in a flat walk and in gait all the way around your arena, changing speed and direction with little more than the weight of the reins on the curb alone. If he starts to throw up his head or resist in any way, **immediately** return to the snaffle rein, reestablish even, light contact, and ride in the snaffle alone for a period of time.

After your horse has mastered working on the curb rein in the arena, ride outside the arena on trails or in the pasture, alternating the use of the reins. Gradually increase the amount of time you ride with light contact on the curb and reduce contact with the snaffle. Always use the snaffle reins alone for control if there are problems, keeping the curb reins in reserve to perfect head and neck position. Remember that when a horse is worked in both reins, the snaffle tends to lower and extend the head and neck, while the curb, when used correctly, raises it and brings the forehead toward vertical. Practice extending gaits on the snaffle, collecting them on the curb. Ride uphill on the snaffle, downhill with light vibrations on the curb. Back your horse on the snaffle alone at first, then gradually try it in the curb, keeping his nose down and his jaw relaxed. Do not, however, work lateral flexions such as the shoulder-in or haunches-in on the curb rein. The curb is not designed for lateral exercises; its function is more suited to head-to-tail collection or containment.

Making the Transition from Bitless Headgear to the Curb

If you are using bitless headgear because your horse is uncomfortable in a bit, stay with that gear! As you have discovered, bits are not necessary to ride or control a gaited horse. If your horse has no objection to a bit in his mouth, however, you may find that you will enjoy riding him in a curb bit from time to time.

There are two options for helping your horse understand the transition from bitless headgear to a curb bit. You can add a snaffle bit under his bitless headgear and make the transition to the curb by first teaching him to respond to a snaffle. Or you can add a curb bit under the noseband bridle and make a direct transition to that from bitless riding. In either case, it is useful to have a bridle that comes equipped with a bit hanger or a light, thin additional headstall that will fit under your bitless headgear and hold the bit.

Carrying the Bit

Start making the transition to the bit by letting your horse carry a bit under his bitless headgear without reins attached for several weeks or even months, until he is completely comfortable with it in his mouth. You can begin this process with a snaffle bit, but if you are making the transition directly to a curb bit, start with a Pelham, a Kimberwicke/Uxeter, or a curb that has slots at the mouthpiece for attaching reins, as well as rings on the end of the shanks. Use a bit with short shanks, preferably less than 4 inches. This type of bit will allow you to teach your horse to respond to the feel of a bit in his mouth without leverage before he must respond to the leverage curb effect.

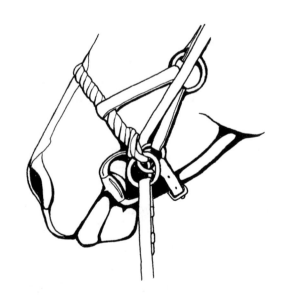

Adding the bit to bitless headgear. Let the horse carry the bit without reins under the noseband for a while until he becomes accustomed to it.

Double Reins

Riding in an enclosed arena, add a set of reins to the top slot of the curb, Pelham, or Kimberwicke/Uxeter bit, but continue to use the reins on the bitless headgear. Don't put any pressure on the bit reins; hold them slack in the top of your hand as you ride with some light contact from the noseband reins in the lower part of your hand. Be very distinct in your seat and leg cues for turning and stopping, using the noseband reins infrequently to reinforce those aids. Gradually add the feel of the bit reins to the pressure/release of the noseband reins, using both at the same time to stop and turn your horse. Ask him to move up into gait and use the bit reins in addition to the noseband to remind him to carry his head and neck in the best position for his gait.

Over time, gradually reduce the use of the noseband reins and rely more and more on the bit reins to ask him to turn, stop, and maintain his head and neck position in gait. It may take several weeks or months for your horse to respond lightly to the bit, or he may learn quickly to transfer the nose cues to mouth cues. As your horse becomes more accustomed to the feel of the bit, ride out on the trail with the double reins, using the bit reins but keeping the noseband reins in reserve for control, if needed.

When your horse responds to light cues from the bit reins while he is still wearing the bitless headgear, move the reins to the shank end of the curb bit or to the lower slot in the Kimberwicke/Uxeter. Follow the same procedure you used when teaching him to respond to the upper slot of the bit, using the noseband and the curb reins simultaneously and then gradually reducing the use of the noseband. If you remember to use weight and leg aids as well as rein aids when you ride, your horse should be able to go in the curb alone after a month or two of practice in the double reins.

Riding on the Curb Rein

If your horse tries to nose out or lug on the bit in the curb, he is not yet ready to work on the leverage rein alone. Return to the snaffle or bitless headgear, remind him to travel in a semi-collected position with light squeeze/release vibrations, then return to the use of the curb when he has reestablished his balance. As long as he has "relapses" and is not able to carry himself in gait on light contact with the curb reins, you should stay in double reins so that you can correct him with the snaffle or noseband. This process can take several months or longer, depending on your skill and your horse's ability. If you hurry it and try to correct your horse on the curb rein, you will find yourself riding with heavier and heavier contact on that rein as your horse develops an increasingly dull mouth. Although he may be ridden in a curb, he will not have "earned" the bit.

Riding with One Hand

As your horse becomes more accustomed to the effect of the curb bit, increase the time you ride him with the indirect or neck rein. If you have been teaching him in the snaffle or noseband to respond to the indirect rein while riding first with two hands, and then one hand, at the walk and his slower easy gait, he should have no problem understanding the use of the reins against his neck when you ask for a turn.

It may be awkward to ask for a neck rein response with double reins held in both hands. To make it easier, hold all four reins in one hand, curb reins in the middle, with more slack in the snaffle reins than the curb reins as you practice neck reining on the curb.

If the horse does not respond to the neck rein easily, do not try to pull or push him around with the curb rein. Instead, return to using the snaffle rein to refresh

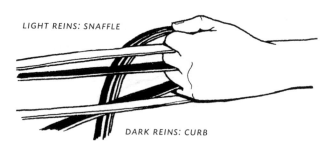

LIGHT REINS: SNAFFLE

DARK REINS: CURB

Riding with all four reins in one hand, another step in making the transition to riding in the curb alone with one hand.

him on the use of leg and weight aids for turning. Practice neck reining with the bit he understands before you try it in the curb.

Riding with One Hand on the Curb Rein

Once your horse is responsive to the curb rein, understands the aids for neck reining, and will maintain his gait without constant pressure on his mouth from the bit, you can start to ride him with one hand in the curb bit alone.

TWO METHODS FOR HOLDING CURB REINS IN ONE HAND

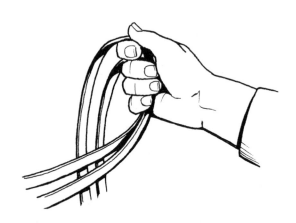

To lower the horse's head, hold the reins through the bottom of your hand with the free ends coming out over your index finger.

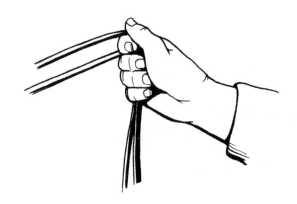

To raise his head, hold them through the top of your hand with the free ends hanging below your little finger.

How to Hold the Reins

How you hold your curb reins in one hand depends on whether your horse is inclined to pace and needs to be reminded from time to time to lower his head, or if he is inclined to hard trot and needs occasional reminders to elevate his head and neck.

If he is pacey, hold the curb reins through the bottom of your hand, the bight (free ends) coming out between thumb and forefinger. This method allows the weight of the rein to remind the horse to keep his head lowered and will give you the option of vibrating your little finger on the reins to bring his nose in if he starts to nose out. If he is trotty, hold the curb reins through the top of your hand with your index finger between them and the bight coming out through the heel of your hand. This will allow you to raise his head with a light upward twitch of your index finger.

Going "On Parole"

With the snaffle rein removed, your horse is "on parole" in the curb. If he stays light in your hands and travels with a relaxed jaw in gait, you can ride one-handed in the leverage bit. You may want to switch to a low port-grazing curb in place of the Pelham or continue to use the Pelham as a curb without the snaffle rein. At the first sign of resistance in the curb, from nosing out to overtucking, return to the snaffle action on the Pelham or the bitless headgear.

Don't dull your horse's mouth to the curb by correcting his behavior in it. It is a "party manners" bit, not an instrument of punishment or a retraining tool. A horse that has been ridden correctly in a curb can always go back to the snaffle for a refresher should it be necessary.

What's Next?

Once he has made the transition to a curb, your horse's basic training qualifies him as a true gaited pleasure and trail horse. There are also plenty of other things you can train him to do, if you are interested in doing them. You can teach your horse to work cattle or do reining if he has the temperament and conformation for those things. If you are interested in it, you can try jumping in a snaffle bit with your gaited horse, again, if he has the conformation and personality for that. You can "gun break" and teach him to pack game if you enjoy hunting. You can also try pleasure driving with a cart. If you are interested, find someone who specializes in those types of training and learn how to do them with your horse.

You will find that you train a gaited horse for those activities the same way you would train any other horse. Easy-gaited horses were originally bred to be using horses; go ahead and use yours for those activities if his conformation allows.

If you have imagination and skill, and he has athletic ability, you are never finished training your horse.

What you have been working for: A finished pleasure horse moving easily in gait down the trail on slack reins in a curb bit. The rider has one hand on the reins.

CHAPTER THIRTEEN

Foals & Young Gaited Horses

Time and patience . . .
— BRADBURY FAMILY MOTTO

There are plenty of resources available for those who want to know how to raise young horses and start them under saddle. Gaited horses are just regular horses with a little extra talent, so most of this information applies equally to easy gaited and non-gaited horses. If you plan on breeding mares, raising foals, and later training young horses from scratch, apply methods that work to produce well-behaved pleasure horses in any breed, with a few modifications to fit the needs of your gaited horse.

Working with Foals

Good horsemen have known since before the time of Xenophon that it makes sense to handle foals early. Whether you call it imprint training, gentling, or simply handling, early contact with a human can help a foal develop the trust and respect that make all later training much easier. Unfortunately, there are some people who go overboard, either by treating foals like lap dogs or by failing to understand that respect is as important as a lack of fear in a young horse. That sort of handling often creates spoiled, obnoxious, and even dangerous adult horses. It is better to leave a foal completely to his own devices with other horses than it is to mishandle one. If you do choose to handle very young foals, do it the right way!

"Imprinting" and Other Early Handling

If you are going to handle a foal, remember that every time you interact with him, you are teaching him something. Review the basic attributes of good training in chapter 3 and apply them to the foal. Remember that you are the boss mare in the relationship, and act accordingly. Don't play "stupid horse trick" games with him, letting him look for treats in your pocket, "training" him to box by rearing and striking, encouraging him to chase you in games of tag. Those things may be cute in a baby, but in a grown horse they are dangerous and evidence of a lack of understanding of your alpha status. Lower-ranked horses in a herd never display that sort of behavior with the boss mare; if you expect your foal to grow into a willing partner, don't encourage him to behave in ways that to his horse mind mean he is dominant to you.

The premise behind imprint training is that if a newborn foal is exposed to a flood of sensory stimuli that includes things he will encounter later in life, he will retain this information in his immature neurological system and be willing to accept these things with ease as he gets older. A foal, however, does not "imprint" the way a baby goose does. A gosling retains for life everything it sees the instant it hatches, identifying with whatever it sees first as "mama." A foal's mind does not work that way, probably because he is a much more intelligent creature than a baby goose!

For young horses, the early experiences of imprinting tend to fade unless reinforced periodically as they mature. If you want to imprint your foal, be aware that you will probably need to follow up once a month or so with at least some of the things you did with him at birth. It can be just as effective to introduce those stimuli one at a time, in a nonthreatening way, as your foal matures. Start with easy activities such as being touched all over, then progress to more complicated actions such as restraining with a neck rope, grooming with a brush, hoof handling, halter training, and standing tied. Things taught in small increments seem to stick with the foal better than those taught all at once by force.

Probably the best lessons you can teach a young foal are to stand still for grooming, hoof care, and general veterinary care and to be led on a slack line. This early training has the advantage of making hoof and health care easier and of teaching the foal that he can stand still and obey you without constant pressure on his body. It can also be good preparation for later work on a slack rein under saddle without constant contact on a bit. The easiest method for catching and restraining a young foal is to use a *neck loop*. It reduces the potential trauma to his developing neck that a halter might cause. You can buy ready-made neck ropes that have metal fittings in the form of an eye and snap that can be adjusted to form a nonslip loop. You can also make your own by attaching an eye to a short length of rope or tying a bowline knot in an ordinary lead rope after you have it around your foal's neck. If you are not good with knots, use a rope with adjustable fittings. Adjust the neck rope to form a loop that is small enough to prevent the foal from slipping out of it easily, but not so tight as to choke him.

To introduce a foal under the age of three weeks to the experience of being restrained, put the foal and his mama in a small corral or stall with soft, deep footing. If necessary, tie up the mare with some hay to occupy her so she won't be in the way.

• Carrying the open rope or loop in one hand, walk calmly up to the foal, talking softly. Pet him on the neck and shoulders, then carefully slip the rope around his neck, still talking to him and petting him. You can also give him a

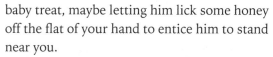

Using a neck loop to restrain and lead a young foal can cause less trauma to his neck than using a halter at an early age.

baby treat, maybe letting him lick some honey off the flat of your hand to entice him to stand near you.

• Fasten the hook to the eye of the rope, or tie the bowline knot under his neck. Slide the loop down toward the base of his neck. Continue to pet him and talk to him. He will eventually notice the rope. Hold on.

• If he fights by trying to run backward or forward, tries to duck out of the loop, or rears, go with him so that he does not escape the loop and is not choked by it. Pet him and reassure him, and allow him some time to get used to this thing around his neck.

• As he adjusts to the feel of the rope, begin to pet him all over. He will probably try to leave. Pull and release and say *whoa* if he starts to move away from you, repeating these actions until he stands still. Instantly reward him by praising him and petting him on the neck for standing still. If he moves again, say *stand* and again pull and slack on the neck rope, until he stands still. Then praise him again. Always use *whoa* for the initial stop, and *stand* to remind him to stay still once he has stopped.

Continue petting and touching him all over, including his ears and sheath (bag if it is a filly), and up and down his legs. If he tries to move, repeat the pull/release on the rope until he stands still. Praise him, pet him a little longer, then remove the rope and let him go back to his mama.

Leave him alone for the rest of the day, then try the neck rope routine again in a couple of days. **Never** work with a foal this age for longer than 10 minutes at a time, and don't work with him every day. He has the attention span of a gnat, and he needs to learn to be a horse as much, or more, than he needs to learn things from you.

Learning to Lead

After a few sessions of standing still near his mama with the neck loop restraining him, you can begin to teach the foal to be led with the neck rope. After you have caught him and handled his body, stand to one side in front of him, facing toward him. Tug and release on the neck rope, turning his neck and shoulders toward you until he takes one step. Praise him, pet him, then repeat the tug and release, this time turning him in the other direction. Remember that releasing pressure is as important as putting pressure on him to ask him to turn.

Build gradually on the one or two steps he takes to the side until he starts to follow you around in a circle in response to the tugs/releases on the neck loop. Ask for very little, but praise him often. Don't drag him around by the neck; teach him to come with you in response to a tug on the line and an instant release of pressure. This is a lesson that will carry over to later riding.

By the time the foal is a month or so old, you can replace the neck rope with a foal halter, letting him wear it **only** when you are giving him his short lessons in handling, a couple of times a week. Use a halter that can be adjusted around the nose as well as at the throatlatch, and fit it on your foal's head so that it is snug but not tight. Don't try to use a halter that is too big; it will flop around and be a distraction to the foal.

- Catch and restrain the foal with the neck rope. Let him see and smell the halter, then rub it over his body and neck. He should not be afraid of it because he is used to you touching him by now.
- Gently slip it on his head and fasten the crown piece so it will stay in place. Do not attach a lead rope to the halter. Let him become accustomed to the halter while still wearing the neck loop.
- The foal may fight the feeling of the halter, shaking his head and stomping his feet. Allow him to play a little, then remind him to stand still with a pull and slack on the neck loop, pet him, and reassure him that the halter is not going to hurt him.
- Attach a cotton lead rope to the halter, but keep the neck loop in place. Begin to lead the foal around using the neck rope, moving him to the side using the command *come on.*
- Gradually introduce a pull and slack on the halter lead rope in addition to the sideways motion with the neck loop. Be prepared for the foal to rear, strike at the lead rope, or even throw himself over backward when he first feels the tugs on the halter over the top of his head. Keep slack in the lead rope and go with him if he acts up.
- Talk quietly to calm him, restrain him with the familiar neck loop, then repeat the small tugs to the side with the halter rope. Soon he will take a step toward you when you tug and release the halter rope. Practice leading from both sides, using the neck rope for backup.

After he has been led with both for a little while, you can discontinue the use of the neck loop and lead the foal around with the halter just as you did with the neck rope. It is not very difficult to teach a foal to be led in a halter this way, if you start first by using the neck loop and do not force him. You won't need to use rump ropes or body ropes to move him forward because he will respond to your simple pull and slack on the lead rope.

The foal should now follow along behind you on a slack rope with an occasional reminder that he is supposed to keep up with you. If you work with him for a few minutes every other day, he will not forget what he has learned and will be able to build on it as you add a few new things to his lessons each time. Practice leading him behind his mother whenever you can, first leading him with her, then stopping and going away from her a short distance. Never try to pull him anywhere with a tight rope. Keep using the pull and slack motion, and unbalance him by tugging to the side if he tries to lock up his legs and balk. Be sure to take the foal halter off when you are finished with a leading session. To prevent accidents, never leave a halter on a horse at liberty.

Always teach a foal to lead on a slack line. The slack line will prevent him from becoming stiff and resistant to being led and can prevent him from developing a poor use of his neck. In addition, a slack lead line will give him free use of his head and neck, allowing him to develop looseness and rhythm, important elements of the easy gaits.

More Lessons for Baby

Once your foal understands being led in a halter, re-inforce his baby lessons with the commands *whoa* and *stand* as you would an adult horse. Begin to do a little ground work with him, as well. Teach him to back up, to stand square, to lead from both sides, and to walk over a few poles, and desensitize him to fly spray and other ordinary things. (Follow the techniques given in chapter 4 for pole work and desensitization methods.) Again, keep your sessions very short and let your foal spend most of his time being a horse with other horses.

Ponying a young horse is good exercise and a great way to teach him about the world, as long as you keep the lead line slack between your hand and the colt's head.

Ponying

Being ponied is an excellent experience for any foal that's learning about the world, and for a gaited foal, it has the added benefit of helping him begin to establish his easy gait. Once your foal is well trained in the halter and will lead on a slack line from your side at a fast walk, at about three months of age, you can teach him to go along next to his mother for short distances as you ride her. Obviously, this will work only if the mare can be ridden safely. If she is one of those broodmares that never made it beyond "green broke" or is not sound, wait until the foal is weaned, then teach him to pony from another older horse that is calm and friendly to him.

Equipment
You will need a sturdy foal halter, an 8-foot-long cotton lead rope, a long crop or dressage whip (which you may not need), a stout Western saddle with breast strap and back cinch, and a calm, easily managed mare (preferably the mother of the foal), who can be ridden with one hand and has had some experience as a pony horse. Do not try to pony a foal from a horse that is aggressive. You will want to start in a fenced pasture, arena, or field away from other horses, if possible.

The First Lesson
Saddle the mare and hang the crop or whip from the saddle horn. Halter the foal using the long lead, place him at the right side of the mare, and wrap the end of the lead around the horn. Mount up.

- Hold the lead in your right hand, about 3 feet from the horn, leaving the end dallied to the saddle, but keeping slack rope between your hand and the foal.
- Move the mare out a couple of steps in a slow dog walk (not a flat walk) while pulling and slacking on the lead line to bring the foal along with you. He should walk with his head about even with your knee, no more than 3 feet away from the mare.
- If he balks, tap him with the crop on the croup and move him forward.
- If he jumps ahead of the mare when you touch him with the crop, use a strong pull and slack to restrain him.

Practice until he will walk quietly beside the mare at a slow walk on a slack line. This may take some time, or he may figure it out instantly. Do not try to drag him along beside you with a tight rope; use a tap from the crop on his rump to motivate him instead.

Remember that ponying is just another way to lead him; keep the line slack unless you are correcting him for going ahead or hanging back. Practice riding the mare and ponying the foal in a flat pasture or arena until he is very comfortable with the lesson, then take him out and go around your driveway or some other safe place close to home.

Exploring

Most people pony colts to condition them and to teach them to accept the types of things they will encounter later when they are ridden. With a foal under six months of age, you are not going to be doing much conditioning, but you can certainly teach him about going up and down hills in a controlled way, crossing small streams with his mother, and walking calmly along the side of a gravel road with light traffic. If you practice riding next to roads, be sure to keep the foal on the far side of his mother so that any cars that come by are well away from him and he will not be in danger of spooking into them. Take the foal on short rides in your pasture or other terrain that is not too rough. Avoid dense trees, if possible, so that he does not wrap the lead line around one. Try to take him through small bogs or up and down short steep banks if they are available. Some people take young foals on trail rides with their dams, reasoning that if wild horses can travel all day with foals at their sides, it should be possible for domestic ones as well. A slow, short trail ride of no more than 35 minutes will not hurt a four- to five-month-old foal, but a much longer ride is not a good idea. At this point in his life, you are not trying to get him ready for an endurance contest, you are just teaching him about the world with his mother for reassurance.

Gait

If you have a well-gaited mare and are on smooth, flat footing, you can move her out of a slow walk once the foal walks easily next to her. Keep the mare at a slow speed in her gait, allowing him to keep up and maintain the rhythm of the gait with his shorter legs. Take it slow and easy, and eventually he will start to do his gait a few steps at a time along with his mother.

If the colt moves into a flat walk or other gait with head nod, you may have a problem with the lead rope on the halter swinging and hitting him under the chin as he nods his head. This can be very annoying to the foal and may cause him to start throwing his head instead of nodding it naturally in his gait. To overcome this problem, attach the snap on the lead rope on the far side of the halter, run the rope through the metal halter fitting on the noseband, under the foal's jaw, and out the near fitting so that the snap does not hang down from the ring under his jaw. This arrangement will keep the snap and rope from swinging under the foal's head, and will also give you a little more leverage in case he tries to rush ahead of the mare.

As the foal grows and matures, you can pony him at a flat walk and in his easy gait for a short distance, but keep an eye on what he is doing. At the first sign of a pace or other unwanted gait, slow down and walk.

Weanlings and Yearlings

Once your foal is weaned, at about six months of age, his attention span may be a little longer and his body a little more mature. If you have not taught him to lead in a halter or other basics as a baby, teach him these skills as soon as possible after he is weaned. Between the ages of six months and a year, he will grow and change constantly and will need regular hoof care and worming, at the very least. Make these experiences easier for him by routinely leading and tying him up for grooming and handling, as well as taking him out to pony next to his mother or another compatible horse to accustom him to the sights and terrain away from home.

Teaching a Colt to Stand Tied

Once your colt has learned the commands *whoa* and *stand* on a slack line while being led with a halter and has developed more muscle in his neck and back, it is time to teach him to stand tied. There are two approaches to this type of training. One holds that the foal should be tied to a stout object with a heavy rope and halter and left alone to fight it out on his own until he develops respect for the halter and learns to stand still. The other believes that a struggle should be avoided and that the foal should learn to stand still while tied in response to the verbal commands *whoa* and *stand*.

To follow either method, use a well-fitted, sturdy halter, strong lead rope with a heavy-duty snap, a piece of rubber inner tube wrapped at the foal's head level around a fairly large tree or strong post, and good judgment. Lead the colt into the enclosure with the post, and tie the lead rope to the inner tube with a quick release–type knot that will untie easily if you pull on the loose end but will not come undone if the foal pulls on it. The inner tube will allow some play in the lead rope and can prevent injuries to the colt's neck and back if he should fight it. Groom him and handle his feet, then step to the other side of the corral for a few minutes, keeping an eye on him.

You now have two choices, depending on his reaction to being left tied up. If he just stands there half asleep, you won't need to do anything at all. If he starts to panic or pull back on the lead rope, however, you can either command him to *stand*, go to him, reassure him, and urge him forward to release tension on the rope with a tap on the rump, or you can stay away from him, let him pull until he figures out that he can't get away and, when he is standing still, go back to him, pet him, and reward him for not pulling.

Whatever you choose to do, remember that your final goal is to convince him to stand tied on a slack rope, quietly, without you standing next to him. You do not want him to stand snubbed to the post or tree, forced into immobility by a tight rope. Maintaining a slack line is the key to his future training.

Basic Ground Lessons

In addition to the routine grooming and handling that you might do every day, as he gains some maturity, you can begin short 30-minute lessons with your colt a couple of times a week. Mini-lessons will build on the things he has already learned. Lead him over a couple of poles and ask him to stand on a slack line while you desensitize him to flapping towels and plastic bags along his body. Practice flexing and bending his neck as he wears a lead rope and halter. Teach him to move away from pressure by practicing the basic rotations and side step. Don't overdo these exercises; just ask

him to move a step or so in each direction once in a while. Praise him often and keep all work sessions short, following the same ground work techniques you would use with an adult horse (see chapter 4). You can also begin to add a couple of new skills to those he already knows.

Introducing Longe-Line Work

When he is nine to ten months old, you can introduce your youngster to the idea of the longe line to help him develop lateral flexibility. Because it is very hard on a young colt's legs and body to move with any speed around a small circle either at liberty in a round pen or on a longe line, don't use these methods with a baby horse to teach gait, to wear off excess energy, or even to develop good manners. Work on manners and respect with a lead rope and halter, not by running your colt around in circles.

At his young age, you can introduce him to the idea of circling you on the longe at a **very slow walk** in both directions, asking him to bend his head and neck toward the center of the circle and stopping at a distance from you with the command *whoa*. Keep these sessions very short, no longer than 15 minutes total, and use the line only to help the colt develop lateral flexibility, preparing him for later work at a more advanced level on the longe and under saddle. If you start this work early and carefully, you can reduce any problems he may have with being one-sided in later training. The consistent, gentle bending work on the longe line will help him stretch his stiff side and strengthen his weak side.

Ground Driving

Although you can't ask very much of your colt on the longe, by the time he is a year old, you can begin a little ground driving with him to teach beginning rein cues and help him develop a little more independence when walking over obstacles. Keep all sessions of ground driving short, nonthreatening, and simple. Again, do not do this sort of work every day. Once or twice a week is plenty for any colt. Let him be a horse most of the time, with only a few lessons from you to keep his life interesting.

Very light work on the longe line, at a walk, can give your colt a head start on flexibility.

Equipment

You can drive your colt in a halter, sidepull, longeing cavesson, or snaffle bit and bridle. It is advisable to start a young colt with a halter, then proceed to a bit when he is two or more years old. You will also need two long lines (two longe lines will work), a longe whip, and a surcingle (and maybe a crupper) or a bareback pad with stirrup Ds. With older colts, you can also use a Western saddle (see page 227 for the method to introduce the saddle to a colt). You will also need a large enclosed area or ring in which to work. Finally, the help of a friend can make the first couple of lessons easier.

Teach your colt to accept the surcingle or bareback pad. Tie him, let him sniff and examine it, rub it all over his body on both sides, and, when he is no longer worried about it, set it softly over his back. Gradually tighten the girth so that it is snug but not tight. Be prepared for him to react as he feels it circling his body. Reassure him, then try again, until he will stand still as you adjust the girth. Lead him around with this new article on his back, keeping him quiet with tug/slacks on the lead line if he acts excited, until he shows no interest in it. It may take a couple of lessons for him to accept the feel of something around his middle. Take your time; let him settle down with this new sensation before you start to use it for anything.

Longeing with Two Lines

At the end of a typical short walking lesson on the longe, stop your colt and go to him.

• Attach a longe line to each metal fitting on the side of the noseband of his halter or to the side rings on the longeing cavesson.
• Run the second longe line around the far side of his neck, through the far ring on the surcingle or D of the bareback pad, and across his back.
• Run the near line through the ring or D of the bareback pad on the near side of the colt. The ends of both lines should be on the near side.
• Take up the lines, keeping the one across the colt's back slack.
• Longe the colt at a slow walk in a small circle, holding one line in each hand, holding your longe whip in one hand, and carrying the lash with the stock. Do not let the lash trail in the dirt or hang free. Let him circle you at the slow walk several times, with both lines on one side of the colt, using occasional light tugs on the outside line to cue the colt into a larger circle. Repeat from the other side of the colt.

Ground driving a colt is good preparation for being ridden and will give him a chance to work on his obstacle skills.

To change to the driving position:

- Begin by longeing the horse in double lines at a very slow walk.
- Ask your helper to walk at the colt's head to keep him moving straight.
- Move toward the rear of the colt, keeping slack in the near line, but slowly tightening the far line.
- While you helper walks at his head, drop behind the colt, moving the line from across his back so that it runs parallel to the far side of the colt. Keep your hands up so the lines do not drag on the ground or hit the colt in the hocks. Take up the excess slack in both lines and walk 5 to 6 feet behind the colt.
- Walk around your enclosure with your friend leading the colt for a few minutes, then have her move away from the colt toward the center of the corral. If he tries to follow her, use small tugs and slacks on the outside line to keep him going forward. If he tries to stop or turn to the outside of the circle, repeat the word *walk* and touch him on the rump with the tip of the whip; do not snap the lash behind him.
- Adjust the long lines to keep moving in a straight line.

Driving may be a little awkward for a while as you use first one line, then the other, and your colt overcorrects in response to your tugs. You may need to have your friend go back to his head and walk with the colt until he is more comfortable with the idea of being driven in place of being longed. In time, however, your colt will walk by himself in front of you as you guide him with the long lines. He is then ready to learn to halt and change directions.

- As your colt walks forward, say the word *whoa* while giving a quick pull and slack on both lines. He should stop at once at the familiar word.
- If he moves, give a strong, quick pull and immediate slack on the lines, repeating until he comes to a halt. Praise him for a job well done. Let him stand still for a moment, then move him out again in the slow walk.
- Turn him to the right, pulling and slacking the right line to the side. Use a light pull on the left line to prevent him from making too sharp a turn.
- Straighten him, using the left line a bit more strongly while slacking off with the right, go forward a few steps, then turn him to the left, using the same technique with the left line.

Drive him around the ring, changing directions several times. Try a few large figure eights or serpentine loops, then halt him again. Practice driving in a straight line again, then end the session. Go to your colt, praise him, and pet him!

Over the next few lessons, drive your colt in smaller circles, changing direction often. Drive him around some cones, over your spaced poles, and over a tarp or bridge. Take him out and drive him in your pasture, stopping and changing directions frequently. All of these experiences will be new for him when he is driven through them instead of being led through them. He may be hesitant at first, or he may go forward boldly. Practice a few times a month until he drives easily wherever you send him.

Learning and Growing

Pay attention to your colt. Notice how he reacts when you work with him and how his body develops. If he is lazy or bored with what you are doing with him, stop working with him for a month or so and let him just be a horse for a while. If he goes through a sudden growth spurt, leave him at liberty for a while to let his muscles and nerves catch up with his bones. You can discontinue lessons with a colt for several months without causing him to forget what he has learned, although you should continue to handle and groom him even if he is not doing ground work. After a long vacation he may be a bit silly the first time you longe him or drive him, but he will soon remember your commands and respond to them.

Two-Year-Olds

Conventional wisdom says that it is appropriate to start young two-year-old horses under saddle. In physical terms, this is equivalent to putting 10-year-old children to work in the coal mines. We don't work human children like that anymore; there is no good reason to work immature horses that way, either. Don't be in a hurry to start your colt under saddle; instead, do a little more ground work with him, helping him begin to develop his body and his mind so he

can perform his gaits more easily when you do start him under saddle.

Each colt matures, mentally and physically, at a different rate. Keep this in mind as you work with your colt. Some learn easily and work athletically at an early age. Others may be slower to learn and awkward as youngsters. This does not mean that the easy ones will be better riding horses than the awkward ones. Often the colt that takes a while to learn something is more willing to work for you, while a smart one gets bored easily and finds ways to entertain himself that may not fit in with your lesson plans. Those that are athletic early on usually stay that way, but an awkward colt may just be slow to grow into a large body. Don't write him off because he stumbles over his own feet at two. At six, he may be outstanding in his gait and movement. Some colts will automatically go into their easy gait while others seem to do every gait but the one you expect. While it is easier to work with a colt that never does anything but the gait expected of him, others usually do the gait just as well. Give your colt time, help him condition the muscles and nerve paths he needs to do his gait, and he will eventually reward you with the wonderful smooth gait you hope for.

Longe-Line Work for Two-Year-Olds

As a long yearling and early two-year-old, your colt is still pretty gawky and his legs have not finished growing. Work him very lightly on the longe in both directions, at both a walk and a slightly faster walk, for no more than 15 minutes per lesson. Practice frequent stops on the command *whoa*, and let him learn to stand still at a distance from you with the command *stand*. As he matures into a two-year-old, very gradually increase the time he spends on the longe during lessons to about 20 minutes total. This is the absolute maximum for a young horse, and it ought to be a maximum for an adult horse, as well. Begin to introduce the flat walk and a little of his easy gait, along with numerous speed changes and halts. Work over poles if your colt starts to show signs of pacing. Continue to practice asking him to bend his head and neck so that he makes good, round circles on the longe in a walk and slow speed of his gait.

Introduce the Saddle

By the time he is two-and-a-half, you can start longe-ing your horse in a light saddle. First, introduce him to the saddle in a nonthreatening way and place it on his back gently and quietly.

• Tie the colt in a quiet place, away from other horses or distractions. Hold the saddle pad out for him to examine, let him sniff it, and rub it over his body. Then place it on his back. This should not bother him because the pad is about the same as the bareback pad he has been work-ing in for ground driving.

• Fold the stirrups and cinch over the seat of the Western saddle or tie up the irons on an English saddle. **Place** it quietly on his back, over the pad. Do not throw the saddle up on the colt's back or swing it up with stirrups dan-gling. This practice can bruise his back and make him reluctant to be saddled. Most colts that flinch or dance around when they see the saddle pad coming have had the unpleasant experience of having a saddle thrown on them. Since you want your young gaited horse to work with a fluid body so he can do his best gaits, don't cause him to stiffen his back in anticipation of a saddle thudding down on him. Use your arms and lift the saddle up carefully, and avoid hitting the colt in the side with any part of it. He should stand perfectly still for you to put the saddle on if he is not being hurt or frightened by it. He may, however, reach around and take a bite out of a stirrup leather.

• Quietly reach under the colt and take up the cinch, one notch at a time.

• Untie the colt and lead him forward a few steps, then tighten the cinch or girth gradually so that it is just snug enough to keep the saddle from slipping. If you are using a Western saddle, gently flap the stirrups and fenders a few times until the colt is not upset by them bouncing against his sides. Your colt will prob-ably not be bothered by the stirrups after his experience with the bareback pad. If he seems upset by the stirrups, tie them over the saddle with a piece of twine. Make this first saddling experience as nonthreatening as possible for your colt.

• Work the colt on the longe, first at the walk, then at the flat walk. Keep him concentrating on his gaits, not on the saddle. If he gets excited, calm him with your voice and pulls and slacks on the longe line until he will walk qui-etly again.

• Longe him for a while with the stirrups tied up, then let them down and gently slap them against his sides, make noise with them, and let them fall into his elbows while he stands still on a slack line. Then repeat the longeing lesson, this time with the stirrups hanging free. The colt may be startled the first time he is hit on the elbow by a flopping stirrup. Watch for that reaction, and be prepared to calm him with your voice and keep his attention on his work with pulls and slacks on the longe line.

In a very few lessons, your colt will accept being saddled better than many older horses and will work willingly on the longe while wearing a saddle. This acceptance of the saddle is another step in the process of teaching him to respond to a rider calmly, with respect but without fear. You can then go on to longe-ing him in the saddle with a plastic bag or even a slicker attached to it, after first desensitizing him to the bag or slicker as he stands still on a lead rope.

Gaits and Cantering on the Longe

As your colt matures into a long two-year-old, you can begin to introduce periods of longe-line work in his easy gait, as well as teach him to rate his speed in gait. Practice the type of longe-line work you would do with an adult horse, but keep sessions short and slow to prevent damage to his legs. If he shows problems with the pace or other unwanted gaits, begin working him over poles to change his timing, and work on frequent transitions in speed and between gaits. Again, don't longe him for longer than 20 minutes, most of that at a walk or flat walk.

If your colt shows an inclination to canter in the pasture, and you later expect to ride him at that gait, go ahead and teach him to do it in a controlled way. It may be better to use the longe rather than the round pen for this work so that you can ask for the gait in only short bursts, never allowing him to do a complete circle in the canter. This will prevent some of the stress of canter work on his young legs. Use very short sessions of trot work over poles or a low cavalletti to help him strengthen his back and hind legs for canter work. Practice cantering about every third lesson, not every time, and only for a couple of repetitions in each direction. Walk often, canter little!

Ground Driving in a Bit

In addition to learning about a saddle and working in gait on the longe line, your two-year-old colt can also do some more ground driving, this time away from home. You can continue to drive him in a halter, or use a sidepull for excursions away from a fenced-in area. If you intend to start him under saddle in a bit, you can also fit him with a snaffle bit under his halter, and let him become accustomed to feeling the bit in his mouth. When he seems comfortable in the bit, you can drive him with the lines attached to it rather than to the halter. The pressure in his mouth will give you more direct communication than the feel of the halter or cavesson on his nose, and it may help him turn and stop more quickly than he did with only noseband pressure. Be careful to avoid driving him with steady pressure on the bit because that will create a dull mouth for later riding. Keep your lines slack most of the time, whether you use a halter, cavesson, or a bit to drive in. Allow the colt as much freedom as possible in the way he uses his head, but do not let him put it down to graze or sniff the ground. Keep him alert and moving forward.

If you are fairly athletic, you can drive your colt in a flat walk or slow version of his easy gait. To work in the flat walk, push him forward in the ordinary walk, tell him to *walk OUT* the same way you did on the longe, and be sure to keep slack in your lines. Use pulls and slacks or vibrations on the lines to slow him if he goes too fast and a touch from the whip to move him out if he is slow.

If he tries to pace-walk, lower your hands to help him lower his head, and continue to drive him forward at a good walking speed. He may discontinue the pace. If he doesn't, slow down to a walk. Don't drive him in the pace or at a speed faster than you can follow! Remember, he must have the free use of his head and neck to work well in his gait, so you must be careful to avoid driving him with constant pressure on the lines. Ground drive your colt over poles and trail obstacle bridges, up and down hills, and in most places you plan to ride him. This will help him build confidence so that he can eventually carry you over that same ground without fear.

Starting the Young Gaited Horse Under Saddle

When your horse is a full three-year-old, you can start him with light work under saddle and rider. This process should be relatively painless if you have been working with him in short lessons all his life. Being ridden is really just another logical progression in the lesson program; it is not something to rush through in one day.

Do all of this work in a small, well-fenced round pen or ring. While it is possible to start colts under saddle in large pastures or even in barn aisles, neither is a safe way to go about it. Work in a location where you can turn your horse easily but not give him the room to bolt.

There are few moments in life more exhilarating than the first ride on a young horse. As much as you may think you know about your colt, there are still questions. What will he do when he feels your weight? How will he move under saddle? And, perhaps, from a tiny voice in the back of your brain, "Why am I **doing** this?" Relax. There should be no problems if you have done your ground work well. Most gaited horses have even, sensible dispositions. They are not likely to buck or act rank unless provoked into it by fear.

Review and Prepare

You may have been working with your colt for 45 minutes once or twice a week, longeing, ponying, and

How to Introduce a Bit

IT TAKES A LITTLE PRACTICE to teach a colt to accept a bridle with a bit attached. If you rush or force him, he may clamp his teeth shut against the bit. Take your time and he will open his mouth willingly.

▶ Using a bridle with buckles that are easy to undo, pre-adjust the bridle so that it will fit loosely over the colt's head.

▶ Detach the bit from one side of the bridle.

▶ Put honey or molasses on the bit and then hold it to his lips, letting him smell the sweet stuff and lick his lips.

▶ Place the crownpiece over his poll, leaving the bit outside his mouth.

▶ Insert one finger on the off side of his mouth at the corner of his lips, between his molars and incisors, where there are no teeth.

▶ Wait until the colt opens his mouth for the finger and the scent of sweet, and then slide the bit into his mouth. **Avoid hitting him in the teeth with the bit.**

▶ Reattach the bit to the bridle. The colt will lick and chew the bit, enjoying the sweet.

▶ Remove the bit by loosening the crownpiece and dropping it slowly, letting him spit out the bit to keep it from hitting him in the teeth.

Repeat this process each time you put on the bit and bridle. When your colt will open his mouth readily for the bit, leave it attached to the headstall. If he later becomes resistant to bridling, detach one side of the bit and sweeten the bit for a couple of lessons until he accepts it again.

---

doing other ground work or exercises. Before you mount up the first time, increase these lessons to once a day for at least a week. Work with your colt until he is completely obedient and quiet, no matter what spooks or obstacles he faces.

A typical lesson might look like this:

• Longe him in all his gaits, using either the halter or the longeing cavesson.
• Ground drive him in a straight line and in large circles or figure eights.
• Lead and drive him over obstacles.
• Saddle and unsaddle him.
• Shake plastic bags around him.
• Lead him, then longe him with a slicker tied to the saddle.

During this preparation period, if you have been longeing your colt in a halter or longeing cavesson and you plan to start him without a bit, switch to a jaquima or California bosal with fiador, using the mecate as your longe line and tying it to form reins as well as a line. If you plan to do your early riding in a snaffle bit, fit a simple headstall with a snaffle bit under the cavesson or halter. (Do not use a bridle with a noseband, which will interfere with the signals from the longeing cavesson or halter.) Carrying the headstall under his longeing headgear will help the colt accept the feel of a bit in his mouth and give him time to adjust to it before he is required to go to work in it. He will chew and play with the bit at first. Don't try to prevent him from mouthing the bit by tightening the cavesson over his jaw. Allow him to learn to pick up the bit without forcing his mouth shut over it.

Experiencing Weight

It is possible to accustom a colt to feeling weight on his back by teaching him to carry a packsaddle or tying bags of sand over a regular saddle. This certainly does no harm, but it is unnecessary. Carrying dead weight has little relationship in the colt's mind to carrying a rider on his back. It takes a human being to teach a colt to carry a rider.

Step One

Teach the colt to accept the presence of a person standing close to him, higher than his back. You will need a portable mounting block of some sort. Use something solid. Do not stand on anything that could tip over or in which a colt could catch a foot. Do not try to stand on a fence for this. You need solid footing to support your weight and must avoid slipping and frightening the colt.

• Saddle and work the colt as usual on the longe, in all gaits, with frequent stops and transitions.

• Stop him, lead him to the center of the longeing circle, and go to him, carrying the mounting block.

• Allow him to examine it, then place it by his side, even with the stirrup.

• Keep him standing quietly with the block next to him. Command *stand* and pull and slack instantly on the longe line if he starts to move.

• Stand on the block, close to his side, *keeping the line slack*. He may turn his head to look at you, but should not move his feet.

• Lean your weight over his back, standing on the block. Pat him on the off side, talk to him while you lean on him for a few moments, then get down.

• Carry the block to his other side and repeat the exercise.

Practice this for a couple of lessons, on successive days, until the colt will stand still on a slack longe line and pay no attention as you lean on him from either side.

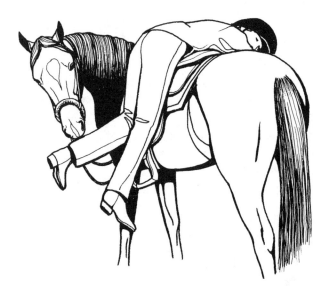

Let your horse feel your weight over his back before mounting up using a stirrup.

Step Two

Teach the colt to accept your weight across his back.

• Give the usual longe-line lesson and repeat step one.

• Lever yourself across his back with your arms, lying over the saddle on your stomach, your feet free of the block.

• Keep your head low, talking to the colt in a calm tone. Stay across his back a moment or two, then slide down so that your weight is back on your feet, supported by the block.

• Repeat several times on both sides.

If he tries to move, remind the colt to stand still with a quick pull and slack on the longe line. Never try to hold him still with a tight line as you lie across him.

Step Three

Teach the colt to accept your weight as you sit astride him. After several sessions of just lying across his back, when he is comfortable and unafraid of your weight:

• Give the usual longe-line lesson and repeat step two.

• Swing one leg over his back, keeping your head and torso low, then lie astride him. Pet him, praise him, and reassure him.

• Slowly sit up. He may turn his head and sniff your boots. Continue to pet him and talk quietly to him for a few moments.

• Do not ask the colt to move and do not put your feet in the stirrups.

• Slip off his back. **Do not** use the stirrup to dismount; this can cause the saddle to slip and throw him off balance, confusing and upsetting him.

• Repeat several times, then move the block and practice on the colt's other side.

If your colt tries to move, pull and slack on the longe line and command *stand* to keep him still. Continue a series of pulls and slacks on the line until he stands, then praise him. He must stand still while you sit on his back.

For the next few days, end your lessons by sitting astride the colt, petting him and talking quietly to him. He will soon accept this new experience and stand calmly as you sit astride.

Step Four

Teach the colt to stand quietly as you mount using the stirrup.

- Work the colt on the longe at all gaits, with frequent halts on the command *whoa*.
- Slowly tighten the girth just enough so that the saddle will not slip when you put weight in the stirrup.
- Using the mounting block, practice lying across his back several times from both sides.
- Pull down on the stirrup, first on one side, then the other.
- Standing on the block, put your foot in the stirrup with a little weight on the stirrup, but do not stand in it. Remind the colt to stand still with a pull and slack on the longe if he tries to move.
- When he is still, place one hand on his withers in front of the saddle holding the slack mecate reins and the other on the cantle of the saddle, keeping your torso close to the colt.
- Take a light step in the stirrup and swing your free leg over the colt, using both your foot and your arms to lever yourself up. Sit quietly astride. Pet and praise your colt for standing still. Sit and breathe in and out a few times, relaxing on the saddle.
- Dismount by swinging your free leg back over the saddle, balancing over the seat, taking your foot out of the stirrup, and sliding to the ground.
- Repeat a couple of times on both sides, then end the lesson.

Do not stand with all your weight in the stirrup or pull yourself up with your hands on the saddle. This can make the saddle twist on a horse's back, digging into his spine and throwing him off balance. The mounting block will give you sufficient added height to allow the saddle to stay centered on the colt's back as you mount. Even after your horse is trained, it is a good idea to use the block whenever you mount up to preserve his back. It may be easier on your knees, as well.

If you follow this gradual method for teaching the colt to stand for mounting, he will accept it as just

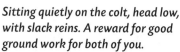

Sitting quietly on the colt, head low, with slack reins. A reward for good ground work for both of you.

another lesson. Continue to mount on a slack rein and he will never develop the bad habit of taking off when you have one foot in the stirrup. He will also be willing to wait for your cues before he moves out once you have settled into the saddle because he has not automatically associated moving out with you mounting up.

The First Ride

Your colt now stands still for you while you mount. Practice mounting from both sides at the end of several lessons, then continue his training by asking him to move forward with you on his back. It is a good idea to have a friend help the first few times you try this. You may need an extra pair of hands on the ground when your colt first learns to carry you.

Equipment

You will need a thick dressage whip without a lash. You will also need some reins to attach to the longeing cavesson, halter, bosal, or snaffle bit. Cotton or mohair mecate reins are necessary if you use the bosal. Do not use braided leather reins or heavy reins of any type when starting your colt. They will be stiff and difficult to pay out or take up and will interfere with the feeling of contact between your hands and the colt's nose. Braided reins can also give you nasty rope burns if they are pulled through your bare hands.

Avoid spurs of any type, tie-downs, trip ropes, running Ws, or other equipment suited to breaking broncs. Your colt is no bronc and will not be acting like one. You should not have to throw your colt with a running W or other apparatus to gain his respect. This treatment is the last resort of a wise horseman. May

A calm first ride, in a California bosal, on a young three-year-old. If you have done your ground work well, there will be no bucking or running.

you never have the misfortune of dealing with a horse that requires it. Your young horse should accept moving with you mounted up as just another lesson. If he acts up, remind him to obey with strong pulls and slacks on the longe line. If he continues to act silly, quiet him, dismount, and give him a major lesson in *whoa* on the longe line until he obeys. Then continue your mounted work.

The Lesson

Saddle your colt and put on whatever headgear you plan to use to longe and then ride him. For the first few rides, a halter will work almost as well as a bit, jaquima, or bosal. Work the colt for at least 20 minutes on the longe line in a small enclosure. Stop him frequently and practice transitions to all of his gaits. Stop him, attach your reins if necessary, and coil the longe line, either tucking it in your belt or tying it up with your saddle strings. (The longe becomes your "get down" line for the first few rides. With it still attached you can quickly dismount and remind a disobedient colt of his earlier lessons.) Allow the colt to examine the dressage whip, then hang it from the saddle horn or from your wrist with a loop. Place your mounting block next to the colt, then practice leaning over him and mounting with the reins slack. Keep your friend nearby, talking quietly if necessary, but not holding the colt still for mounting.

• Mount up. Have your friend remove the block so the colt will not step on it.
• Pick up the reins, one in each hand.
• Squeeze/release your legs from thigh to calf and say *walk*. At this point in the process, your legs mean nothing to the colt, but he may respond to the familiar verbal command. Do not kick him, and do not lean forward as you ask him to move.
• Allow him to walk slowly for a few steps, guiding him from left to right with light pulls and slacks, on one rein at a time. Hold your "leading" hand (direct rein) low and to the side as you guide him.
• Ride at the walk for a short time, guiding the colt away from the rail.

• Turn in a gradual curve in both directions, as you did when driving in long lines.
• Command *whoa* while squeezing/releasing with your upper thighs, tilting your pelvis slightly toward the rear, breathing out, and squeezing/releasing on the reins.
• Stop the colt, pet him and praise him, then dismount.

All first rides should go so smoothly!

Possible Problems

Although many colts will move out quietly the first time they are asked, some are not quite so cooperative. Many will refuse to move, despite leg and verbal cues. Others will take off in a fast gait and refuse to slow down. Once in a while one will try a crow hop or two. To deal with these problems, make use of your friend on the ground.

Won't Move

After you have spent several lessons teaching your colt to stand still when you mount up, he may think he is never supposed to move with you on his back. Do not kick or spur a green colt that stands still when you want him to move. He is probably confused, not stubborn. Give him a chance to understand what you want by using diagonal aids. Pull to the side with one rein to turn his head and neck and press straight into his side with the opposite leg, repeating the command *walk*. The pull to the side may work to "untrack" him the same way it works to move a foal that is learning to be led.

If this fails, have your friend lead the colt from the ground. This will let him know that nothing terrible will happen if he moves with you on his back. After he has been led for several steps, try to move him out again, without your friend leading. He may walk forward easily, responding to the verbal command *walk* followed by the squeeze of your legs. Or he may not understand what you want. Try again. Be sure to keep your reins slack, squeeze with your legs as you say *walk,* and follow up with a single tap on his rump (haunches) with your crop.

The colt will probably walk forward, then stop after a few steps. Move him out again, squeezing first with your legs, then backing up the leg aid with another tap from the whip. Release all leg pressure as soon as he moves. If he is slow to respond, instead of squeezing harder or kicking, use a light tap from the whip to reinforce the leg signal. He will soon learn to respond to a light squeeze by moving forward with some energy.

Do not get into the habit of using constant leg pressure or kicks to move him. Squeeze/release with both legs and follow up with a tap from the crop if he is slow to respond. If you must kick him, give one solid, hard kick, and then leave him alone. Avoid the habit of constant nagging little kicks to move him forward; it will make him very dull to leg aids. Don't use spurs to force him to move; they can make a horse resistant and stiff in his back, working against good gait in young horses.

Too Fast

If your colt takes off faster than a walk, pull and slack on the reins, say *easy* in a quiet tone, and ask your friend to walk next to him, leading him at a slower speed. When the colt has been led a while, ask your friend to step away and then use pulls and slacks on one rein at a time to control the colt. Keep your reins slack in between pulls. Do not try to hold the colt in with a steady strong pull on the reins. Pull and slack, pull and slack until the colt slows down and relaxes at a walk on a slack rein.

Crow Hops

This is not serious bucking. The colt crow hops because he is a little uncertain when he feels your weight shift as he moves. Have your friend lead him with you in the saddle, stepping away after a couple of trips around the enclosure. If the colt tries to crow hop again, pull and slack on the reins, say *whoa*, stop him, then start out again at a walk. If he persists in acting up, check to make sure your saddle fits him. A saddle that is too narrow or too wide can press on the colt's spine and may be enough to cause him to act up. If the saddle is not the problem, double him to regain his obedience and attention, then continue around the corral. (See chapter 5 for the doubling technique.)

Following Up

Give your colt a lesson every day for the next two weeks. Longe him, then mount up and ride him at a walk around the corral, round pen, or small ring. At first, ride him about 10 minutes of the 45-minute lesson, practicing frequent stops and changes of direction at a walk, then gradually increase the time in the saddle to about half of the lesson period.

The colt's balance will be poor at first. He may feel as if he is walking on eggshells as he carries you slowly around the corral. Help him adjust to your weight by staying centered in the saddle, weight even on your seat bones. Ask for wide turns, using light tremors on one rein low and to the side while pressing your opposite leg directly into the colt's side. Avoid leaning into turns, which may unbalance him.

By the third or forth ride, urge the colt out of the ordinary walk for a few steps. Use the verbal command *walk OUT* and a strong squeeze/release from your legs, followed by a light tap from the whip if necessary. He may go right into a flat walk as a result of his longe-line training. He may do some other gait. Do not worry if he does not flat walk. At this point, gait is less important than controlling him at a speed faster than a slow walk. Ride in the faster gait for part of each lesson, first on the rail, then in wide turns. Practice increasing and decreasing speed in the walk, as well as frequent halts on the rail.

Your colt may work very well for the first two or three rides, then, when he feels his feet are firmly under him, he may try a little rebellion. He may decide he can't turn in one direction, refuse to move out of a stop, "forget" he knows what *whoa* means, or even try a crow hop or two. Be prepared for this. Ride centered in the saddle and double him to keep his attention on business, if necessary.

Beginning Training

After the initial starting period of about two weeks, during which it is best to ride your colt every day, you can reduce your lessons to four or five a week. He should have adjusted to your weight, learned the basics of turning right and left and stopping, and generally settled down under saddle. If you have been using a California bosal or longeing cavesson for early work, change to a sidepull. Once past the early discipline stage, the motion of the heavy rawhide bosal will be distracting to a colt with much natural head nod in his easy gait. You can continue to longe him in the bosal or cavesson, then change to the sidepull when you start the ridden part of your lessons. If you have been longeing and riding in a jaquima or snaffle bit, you can continue in that headgear.

Now that your colt has better balance, in addition to riding around your ring on the rail at a walk and turning frequently, begin riding him over some of the obstacles you have led and driven him over in the ground work part of his training. Ride over a few low poles, over the bridge or tarp he learned to cross during his ground work, and around some cones or other markers in wide turns and figure eights. Ride with another ridden horse in the ring, if possible. Have another rider go in front, to the side, and behind your colt so he learns that he can be ridden in company as well as alone. Ask the other rider to pass you with some speed while you keep the colt moving at a slow walk. If he tries to speed up to keep up with the other horse, pull and slack on the reins and remind him to obey with the double, if necessary. He must pay attention to you, not other horses in the ring or on the trail.

Begin to ask your colt to back a step or two and to neck rein, still at the walk, during each session. Use weight and leg cues as much as rein cues to ask for these things, and he will soon respond without the action of the reins. As your colt becomes more obedient under saddle, take him outside the ring for short rides. Ride him alone and with an older "schoolmaster" horse to help him accept the wide world more calmly. Go back to the areas where he has previously been ponied or ground driven. Ride up and down some gentle slopes so that he can learn to keep his balance under you. Build his confidence in you and himself and give him something to think about besides going around in circles in a ring. This will keep him fresh mentally and willing to work.

Shoes

Although it is a good idea to start colts barefoot and to ride them that way as long as possible, once you start riding frequently, your colt's hooves may begin to wear down. If necessary to protect his hooves from wear, have him shod at his natural angle in ordinary keg shoes without caulks, grabs, toe weights, or trailers. Shoes are to protect his hooves, not "improve" his gait. If you ride on soft ground, you may not need them.

Graduating from Kindergarten

Early training for a gaited horse is a little different from that of a non-gaited type. Most trainers work trotting horses in all three gaits within the first week or so and do not consider a horse broke to ride if he can't be ridden in a walk, trot, and canter/lope. Because trotting horses have so few options, their trainers can let gaits take care of themselves and determine which one the horse uses by speed. Easy-gaited horses have so many possible intermediate gaits that the correct gait is a bigger part of their training program. It is important to lay a strong foundation in the ordinary and flat walk before asking for more speed in an intermediate gait.

This work in the walk will strengthen the muscles needed for the easy gait and make it more likely the colt will do that gait when asked for it. Although you can try short bursts at a faster-than-walking speed to work on control with your colt, most of your training for quite a while must be done in the walk and flat walk. Review the discussion of the walk (chapter 5) and work with your colt as indicated in this foundation gait. In time, this slow work will pay off in a rhythmic intermediate gait. Your colt will eventually be just as obedient under saddle as a trotting horse that has been loping from the first week of training. And he will be a pleasure to ride, at any speed!

Sample Lesson Plans for Developing and Improving Gait

EACH HORSE IS DIFFERENT. Once you know your horse's ability and learning style, you can tailor specific plans to help him do his best gait. Build gradually on what he knows while his body develops strength and flexibility. These lesson plans are only suggestions of things you can incorporate into your riding sessions; don't expect your horse to do everything in them every ride. Experiment with adding or substituting exercises and with increasing or decreasing the number of steps in each. Don't ask for more than your horse can honestly do.

To keep your horse supple, always start and end each lesson with a short session of ground work. Practice several repetitions of the neck flexions (both lateral and direct), back lifts, and the head/neck lowering and stretching exercise discussed in chapter 4. Start and end each ridden session by riding at least three minutes of the neck-stretching exercise on a loose rein. Keep all ridden lessons to no more than 45 minutes, unless you are incorporating lessons into trail riding.

LEVEL ONE:
Basic Skills for Flexibility

• Ride with two hands, using light "plum-feel" contact, in the ordinary walk twice around the arena in both directions. Halt on the rail for a count of 10 one time in each direction.
• Ride at least two 20-meter (approximately 60-foot) circles in the walk in each direction, changing directions through the circle.
• Ride at least two figure eights with 20-meter circles on each end.
• Ride at least two 10-meter (approximately 30-foot) circles in the walk in each direction, changing directions through the circle.
• Ride at least two spirals from 20 meters (60 feet) down to 10 meters and back out again in the walk in each direction, changing through the circle at the 20-meter size.
• Ride a three-loop serpentine at least twice at the walk.
• Ride at the flat walk or fast ordinary walk with light contact at least twice around the entire arena, change directions by crossing the diagonal of the arena, and repeat going twice in the opposite direction.
• At the slow walk, ride a two-loop serpentine using the neck rein.
• Practice alternating neck stretches down and forward on a loose rein, then into contact at the ordinary walk, at least three times around the entire arena.
• Return to the normal head position on light contact at the walk. Ride into a halt. Praise and pet your horse. Ride in the relaxed neck-stretched position on slack reins, stop in the center of the arena, and dismount.

LEVEL TWO:
Beginning Gait Work

Practice all skills in Level One.

• Warm up at the ordinary walk, riding large and small circles, serpentines, and the first two phases of the neck-stretching exercise in each direction.

• Riding in a flat walk, alternate riding with contact in the lowered head position and in the "up and in" position, no more than 10 steps in each. Change directions across the diagonal of the arena and repeat in the other direction.

• Ride one 20-meter circle in the flat walk. Return to the ordinary walk, change through the circle, then ride one 20-meter circle in the flat walk in the other direction.

• Ride across the center of the arena and come to a halt in the middle. Stand for the count of one, back one step, then go forward at the ordinary walk. Repeat twice during the lesson.

• Ride at the flat walk for 10 steps, then ask for the intermediate gait for 10 steps in the third phase of the neck-stretching exercise, maintaining light contact as your horse carries a slightly raised head and neck, with his mouth relaxed on the bit. Return to an ordinary walk. Repeat in each direction.

• Halt on the rail, back two steps, then walk forward at the ordinary walk. Repeat twice during the lesson, in each direction.

• Ride once around the arena in the intermediate gait, change across the diagonal, and go around in the opposite direction once. Return to the flat walk. Repeat in both directions.

• Play the scales in the ordinary walk, increasing and decreasing speed. Go 10 steps in each speed.

• Ride a two-loop serpentine at the flat walk in each direction on slack reins, using the indirect (neck) rein.

• From the ordinary walk, ride into a halt at the center of the arena. Pet and praise your horse. Ride in the relaxed, neck-stretched position on slack reins. Stop at the center of the arena and dismount.

LEVEL THREE:
Improving Gait and Flexibility

Practice all skills in Levels One and Two.

• Warm up in the ordinary walk, practicing large and small circles, serpentines, and figure eights, and in the flat walk, practicing large circles and the three phases of the neck-stretching exercise.

• Ride twice around the arena in the flat walk in each direction, changing directions across the center.

• Ride once around the arena in the intermediate gait in each direction, changing directions across the center. Return to the flat walk.

• Alternate the flat walk and the intermediate gait every 10 steps, practicing smooth transitions between the gaits at least twice around the arena in each direction.

• Play the scales in the flat walk, increasing and decreasing speed and step length in that gait.

• Return to the ordinary walk, ride a 10-meter circle to the right in the corner of the arena, and come out of it into two steps of the shoulder-in. Finish the shoulder-in by returning to a 10-meter circle, change directions through the circle, and continue on in the ordinary walk. Repeat, starting with a 10-meter circle to the left. Practice twice in each direction.

• Ride in the flat walk, asking for speed and extension in the gait, once around the arena.

• Ride in the intermediate gait, playing the scales in it, once around the arena. Change directions across the middle in the slow intermediate gait, then repeat, playing the scales in the opposite direction.

• Lower the horse's head in the neck-stretching exercise on light contact at the flat walk. Ride twice around the arena in each direction with the horse's head lowered into contact.

• Return to the normal head position in the flat walk. Ride a three-loop serpentine on slack reins using the indirect (neck) rein. Riding with one hand, practice a large 20-meter circle, change through the circle, and repeat in the other direction.

• Return to an ordinary walk, still with one hand, then ride into a halt. Stop and praise your horse. Dismount.

LEVEL FOUR:
Increasing Flexibility in Gait

Practice all skills in the first three levels.

• Warm up with circles, serpentines, and playing the scales in the walk and flat walk. Practice all three phases of the neck-stretching exercise in the walk and flat walk.

• Ride three circles around the entire arena in the flat walk and in the intermediate gait, asking for a moderate speed. Change directions across the diagonal and repeat in the opposite direction.

• Riding on the rail in the flat walk, come to a halt. Back one step and, as the horse finishes stepping back, immediately ask for the flat walk forward. Ride halfway around the arena in an energetic flat walk, then halt and repeat. Change directions and repeat the entire exercise in the opposite direction.

• Return to an ordinary walk. Ride from a 10-meter circle into a shoulder-in, go five steps in the shoulder-in along the rail, then return to the 10-meter circle. Repeat in the opposite direction.

• Go immediately from the ordinary walk into the intermediate gait, ride 10 strides, then return to the flat walk.

• Return to the ordinary walk, ride to the center of the arena, and come to a halt. Ask for one step of a turn on the forehand in each direction.

• Ride back on the rail at the ordinary walk. Then, in a corner of the arena, ride a 10-meter circle, this time coming out of it with a haunches-in at the rail. Ride three steps of the haunches-in along the rail, return to the straight track, and continue on at a flat walk. Practice twice in each direction.

• Return to the center of the arena, halt, and ask for one step of a turn on the haunches in each direction. Return to the rail in the ordinary walk.

• Ride two 20-meter circles at the flat walk, then one at the intermediate gait, changing through the circle at the flat walk to repeat in the opposite direction.

• Ride one 10-meter circle in the flat walk in each direction, changing through the circle in an ordinary walk.

• On the rail, play the scales in the flat walk. Ask for stride lengthening along the long side of the arena, shortening along the short side. Ride one 20-meter circle in the shortened stride, then reverse directions and repeat.

• On the rail, play the scales in the intermediate gait, asking for stride lengthening along the long side of the arena, shortening along the short side. Ride into the corners at the shortened stride and ask for lengthening as you come out of the corner. Repeat at each corner of the arena, change direction across the diagonal in the ordinary intermediate gait, then repeat in the opposite direction.

• On light contact, ride a three-loop serpentine in the flat walk followed by a two-loop serpentine in the intermediate gait. Repeat twice in both directions. Gather your reins into one hand and ride with slack reins, at the slowest speed of the intermediate gait. Ride first a two-, then a three-loop serpentine using the neck rein. Return to the rail at a flat walk.

• Ride into a halt on the rail from the flat walk with one hand on the reins.

• Praise and pet your horse. Ride in the neck-stretched position at an ordinary walk with one hand. Stop and dismount at the rail.

You can go on to devise more complicated lessons, incorporating the canter or other gaits beside the main intermediate gait. You can also add side passing and leg yields to this, although those are mostly useful as maneuverability exercises. For trail and pleasure riding, you may not want to do much beyond the first two levels of gait work. Practice the skills that are suited to your horse.

Names of Gaits and Gaited Breeds

Gait names from around the world, from research by Lt. Col. J. W. Bradbury and the late Dr. Hanneke Receveur.

Names for the Pace (Hard Pace)

Ambladura (Spain)
Ambladura lanzada (Spain)
Amble jété (France)
Dazo or Ta tsou (China)

Huachano lanzada (Peru)
Huambi (South America)
Paso huambeado (Peru)
Passgang (Germany)

Skeith/Flug skeith (Iceland)
Telgang (Netherlands)
Tsouma/Zoma (China)
Zelt (Germany)

Names for the Broken or Stepping Pace

Ahthacha (Burma)
Ambio (Italy)
Ambladura retardada (Peru)
Amble (England)
Amble rompu (France)
Amble surpassé (France)
Andadura (Spain)
Argulillo (Peru)
Compas (Peru)

Entrepaso (Puerto Rico, Colombia)
Gangstapp (South Africa)
Halb pass (Germany)
Hetwahr (North Africa)
Hsiaotsu (Mongolia)
Kortgang (South Africa)
Marcha picada (Brazil)
Paso ligero (Spain)
Paso portante (Nicaragua)

Perestrup (Russia)
Pottok (Provence, France)
Schritt (Old German)
Skeith tolt (Iceland)
Soberandando (Peru)
Sobre paso (Brazil)
Stap telgang (Holland)
Takama (West Africa)
Tropota (Russia)
Verlengede Stap (Holland)

Names for the Running Walk

Amble plan (France)
Flugskref tolt/Hlanpandc fetgan-gur tolt (Iceland, per Gunnar Bjarnason)

Paso llano (Peru)
Snelstap (Holland)
Strykstapp/Strijkloop (South Africa)

Vorlengende stap (Indonesia/Dutch)

Names for the Saddle Rack/Rack (Determined by Speed, Same Basic Gait)

Kathiawar (India)
Marcha (Brazil)
*Paso corto (Colombia, Puerto Rico)
*Paso fino (Colombia, Puerto Rico)

*Paso largo (Colombia, Puerto Rico)
Paso menudeado (Peru)
Paso travado (Galicia)
Poroszkalni (Hungary)
Rakhwan (Turkey)

Siar (Saudi Arabia)
Tolt/Hreina tolt (Iceland, second form, per Gunnar Bjarnason)
Tranco (Argentina)
Trapatka (Russia)
Trippel (South Africa)

*Note: Speed determines difference between these three gaits.

Names for Fox Trot

Adiestramiento (Chile)
Draf tolt/Brokk tolt (Iceland)
Halb trab (Germany)

Marcha Batida (Brazil)
Pasitrote (Peru)
Traquenard (France)

Trocha (Colombia, Puerto Rico)

Names for Mixed Canter Gait (Canter in Front, Trot/Walk in Back)

Aubin (France)
Dreischlag (Germany)
Dreislag (Holland)

Halb-gallopp (Germany)
Overpace (England)
Valhopp (Iceland)

Wicky wack (colloquial Southern
    United States)

Gaited Horse Breeds, an Ever-Expanding List

EUROPE	ASIA	AMERICAS	AFRICA
Asturcon	Altai	American Saddlebred	Afrikan Saalperd
Bosnian	Azerbaijani	Andadores	Basuto
Breton/Roussin	Bhutan	Bolivian Paso	Berber
Dales	Birman	Calentero	Boerperd
Fell	Bokhara	Campolino	Fulani
Galician	Hokkaido	Costeno	Hausaa
Garrano	Jaf	Cracker Horse	
Highlander	Jomud	Criollo Argentina	
Icelandic	Kabardiin	Galiceno	
Merens	Kachin	Kentucky Mountain Horse	
Mysekaja	Kirgis	Llanero	
Nordlandhest	Marwari	Mangalarga Marchador	
Norman	Mongolian	McCurdy Plantation Horse	
Pottok	Nepalese	Missouri Fox Trotter	
Skyros	Sandlewood	Morochuco	
	Siamese	Mountain Pleasure Horse	
	Soemba Pony	Paso Fino Horse	
	Tibetan	Peruvian Paso Horse	
	Timor Pony	Racking Horse	
	Tongan Singlefooter	Rocky Mountain Horse	
	Turkmene	Singlefooter (Appalachian)	
	Tuschin	Spotted Saddle Horse	
	Tuva	Standardbred	
	Viatka	Tennessee Walking Horse	
		Tiger Horse	
		Virginia Pocket Horse	

Breeds That Include at Least Some Gaited Individuals

American Bashkir Curly, American Quarter Horse, Andalusian, Appaloosa, Arabian, Canadian, Friesian, Hackney, *Hanoverian, Morgan, Mustang, Spanish Barb, *Thoroughbred, *Trakehner

* Breeds specifically known not to be gaited that will produce gaited individuals on rare occasions

Bibliography

Adams, O. R. *Lameness in Horses*. 2nd ed. Philadelphia: Lea and Febiger, 1977.

Albright, Verne. *The Peruvian Paso and His Classic Equitation*. Ft. Collins, Colorado: Caballus, 1975.

Anderson, J. K. *Ancient Greek Horsemanship*. Berkeley: University of California Press, 1961.

Ascasubi, L. de. *El caballo de paso y su equitacion*. Lima: Asociacion Nacional de Criadores y Propietarios de Caballos Peruanos de Paso, 1968.

Back, Willem, and Hilary Clayton. *Equine Locomotion*. New York: W. B. Saunders, 2001.

Barclay, Harold. *The Role of the Horse in Man's Culture*. London: J. A. Allen, 1980.

Beery, Jesse. *Prof. Beery's Saddle-horse instructions*. West Carrolton, Ohio, 1934.

Belasik, Paul. *Riding Towards the Light*. London: J. A. Allen, 1990.

Bennett, Deb. *Conquerors, the Roots of New World Horsemanship*. Solvang, California: Amigo Publications, Inc., 1998.

——. *Principles of Conformation Analysis, Vols.1–3*. Gaithersburg, Maryland: Fleet Street Corp., 1996.

Beudant, E. *Horse Training*. New York: Charles Scribner's Sons, 1931.

Bjarnason, Gunnar. *Aettbok og Saga, Vols. 1–4*. Iceland: Bokaforlag Odds Bjornssonar, 1982.

Browne, William. *Browne his fiftie yeares practice*. London: 1624.

Cavalry School, the Academic Division. *Horsemanship and Horsemastership, Vol, 1*. Fort Riley, Kansas: The Cavalry School, 1942.

Ceram, C. W. *The Secret of the Hittites*. New York: Alfred A. Knopf, 1956.

Crowell, Pers. *Cavalcade of American Horses*. Garden City, New York: Garden City Books, 1951.

Dent, Anthony, and Daphne M. Goodall. *The Foals of Epona*. London: Galley Press, 1962.

Dent, Anthony. *Horses in Shakespeare's England*. London: J. A. Allen, 1987.

——. *The Horse Through Fifty Centuries of Civilization*. London: Phaidon Press, 1974.

Eisenberg, Baron Reis d'. *Description du manège modern dans sa perfection*. Paris, 1727.

Escobar, Jaime Mejia, and Camilo de Francisco Saavedra. *El Caballo de Paso Colombiano/The Colombian Paso Fino Horse*. Bogota, Colombia: Lito Camargo Ltda., 1986.

Farshler, Earl R. *Riding and Training*. New York: Arco Publishing, 1975.

Fraser, Andrew F. *The Days of the Garron: The Story of the Highland Pony*. Midlothian: Macdonald Publishers, 1980.

Goubaux, Armand, and Gustave Barrier. *The Exterior of the Horse*. Translated by Simon Harges. Philadelphia: J. B. Lippincott, 1891.

Guérinière, François Robichon de la. *Ecole de Cavalrie*. Paris: 1733.

Harris, Charles. *Fundamentals of Riding*. London: J. A. Allen, 1985.

Henriquet, Michel, and Alain Prevost. *L'Equitation, un Art, une Passion*. Paris: Editions de Seuil, 1972.

Henriquet, Michel, and Catherine Durand. *Gymnase et Dressage*. Paris: Editions Maloine, 1991.

Hildebrand, Milton. "The Adaptive Significance of Tetrapod Gait Selection." *Amer. Zool.*, 20 (1980): 255–267.

——. "Symmetrical Gaits of Horses." *Science*, 150 (1965): 701–708.

Howell, A. Brazier. *Speed in Animals: their specialization for running and leaping*. New York: Hafner, 1965.

Hrozny, Bedrich. "L'Entrainement des chevaux chez les anciens Indo-Europeens d'après un texte Mitannien-Hittite provenant du 14e siecle av. J. C." *Archiv Orientalni*, 3 (1931).

Hunt, Ray. *Think Harmony with Horses*. Edited by Milly Hunt. Fresno, California: Pioneer Publishing Company, 1987.

Imam, S.A.H.A.A. *Seduction, or the Hackamore and the Mise en Main*. Bihar, India: The Indian Heritage, 1992.

Isolfsson, Eyjolfur. *A Hestbaki*. Reykjavik, Iceland: Eidfaxi, 1981.

Jackson, Noel. *Effective Horsemanship*. Princeton, New Jersey: D. Van Norstrand, Inc., 1967.

Jeffcott, L. B. *The Jeffcott Collection*. North Carolina: Le Club, 1996.

Kimke, Reiner. *Cavalletti*. Translated by Daphne Machin Goodall. London: J. A. Allen, 1969.

La Hood, George J. Jr., and Rosalie MacWilliam. *The American Paso Fino*. Columbus, North Carolina: Friendship Enterprises, 1976.

Laracuente, Jose M. *The Paso Fino Horse*. Hato Rey, Puerto Rico: Ramallo Bros., 1983.

Loch, Sylvia. *The Classical Rider*. London: J. A. Allen, 1997.

———. *The Classical Seat*. Haslemere, Surrey: D. J. Murphy, 1987.

Mackay-Smith, Alexander. *The Colonial Quarter Race-Horse*. Middleburg, Virginia: Colonial Quarter Horse Publications, 1983.

Marey, Etienne. *La Machine Animale. Locomotion Terrestre et Aérienne*. Paris: Germer Baillière et Cie, 1882.

Markham, Gervaise. *Cavalrice*. London: 1607.

Miller, Robert M. *Imprint Training of the Newborn Foal*. Colorado Springs, Colorado: Western Horseman Books, 1991.

Müseler, Wilhelm. *Riding Logic*. New York: Arco Publishing, 1981.

Muybridge, Eadweard. *Animals in Motion*. Edited by Lewis S. Brown. New York: Dover Publications, Inc., 1957.

Racinet, Jean-Claude. *Another Horsemanship*. Cleveland Heights, Ohio: Xenophon Press, 1994.

Rooney, James R. *Biomechanics of Lameness in Horses*. The Williams and Wilkins Company, 1969.

———. *The Lame Horse*. A. S. Barnes and Co. Inc., 1974.

Rostock, Andrea-Katharina, and Walter Feldmann. *Islandpferde Reitlehre*. Bonn: Thenée Drück K.G, 1986.

Saurel, Etienne. *Pratique de l'équitation d'après les Maîtres Français*. Paris: Flammarion, 1964.

Scharf, Emily Ellen (pseud. Susanne). *Training and Gaiting, Vol. 1*. New York: Hobston Book Press, 1947.

Sevy, L. de. *Seat, Gaits and Reactions*. Fort Riley, Kansas: The Cavalry School, 1930.

Smythe, R. H. *The Horse: Structure and Movement*. London: J. A. Allen, 1967.

Swift, Sally. *Centered Riding*. North Pomfret, Vermont: Trafalgar Square Farm Books, 1985.

Taylor, Louis. *Bits: Their History, Use and Misuse*. North Hollywood, California: Wilshire Book Company, 1974.

———. *The Horse America Made*. Louisville, Kentucky: Kentucky American Saddle Horse Breeders' Association, 1944.

Twelveponies, Mary. *Everyday Training, Backyard Dressage*. London: The Tantivy Press, 1980.

Van Schaik, H. L. M. *Misconceptions and Simple Truths in Dressage*. London: J.A. Allen, 1986.

Vasko, Kent Allen. *The Equine Athlete — Structure and Function*. Ohio: Stallion Road, 1982.

Wheatley, George. *Schooling Your Young Horse*. North Hollywood, California: Wilshire Book Company, 1971.

Williamson, Charles O. *Breaking and Training the Stock Horse*. Caldwell, Idaho: The Caxton Printers, Ltd., 1971.

Womack, Bob. *The Echo of Hoofbeats*. Shelbyville, Tennesee: Walking Horse Publishing Company, 1973.

Saddle Fitting Resources

About the Horse
www.aboutthehorse.com
General information, *About the Fit* (video)

The Port Lewis Workshop
www.rocler.qc.ca/portlewis
The Port Lewis Saddle Fit System (gel pad)

Equine Management, Auction, and Appraisal Services, Inc.
www.saddlefitting.net
The Equiscan Computer Saddle Fitting & Pad Analysis Service

Saddletech
www.saddletech.com
Saddletech Gauge (software)

Video Resources on Round Penning

Anderson, Clinton. *Feel the Difference, Groundwork Series 1, Round Penning Made Easy, Part 1, 2, 3*. Equi-Management Group with Media Consultants, Inc., 2001. VHS.

Lyons, John. *Video Collection II, Controlling the Mind and Body of Your Horse*. Parachute, Colorado: John Lyons Symposiums, Inc., 1999. VHS.

Index

References in *italic* denote tables or boxes. References in **bold** denote illustrations.

Other Storey Titles You Will Enjoy

Among Wild Horses, by Lynne Pomeranz.
An extraordinary photographic journal of three years in the lives of the Pryor Mountain Mustangs of Montana and Wyoming.
148 pages. Hardcover with jacket. ISBN-13: 978-1-58017-633-0.

Equipping Your Horse Farm, by Cherry Hill and Richard Klimesh.
A guide to every aspect of selecting, maintaining, and operating essential equipment for your horse operation.
192 pages. Paper. ISBN-13: 978-1-58017-843-3. Hardcover. ISBN-13: 978-1-58017-844-0.

The Horse Behavior Problem Solver, by Jessica Jahiel.
A friendly, question-and-answer sourcebook to teach readers how to interpret problems and develop workable solutions.
352 pages. Paper. ISBN-13: 978-1-58017-524-1.

The Horse Conformation Handbook, by Heather Smith Thomas.
A detailed "tour of the horse," analyzing all aspects of conformation and discussing how variations will affect a horse's performance.
400 pages. Paper. ISBN-13: 978-1-58017-558-6. Hardcover. ISBN-13: 978-1-58017-559-3.

How to Think Like a Horse, by Cherry Hill.
Detailed discussions of how horses think, learn, respond to stimuli, and interpret human behavior – in short, a light on the equine mind.
192 pages. Paper. ISBN-13: 978-1-58017-835-8. Hardcover. ISBN-13: 978-1-58017-836-5.

The Rider's Problem Solver, by Jessica Jahiel.
Answers to problems familiar to riders of all levels and styles from a clinician and equine behavior expert.
384 pages. Paper. ISBN-13: 978-1-58017-838-9. Hardcover. ISBN-13: 978-1-58017-839-6.

Storey's Illustrated Guide to 96 Horse Breeds of North America, by Judith Dutson.
A comprehensive encyclopedia filled with full-color photography and in-depth profiles on the 96 horse breeds that call North America home.
416 pages. Paper. ISBN-13: 978-1-58017-612-5. Hardcover with jacket.
ISBN-13: 978-1-58017-613-2.

Trail Riding, by Rhonda Hart Poe.
Fundamental instruction and detailed advice on every aspect of preparing for and executing a pleasurable trail ride.
336 pages. Paper. ISBN-13: 978-1-58017-560-9. Hardcover. ISBN-13: 978-1-58017-561-6.

These and other books from Storey Publishing are available wherever quality books are sold or by calling 1-800-441-5700.
Visit us at *www.storey.com*.